What the World Might Look Like

What the World Might Look Like

Decolonial Stories of Resilience and Refusal

SUSIE O'BRIEN

MCGILL-QUEEN'S UNIVERSITY PRESS
Montreal & Kingston • London • Chicago

ISBN 978-0-2280-2133-9 (cloth)
ISBN 978-0-2280-2134-6 (paper)
ISBN 978-0-2280-2150-6 (ePDF)
ISBN 978-0-2280-2151-3 (ePUB)

Legal deposit second quarter 2024
Bibliothèque nationale du Québec

Printed in Canada on acid-free paper that is 100% ancient forest free (100% post-consumer recycled), processed chlorine free

This book has been published with the help of a grant from the Canadian Federation for the Humanities and Social Sciences, through the Awards to Scholarly Publications Program, using funds provided by the Social Sciences and Humanities Research Council of Canada.

Funded by the Government of Canada | Financé par le gouvernement du Canada | Canada
Canada Council for the Arts | Conseil des arts du Canada

We acknowledge the support of the Canada Council for the Arts.
Nous remercions le Conseil des arts du Canada de son soutien.

McGill-Queen's University Press in Montreal is on land which long served as a site of meeting and exchange amongst Indigenous Peoples, including the Haudenosaunee and Anishinabeg nations. In Kingston it is situated on the territory of the Haudenosaunee and Anishinaabek. We acknowledge and thank the diverse Indigenous Peoples whose footsteps have marked these territories on which peoples of the world now gather.

LIBRARY AND ARCHIVES CANADA CATALOGUING IN PUBLICATION

Title: What the world might look like : decolonial stories of resilience and refusal / Susie O'Brien.
Names: O'Brien, Susie, author.
Description: Includes bibliographical references and index.
Identifiers: Canadiana (print) 20230622364 | Canadiana (ebook) 20230622410 | ISBN 9780228021339 (hardcover) | ISBN 9780228021346 (softcover) | ISBN 9780228021506 (PDF) | ISBN 9780228021513 (ePUB)
Subjects: LCSH: Decolonization in literature. | LCSH: Indigenous peoples in literature. | LCSH: Black people in literature. | CSH: Indigenous fiction (English)—History and criticism. | CSH: Canadian fiction (English)—Black Canadian authors—History and criticism.
Classification: LCC PS8191.R48 O27 2024 | DDC C813.009/353—dc23

Contents

Acknowledgments

THIS BOOK WAS WRITTEN in Ohròn:wakon/Hamilton, traditional territory of the Mississauga and Haudenosaunee people within the land protected by the Dish With One Spoon wampum agreement. Worn out with repetition as the *pro forma* opening of meetings in settler institutions – a virtue-tinted version of "let's get things started!" – the Land Acknowledgment is still a good place to begin to recognize the foundations of this project. Indigenous people offered European settlers, including my Scottish and Irish ancestors, tools necessary for living on this land. Settlers took those tools and much more while failing to take up the habits of gratitude and practices of diplomacy for working out the terms of shared caretaking responsibility that Indigenous people showed us. The Land Acknowledgment is a starting place to express thanks to the land, air, and waters of Hamilton that have nourished me during the time of writing and most of my life before it. I am also grateful to the Haudenosaunee, Anishinaabe, Waanyi, and other Indigenous thinkers and writers I draw on in this book who continue patiently to offer lessons on how to live well on this planet amidst their ongoing struggles for decolonization. This book depends on their work; I hope it will also advance it.

The idea for this project emerged far from Hamilton, during a visiting fellowship in the Department of Media, Film and Communication at Otago University in Aotearoa New Zealand in 2009. I thank colleagues there who offered patient feedback on its tentative, not at all coherent, early iteration. In the following years, the seeds of its arguments germinated in papers delivered at successive Canadian Association for Commonwealth Literature and Language Studies (CACLALS)/Canadian Association for Postcolonial Studies (CAPS) and Association for Literature, Environment and Culture in Canada (ALECC) meetings; I am grateful for questions and suggestions from colleagues there that helped them grow.

Assembling a raggedy bunch of thoughts into a book depends on both critical feedback and encouragement. Mary O'Connor, Melinda Gough, and Chandrima Chakraborty offered both, in our writing group from way back when. Many others at McMaster contributed to an environment of intellectual richness and warmth that allowed ideas to flourish, beginning with Don Goellnicht, the chair who hired me and who did so much to make English and Cultural Studies an inspiring department to work in. My colleagues, including Lorraine York, Peter Walmsley, Grace Kehler, Sarah Brophy, Gena Zuroski, Nadine Attewell, and Ki'en Debicki all embody the kind of innovative and ethical scholarship to which I continue to aspire. Many thanks too, to Sophie Goellnicht, whose hard work and common (and uncommon) sense secure the foundations of everything we do. In addition to being excellent colleagues, Amber Dean (Blaze), Christina Baade (Cassie and Saura) and Devon Mordell (Angus), have been outstanding talking, walking, sniffing, ball-thieving, and occasionally drinking companions. Graduate students in ENGLISH 773 "Revolt and Remember" kept the spark of my curiosity about resilience alive, encouraging me to see it in more nuanced ways while also modelling incisive and joyful ways to think together.

I also owe much to collaborations that took me beyond the bounds of this project and out of the grooves of my regular habits of thinking. Members of the Time and Globalization Working Group taught me to relish the pleasures and rigours of interdisciplinary work and to avoid tossing around words like "neoliberalism" without clearly defining them. In formal and informal collaboration, Petra Rethmann continues to be an amazing thinker with whom to push against and periodically jump the fences of our respective fields to get a better view of things. I have also learned, am still learning, so much from Cheryl Lousley, whose work brilliantly illuminates the big, historical view as well as the stakes of work in the environmental humanities. Jordan Sheridan and Nandini Thiyagarajan have expanded my imagination in many ways, not least by helping me always to see resilience – and life in general – through a multispecies lens. The critical (and linguistic) agility of members of the Narrating Resilience, Achieving Happiness (RESHAP) group, led by Ana Fraile and Eva Darius-Beautell, has been a wonderful source of ideas and inspiration. And the

Reckoning, Repairing, Reworlding Working Group (RRR) continues to provide sanctuary for confronting what's broken in the humanities and collectively imagining scholarly and creative off routes from colonial institutional structures and practices. Sue Spearey, Jesse Arseneault, and Helene Strauss dreamed RRR into being and continue to work to make it thrive. They have also sustained me with wisdom, gossip, and hilarity during periods of doubt about academia and life in general.

I have leant on the brains and good graces of many people in the course of getting words onto pages. Daniel Coleman, Leigh Dale, Julie McGonegal, Simon Orpana, Tony Porter, S. Trimble, Carolyn Veldstra, Bridget Mountford, Nandini Thiyagarajan, and Cheryl Lousley all read and offered invaluable commentary on the chapters as they emerged; I also owe many thanks to Lisa Kabesh whose professional editing services I wish I had thought to contract a lot earlier and to Amber Meadow Adams for advice frantically solicited and graciously given just under the wire. I appreciate tremendously the work of Khadija Coxon at McGill-Queen's UP; her sage and supportive professionalism and especially her patience have eased the arduous process of shaping a manuscript into a book. Boundless gratitude too, to the two anonymous reviewers whose careful detailed reading and constructive advice helped to strengthen its ideas and their expression, and to Candida Hadley for her exceptionally perceptive copyediting.

The labour of writing a book is different from – maybe even antithetical to – the labour of looking after people and things. This became embarrassingly clear to me many years ago when my youngest child came home from kindergarten with an assignment in which, in answer to the question, "What do your parents do?" he wrote: "My dad takes care and my mom eats." Not completely accurate but certainly not wrong, this statement has become a family joke about the way things work in our house. So from my perch at the dining room table, I offer thanks and love to my children, Bridgy, Tom, and James, for turning out so thoughtful, curious, funny, and kind in spite of my constant working, complaining about working, thinking about working, and eating; to the fur suit crew, Santa and Fred, and sometimes Franny, for their frank and frequently irritating expression of devotion, and finally, to Peter for taking care, for always being right and mostly not saying "I told you so," and for putting all the pieces together.

Thanks to the Social Sciences and Humanities Research Council of Canada for funding that helped to launch this project. Parts of chapters 4 and 5 began as a keynote talk delivered at Association for Commonwealth Literature and Language Studies (ACLALS), subsequently developed into a paper published in *Studies in Canadian Literature* in 2023.

What the World Might Look Like

INTRODUCTION

Unsettling Resilience Narratives

THE WORLD IS COMPLEX. From this broad, seemingly self-evident idea, others follow: that things are mixed together and always in flux and that surprises will occur, some of them bad. This view of the world in turn creates an imaginative framework for how we should be in it. It suggests, for example, that, given the complexity, multiplicity, and volatility of everything, it's difficult and maybe a bad idea to try and control too much. That the best, or maybe the only, way to live in this kind of world is not by resisting or trying to smooth its jagged bits but by learning how to adapt to and even embrace them. This constellation of ideas about how things are and about what we should do and how we should be with them provides a foundation for the concept of resilience, an idea that has itself achieved the status of a self-evident description of how the world works. Resilience logic tells us that systems, populations, organisms, organizations persist – or that the ones that *do* persist do so – by successfully adapting to conditions of permanent instability.

This book is interested in how the idea of resilience has come to assume such prominence in the late twentieth and early twenty-first centuries, with a focus on its currency in settler-colonial cultures, where, I argue, it has found a particularly hospitable home. I am not interested in invalidating resilience as a way of empirically describing how things or beings work or even how they *should* work. I aim, rather, to think through the way the idea of resilience gets enlisted in dominant narratives about what or who needs to learn how to persist in the face of what kinds of dangers and disruptions. The emergence of resilience thinking in the 1970s has been persuasively linked to recognitions of planetary connectedness and precarity (Robin 2014) and to the burgeoning of the Hayekian economic theory that would birth neoliberalism (Walker and Cooper 2011, 143–61). I build on these accounts to think through how the concept of social-ecological resilience, which developed in tandem and increasingly together with psychosocial resilience, served the interests of a Western world that was increasingly anxious about how to manage the erosion of its hold (or the illusion of its hold) on things. Pressures ranging from Civil Rights and decolonial movements to the arrival of nonwhite immigrants on the shores of the UK, US, Canada, Australia, and Aotearoa New Zealand all contributed to the startling, anxious recognition in the global North that the world was not as ordered – was not as amenable to ordering – as they'd assumed. New ways of describing the world, corresponding to new modes of hegemonic regulation that nodded to these changes without succumbing to them, would have to be found. The concept of resilience – the idea of persisting in the face of (at least a certain amount of) disruption – answered this need.

Resilience presented itself as a way of seeing the world as it *really* was: more entangled and messy, more volatile, than had previously been assumed. It felt – still feels – realistic in distinction to older ecological models, which saw bodies and systems as discrete, unified wholes governed by the principle of homeostasis. The idea of resilience also has a politico-aesthetic resonance that has affinities with liberalism. Where conservatives tend to see the world in black and white, with identities (of both individuals and nations) possessing fixed, essential qualities, liberalism, especially the iteration that Elizabeth Povinelli calls "late liberalism" (2011, 11–12), which blends the market maximization of neoliberalism with cultural values of cosmopolitanism and multiculturalism, has a much higher tolerance for difference and change.[1] In fact, this tolerance is a hallmark of liberalism, a source of its belief that it is both smarter and morally better than conservativism. That belief may be correct, but it also helps to nourish liberalism's denial of its complicity with racial capitalism and settler colonialism. The idea of resilience, as it applies to the putatively natural, appropriate survival of complex adaptive systems and beings, is part of this denial.

In spite of its tight embrace of realism, this – liberalism – is not the only way of truly seeing the world. And it doesn't supply the only terms for thinking about resilience. Understood as a mode of survival *in relation* – to an environment, to other beings and forces – resilience was a key element of many traditional Indigenous cultures, even if it is irreducible to a single term. In fact, the centrality of the principle of what Potawatomi scholar Kyle Powys Whyte calls "collective continuance" (2018, 126) to Indigenous cultures arguably obviated the need for a word that separated that quality out from other values like responsibility, interdependence, and environmental justice (chapter 5 offers a more detailed consideration of the [ir] relevance of resilience to Indigenous cultures). The point of emphasizing the embeddedness of resilience in Indigenous culture is to say, first, that the idea long predated its 1970s "discovery" and, second, that the processes of colonialism and racial capitalism – in which I am arguing the dominant, contemporary concept of resilience has functioned as a tool – set about deliberately to destroy that quality of collective continuance. This destruction was not just incidental to the projects of eliminating Indigenous people in Canada, the US, and Australia to clear the land or of enslaving and transporting Indigenous Africans to work it; it was an essential component of those projects. So, while one goal of this project is to think critically about the way the idea of resilience is mobilized in support of settler colonialism, peeling back its realist claims to reveal its entanglement with myths of progress combined with fears of degeneration, another goal is to understand how resilience has been and can be "repatriated," as Ana María Fraile-Marcos puts it (2019, 12), as a necessary but insufficient component of decolonization. Resilience predates colonialism; it can also be a mode of struggle and survivance in defiance of it.

One governing premise of this project is Donna Haraway's statement, adapting the words of Marilyn Strathern (1992), that "it matters what stories we tell to tell other stories with ... It matters what stories make worlds, what worlds make stories" (2016, 16). In trying to understand how resilience gets expressed through stories, I'm interested in the ways hegemonic stories – specifically, stories about childhood, urban life, health, education, and environment – congeal into dogma such that their storyness recedes into what passes for common sense. But I'm also interested in the stories that foreground their status as stories, as fiction, to shake up the terrain of common sense, or what Mark Fisher terms "capitalist realism" (2009), to highlight the hidden violence in conventional conceptions of resilience and offer other takes on the world, other modes reckoning with the past and working towards a liveable future. According to Waanyi writer Alexis Wright, whose novel *The Swan Book* is the focus of chapter 6, "It is the work of the writer to try to imagine ... what the world might look like. It's not a simple thing like going out into the backyard and seeing a hornet's nest – it's describing the hornet's nest of the world" (Wright and Zable 2013). If we accept this assertion, a few things follow. One is the central role of the imagination. The phrase, "what the world might look like" can be read in different ways: in the cautionary "if-this-goes-on" vein of warning, as Octavia E. Butler (1998) memorably described her goals in writing speculative fiction, but also in the sense that the whole world is impossible to grasp. It is necessary to extrapolate from what can be seen by "going out into the backyard" to what things *might* look like at the scale of the planet. Wright is talking about scale in the sense described by Métis/Michif scholar Max Liboiron, which is significantly "not about relative size. Scale is what relationships matter within a particular context" (2021, 84). Wright's invocation of the "hornet's nest of the world" is an observation about scale and also about positionality. Unlike the "real" world conception of resilience as a universal, visible measurable capacity of systems and individuals, Wright's meditations on the world of the writer remind us that the writer (and the reader) is always *somewhere*, looking at particular hornet's nests from a particular vantage point.

That observation about scale and positionality has significant bearing on this book. I am a white, heterosexual, cis-gendered, and able-bodied settler woman (one who, not incidentally, owns a house with a backyard). I embody the settler-colonial concept of resilience, which is to say that I am both hailed by the *idea*, with its idealization of the white liberal society of which I am a part, and materially advantaged with tools for survival – whiteness, wealth, and education – that make me, if not adaptable, then at least fine for now. Wright's characterization of "the work of the writer" gestures to the effort that is required to leap from the hornet's nest of the backyard to the hornet's nest of the world. Recognizing the insensibility that comes with privilege, that isn't necessarily overcome (in fact it might be deepened!) by scholarly training, I embrace the obligation and the possibility of that leap, of that work. I am interested in resilience, which is to say that I'm curious about it, as a concept that's bristling with promise and danger, but I'm also invested; I want the world to keep going. I want to keep going! But not as things currently are, not as I currently am, as the beneficiary of a planetary regime that is sinking under the weight of accumulated horrors. Which means, as a start, learning how to see differently, and this leads back to the hornet's nest. The question for me isn't whether or not the world *is* a hornet's nest but what seeing the world as a hornet's nest brings into view. For example, it is a simple fact that the world is a home and a habitat for different beings, beings who are not necessarily like (or liked by) humans – beings who have their own communities, interests, and perspectives. It is the singular capacity of creative writers (and other cultural producers) to invite us to inhabit the energetic nexus of metaphor and materiality in a way that allows us to think both critically and creatively about where we are and where we might be going. Using Wright's statement as a launching pad, we can start to stretch and unravel the stories that underpin capitalist realism. From "the world is complex," we can move to "the world is more complicated than you think it is." "The world is a hornet's nest."

To work through the different resonances of resilience and the worlds these resonances understand and anticipate, this book considers the concept as it is expressed through narrative, illuminating certain actors and storylines, imagining certain futures, and foreclosing others. The goal is not only to compare definitions of resilience, positing some as better, more equitable, inclusive, or emancipatory than others, though that is frankly part of it. It is also to compare *kinds* of narratives – to think about those popular resilience narratives whose commensensical authority tends to suppress their status *as* narratives and about fictional ones that self-consciously stage troubling questions about categories of humanity and nature, health and disability, identity and transformation. This book gratefully, in recognition that they have not offered themselves up in this particular role, takes Alexis Wright along with Trinidadian-Canadian writer David Chariandy and Michi Saagiig Nishnaabeg writer Leanne Betasamosake Simpson as guides to thinking about the idea of resilience differently, with an eye to its potentiality as an imaginative resource for decolonization and planetary health. It begins, though, in the thick of late liberalism and settler colonialism where the popular concept of resilience has so firmly taken root.

Historicizing Resilience: Managing Systems, Managing Individuals (and Having Fun)

The modern origin story of resilience begins in the 1970s, developing from different disciplinary roots that became entwined over time. In ecological terms, resilience describes a system's capacity to retain its basic function and structure in the face of disturbance (Holling 1973; Walker and Salt 2006, xiii). Key to resilience thinking is the challenge that it poses to traditional ideas of a harmonious balance in nature. Rather than existing in a state of homeostasis that occasionally gets sent out of whack by some external force, the natural world is in a perpetual state of flux in which continuity is maintained by constant adaptation. As articulated in forest ecologist C.S. ("Buzz") Holling's 1973 article, "Resilience and the Stability of Ecological Systems," a piece that is often cited as the origin of the concept, resilience thinking takes account, in a way that traditional ecology did not, of the pervasive factors of change and spatial heterogeneity.

The decade preceding Holling's paper, beginning with the publication of Rachel Carson's *Silent Spring* (1962) and culminating in the appearance of the much-debated *Limits to Growth* report (Meadows et al. 1972),[2] generated awareness of the earth as an interconnected system and sounded a warning about its capacity to withstand human pressures, particularly population growth. These texts represented part of a burgeoning recognition of the effects – cumulative, pervasive, nonlinear, and irreversible – of human activity on ecosystems such that the idea of equilibrium was increasingly untenable. At the same time, the old model of ecological research, based on the idea of self-contained systems, appeared to be increasingly inapplicable to real-world situations. While the discipline of ecology began by focusing on specific local ecosystems, as the twentieth century progressed, the ideal microcosm that could be studied as a "little world within itself" proved increasingly elusive (Forbes 1925, 1, quoted in Robin 2014, 48). Urbanization, industrial pollution, and the proliferation of invasive species invalidated the "stability view" of ecological systems, which "emphasizes the equilibrium, the maintenance of a predictable world, and the harvesting of nature's excess production with as little fluctuation as possible" (Holling 1973, 21). In contrast, the resilience view of ecological management "would emphasize the need to keep options open, the need to view events in a regional rather than a local context, and the need to emphasize heterogeneity" in an effort "to absorb and accommodate future events in whatever unexpected form they took" (21). Resilience ecology provided models that explained the flux and multifariousness that characterized real-world ecosystems. Systems ecologist Carl Folke used the metaphors "revolt" and "remember" to describe the contradictory energies at play across different scales of a system that enabled – required, even – periodic, localized breakdowns to enable the preservation of the whole (2006, 259).[3]

One shift in focus implied by the resilience approach was to cast disruption (e.g., in the form of invasive species) not as a periodic violation of a natural order but as a functional part of natural *dis*order. "Perhaps," environmental historian Libby Robin speculates, "the world was ready for this new idea in 1973. The year was significant for the international political context that was all about shocks, particularly the oil shocks that suggested that western society could not continue to grow indefinitely on the basis of fossil fuel economies ... The first oil shocks in 1973 underscored the limits to growth, and turned thinking toward new paradigms for the relation between humanity and nature. Scientific and social questions cast long shadows on each other, and created an atmosphere of support for an integrative imagination" (2014, 53–4). Robin traces the shifting material contours of the world for which resilience supplied a useful descriptive theory. Implicit but unexamined in her account are the political and cultural currents that buoyed its enthusiastic uptake. What Robin's analysis makes clear is that a new focus on conservation emerged in the 1970s alongside, and in tension with, a geopolitical reckoning with shifts in global power that threatened the solidity of a belief in the inevitability of Western, particularly US, dominance. The idea of resilience presented itself as a tool that could be used to think through – and eventually to manage – the ramifications of unanticipated and potentially threatening change.

In this respect, the emergence of resilience follows the development of the discipline of ecology more generally – a discipline whose roots

Robin and others (Grove 1995; Griffiths and Robin 1997) have traced to nineteenth-century European efforts to manage the environmental effects of colonialism. As Richard H. Grove makes clear in his book *Green Imperialism*, colonial invaders encountered "a highly unfamiliar set of circumstances, in which risks in the physical environment ... were paralleled only by the dangers apprehended as being posed by an often equally poorly understood indigenous population. The instability of power relations between coloniser and colonised was thus frequently paralleled by the terms of a new dispensation of power defined in terms of an unknown ecology. In other words, an unfamiliar environment and populace might both present untold risks in knowing and controlling" (1995, 479). Environmentalist concerns were often coupled with concerns about human health. These concerns were both medical, focused on the risks unfamiliar diseases posed to colonists (bolstered by fears of the enfeebling effects of the tropics),[4] and metaphysical, reflecting "anxieties about the survival, nature and integrity of the human individual and human society" (483). Darwin's *Origin of Species* (1859) resonated in exciting and disturbing ways with the whole colonial project in its illumination of the constitutive role of change in defining identity and, by extension, the contingency of the human. Surveying ecology's colonial origins reminds us that ideas about natural order never stray far from concerns about (selectively defined) human flourishing – a relation that holds in contemporary thinking about resilience. The question of what structures of governance work "best" to manage unpredictable environments is one that continues to preoccupy resilience ecologists. Anxieties about environmental change, tangled with questions about being and becoming that strike at the very heart of what defines the human, continue to haunt resilience science in its pursuit of "the mathematics of heterogeneity" (Robin 2014, 58).

In ecology, resilience thinking focuses on systems but carries with it a trail of ideas about human identity. In psychology and allied fields, the reverse is true: resilience is attached to individuals, who are understood to be acting within a field of complex forces that translates into unpredictably and unevenly distributed life chances. In its early iterations, psychosocial resilience research focused on children exposed to risks such as parental mental illness, family conflict, and poverty (Garmezy 1974; Werner and Smith 1982). Departing from deficit-based approaches to development, resilience research sought to understand the factors contributing to "good outcomes" where they would not otherwise be expected (Masten 2001, 28). As resilience came to be understood less as an intrinsic quality that some individuals possessed than as a set of natural capacities or "ordinary magic" that individuals could cultivate to help them to thrive in challenging circumstances (Masten 2001), the concept of psychosocial resilience came to take on an increasingly regulatory flavour.

Psychosocial resilience is concerned with individuals rather than ecosystems. However, like social-ecological resilience, it emerged in the context of a shifting understanding – and governance – of the world. Ideas of an ideal balance that should be maintained or returned to had given way to an understanding that social and physical orders existed within a landscape of more or less ubiquitous, more or less perpetual risk (Beck 1992; Castel 1991). This recognition had both negative and positive implications. As the assumed stability and integrity of ecosystems gave way to a sense of volatility, interactivity, and ever-imminent disruption, ideas about human subjectivity also morphed into something more fluid: freer, more flexible but also more precarious. The late twentieth century saw the emergence of a "new ethical vocabulary" in which the poles of conformity/deviance, defined in relation to a relatively stable social order, were shaken by ideas of "autonomy, freedom, choice, authenticity, enterprise, lifestyle" (Rose 1996, 320). In psychosocial resilience theory, an emphasis on the achievement of "competence" (Garmezy, Masten, and Tellegen 1984) and "positive adaptation" (Luthar, Cichetti, and Becker 2000, 545) reflected this emerging ethical landscape defined not by adherence to a singular norm but by constant self-modulations in response to ever-changing environmental conditions (see chapter 1 for a more detailed discussion of this development).

If the conceptualization and application of resilience in ecology and the psychosocial sciences emerged in seeming opposition to one another – the former with a focus on ecosystems and the latter with a focus on the individual – the 1980s saw a convergence of these two streams of resilience thinking, which continues today, such that psychosocial resilience is understood to encompass individuals and their environments and social-ecological resilience describes complex adaptive systems characterized by human and nonhuman interactions. The consolidation of resilience as a measure of adaptability to a constantly changing physical and social environment corresponds to the political mood of settler colonialism, as I will elaborate below. First, it's worth looking a little closer at the ways resilience attends to, and even conflates, the scales of the individual and the system. This convergence might seem natural if we accept, along with the apparently self-evident statement "the world is complex," the truism that "the world is made up of individuals." These ideas, ideological pillars of late liberalism, find interesting expression not just in resilience thinking but also in how resilience scientists talk about themselves.

This talk merits attention because popular accounts of the emergence of resilience thinking and the people who engage it express something of the worldview that resilience purports to describe. Andrew Zolli and Ann Marie Healy's account, *Resilience: Why Things Bounce Back* (2012), is typical in its punctuation of discussions of resilience theory with portraits of its quirky, brilliant creators. There's the story of the boy whose nerdy obsession with fish blossomed into a PhD, followed by a career conducting groundbreaking research into the complexity of aquatic ecosystems (55); the Iranian immigrant who developed a think tank focused on improving critical infrastructure security after 9/11 and came to be regarded as "the father of the smart grid" (80); and the theoretical physicist with an eclectic wardrobe: "a breezy blue striped shirt and white pants – the quintessential sartorial choice of the summering Englishman" along with a belt-buckle embedded with turquoise stone from New Mexico, where he leads complexity research at the Santa Fe Institute (95). Unremarkable on their own, together these biographies shape the story that has helped to usher resilience science into popular culture. If that story has a moral, it may be expressed through these singular scientists' collective recognition that the world is untidier than we previously thought: more interconnected, more heterogeneous, and more unstable, full of surprises. The sketches of the scientists gesture towards this element of resilience thinking in highlighting curiosity and quirkiness (intellectual and sartorial) as well as diversity, exemplified in the story of the Iranian immigrant working on US security post-9/11.[5]

It is worth noting that, underlying the novel account in which resilience science itself takes on the character of a complex system, even as the scientists are cast as autonomous figures outside a world that is the object of their discovery, a more familiar story emerges. The details of the scientists' biographies describe a fairly conservative trajectory: each pursues a traditional path through university, on to higher degrees, and finally leadership within a particular field. Far from being outliers, they are celebrated as part of a socially dominant group whose views about change, diversity, and systems happen to correspond to prevailing wisdom. Nowhere, perhaps, is the myth of the resilience leader more exuberantly upheld than in the representation of Buzz Holling, the "father" of resilience thinking, who begins his reflection on his pioneering role this way: "I am writing now to give a personal view of what I believe I have discovered – my personal, explorers' guide of intellectual journeys that truly excited me when, as it seemed to me, wondrous new lands periodically suddenly emerged that no one had seen or remarked on before. For scientists, those are the times when a tsunami wave of excitement triggers a passion for discovery" (2007, 3). Holling's reflection is noteworthy not for its hubris – his comments on the field contain many generous extensions of credit to other scientists, such as Steve Carpenter, "a great ecosystems scientist" (8); Carl Waters, "a truly brilliant, maverick scientist" (8); and Larry Dill, "a well known behavioral ecologist, who, in my view, is simply the best whole animal experimentalist in the world!" (5) – nor is it my intention to deny the importance of his work. What invites interrogation is the recourse, here and elsewhere, to metaphors of singular individuals set on voyages of discovery to "wondrous new lands."

These creation stories of the field of resilience ecology highlight in concentrated form some of the tensions that animate popular resilience discourse. The easy movement between complex systems and individual human(ist) subjects – sometimes verging on conflation of the two scales – relates to another contradiction, that between an emphasis on the "incomprehensible complexity, interconnectivity, and volatility of the modern world" (Zolli and Healy 2012, 4) and a conservative vision of a world led by exceptional, enterprising men. These contradictions emerge, to recall the earlier discussion about the history of resilience ecology, during a period of decolonization and globalization in which the West was starting to experience the wavering of its assumed solidity and authority. The idea of resilience enabled a reckoning with the danger of dissolution while holding to the (nostalgic) vision of continued dominance, exemplified by the figure of the colonial adventurer.

The element of pleasure is not incidental. More than an index of a willingness to undertake risky pursuits, pleasure is a critical aspect of the resilient individual's (or the resilience scientist's) interface with the world. The importance of this quality emerges in interviews with the scientists who make up the Resilience Alliance conducted by John N. Parker and Edward J. Hackett (2012).[6] Musing about the personal qualities that characterize members of the alliance, one member notes that, in addition to being knowledgeable and curious, "they had fun ... After five days on an island in a workshop, these were the ones that would sing the songs and make the limericks and ended up as good friends" (Parker and Hackett 2012, 29).[7] Another Resilience Alliance leader notes that participants "are all empathetic people; they really try and understand other people. So that is a good quality – they enjoy happy hour. They enjoy fun" (29). Yet another scientist explains the strategy of inviting participants who "are willing to cross the boundary, people who are willing to invest time to learn the language and the necessary jargon of other disciplines. And people who are just fun, and people who are willing to take those challenges" (29).

In some ways, the personal qualities highly rated by resilience scientists are unremarkable (though perhaps not stereotypically associated with scientists); collegiality is important in any academic endeavour – or any collaborative work. However, the characterization of the Resilience Alliance and its ideal members also bears significantly on the concept of resilience itself, in its contrary tendencies towards openness and closedness. One of the hallmarks of resilience thinking is the recognition that borders – of ecosystems, of organisms, of organizations – are more porous than previously recognized. The normative behavioural corollary of this recognition is a facility and enthusiasm for crossing them, whether the borders are between disciplines, between professional and nonprofessional realms of activity – for example, scholarly dialogue and limerick contests – or between public and private life (another unusual aspect of the Resilience Alliance workshops was the inclusion of family members). The net effect of this boundary crossing is merging of selves such that, in the words of one Resilience Alliance workshop participant, the group became like "more or less a collective brain, or a collective soul" (Parker and Hackett 2012, 32) in which, another notes, "you interact with the same people ... so you can almost communicate by minimal sounds. It's almost like you know people so well that one of them makes a head gesture like that [nodding] and it just communicates a whole subroutine of knowledge at once" (32). The impression these comments give is of the group as organism, its parts relating to one another effortlessly, as if by nature. Another way of seeing it is as a tight, closed community whose existence depends on the exclusion of outsiders. Consistent with this view is the interpretation members offer of the upheaval that occurred in the original network in the late 1990s, precipitated by the admission of new members, as reflecting the natural cycle of complex adaptive systems in which periods of growth and conservation give way to disruption and reorganization. This ecological account of the group's identity and dissolution makes no reference to the role of power in shaping dynamics of belonging, conflict, exclusion, and fragmentation.

It is against this ambiguous backdrop – the official portrait of heterodoxy and flexibility and the less acknowledged dynamic of familiarity and homogeneity – that "fun" becomes possible. That is, fun as an orientation to the world that celebrates risk and sanctions the transgression of borders, according to unspoken rules governing membership in an exclusive group (see chapter 1 for an elaboration of this idea). The seven senior scientists who make up the core of the Resilience Alliance include six men and one woman from North America, Western Europe, and Australia. We may assume that the relative homogeneity of the group contributed to their ease of interaction and the related premium placed on (an apparently generally agreed upon definition of) fun. While we should be cautious about drawing a too-neat line from the composition of this small group of scientists to the insights of resilience science in general, there are some elements of resilience science that make the politics of its production especially salient. One is the conception of the social-ecological system, an extrapolation from the physical to the social world that has drawn much criticism (Olsson et al. 2005; Cote and Nightingale 2012; Evans and Reid 2014; Hornborg 2013; Davidson 2013). A significant concern is the move to naturalize particular social configurations; as Olsson et al. put it, "assumptions of self-organization and function tend to hide power, ignore the dynamics of conflict, and bracket agency" (2005, 6).

The conflation of different kinds of research objects (ecological systems/social groups) reflects the totalizing impulse of resilience theory, which strives for globality not just in terms of ecosystemic comprehensiveness but also of disciplinary knowledge. Citing environmental scientist Roderick J. Lawrence's work on transdisciplinary studies, Seema Arora-Jonsson identifies in resilience science an "aspiration to epistemological transcendence" (2016, 100) and corresponding lack of awareness of its situatedness (103).[8] As feminist and postcolonial scholars such as Sandra Harding have pointed out, "northern sciences ... tak[e] their problems, ontologies and other background assumptions, and preferred methods of collecting and evaluating data from their local historical contexts" even as they aim to universalize those problems, ontologies, and methodologies (2008, 140; Arora-Jonsson 2016, 103). Arora-Jonsson follows Harding in arguing that, "instead of a unified and integrated whole, resilience too is an 'ethnoscience'" (2016, 103). The portrait of resilience scientists cited above clearly bears out this characterization.

This does not mean that we can simply graft markers of privilege, including gender, citizenship, and race, directly onto the composite sketch of the exemplary resilient subject – the individual who is courageous, curious, flexible, and fun (and possibly sporting a turquoise emblazoned belt). It does mean that the privileged location of the scientists who form the Resilience Alliance – a group who are "friends first and also collaborators" (Parker and Hackett 2012, 29) – shapes and limits the kind of world they imagine: its systematicity as well as its risks and pleasures, its exclusions and oppressions. The scientists' location may partly explain resilience theory's hospitality to capitalism and the idea of the market as a self-correcting mechanism (Walker and Cooper 2011; Joseph 2013; Zebrowski 2015; Evans and Reid 2014). More specifically, it establishes a cultural context for Hollings' conception of himself as an "explorer" who embarked on the discovery of "wondrous new lands" riding a "tsunami wave of excitement" (Hollings 2007, 1).

The ambiguous connotations of the tsunami wave, for which "excitement" might not be the only or most obvious response, recalls the historical context of the advent of resilience ecology described above: the 1970s was a period of simmering global economic and ecological crisis to which neoliberal and resilience theories respectively offered provisional solutions (Walker and Cooper 2011). The turmoil of the period might be aptly summed up in the rueful nostalgia expressed by a Royal Dutch Shell executive in a 2004 interview,[9] who recalled a time before the burgeoning of computer technology, roiling currencies, and oil crisis of the 1970s when "we thought the world was makeable" (Heinzen and Muliro 2004, 9). Hayekian economics and resilience theory each supply, in separate realms that would eventually be synchronized, templates for what "we" – a group the Royal Dutch Shell executive later characterizes vaguely but tellingly as "a fraternity" (12) – should do to manage a world that had begun to reveal itself as unamenable to top-down control (of course, it hardly warrants mentioning that what amounted to a revelation to this fraternity was, and had always been, common knowledge to most of the world's population). The mood of apprehension that accompanied the recognition that the Western-dominated post–World War II order was less stable than previously assumed conditions resilience theory's concern with the capacity for systems to persist in the face of disruption. It also arguably shapes an idea of fun that risk figures predominantly in: the risk for the explorer that he might encounter storms or, even worse, an obstacle – in the form, for example, of hostile natives – that threaten his very freedom to keep exploring.

Resilience, Late Liberalism, and Settler Colonialism

The origin story of social-ecological resilience science, as told by its protagonists, resonates with how resilience has emerged, since the 1980s, as an essential way to understand and to navigate an increasingly complex, increasingly volatile world. Resilience has become an indispensable tool for managing contingency, seeking, in the words of Christopher Zebrowski, "to secure society from unpredictable systemic shocks by improving the evolutionary capacity, or 'fitness,' of the population" (2009, 3). The increasing centrality of resilience as a concept that draws together ecology, urban planning, development, security, and the psy-disciplines[10] cannot be understood apart from this biopolitical imperative. That imperative in turn arises in the context of the growing pains of liberalism, struggling with "a series of legitimacy crises in the way of anticolonial, new social movements, and new Islamic movements" (Povinelli 2011, 25). Formal gestures of recognition towards these movements take place alongside (and work to conceal) the consolidation of prevailing concentrations of political and economic power. The chief function of policies undertaken in late liberalism, as Povinelli defines it, is "to conserve liberal governance and the accumulation of value for dominant social groups" (2016, 169). Accordingly, beginning with Reagan and Thatcher in the US and the UK, neoliberal economic thinking, nourished by Cold War rhetorics of anticommunism, justifies "the killing of all social projects that do not produce market forms of life ... on the basis of a distinction between societies of freedom and those of constraint, and the security risk of allowing the latter to gain a footing in the former" (Povinelli 2011, 29). The preeminence of risk highlights the tension at the heart of late liberalism between a recognition of the centrality – indeed the necessity – of change and a concomitant desire for permanence.

This balancing act is performed with particular acuteness in the settler-colonial state. In support of her thesis that settler occupation of Indigenous lands becomes the model of the liberal nation, Povinelli cites Benedict Anderson's observation that "one of the justifications, sooner or later for the new nationalism[s] was their creole nature: 'their distinctive history, and especially their demographic blending of settler and indigenous peoples, to say nothing of local traditions, geographies, climates, and so forth'" (Povinelli 2011, 36). Reconciliation, a political project that aims to undo centuries of violence towards Indigenous people (while denying its continuation in the present) in some ways describes a more general, existential objective for settler-colonial nations, which derive their legitimacy from their successful metabolization of difference. Settler-colonial nations embody (for settlers) the contradiction between potentiality for growth and progress – the biopolitical end of statehood – and rootedness in place. This contradiction is spatial, in the sense of belonging to the land while also using it as capital, as well as temporal: future persistence and growth derive their legitimacy from a sense of historically justified self-possession.

This contradiction, between conservation and transformative movement, also informs the idea of resilience, which assumes a distinct character and finds special resonance in settler-colonial culture. In its emphasis on heterogeneity and the tension between change and persistence, resilience replaces older ideas of meaning (whether personal, organizational, or ecosystemic) defined by homogeneity and stasis. Another way of thinking about this feature of resilience thinking might be to emphasize the distinctly modern nature of settler-colonial nations, which focus, at least in official liberal iterations,[11] on *formal* aspects of identity (democratic capitalist, liberal) rather than its specific content (some version of "blood and soil"). While settlers might be plagued by a desire to claim Indigenous legitimacy, or to naturalize their presence in a particular place, this desire remains always haunted with the ongoing displacement of Indigenous people on which settlement is predicated. Thus, the emphasis in resilience thinking on navigating the future – a path often eased by downplaying the past (see, for example, Colombino and Vanolo 2017) – is conducive to settler-colonial sense, which, Povinelli suggests, divides humans into two fundamental categories: "autological subjects," agential, future-oriented human beings (white settlers), and "genealogical societies," groups of (Indigenous) people whose whole existence is seen to be subsumed by tradition and will accordingly be superseded or subsumed by progress (2016, 172).

Extending Povinelli's formulation of late liberalism, its rhetoric of heterogeneity, its market fundamentalism and celebration of the entrepreneurial individual, we can identify three common elements in the way resilience thinking appears in contemporary culture. The first is an emphasis on heterogeneity or diversity as a key property of resilient systems that operate in tension with the concept of coherent identity. This tension also expresses itself in an orientation to a future that draws together discourses of sustainability and change, working to reconcile opposing dynamics of preservation and disruption. The second, which underlines the focus on diversity, is a focus on the system as the key locus of meaning, understood in terms of a relatively seamless integration of economy, environment, and society. The third, drawing on the "new ethical vocabulary" outlined by Nikolas Rose (2011, 145), is a model of ideal personhood, defined by a capacity to understand, accept, and successfully leverage these complex forces (deemed to be the unavoidable realities of modern existence) into a productive life. These strains of thought nourish the diverse resilience narratives that circulate in settler-colonial society, a select few of which this book analyzes. These include the quest to restore a childhood defined by "old-fashioned" outdoor fun, whose elements of risk and adventure are now understood to be compromised by a culture of safety – we could call this the "resilience lost" narrative – as well as narratives of "resilience found," like those seen in blueprints for urban futurity in the face of threats ranging from environmental disaster to pandemics to homelessness. Implicit in each of these narratives is an idea of the future that is infused with optimism (the belief that change brings opportunity), anxiety (the fear that things will change irrevocably), and nostalgia (the sense that they already have). Acknowledging these tensions serves as a reminder that resilience as a concept is always contingent on what is outside it and on the ever-present possibility of its failure in the face of an unassimilable other. One is always resilient *to* something: to a disruptive disaster or force that would make one other than oneself.

Policing Resilience

Considering resilience in this way, as an index of the capacity to successfully leverage difference without being undone by it, illuminates its conceptual usefulness to the preservation of white supremacy through settler colonialism and racial capitalism.[12] Settler colonialism justifies itself through an awkward dance between the symbolic poles of identity and belonging on the one hand and the ideas of infinite expansion on the other. Indigenous people are necessary to this dance, as a source of (stolen) cultural markers of belonging, but also obstacles to it; their connection to the land impedes its exploitation. They are likewise enlisted by the discourse of resilience – Indigenous people exemplify resilience! They have been here forever! – and cast out by it, their attachment to the land inimical to the kind of flexible accumulation settler futurity is based on. In a similarly twisted way, the idea of resilience works in concert with the discourse of multiculturalism, which functions via what Ghassan Hage terms a "dialectic of inclusion and exclusion" (2000, 136–8). Racial capitalism prescribes both the movement and the limits of that movement within the terms of a foundational inequality that amounts to an "extrinsic relation between a White possessor and a non-White possessed" (140). That is to say, racial capitalism depends on the *existence* – as necessary predicate to the *containment* – of difference and movement to sustain its power.

The tension between identity and sameness, stability and movement also inspires the allure of resilience. Though it acknowledges that things are complicated and getting more so, and though it recognizes difference as inherent in, rather than opposed to, systems, resilience as it is conventionally evoked speaks to the possibility of conserving (with minor adaptations to changing environments both natural and social) the white, heteronormative, patriarchal, and colonial foundations of late liberalism. Thus, as Povinelli observes, mainstream environmentalists converge with "laissez-faire liberals, Keynesian liberals and neoliberals" in their support for what Jacques Rancière defines as the role of police – that is, "the management of a given distribution of social places of roles, ways of being and saying such that some activities are visible and sayable … while other activities appear to be nothing more than noise" (Povinelli 2011, 50). Dominant understandings of resilience are not only inseparable from contemporary relations of racial capitalism and, in places like Canada, the US, Australia, and Aotearoa New Zealand, settler colonialism; those relations are their ultimate referent. In other words, whether the term resilience is nominally applied to ecosystems or individuals, it is the sustenance of the system as a whole – the extractive, exploitative, and infinitely growth-oriented system – that is fundamentally at issue.

What is the role of policing in relation to the goal of sustenance and the value of resilience? The question is not just metaphorical. The value of resilience has assumed particular salience in the realm of security, focused variously and sometimes together, as in the US Department of Homeland Security, on threats ranging from terrorism to epidemics to natural disasters. The risk of these threats has grown proportionately with the extension and intensification of networks associated with globalization, though they are notoriously not new. Foucault identifies the emergence of this tension in the governance of space in the eighteenth century, particularly with respect to site of the town. On the one hand, in accordance with the intensification of capitalism, there was a need for circulation. On the other hand, circulation threatens to compromise sovereignty; it presents a problem of security. Therefore, the challenge arises "of organizing circulation, eliminating its dangerous elements, making a division between good and bad circulation, and maximizing the good circulation by diminishing the bad" (Foucault 2009, 34). This approach to governance anticipated the modern understanding of social space, organized around the nodes of cities, as comprising an ecological system whose heterogeneity and interconnected complexity – the key to its resilience – also demanded new forms of regulation.

The understanding of space as an *environment* goes hand in hand with the mode of governance Foucault termed biopolitics, which is concerned with human beings "insofar as they are a species, insofar as they are living beings" navigating a particular milieu (2003, 245). The central aim of biopolitics is maximizing fitness, a population-scale imperative for which individuals are enjoined to take responsibility. As Rose points out, the "new ethical vocabularies" that define this model of fitness don't just codify rules for how to be. They also

> establish new "dividing practices" within and between subjects. Thus the language of responsible self-advancement is linked to a new perception of those outside civility – the excluded or marginalized who through willfulness, incapacity or ignorance cannot or will not exercise such responsibility. On the one hand, pathologies are re-individualized, removed from a "social" determination into a moral order, thus providing the basis for new and harsher strategies of surveillance and control of those who, after all, bear the responsibility for their fate within their own hands ... On the other hand, these new sectors of the population are opened up to new forms of intervention by experts, which would re-educate or "empower" them, equipping them with the techniques of life planning and personal conduct to cope as autonomous subjects, deploying psychological techniques from social skills training to group relations. (N. Rose 2011, 145)

The dividing practices Rose describes operate at the level of individuals, subjecting them to surveillance and administration by the psy-disciplines. But their goals are also broadly social, the sequestration of "at-risk" individuals aimed at protecting the population at large. In the arena of security, the discourses of psychosocial and social-ecological resilience converge.

As noted above, the key element in their convergence – the core element of biopolitics – is racism. Sylvia Wynter has shown that the ideal of population "fitness" rests on an evolutionary story, an "origin narrative of survival-through-ever-increasing-processes-of-consumption-

and-accumulation" (Wynter and McKittrick 2015, 11) that culminates in the figure of *homo economicus*, whose supremacy not coincidentally corresponds to what Wynter describes as the "law-like normalization of the corporeal features of Western Europeans in their now ethno-class bourgeois aesthetic configuration" (18). This narrative, as already noted, is part of the climate of resilience's emergence as a key concept: the idea of resilience is steeped in discourses of race and specifically of white supremacy. That does not mean that resilience is understood to be the hallmark of whiteness or even that the concept attaches itself primarily to white bodies. Resilience slips and slides between referents, in part because its meaning is unstable and changes according to the context in which the term is used. For example, Sarah Bracke cogently highlights distinctions between the way the idea of resilience interpellates "First World subjects," for whom the term "resurrects a form of self-sufficiency, and hence, a fantasy of mastery" (2016, 58) and the way the term adheres to subaltern subjects whose survival in the face of colonialism, war, and globalization is recast as a valiant capacity to "absorb the impact of austerity measures and continue to be productive" (61). Resilience is also slippery because it emerges from and describes conditions of instability and change. It speaks to anxiety about how to secure ways of being that are oriented not only around ecological sustainability but also around racial capitalism, Western dominance, and settler colonialism.

Reckoning with Resilience Narratives

The diverse and even chaotic strands of thinking that energize the idea of resilience take coherent shape via narrative. As Michael Basseler puts it, "The very notion of resilience, as the capacity to bounce back from stress and pain, rests intrinsically upon the narrative sequencing of events, responses, and adaptive processes" (2019a, 26). However resilience is invoked, whether in the service of disaster strategy, ecosystem management, corporate planning, or social justice work, it rests on the idea of an entity (a system, an organization, a community, an individual) carrying on through time, either persisting in its current form (staying resilient) in the face of disruption or becoming something else. Resilience narratives convey assumptions about the present (what or who counts as an entity that can – or should – persist into the future? How does that entity exist in the world, in a particular environment?); the future (what would persistence look like? How would we measure it? How much change is tolerable or desirable?); and even, implicitly, since it is not an obvious feature of resilience, the past (how did the current environment come into being? What traces of past actions and processes persist in the current configuration of things and with what effects or implications?) In most iterations of resilience – for example, when we talk about cultivating resilience as a mental health strategy or promoting the resilience of a community to climate change – these elements of the narrative remain hidden, buried in the thickets of common sense that tell us *of course* it is clear what (or whom) we are seeking to preserve against what.[13]

To highlight the narrative aspect of resilience thinking is not to unmask it or discount its conceptual power as a tool for illuminating what Bruno Latour (2004) calls "matters of concern."[14] Perhaps the most useful approach to narrative in the context of resilience is to see it not as lifeline to solid historical ground[15] nor as the ideological underpinning whose exposure renders the whole idea of resilience suspect but as a mode of thought that exemplifies resilience while also allowing us to think critically about it. Sylvia Wynter's theory of *homo narrans* offers a way into understanding this paradox. In Wynter's formulation, the hierarchy that once prevailed through the decree of medieval Christianity's Great Chain of Being has yielded to a modern, no less immutable law sanctioned by the discourse of biology, which divides forms of existence, including human groups, into categories of "the naturally selected (i.e., eugenic) and naturally dysselected (i.e., dysgenic) beings" (Wynter and McKittrick 2015, 17). Wynter complicates the naturalness of this division by noting a missing piece of the biological story, which is humans' evolution as a storymaking species, as evidenced by one-hundred-thousand-year-old archaeological findings in Blombos Cave, South Africa. What Foucault calls the "invention of Man" – an invention that emerged simultaneously with, and as a rationale for, capitalism, slavery, and colonialism – is not scientific fact but narrative creation, a secular extension of the earlier Christian idea of the Great Chain of Being (Wynter 2003, 263). Katherine McKittrick elaborates Wynter's conception of the biosocial aspect of human evolution this way:

> Humans are ... a biomutationally evolved, hybrid species – *storytellers who now storytellingly invent themselves as being purely biological.* With this, particular (presently biocentric) macro-origin stories are overrepresented as the singular narrative through which the stakes of human freedom are articulated and marked. Our contemporary moment thus demands a normalized origin narrative of survival-through-ever-increasing-processes-of-consumption-and-accumulation. This is reinforced by the epistemological discourses of natural scarcity, the bell curve, and so forth, together with the "planet of slums" reality that is before us – which is nevertheless made to appear, in commonsense terms, as being naturally determined. This commonsense naturalized story is cast as the only possible realization of the way the world must be, and "is." (Wynter and McKittrick 2015, 11)

This translation of a partial narrative into natural and inevitable truth has powerful political effects. It "enables the interests, reality, and well-being of the empirical world to continue to be imperatively subordinated to those of the now globally hegemonic ethnoclass world of [white, Western, bourgeois] 'Man'" (Wynter 2003, 262). As it settles into the status of a realist picture of the-way-things-are, the narrative foundations of this arrangement disappear from view.

Dominant resilience narratives rest on the foundations of the narrative of evolution. Central to both is the principle of adaptation, along with its implied opposite: failed adaptation or the absence of resilience can be read as the ontogenetic manifestation of the phylogenetic process of "dysselection" (Wynter and McKittrick 2015, 37). Models of psychosocial and social-ecological resilience converge in their naturalization of what Wynter identifies as "the Malthusian storytelling trope of *natural scarcity*" (65), adherence to which she suggests "has replaced what had been its/our enslavement to original sin" (26). Resilience represents, if not salvation, then success in the game of natural selection, for which racial capitalism (foundationally bound up with colonialism) is understood to serve as proxy. As economics becomes the principal mechanism of selection/dysselection, with primacy granted to the figure of the "jobholding Breadwinner" (Wynter 2003, 321), it does not entirely overwrite but instead builds on prior hierarchies of humanness. The narrative of human progress continues to pivot around what Wynter, following W.E.B. Dubois, calls "the Color Line" (310), policed by the dynamic of selection/dysselection.

Wynter's theorization of the process by which the narrative of (white, bourgeois, Western) "Man" comes to overwrite the experience of the human bears on resilience in two ways. First, in the same way as the narrative of the ascendance of the "jobholding Breadwinner" recapitulates Darwinian evolution as that process is commonly understood, it also accords with the dominant view of resilience, whereby good life outcomes are understood to reflect successful adaptation to the inevitable ups and downs of existence in complex economic/ecological systems. Second, Wynter's argument about narrative resonates with the concept of resilience in a way that at first glance might seem contradictory. Her reconceptualization of the conventionally understood figure of the human as not *homo economicus* but *homo narrans* points to the fundamental significance of humans' capacity for storytelling to our persistence as a species: that is, storytelling conditions our resilience. To accept this argument is to recognize that, in her thorough dismantling of the conventional narrative of Man, Wynter is not asking us to dismiss the meaningfulness of narrative but, rather, to accept its centrality to humanness, its material necessity to our survival, *and*, by extension, to acknowledge the narrative foundations of the things we tell ourselves about our species, about what it means to be human. To recognize that what we take to be true is founded in stories, constructed out of the interests and material conditions that coalesce in different places for diverse peoples at particular historical moments, is to recognize that other stories are possible, articulating different constellations of interest and circumstance.

Geographers Kevin Glynn and Julie Cupple illuminate this possibility by drawing on Wynter's concept of *homo narrans* to analyze decolonial resilience stories created by Indigenous groups in Guatamala who have been displaced by the slow and fast violence of volcanoes, hurricanes, and government indifference and brutality: "Neoliberal imaginaries and the narratives they generate are not yet the only ones that are active and effective in the world," Glynn and Cupples assert (2022, 25). Indigenous communities of La Rochela and La Trinidad employ modes of "narrative disarticulation and rearticulation" (18) to contest dominant (neoliberal, nationalist) resilience narratives and assert new ones. Their tactics are both critical – for example, highlighting connections between state responses to "natural" disasters and practices of racial and colonial violence (21) – and creative, engaging in "border thinking" (Mignolo and Tlostanova 2006) that emerges from the space of the dispossessed to build alliances across groups and develop hybrid epistemologies (Glynn and Cupples 2022, 23). They also refuse the "necronationalistic" practices of the state by exhuming the disappeared bodies of those who have died from state neglect and violence and telling survivors' stories (23) and – perhaps most importantly – continue to express and practice Indigenous knowledges and ways of being (20). "Indigenous communities have been learning to negotiate and contest colonial imports such as *homo economicus* and neoliberal narrativity for a long time," Glynn and Cupples point out (25). As far as resilience goes, they note that "decolonial modes of thought and social movements arise from struggles against five hundred years of disastrous coloniality, and generate sharply different conceptions and narratives of what it might mean and look like to practice resilience in the age of contemporarily expansive disasterscapes" (25).

Drawing on Wynter's insights into humans' adaptive capacity as storymaking animals, Glynn and Cupples' research makes clear that resilience cannot be dismissed as a structuring principle for the lives of those in the shadows of settler colonialism. This study applies this insight in the context of literary critical analysis of resilience fiction. Following Wynter's invitation to develop a "meta-Darwinian/neo-Darwinian account" of our origins in the interest of "giv[ing] humanity a different future" (Wynter and McKittrick 2015, 72), I suggest we can start to think about a "meta-resilience" narrative – one that acknowledges the constructedness and historical specificity of our understanding of the stakes of resilience. What constitutes resilience, who or what is understood to be resilient, against what, and to what effect? In support of Basseler's aim to create a "cultural narratology of resilience" (2019a, 30), asking these questions recognizes that all formulations of resilience are partial, bound by time, place, and circumstance, while going beyond ideological critique to recognize the usefulness – perhaps even the inevitability – of resilience as a measure of the capacity to go on. Wynter invites us to imagine what writer, activist, and self-described "Queer Black Troublemaker" Alexis Pauline Gumbs calls "a poetics of possibility," which is "based on the hope that we can tell ourselves (and believe) a story that allows our species to continue to live on this planet before it's too late" (Gumbs 2019, 336).

"A Poetics of Possibility"

Many Indigenous cultures recognize a connection between resilience and storytelling. For Leanne Betasamosake Simpson, "stories direct, inspire, and affirm an ancient code of ethics" (2017, 152). This conception of story is more radical than the process advanced by some psychotherapists of "knitting together a broken self" (Cyrulnik 2005, 5).[16] Following Nishnaabeg tradition, Simpson represents story as integrally tied to the project of radical Indigenous resurgence, an "algorithm" that operates, together with ceremonies and the land itself, as "coded processes that generate solutions to the problems of occupation and erasure and to life on earth" (2017, 23, 34). In its fundamental, adaptive significance, this version of story has parallels to Wynter's conception of *homo narrans*, whose understanding of the function of narrative extends from the level of the individual/therapeutic to the level of the species/socializing: storymaking is an indispensable tool for survival. Indigenous stories and storymaking capacity are accordingly part of what colonialism sets out to destroy.

One of the main arguments of this book is that dominant conceptions of resilience are complicit in colonialism. If, as Glen and Cupples argue, the problem is with the frame and not with the idea of resilience itself, what do anticolonial literary narratives look like? One approach to this question is offered in the idea Anishinaabe writer and scholar Gerald Vizenor calls "native survivance," a dynamic that is characterized by "an active sense of presence over absence, deracination and oblivion" and the renunciation of "the unbearable sentiments of tragedy, and the legacy of victimry" (2008, 1). Survivance is not about survival in the sense of an identifiable referent – "the native" – persisting through time. Noting that "the Indian" was a colonial invention, Vizenor gives voice to the perspective of the "postindian," a figure whose ironic indeterminacy embodies the "protean" nature of native creation stories whose "tease and weave of ironic gestures were badly translated by pioneers, missionaries, federal agents, and scholars" (2019, 1).[17]

Against those translations, which reduced the living truth of oral narrative into "catechism or liturgy" (3), Vizenor calls for writing that retains a sense of mobility, comedy, and irony.

This sense is crucially different from the "fun" associated with dominant resilience narratives, discussed above and in chapter 1, which is defined in terms of escapist freedom. By contrast, Vizenor argues that "the grasp of irony is crucial to fully recognize the chancy contradictions of historical, political, and critical historical and literary narratives, and the consent of irony creates a lively and humane discourse" (2019, 12). Irony is wedded to context and entails a kind of contract between speaker and listener to attend to the contradictions and silences that underlie communication. Rejecting efforts at complete representation that seek to "'steal [the object of their description] with words'" (Blaeser 1996, 171), Vizenor employs a writing style that is deliberately elusive and indeterminate, embodied in metaphors that hover between meanings, nonlinear narratives, and an attention to the ambiguity that surrounds what passes for reality. "Shadows are a natural presence in native stories and artistic scenes," he notes. They are "vital motion, visionary and animate, and create a sense of presence. The Anishinaabe word *agawaatese*, for example, is translated as a shadow of flight, a totemic image of presence, not the mere absence of light, or a passive cast of the source. The traces of shadows are a presence in stories and art" (Vizenor 2019, 20). The emphasis on traces and shadows is not fun, nor is it merely deconstructionist (though Vizenor cites Derrida liberally). Rather, this emphasis speaks to a crucial component of survivance whereby presence and intelligence are flickering, conferred not only on the living – those conventional resilience theory might celebrate as survivors – and not only conferred on humans.

Vizenor notes that "survivance" has multiple roots, associated with "'survival of the soul (after death), afterlife' ... and the 'succession to an estate ... the right of such succession in case of survival' (*New Shorter Oxford English Dictionary*)" (2008, 19). He goes on to note that the suffix *ance* connotes action, such that "survivance ... is the action, condition, quality, and sentiments of the verb *survive*, 'to remain alive or in existence,' to outlive, persevere with a suffix of *survivancy*" (19). The emphasis on movement is worth noting, as is the idea of succession. Survivance succeeds death – a fact that does not contradict irony but is bound up in it. The death that haunts survivance shapes both the kind of narrative that can be told and the means of telling it. To the extent that colonial violence is enacted not just on a people but on their meaning-making systems, storytellers face the task of expressing the life of a world in a language – English – whose grammar has evolved through the conquest of that world. Narratives of survivance differ from straightforward conventional resilience stories in this important respect: they are told ambivalently, in swirls of allusive and ironic misdirection against the terms of their expression.

Another sort of scaffolding for decolonial resilience stories speaks to the experience of writing through the violence of chattel slavery and its surrounding mythologies. Christina Sharpe's theory of Black life in America as a mode of living "in the wake" has been enormously generative in figuring the struggle to articulate "what, if anything, survives" the objectification of Black humanity that is also the strangulation of ways of knowing and imagining (2016, 14). "Wake" figures the aftermath of tragedy, both in the sense of the displacement of water behind slave ships and the rituals that attend a death, while also connoting the form of consciousness that Sharpe calls "wake *work*" (10, italics added). And in the same way that a wake, in the gathering of mourners together to eat, drink, and remember, also affirms life, Sharpe's method is "interested ... in tracking the ways we resist, rupture, and disrupt that immanence and imminence aesthetically and materially" (13). Her process involves turning to Black creators such as M. NourbeSe Philip, Dionne Brand, and Kamau Brathwaite to understand how their works "observe and mediate this un/survival" (14).

Conventional resilience narratives fall into a couple of familiar forms: a description of a complex adaptive system that subsists through levels of cyclical change, an account of an individual working through trauma to find renewed agency and possibility, or a combination of the two. This combination can be seen, for example, in the story of an individual or a community who survives by learning to adapt to the volatile environment they live in. As it tracks the meaning of living on in what Saidya Hartman calls the "afterlife of slavery" (2007, 6, quoted in Sharpe 2016, 33), Sharpe's *In the Wake* tells a story of resilience that weaves together critical race theory, history, and personal anecdote in a way that does not conform to any of these narrative forms. It is punctuated by silences, gaps in stories, places where things don't add up. These silences are part of the story of slavery, the outcome of what Sylvia Wynter calls Black people's "narratively condemned status" (1994, 15, quoted in Sharpe 2016, 13). While wake work, as a form of attention and imagination, cannot restore the presence of those whose lives have been effaced or suture over the space left by their absence, it can, through narrative techniques such as Black annotation and Black redaction, serve to "make Black life visible" (123).[18]

A popular way of figuring the dominant version of resilience is through the image of a kayak navigating white water.[19] Against the backdrop of the turbulent water is the human subject(s), the kayaker or paddler(s) who navigate through chaos without ever being themselves undone by it.[20] How wake work departs from this metaphor is instructive. The emphasis in the whitewater image is on adrenalin-fuelled agency, choice (shooting the rapids connotes seeking them out, a recreational simulacrum of an accidental encounter with danger), and forward motion. The human or humans in the boat are affected by the water, dependent on it to buoy them up and threatened by its ability to submerge them, but they are separate from it; the relationship is, ideally one of mastery. Being in the wake – in the wake of the slave ships, in the "disturbed flow" of history – is an experience of immersion, of drowning, in circumstances beyond your control. The dangers that must be navigated, moreover, are not just the shoals and eddies, the acts of violence, that loom ahead but those that rise up from the past, experienced in the form of intergenerational trauma. Being in the wake is an encounter with death, but it is importantly not a solitary experience; it is defined by kinship with those who have died and those who live to mourn them while continuing to face their own risk of premature death. Unlike the resolutely forward trajectory of shooting the rapids, in which speed is of the essence, being in the wake means reckoning with memory, in the sense of honouring the dead and also of understanding the forces behind current circumstances, the presentness of the past.

The narrative mode of wake work fosters resilience not only incidentally, as a means of representing particular ways of living on, or even instrumentally as psychosocial resilience theories have it, by "shedding light on the world and giving it back its coherence" (Cyrulnik 2005, 37). More fundamentally, it is as an embodiment of loss and endurance, contingency and meaning, transformation and continuity. These contradictions emerge not just in the kinds of stories that can be told, but in their very structure. Survivance and wake work take different forms, emerging from related but distinct histories of racial capitalism and colonialism.[21] Together, they offer a repertoire of thematic and formal methods for writing resilience against/out of conventional resilience narratives. Both are haunted by death and reject conventional tropes of resurrection; both occupy a temporal zone in which present, past, and future converge; both depart from the conventional resilience reference points of individuals and systems, locating meaning instead in systems of relationality, citation, and kinship that encompass the living and the dead and, in Vizenor's case, the more-than-human. And finally, both vigorously contend with the constraints of the forms (linguistic, syntactic, generic) that English (the language and the discipline) affords them. The contradictory impulses of resilience, to conservation and transformation, inhere in the form of their work, which exploits the indeterminacy and metaphoricity of language, sometimes paring it down to its genealogical roots, as Sharpe does with "wake" and Vizenor with "survivance."

If the grammar of resilience is declarative, "I endured, I survived," the grammar of wake work and survivance is knottier, more circumspect. Of writing in the shadows of slavery, Saidiya Hartman asks, "How can narrative embody life in words and at the same time respect what we cannot know? How does one listen for the groans and cries, the undecipherable songs, the crackle of fire in the cane fields, the laments for the dead, and the shouts of victory, and then assign words to all of it?" (2008, 3). Hartman raises the possibility that narration might be "its own gift and its own end, all that is realizable when the past and redeeming the dead are not. And what do stories afford anyway? A way of living in the world in the aftermath of catastrophe and devastation?" (3). Decolonial resilience stories emerge from the recognition that the Anthropocenic cataclysm that settler-colonial society anticipates (that it seeks to contain within conventional resilience stories) began a long time ago. In place of the wish that the present world might be sustainable, that things could return to "normal,"[22] this recognition can energize the renovation of centuries-old habits of coping in the interests of imagining different futures.

The world-building form that Anishinaabe scholar Grace Dillon labelled "Indigenous futurisms" is an important expression of this imagining.[23]

Within this form are several mobile and overlapping categories, including "Native slipstream,"[24] "Contact," "Native apocalypse," and *Biskaabiiyang*, an Anishinaabe word meaning "Returning to Ourselves" (Dillon and Marques 2021, 3), or more literally, "returning to the woods" because, as Dillon notes, alluding to her Anishinaabe kin, "we're woodland peoples" (4). Against the global currents of colonial extraction, Indigenous futurisms speak to Indigenous ecologies, to modes of "collective continuance" that derive from place-based relations of interdependence (Whyte 2018, 131) even as they address the situation of the planet.[25] In the words of Yorta Yorta social worker Cherie Minniecon, Indigenous futurism offers "a space for ancestral imagination to be explored, reminding us that the future is not colonised; it is an open and contested place that we have every right to create and lead into" (2020, 5). Indigenous futurisms, together with survivance and wake work,[26] provide conceptual frameworks for reading the stories of decolonial resilience that are the focus of the second half of this book. The book begins, though, with an exercise in unlearning the resilience stories those of us living in settler-colonial societies are most familiar with.

Decolonial Resilience Stories

The texts taken up in the first three chapters might at first blush seem disconnected – chapter 1 analyzes resilience education literature alongside a Hollywood action film, chapter 2 explores how resilience stories shape how we think about two major metropolitan centres in Canada and Australia, and chapter 3 looks at academic antiresilience thinking and its connection to dominant, white models of resilience. Each of these disparate analytical sites demonstrates how resilience and antiresilience are invoked and operationalized to entrench the status quo of settler colonialism, racial capitalism, and white nostalgia.

The strand of settler-colonial resilience thinking that chapter 1 analyzes finds expression through a common preoccupation with restoring "old-fashioned fun." I suggest that this narrative speaks to white anxiety in the anglosphere about declining racial and national dominance in the world. The campaign to restore resilience by reviving the element of risky play associated with an idealized childhood of the recent past in which children (some children, anyway) were allowed to roam free in nature speaks to fears of diminishing Anglo-American strength, global mobility, and power. Chapter 2 shifts from the psychosocial to the social-ecological and (at least superficially) from a mythical past to a speculative future as embodied in Melbourne's and Toronto's urban resilience strategies. Urban resilience thinking imagines the city as a locus of diversity, risk, and possibility; cities are engines of poverty, epidemics, and climate change and sites from where remediation might emerge. But imagining the "resilient city" – an exercise that is simultaneously speculative and mythological – conceals the displacements of Indigenous peoples and the processes of racial capitalism on which settler-colonial urbanism is materially and imaginatively predicated, foreclosing the imagination of different ways of being in place.

Chapters 1 and 2 engage with the stories that pass as common sense and that interpellate white settlers into a vision of a secure future, whose enduring coloniality is masked with the rhetoric of diversity and change. Less obviously, the stories that sustain settler colonialism also enable a strain of *anti*resilient thought that finds a home in some enclaves of the (white) academic left. This strain of thought, which I explore in chapter 3 through texts such Roy Scranton's *Learning to Die in the Anthropocene* (2015a) and Brad Evans and Julian Reid's *Resilient Life: The Art of Living Dangerously* (2014), offers a mix of well-reasoned critiques of the neoliberal resonances of resilience and melancholic appeals to an older tradition of Marxist humanism. Like the dominant conception of resilience it purports to challenge while living comfortably within it, this mode of critique represents a failure of imagination.[27] With its vision of collective survival (or its preferred trajectory of collective doom) locked in the abstract, universal, and "realistic" framework of settler colonialism and racial capitalism, it is largely uninterested in the stories of IBPOC writers and activists that enlist the past in their imagination of a decolonial future.

Beyond articulating that failure of imagination, this book takes small steps towards illuminating remedies to address it. It aims to contribute to the project described by Amit R. Baishya and Priya Kumar in their introduction to a 2022 special issue of *Postcolonial Studies* of "unearthing multiple genres of the human as arts of living in an increasingly damaged planet, instead of repeating melancholic paeans on learning to die in the Anthropocene" (307). To this end, the final three chapters take up a selection of stories by Black and Indigenous writers in Canada and Australia, not to synthesize them into a nicer, more inclusive vision of resilience (Resilience 2.0?) but to understand the work they are doing to dismantle colonial ideas of futurity and articulate in their place visions of Black and Indigenous survivance. Thus, these chapters focus on stories that imagine and enact such models of resilience in the contexts of the world-ending processes of colonialism and climate change.

Chapter 4 focuses on David Chariandy's 2017 novel *Brother*, which narrates the aftermath of a Black teenager's murder by police from the perspective of his younger brother. In this chapter, I read the novel against dominant resilience narratives that figure Black children as alternately too resilient (read: powerful and dangerous) and not resilient enough (read: in need of character-building discipline). *Brother* challenges both of these narratives in its account of the ways Black youth and their families are made vulnerable by racism, as well as the ways they foster collective resilience through community, music, and connection to more-than-human nature. Chapter 5 continues the exploration of decolonial modes of resilience through Leanne Betasamosake Simpson's 2013 collection *Islands of Decolonial Love*. It focuses primarily on the story "it takes an ocean," which I read as a critical meditation on the ways organizations such as Health Canada deploy "resilience" as a solution to the problem of Indigenous youth suicide and explores the potential of resilience (anticipated by Indigenous philosophies of human and nonhuman thriving) as well as its limitations in addressing the mental health of Indigenous youth, both of which Simpson's writing creatively engages. Finally, chapter 6 continues the discussion begun in chapter 5 on the biopolitics of resilience as they play out in relation to narratives of planetary futurity and the concept of the Anthropocene. Here, I read Alexis Wright's 2016 speculative novel *The Swan Book* as a meditation on enduring the intertwined catastrophes of postcolonial capitalism and environmental devastation. While it offers a powerful decolonial take on the meaning of mathematician Nasim Nicholas Taleb's "black swan" theory (2007), which concerns our capacity to navigate and leverage an increasingly volatile future, the novel presents a more capacious view of resilience in which neither humans nor even life can be assumed to hold a central place.

There is a risk, in highlighting the role of literary narrative in fostering Black and Indigenous resilience in/to settler colonialism, of falling into the "cultural resurgence" trap – the dynamic whereby the celebration of Indigenous cultural production is understood to be an obvious precursor to – or an acceptable stand-in for – radical political transformation (Simpson 2017, 49–50). Without underestimating the significance of that problem (an error to which white academics in the literary humanities are especially prone), it is worth noting that the problem is *not* that the land is real and necessary for Indigenous survival and stories are not; it is that settler culture fundamentally misreads the connection between the two. "The world is complex" is a disembodied, view-from-nowhere pronouncement that makes some things visible while concealing others and licences certain actions and inactions. Survivance stories, as they engage with the more-than-human vibrancy that persists in the wake of violence and loss, don't just offer different vantage points; they also highlight their own partiality, along with the implication of readers in the worlds they half describe and half invent. It is important to read these stories as testaments of and manuals for decolonial resilience. The world is a hornet's nest. What does that look like and how can we learn to live responsibly in it? What else do we need to learn before we can become resilient?

1

Old-Fashioned Fun

"FOR GENERATIONS, Canadians have been scraping off ponds and rivers for informal games of shinny" (Goldman 2016). So begins an episode of the Canadian Broadcasting Corporation (CBC) call-in show *Cross Country Checkup* on the question: "Has old-fashioned fun been trumped by fears of injury and legal action?" The question feels a bit rigged, so it's not surprising that the callers responded with a resounding "Yes!" Unlike the children of yesteryear, who reportedly ran around outside from dawn to dusk, building forts in the woods, falling off skateboards, and exploring construction sites, callers agreed that today's kids are encased in bubble wrap, protected by hovering parents and liability-wary school and park boards, who amp up the safety of their equipment and impose draconian rules ("no running," "no sharing food") to the point that there's little opportunity to engage the world at all, let alone risk getting hurt by it. Among the guests was Michael Ungar, Canada Research Chair in Child, Family and Community Resilience and professor of social work at Dalhousie University, who posited a direct connection between overprotection of children and a rise in their anxiety levels. The consensus was clear: our safety-obsessed culture has resulted in a reduction in not just fun but resilience. In the absence of "manageable risk," today's children are growing up without the skills they require to navigate the challenges of life.

This was not the first occasion on which fun emerged as a subject of Canadian worry. Several years earlier, an article in *Macleans* magazine titled "Too Asian" worried about the changing culture on Canadian university campuses. The article focused specifically on an issue identified by "a growing cohort of students": the overrepresentation and self-segregation of Asians in Canadian universities (Findlay and Kohler 2010).[1] Spurred by overly ambitious parents, the article suggests, Asian students focus extreme amounts of energy on their schoolwork, leaving no time for the traditional university pursuits of joining clubs, playing sports, and partying: "an 'Asian' school has come to mean one that is so academically focused that some students feel they can no longer compete or have fun" (Findlay and Kohler 2010). Though the principle victims of the story appear to be the uncompetitive white students, the authors also make a point of expressing concern about the social fate of the striving Asians, who "risk alienating their more fun-loving peers" (Findlay and Kohler 2010). The article generated a lot of controversy, resulting in *Macleans* temporarily removing it and eventually reinstating it on the magazine's website. It forms part of a broader conversation taking place in universities and other educational sites about the role of co-curricular elements (in which "fun" features alongside and in conjunction with other values, such as work-life balance, diversity, and risk) in fostering student development. These conversations are also, implicitly or explicitly, as in the *Macleans* story, about race.

I cite the *Macleans* story alongside the CBC call-in to offer entry points into an analysis of how what Martha Wolfenstein ([1951] 1958) terms "fun morality" has come to serve, in a range of popular media and parenting and education literature, as an index for an idea of resilience. Fun morality represents the flourishing of a particular way of life – one that sees itself as under threat in the late twentieth and early twenty-first centuries from a variety of culprits, including overdevelopment of natural spaces, technology, and a culture of regulation and litigation. This chapter argues that narratives about the shrinking horizon of fun express a concern about diminishing opportunities for white Anglo-American youth as the seemingly assured trajectory of settler colonialism is shaken by the turbulence of globalization, Indigenous resurgence, and racial justice movements. Worries about the disappearance of fun and calls for its restoration contain, and seek to resolve, a number of contradictions characteristic of the present neoliberal era: between forays into an uncharted future and conservation of an ideal past, between risk and safety, between the dynamics of "flow" and the fortification of the rugged individual.

Part of the work of this chapter is to analyze the significance of claims for the naturalness of fun that dominate discussions about its imperilled status. Some commentators, including callers to the CBC show, echo concerns raised in Richard Louv's bestselling 2005 book, *Last Child in the Woods*, about the decline in outdoor play – literally, play-in-nature; for Louv, this decline hurts both children and the environment. Nature in most discussions of fun, including the "Too Asian" article and other conversations about education, emerges as an abstraction, one related to ideas about evolutionary fitness. It is in this context that the relation between fun and risk becomes particularly significant. But it is here, too, in the conception of fun as an inherited capacity, something that is passed down through generations via the institutions of family and education, that fun assumes a more explicitly white (and heteronormative) flavour; eliding the defining role of race and class privilege, it describes a mode of ease and mobility that come to be seen as an index of character. This chapter goes on to consider how character education, a popular approach to boosting youth resilience, works to harness fun morality (symbolized in traits like humour and optimism) to a project of white, Anglo-American empowerment. It concludes with a reading of the Ridley Scott film *The Martian* (2015), which offers, via its plucky, wise-cracking hero, Mark Watney (Matt Damon), a vision of fun/resilience restored and directed confidently towards the realization of US/planetary settler futurity.

Having/Being Fun: The Emergence of "Fun Morality"

The fun that emerges in current conversations under the shadow of endangerment describes a form of activity that is characterized by equal parts exhilaration and ease. It involves the periodic (and pleasurable) overcoming of challenges – what Ungar terms "managed risk" – that helps to build resilience by enabling children to learn through trial and error (Goldman 2016). "Fun," as it is invoked in this context, is multivalent. It is at once an adjective, a quality of experience, and a noun, something that you can both engage in *and* have. Moreover, it is a quality that cleaves to those who have it; its diminution is associated with (as cause but maybe also an expression of) a weakened capacity for life. Fun is thus understood to serve an evolutionary function, equipping children with survival tools for an uncertain future. The qualifier "old-fashioned" lends a complicating dimension to this function, suggesting that the fun we want to have isn't just adaptive but conservative, emblematic of a certain way of life that is in danger of being lost.

Fun was not always in danger; in fact, until recently, fun was dangerous, a threat to healthy child development that it was parents' job to curb. Martha Wolfenstein's 1951 article, "The Emergence of Fun Morality," cogently describes a transformation in American attitudes to fun over the first half of the twentieth century. By the mid-forties, "fun, from having been suspect if not taboo, has tended to become obligatory. In contrast to early twentieth-century feelings of guilt for having too much fun, one is now inclined to feel ashamed if one does not have enough" (Wolfenstein [1951] 1958, 86). This change assumes special significance in relation to infant and childcare.

Wolfenstein traces a marked shift between the years of 1914 and 1945 from curbing babies' natural impulses, manifested in such behaviour as thumb-sucking and masturbation, to nurturing them. If such behaviours are not restrained, the 1914 US Children's Bureau's *Infant Care* bulletin warns, "children are sometimes wrecked for life" (Wolfenstein [1951] 1958, 88). The 1940s bulletins take a different, and much more benign, view of infant development. For example, while babies were once thought to have insatiable appetites, at constant risk of overfeeding, the 1944 bulletin advocates self-directed feeding, reassuring parents that "the baby's appetite usually regulates successfully the amount of food he takes" (90). A similar logic applies to other pleasures. With respect to mobility, "A baby needs to be able to move all parts of his body. He needs to exercise ... At a very early age the baby moves his arms and legs aimlessly ... As he gets older and stronger and his movements become more vigorous and he is better able to control them he begins to play" (91). His play is outwardly directed: "The baby is interested in exploring his world" (88), they explain, and thus, presumably, only intermittently and mildly interested in exploring his genitals (the masculinity of this scene seems like more than an accident of historical pronoun convention): "For the baby who is concerned with exploring his world rather than with sucking and masturbating, play becomes safe and good" (91), an activity that "is now to be fused with all the activities of life" (91).[2]

The new enjoinment to play expresses a contradiction, to which Wolfenstein is keenly attuned. She notes in the beginning of her article that the new fun morality "appears to be at marked variance with an older, puritan ethic, although as we shall see the two are related" ([1951] 1958, 87). Puritanism persists in the transformation of fun from taboo to obligation: "Where formerly there was felt to be the danger that in seeking fun, one might be carried away into the depths of wickedness, today there is a recognizable fear that one may not be able to let go sufficiently, that one may not have enough fun ... Not having fun is not merely an occasion for regret but involves a loss of self-esteem. I ask myself: What is wrong with me that I am not having fun? To admit that one did not have fun when one was expected to, arouses feelings of shame" (92). Thus, while this shift might appear as a sea change away from the earlier suspicion of fun, it might actually work to further the Puritan position: by turning fun into an imperative, guilt and shame are preserved, while fun itself, robbed of its sense of transgression, becomes even more elusive. Here Wolfenstein identifies a significant distinction between "fun" and "play." Very simply, play is a kind of activity, defined by (an implicitly masculine) freedom of movement and exploration, while fun is what you are meant to have while you are doing it; fun is a disposition, and herein lies its moral character.[3]

One more aspect of Wolfenstein's essay merits consideration. In a postscript, she briefly addresses the contents of the 1951 *Infant Care* bulletin, published after she had completed her research for this article. The new bulletin follows the pattern of the previous two in stressing "the exploratory impulse of the baby" (95) and advocating fun morality; however, it also contains a cautionary note. While continuing to advocate the insertion of fun into all activities (a move that, she sagely observes, can only result in its dilution – thus fulfilling the objective of the new, trickier Puritanism [93]), the 1951 bulletin also demonstrates a resurgence in "the belief in the dangerousness of impulses" (95): "'We know that if we leave [the baby] free to creep everywhere he'd get into trouble.' Thus we must 'set a limit' for the baby 'while he explores'" (95). Wolfenstein concludes her essay by observing that fun morality remains paramount while concerns "that impulses in one form or another will tend to grow beyond control" remain (95).

Wolfenstein's analysis shows how a belief in the importance of fun, coupled with anxiety about what constitutes the right amount, conditioned parenting in the last half of the twentieth century. The discussion that follows will reveal how contemporary conversations about fun's disappearance pick up that mix of confidence and anxiety, folding it into concerns about the development of today's children and the future more generally.

Natural Fun

One of the chief recommendations of fun in the *Infant Bulletins* of the 1940s is that it is natural. This is true in both a descriptive and a normative sense. First, it is associated with infantile "impulses" that can only be curbed through artificial measures, for example, feeding schedules and mechanical restraints that restrict movement; and second, the exercise of these impulses is seen to be a critical part of development: "A baby needs to be able to move all parts of his body. He needs to exercise" (Wolfenstein [1951] 1958, 91). This is an article of faith to those who seek to restore fun in the early twenty-first century, for whom concern is no longer for the baby prevented from sucking his thumb but for the older child who is restricted from natural outdoor adventure that is deemed, by overprotective parents, to be too dangerous.

Amongst the strongest contemporary proponents of the restoration of "common sense" when it comes to letting children follow their "natural" inclinations is Richard Louv, whose *Last Child in the Woods* stresses the importance of fun in nature, asserting, "In our bones, we need the natural curve of hills, the scent of chaparral, the whisper of pines, the possibility of wilderness. We require these patches of nature for our mental health and our spiritual resilience" (2005, 262). Louv contrasts the situation of children today, many of whom suffer from what he terms "nature disorder," with the situation of "Americans around my age, baby boomers or older, [who] enjoyed a kind of free, natural play that seems, in the era of kid pagers, instant messaging, and Nintendo, like a quaint artefact" (1). For Louv, that meant climbing trees in the woods behind his house, "fifty, sixty feet off the ground, far above the Osage windbreak," from which "vantage [he] looked out upon the old blue ridges of Missouri, and the roofs of new houses in the ever encroaching suburbs" (9).

In addition to the element of wilderness, this experience emphasizes two qualities of fun that are also important to callers to the CBC show. First, recalling the 1940s defence of the "infant explorer," fun is associated with action and discovery or, as Louv puts it, "about doing something, about direct experience – and about not being a spectator" (2005, 15). An obvious benefit of this activity is improved physical fitness. Callers to the CBC show concur with the idea that old-fashioned outdoor fun contributes not only to physical fitness – a number of callers link the decline in old-fashioned fun to a rise in obesity, a problem also mentioned by Louv and others (Skenazy 2009), along with Attention Deficit Hyperactivity Disorder[4] – but also to social, psychological, and moral development. Naomi Buck, a freelance journalist and CBC guest, argues that children require the "opportunity ... to explore the world around them in a way that's meaningful, that's challenging and that helps them to become happy, ultimately happy, stable, functional, productive grown-ups" (Goldman 2016). This opportunity is diminished by a culture that "err[s] on the side of safety" (Goldman 2016). Modern children, we can assume, would be barred from the woods, let alone the treetops from which Louv surveyed the Blue Ridge Mountains in his youth. The ambivalent if not dismissive characterization of safety points to another key element of old-fashioned fun: risk.

By "err[ing] on the side of safety," Buck and others argue, we deprive children of the chance to make mistakes and to learn from them – a crucial predicate of resilience. "Risk," as one CBC caller (an outdoor education instructor) puts it, "can be an incredibly powerful teacher" (Goldman 2016). Another comments at greater length:

> You know that by making it harder for kids to play outside because there's too many rules now, you're eliminating a sort of playground Darwinism ... I'm not some kind of sadist who wants to see kids get hurt, but they should have some risk so they learn. Kids are stuck in front of screens so often ... and there's no consequence with a video game when your character gets hurt, but once they're in real life, there are consequences if you are playing dangerously, you will break a bone or, heaven forbid, have some sort of lifelong injury ... There's the whole hand sanitizer thing and everyone is so meticulously clean, kids have weaker immune systems ... It's kind of the

same thing when you're not allowing your kids to have free fun on the playground because you aren't letting them build up a strength. (Goldman 2016)

This comment expresses several common themes, including the identification of "screens" as a primary culprit in the decline of old-fashioned fun and the more or less casual acknowledgment that risk entails the possibility, however statistically slight, of injury or death ("heaven forbid"). We will return to these points below. For now, let's take a moment to consider the "playground Darwinism" part of the argument.

For all the advocates of "free-range" childhood, one of the chief benefits of old-fashioned fun is its cultivation of what Ungar calls the "risk-taker's advantage" (Goldman 2016). In other words, more than constituting a "natural" part of child development, as Wolfenstein ([1951] 1958) showed, it contributes to the fitness of the population, serving a vital evolutionary function. Mistakes, failures, and even "minor trauma," as one CBC caller puts it, are understood as necessary to condition resilience to life's difficulties. "Take [trauma] out of the mix, she asks, [and] what have you got for tomorrow's society? Where are we going with this?" (Goldman 2016).[5] Louv carries the evolutionary metaphor farther than many commentators, conflating psychological and ecological resilience theories in his description of the child-in-nature as an "endangered indicator species" (2005, 159), one on whose recovery the entire planet depends. Others invoke a more limited and even conservative view of evolution, one that works to temper the hazards of playground Darwinism with the reassuring structure of family: just as mothers facilitated fun for their babies in the *Infant Bulletins* of the 1940s, old-fashioned fun is an intergenerational good, one that, under ideal circumstances, parents should pass down to their children.

Louv cites John Johns, "a California father and businessman," on the nature of this obligation and its benefits:

"Intuitively, I believe my kids are better equipped to detect danger because of their time in nature," says Johns. "They've all had adrenalin-thumping white water experiences and spent moonless nights burrowed into their sleeping bags, imagining all manner of evils outside. Whatever neurons were firing then and whatever

> coping/adaptive responses they practice now put them at some advantage in the world." He wonders if this is one of the primal reasons he and his wife have taken their children on so many nature excursions. We just seldom think about it in those terms, that we're helping our kids sensitize themselves to the world. But we sense it. (2005, 182)

Johns's account of his children's experience in nature shares in common with other stories a combination of a psychobiological conception of the "risk-taker's advantage" with a model of parenting – one that draws less on thought than on common sense. Where Johns's take differs from others is in its account of the successful preservation and transmission of the value of old-fashioned fun to his children; mixed with concerns about preparing children for the future is an undertone of nostalgia and loss.

Louv's book begins by recounting a conversation that began with a plaintive question from his son: "Dad, how come it was more fun when you were a kid?" (2005, 1). The certainty, expressed by Louv and most of the CBC callers, that it *was* more fun when they were kids is accompanied by regret that they will not be able to pass on that experience – Louv frequently uses the word "gift" (54, 58, 110, 269) – to their children. A CBC *Cross Country Checkup* caller from Red Deer, Alberta, has fond memories of snowmobiling with his dad and doesn't want to deprive his daughter of something he experienced (Goldman 2016). American novelist and wilderness writer Peter Matthiessen expresses a more general worry, focused specifically on the disappearance of nature: "There's an elegiac quality in watching [American wilderness] go, because it's our own myth, the American frontier, that's deteriorating before our eyes. I feel a deep sorrow that my kids will never get to see what I've seen, and their kids will see nothing; there's a deep sadness whenever I look at nature now" (Louv 2005, 286). In this, as in other expressions of regret about the disappearing landscape of fun (a literal landscape in this example) is a sense of an inheritance that has been lost or stolen from today's children.

In Mathiesson's words we can see another dominant theme in laments for vanishing fun, which is the sense of fun's entanglement in particular geographical and cultural context. It is no coincidence that CBC's *Cross Country Checkup* begins by evoking the image of kids clearing off a pond to play shinny (Goldman 2016). Shinny rates so high on the Canadian mythology index that it might be said to be *the* national pastime: when shinny is threatened, we can infer, the national character is threatened. Louv is even more explicit in hailing the Americanness of the experience he is defending. The American frontier myth (which he presents as fact) provides an overarching framework for his narrative of receding wilderness, which is also a narrative of "ever encroaching suburbs" (2005, 9). Louv's experience of surveying the vastness of the mountains beyond the suburbs is a diminished, but still significant, version of the ideal experience of eighteenth-century settlers, a sense recalled by one of his interviewees in her own childhood wanderings "of being places where no one had quite been before" (273).

That sense of exploration, culminating in arrival on the shores of an undiscovered world, emerges more literally in the contrast Lenore Skenazy, author of *Free-Range Kids: Giving Kids the Freedom We Had without Going Nuts with Worry*,[6] draws between today's children and those of earlier generations: "After all, our moms sent us outside and said 'Come home when the street lights turn on.' Their moms sent *them* out on the streetcars and buses. And their grandmas sent *their* sweet children out on slow, rusty steamers to the New World with only a couple of rubles and a hard salami" (2009, xii). In Skenazy's historical template for free-range kids, the Puritan element of fun identified by Wolfenstein takes on a more literal cast; that is, even though it describes a later wave of immigration than the Puritan arrival on the shores of the so-called new world, the image conjures the same colonial spirit of adventure and sacrifice. The story evokes not only a rosy-hued image of the past but also the implied future of that voyage: those children – "our" ancestors – made America. Embedded in the story is a moral about toughness and risk and the rewards they reap. It is at once a confident story, of continuity and security (things turned out for the best; we inherited the world that those adventurers discovered and created), and an anxious one: the current generation no longer knows how to enjoy it, and, without that spirit of adventure, it may be lost. Haunting this and other stories about old-fashioned fun is a pervasive and paradoxical sense of vulnerability, which extends from individual children to encompass an entire culture.

One element of this vulnerability is elaborated in the *Macleans* article already alluded to in this chapter. "Too Asian" describes a seismic shift in university, or at least in specific Canadian universities, that is characterized by a waning culture of fun (Findlay and Kohler 2010). This decline is associated with the increasing enrolment of Asian students. Though it might seem at first glance that this story has very little connection to recollections about snowmobiling and tree climbing, they have a couple of significant things in common. First and most obviously, they each offer a defence of fun. Each, moreover, associates fun with tradition (this is true even in the absence of the qualifier "old-fashioned"), with ways of life that, in different ways at different stages of development, play a crucial role in the reproduction of a certain social order. Second, each construes fun as under threat. Like fun, the threat is both literal and mythological, seen as somehow emblematic of a moment in history. In the case of the *Macleans* story, the threat assumes an overtly racial character. To understand how race is operating here, even when – I will argue, *especially* when – it does not appear so directly, we need first to consider more closely why fun is seen to be under threat.

Fun-Wreckers

In the "free-range kids" literature, the culprits in the destruction of fun are varied, but a few keep reappearing. Louv suggests that "fear is the most potent force that prevents parents from allowing their children the freedom they themselves enjoyed when they were young" (2005, 123). As an example, he points to the "monster hype" around gun violence based on exaggeration in the media, which contributes to what he dubs "the Bogeyman syndrome" (127). Skenazy elaborates: "Fear, fear, fear. We're always expected to be thinking about fear ... Everyone is exhorting us to watch out, take care, and plan for the very worst-case scenario. Which puts a damper on things, to say the least" (2009, 9). Fear, Skenazy suggests, arises when we allow our common sense to be overridden by paid "experts" – "lawyers, prinicpals and politicians who get a lot of bang for the buck by appearing extremely concerned about our children's welfare" (2009, 44).[7]

One of the most pernicious of these interests, she and other "free-range kids" advocates agree, is the insurance industry. "Everyone these days seems burdened by risk management and liability insurance," *Cross Country*

Checkup host Brian Goldman observes (2016). Louv agrees, contending that "as a powerful deterrent to natural play, fear of liability ranks right behind the bogeyman" (2005, 239). Louv quotes a father's observation that, "in the past, if a child or teen broke an arm on the sidewalk, in a neighbor's yard, or at the school yard, Dad's insurance would pay the bills ... Our parents accepted responsibility for our accidents, careless behavior, or deliberate actions. Today, as seven-figure monetary awards dance in our heads, we open the Yellow Pages and search for attorneys who can fish in the deep pockets of a school district, a city or an insurance company" (244).

All lament the machinations of an industry that in their view has, by adding layers of complexity to what should be a simple calculus of personal risk, eroded the practical and moral structures of individual responsibility. Even lawyer Philip K. Howard agrees that "legal fear has infected the culture" (Louv 2005, 241). Howard is the founder of an organization, Common Good, which advocates "that individual responsibility, not mindless bureaucracy, must be the organizing principle of government" (Common Good n.d.).[8] A critical component of the vision of "neoliberal anti-statism" expressed by the Common Good is what Jennifer Henderson describes as "a politics of community, family, and individual vitalism that presents itself as the alternative to state dependency and names itself *resilience*" (2023, 127). Complaints about the financialization and bureaucratization of risk (discounting and eroding common sense and resilience) are not just antistatist; they also express general anxieties about abstraction, which inform a preoccupation with the negative effects of technology. One caller to the CBC summarizes a shared sense of rueful irony in her observation that "we don't consider risks of putting them in front of screens ... risks [that] are way more serious than the risks of letting them engage in free outdoor play" (Goldman, 2016). "Screens" are a shorthand for a variety of threats, variously identified with TV and the Internet, which both diminish us and scare us away from unmediated experience in the world (not to mention making us fat), and social media, which, by subjecting youth to external sources of validation, erode their internal locus of well-being and control (Gray 2010).

But screen culture, and digital culture more particularly, also constitute a subtler menace. As Louv puts it:

> Today, kids are aware of the global threats to the environment – but their physical contact, their intimacy with nature, is fading. That's exactly the opposite of how it was when I was a child. As a boy, I was unaware that my woods were ecologically connected with any other forests. Nobody in the 1950s talked about acid rain or holes in the ozone layer or global warming. But I knew my woods and my fields; I knew every bend in the creek and dip in the beaten dirt paths. I wandered those woods even in my dreams. A kid today can likely tell you about the Amazon rain forest – but not about the last time he or she explored the woods in solitude, or lay in a field listening to the wind and watching the clouds move. (2005, 1–2)

For Louv, screen culture doesn't only substitute sedentary indoor for active outdoor play; as a vehicle for globalization, it also substitutes an ersatz worldliness for a real purchase on the world. And that world, Louv warns – the natural world – is contracting. Children inhabit a "shrinking home range" (124), the result, he suggests, of the creeping urbanization and suburbanization of natural space: "As long as cities continue to overdevelop housing tracts and underdevelop parks and other sites for natural play, our regional parks and beaches will be crushed by demand, necessitating ever more strict enforcement" (239). Louv sees a direct relation between overcrowding and overregulation, curtailing not just children's play but also their moral development. "One wonders," he provocatively asks, "how the children growing up in this culture of control will define freedom when they are adults?" (129).

He cites as an example of necessary escape from the "culture of control" a weeklong camp held for San Diego sixth graders in the mountains. Noting that the camp "gives some children their first or best experience in nature," he quotes a ninth-grader, Myra, who says of her time at the sixth-grade camp: "There I felt truly comfortable, being among few people and walking down paths that weren't paved ... Sometimes, I feel like I just want to get away from the world, so I dwell in nature through my thoughts and memories" (Louv 2005, 227). Engagement with nature thus serves two fundamental if contradictory functions. On the one hand, it offers a necessary escape from the world – a world that is encroaching on the "home range";

on the other hand, it *is* the world – the real world, the unregulated exploration of which is key to childhood happiness and to adult appreciation for (and capacity to manage) freedom. Once again, a tension emerges between a sense of flow between the individual and her environment and anxiety about the shrinking of that environment, and – maybe worse – the corruption of the *nature* of that relationship.

We should keep these concerns in mind when considering Louv's complaint that the sixth-grade camp has changed in recent years, its central purpose "shift[ing] from a pure nature experience ... [to] become, primarily, a race-relations retreat with nature used as backdrop" (2005, 227). Though Louv does not offer details of this shift, he does issue a warning about its implications:

> The *nature* experience at these camps could be lost if nature camps allow their mission be [sic] become diluted, if they attempt to please everyone all the time. Race-relations and other cultural/political programs at camps across the land are important attempts to imagine a gentler, better world. These are important discussions in a democracy, but childhood is short. If we make those issues our sole priority another generation – or more – could enter adulthood without significant experiences in nature. The great worth of outdoor education programs is their focus on the elements that have always united human kind: driving rain, hard wind, warm sun, forests deep and dark – and the awe and amazement that our earth inspires, especially during our formative years." (228)

Nature is universal in Louv's analysis, while race is divisive and – like culture and politics – more ideological than real. A couple of decades before American conservatives seized on critical race theory as the source of a host of social ills, Louv drew a direct connection between antiracist education (condescendingly described in terms of the vague and idealistic goal of "imagining a gentler and better world") and the erosion of old-fashioned/natural fun. In thus quietly letting race in (or out) through the backdoor, he invites an ungentle question: What is the connection between old-fashioned fun and racism? Louv's comments about the need to stop talking about race and restore the original mission of summer camp raise an uncomfortable historical issue: while we might be united in our subjection to the elements (though surely not in the same way or to the same degree), *nature* as a privileged site of fun, like the university, is not, and has never been, accessible to everyone.

Many scholars have documented the extensive history of displacement, segregation, and violence that has accompanied the wilderness conservation movement in North America. The frontier story of American origins that Louv celebrates inaugurated a wilderness tradition through the violent removal of Indigenous peoples from their land (Cronon 1992). Throughout the nineteenth century and into the twentieth – a period Louv terms the "second frontier," during which the scouting movement inspired "a new politics of preservation [and] an immersion of Americans in the domesticated and romanticized fields and streams and woods around them" (2005, 18) – the establishment of parks (and summer camps named after Indian tribes) consolidated that displacement. During this period, wilderness assumed a powerful, even sacred, significance as a place of refuge for (white) tourists. Tropes of urban decay and pollution were strongly associated with the presence of African Americans. "Sublime nature," Carolyn Merchant notes, "was white and benign, available to white tourists; cities were portrayed as black and malign, the home of the unclean and the undesirable" (2003, 385).

The significance of nature as a place of white refuge was not just symbolic; until the early sixties, many outdoor recreation areas in the US were de facto, if not by law, restricted to whites. With the passing of antisegregation legislation, some states got around the law by privatizing parks, beaches, and pools. Where privatization wasn't possible, facilities were closed and budgets cut: "Against all logic, some white city leaders attempted to end access even to the grass and trees designed to make urban living tolerable" (Wolcott 2012, 169).[9] In spite of national nondiscrimination policies, many national parks enforced race-based segration practices well into the 1960s,[10] and "campgrounds, like urban parks and pools, were largely white spaces that African Americans had limited access to" (170).

It is not surprising that national parks remain inhospitable to racialized people, a trend many groups are trying to reverse. Glenn Nelson, the Asian American founder of Trail Posse, a website that promotes diversity in the outdoors, describes the buzz of "nervous banter" that would start up as he and his friends drove through rural towns, joking about finding a "Whites Only" sign on the gates of their destination. Nelson argues, "We need to demolish the notion that the national parks and the rest of nature are an exclusive club where minorities are unwelcome" (2015). In its campaign to promote "inclusive representation," the Canadian group Colour the Trails works "with brand partners, businesses, and organizations to break barriers and create accessibility" (Colour The Trails n.d.). The goal of making natural spaces more welcoming to racialized people is uncontroversial, but it glosses over a key point: it is not only that nature's "gifts" have not been equitably shared but more that their historical value is partly predicated on inequity and dispossession. It is also worth noting that this inequity and dispossession produces material risks for racialized people in nature, but they aren't the "fun" risks that can straightforwardly be associated with enhanced resilience.

To make sense of the way the uneven risk/resilience landscape is inflected with race, it is useful to recall the two ways of thinking about nature that come together in the concept of old-fashioned fun. "Nature" in the most straightforward sense describes a physical environment for which "woods" might serve as a shorthand in Louv's 2005 book[11] and which may also be loosely equated with the designation "outdoors," which for Skenazy (2009), as for CBC callers (Goldman 2016), is the ideal landscape of old-fashioned fun. But "nature" also describes a broad framework of principles or laws that govern the universe and humans' place in it: fun is natural, in Wolfenstein's ([1951] 1958) outline, in its expression of "impulses." It is also natural in the sense elaborated by advocates for free-range kids, as an evolutionary process through the enactment of "playground Darwinism" (Goldman 2016). In light of the histories of European settlement in North America very briefly surveyed above, that evolutionism assumes pointed significance. In Skenazy's account, early European settlers embodied a spirit of adventure and openness to risk that sowed the seeds of the country's resilience. Put slightly differently, in light of the histories of expropriation outlined above, Skenazy's account frames the colonization of North America as the natural outcome of evolution in which the weaker race gives way to the fitter one.

The mythology of (always-already endangered) old-fashioned fun recalls this colonial history in two ways – that is to say, it seeks to reconcile two different interpretations of it. First, old-fashioned fun is a way of enjoying the world that comes from a sense of natural right, of perfect adaptation to the environment. The idea of entitlement doesn't come into it; fun is, in a sense, just an expression of *who we are*. This interpretation comes closest to the concept of fun outlined in the 1940s *Infant Bulletin*, though some notes of unease have come to creep in. The second, more anxious, interpretation informs directly the worry about the weakening of fun and an associated loss of resilience: fun is a process of learning about and dealing with the contingencies of the world. There is an element of danger in fun, and it doesn't just concern the possibility of falling out of a tree: the danger is that the kind of "old-fashioned fun" that embodies Anglo-American privilege has lost its adaptive edge in a rapidly changing world. In this interpretation, fun is *what we do*, and the ultimate worry is that of losing the "risk-taker's advantage" and, with it, the ability to shape the future.

In a settler-colonial context, that advantage rests on freedom to own and exploit the land, whether conceived as a site for development, fossil fuel extraction, or wilderness adventures. The colonial imperative to secure land supports a biopolitical program of (racist) evolutionism. Foucault explains:

> Basically, evolutionism, understood in the broad sense ... naturally became within a few years during the nineteenth century not simply a way of transcribing a political discourse into biological terms, and not simply a way of dressing up a political discourse in scientific clothing, but a real way of thinking about the relations between colonization, the necessity for wars, criminality, the phenomena of madness and mental illness, the history of societies with their different classes, and so on. Whenever, in other words, there was a confrontation, a killing or the risk of death, the nineteenth century was quite literally obliged to think about them in the form of evolutionism.[12] (2003, 256–7)

In addressing itself to the adaptation of a species to its environment, evolutionism also offers a framework for thinking about contingency and risk – concepts that become central in resilience thinking, as I will discuss further below. First, though, let us briefly consider the disciplinary and biopolitical aspects of fun.

Foucault conceptualizes discipline as a mode of power associated not with repression but with bodily regulation through the enhancement and articulation of pleasure. Fun's disciplinary character emerges clearly in the way it is represented in the 1940s *Infant Bulletins* discussed in Wolfenstein's article. As part of infant training, fun does not entail the loosening of bonds but the erection of new ones. In adulthood, self-scrutiny is critical to the maintenance of these bonds. Considered through the lens of biopolitics, the cost of not having fun is not restricted to individual shame; the fitness of the population is at stake. Michael Ungar expresses the worry that "we parents are accidentally creating a generation of youth who are not ready for life" (2009, 4). In an article in *Psychology Today* that spawned a book titled *A Nation of Wimps: The High Cost of Invasive Parenting*, Hara Astroff Marano (2004) puts it more crudely. Identifying risk-aversion; psychological fragility; anxiety; and the loss of identity, meaning, perseverance, and a sense of accomplishment as "the spreading psychic fault lines of 21st-century youth," she warns, "Whether we want to or not, we're on our way to creating a nation of wimps." In short, it isn't just children who bear the cost of disappearing fun; it is a problem for "a generation" and "a nation." It is a problem for the future.

As fun is biopoliticized, the force of fun morality does not recede but takes on a new intensity. We can liken its regulatory function to that of happiness, which Sara Ahmed incisively analyzes in her 2010 book, *The Promise of Happiness*. Ahmed explores the political implications of contemporary exhortations to be happy such that happiness has become "a disciplinary technique" (8), mastery of which is key to living what psychologist Martin Seligman calls "the good life" (Ahmed 2010, 9). In addition to enhancing individual emotional life, the affective dynamic of happiness works to cultivate a force field of positivity, drawing in good feeling, people, and events. Musing on the characterization of the phenomenology of happiness, "an intimacy of body and world," Ahmed asks, "What if to flow into the world is not simply understood as a psychological attribute? What if the world 'houses' some bodies more than others, such that some bodies do not experience the world as resistant?" (12). Taking up the task of "rewrit[ing] the history of happiness from the point of the wretch" (17), Ahmed traces the circumstances of those bodies she terms "affect aliens" who *do* experience the world as resistant – racialized and gendered bodies whose indissolubility into the flow of the world around them is read as personal failings, crystallized into stereotypes – the "feminist killjoy" (50–87), the "unhappy queer" (88–120), the "melancholy migrant" (121–59).

Of course, that the world *does* house some bodies more than others is not an accident. The right to security, as well as the right to easy movement through the world unencumbered by opposition and regulation, is not – and *cannot be* – enjoyed by everyone in a capitalist settler-colonial society. To the extent that affects like happiness and the related morality of fun operate as norms and as modes of belonging, they are dependent on the production of "affect aliens" – a dynamic of exclusion that is less obvious but no less effective than physical forms of segregation. If it is no longer possible to restrict access to recreational spaces like national parks on the basis of race, it *is* possible to restrict enjoyment of those places (recall the "nervous banter" of racialized campers [Nelson 2015]). And what if enjoyment – the performance of fun – became one of the terms of admission? This is one of the subtexts of "Too Asian," which *defends* under the pretense of simply *describing* the racialized operation of fun quotients at Canadian universities. Asian students "tend to be strivers, high achievers and single-minded in their approach to university ... White students, by contrast, are more likely to build their university lives around social interaction, athletics and self-actualization – and yes, alcohol" (Findlay and Kohler 2010). Asian students, the story implies, miss the point of what university is *really* all about, which is socializing, sport, and booze-enhanced self-discovery – aka fun![13] Less attention is focused on the anxiety that underlies the white students' concern: the academic excellence of Asian students means their success is no longer assured – "they can no longer compete."

The *Macleans* story situates the "Too Asian" problem in a broader dynamic playing out across the US, where many schools have been accused of employing quotas to restrict the admission of Asian students. The story also acknowledges that this practice has a history, in the form of 1920s attempts to exclude Jewish students. Like Asian students today, Jews were seen to be crowding out the traditional (white/Gentile) constituency of students through their academic superiority; thus, supplementary admissions materials like the personal essay came into being, helping to dilute the significance of high grades with an emphasis on extracurricular activities and "personal promise" (Karabel 2006, 326). As Jerome Karabel notes, the evaluation of character did not stop after World War II but became institutionalized. Admission records from Yale in the 1950s, for example, show a candidate with mediocre grades selected over another stronger student because "we just thought he was more of a guy" (327). "Guyness" embodies a particular orientation to the world, one characterized by, among other things, a sense of ease in one's occupation of space. This quality is a mark of privilege not only in the university but also in other elite educational settings. In *Privilege: The Making of an Adolescent Elite at St. Paul's School*, anthropologist Shamus Rahman Khan notes that "what students cultivate" in the New England boarding school "is a sense of how to carry themselves, and at its core this practice of privilege is ease: feeling comfortable in just about any social situation" (2011, 15). Drawing on Pierre Bourdieu, Khan suggest that "this elite ease is also an embodied interactional resource," part of a habitus inscribed on students' bodies through "seemingly mundane acts of everyday life – from eating meals to dancing and dating" and thereby naturalized (16). Structures of inequality become invisible in the process: "In being embodied, privilege is not seen as a product of differences in opportunities but instead as a skill, talent, capacity – 'who you are'" (16). The assumption at St. Paul's, as at elite institutions of higher education, is this: "The world and its innumerable possibilities is a space one can and should navigate with ease" (190). Those who fail in this world are seen as lacking the will or the capacity for openness – and, in the case of Asian students in Canadian universities, for fun.

The perspective voiced in "Too Asian" confirms what Khan's analysis shows: that the capacity to have fun is a mark of privilege. In both instances, hard work is racialized (at St. Paul's, Khan finds that Black and Asian students work harder but receive fewer awards than white students [2011, 186–7]) and generally frowned on. But it would be a mistake to characterize fun as simply the opposite of work; fun, as we have already seen, involves a particular kind of exertion associated with the embrace of risk. If "single-minded" striving compromises fun, by far the greater threat, according to a range of commentators including the free-range parent movement, is the extension of the culture of stifling overprotection to university campuses. Skenazy describes this threat in a 2015 post on her Free-Range Kids website titled "Mob of Yale Students Scream Profanities About Hallowe'en Costume Insensitivity." The much-publicized background to this story was this: Following a party in which white students dressed up in blackface, a message from the university's Intercultural Affairs Committee went out to undergraduate students, cautioning them against insensitive costumes. As Skenazy notes, associate dormitory master Erika Christakis responded to the message by challenging its curtailment of student freedom.[14] Student protest ensued, focused on the problem of persistent, unacknowledged institutional racism.

Skenazy's sense of what she sees as the obvious outrageousness of the protests is signalled in her blogpost by the liberal use of scare quotes around words such as "impact," "safe," and "offensive" (even while mocking what she deems to be unreasonable standards and expectations of safety, Skenazy displays what might be seen as an exaggerated sense of alarm on behalf of Christakis's husband, sociology professor Nicholas Christakis, who is "surrounded" by a "mob" of "scream[ing]" and "swearing" students [2015]). In the spirit of the free-range kids philosophy, the article draws a connection between the fears and concerns of racialized students and a culture in which we have "dangerized" everything from wire laundry hampers to tabs on zippers. Noting that "there's a difference between a real danger (a baby bottle filled with bleach) and a product or practice that could, very rarely and unpredictably, result in serious injury (a laundry hamper, … a zipper pull), the article expresses the fear that "it's quite possible we have bred a generation convinced that everything they encounter that is not an organic avocado (or organic avocado costume) is making them 'unsafe.'" (2015). If the joke about the avocado costume isn't clear enough, Skenazy makes it clear: we all know, or should know, what constitutes a "real" danger vs. the faux dangers identified by "the experts, the universities and/or the government" (to which we can now add, hysterical racialized college students and their allies).

Skenazy's argument finds support in the work of psychologists like Peter Gray, who sees a direct link between overprotected children and a decline in resilience in college students: "Students are afraid to fail; they do not take risks; they need to be certain about things. For many of them, failure is seen as catastrophic and unacceptable" (2015, 2). Dan Jones, past president of the Association for University and College Counseling Center Directors, concurs, observing that students "don't seem to have as much grit as previous generations" (Gray 2015, 4). One remedy many agree on is that "failure and struggle need to be normalized" (3) – a proposal that extends beyond academics to encompass social life more generally. Students must be granted "the opportunity to get into trouble and find their own way out, to experience failure and realize they can survive it, to be called bad names by others and learn how to respond without adult intervention" (4).[15] That students might react with anger or distress to (what "common sense" would deem) minor affronts ostensibly demonstrates their subjection to a culture that promotes hypersensitivity to the wrong things.[16]

(Hyper)sensitivity joins (over)seriousness in infecting the atmosphere of fun that is meant to pervade the university. As Christakis notes in her email to the students, "American universities were once a safe space not only for maturation but also for a certain regressive, or even transgressive, experience" (Friedersdorf 2015, 6). The use of the phrase "safe space" is presumably deliberate, inviting comparison with the (much mocked) demand of racialized students that they be granted a measure of security against insult. It also, probably unintentionally, highlights the racial and gender violence that often attended the socially sanctioned "fun" of hazing rituals that long marked campus life. Like many expressions of nostalgia for the university that once was, Christakis's comment should raise questions about the scope and nature of regression and transgression the university traditionally enabled and when this "safe space" existed and for whom. The use of the term "safe space" in this context is ultimately ironic because Christakis's email resonates with the neoliberal rhetoric of freedom, of which the free-range parenting philosophy is a relatively benign strand, which disparages the call for safety in favour of a healthy exposure to risk that will help to activate their "natural" resilience. *The Atlantic* writer Conor Friedersdorf ("known for his civil libertarian perspectives," according to his Wikipedia page [2023, par. 1]) argues that students "need someone to teach them how empowered they are by virtue of their mere enrolment; ... that they are capable of tremendous resilience; and that they most possess it now despite the disempowering ideology foisted on them by well-intentioned, wrongheaded ideologues encouraging them to imagine that they are not privileged" (Friedersdorf 2015). Among the points we can derive from this awkwardly worded fulmination (who better to dispense ideology than ideologues?) are that most – but not all – students possess resilience; they just don't know it yet. The job of educators is to correct the misperceptions students have internalized from the surrounding ideology that tells them they are not privileged (the implicit assumption here that students are mindlessly reproducing what others have told them regarding their situation is weirdly at odds with the emphasis on intrinsic strength). There is a tension here between the ideas of inherent worth and contingent privilege and empowerment; what combination of these elements conditions the possession or capacity for resilience? Are the students more resilient by virtue of their attendance at Yale or less? Friedersdorf is not alone in suggesting that the latter might be true; in fact, a worry that privilege might be inversely proportional to resilience adds another thread to the knot of race and class anxiety that lies behind much of the current talk about resilience and education.

The Risk of Privilege

Much of the preceding conversation has focused on the way racialized students are enjoined to become more resilient: by being more open and amenable to socialization with white students, by being less sensitive to affronts, and by just having fun. But, as this chapter seeks to show, the concern about the decline of "old-fashioned fun" – and, by extension, resilience – is not only or even primarily about traditionally disadvantaged groups. In fact, the chief target of concern is the white, affluent children that psychologist Madeline Levine identifies as "America's newly identified at-risk group" (2016, 17). Levine bases this assessment on observations of children in her practice in Marin County, just outside of San Francisco. "Regardless of how successful these kids look on the surface," she argues, "they are not navigating adolescence successfully" (7); in fact, they are never given the opportunity to pick up the tools. According to this view, children cosseted by anxious parents, helpful teachers and coaches, and a raft of academic and extracurricular programming designed to help them succeed rarely get to experience failure and the attendant opportunity to bounce back. The loss of resilience, understood as an index of fitness, is a problem to which parents and educators in the independent school community are particularly attuned.[17] "The hot topic in independent schools circles these days is resilience," says Bernie Noe, Head of the Lakeside School in Seattle:

"We are all asking ourselves if we are developing students who will have the tenacity, the toughness, and the determination to compete effectively, over time, in a global marketplace" (2013).

The widespread concern principal Noe describes speaks to a paradoxical situation preoccupying private school educators and their students' parents. A hallmark of these schools' appeal is the sense that they are training future leaders. Proof of the superiority of their constituents can be found in their rigorous admission criteria and academic standards, conditions that allow the schools to claim that they operate on the principles of pure meritocracy. But alongside the confident proclamation of these principles in schools' promotional literature is another, darker view – what Paul Tough describes as "a pervasive, if still somewhat inchoate, anxiety within the contemporary culture of affluence, a feeling that something [has] gone wrong within the traditional channels of meritocratic pursuit" (2012, 183) – that students were graduating without the qualities they required to thrive, let alone lead, in the challenging environment of the twenty-first century. The feeling haunts the students themselves. As Andrew Halls, headmaster of King's College School, Wimbledon, UK, puts it, "We know they will succeed, but they are not always so sure and this can lead to levels of self-doubt that are, for some, crucifying" (Milner 2014).[18] Perhaps unconsciously, Halls puts his finger on the crux of the dilemma for the privileged class: "We know they will succeed" – their success is assured because it is deserved (and, presumably, our own success confirms our ability and our right to determine the criteria for future success). Doubts remain, however, and these come to settle on the uneasy sense that private school students lack something that their public school counterparts have: "The struggle to pull yourself through a crisis ... is exactly what is missing for so many students at academically excellent schools ... And perhaps surprisingly, it may turn out to be an area where the students at [struggling schools] have a real advantage" (Tough 2011, 9).

Of course, the concept of strength through adversity is not a new one. Nor is the fear that naturalized privilege might be snatched away by a lesser but hardier opponent. A 1911 study of Chinese labourers by American sociologist Edward Ross arrived at the disturbing conclusion that Chinese labourers were better able than Americans to cope with adverse environments (Wang 1999, vi). Ross hastens to note that the apparently superior hardiness of the Chinese was not a measure of worth: "Under good conditions, an Anglo-American laborer could beat a Chinese laborer, but the Chinese laborer could better endure spoiled food, poor clothing, foul air, noise, heat, dirt, discomfort, and microbes" (vi). However, he goes on to speculate with alarm that, under the harsh conditions of war, "the hardier men with less of the martial spirit might in the closing grapple beat the better fighters with the less endurance … In the course of a prolonged campaign involving irregular provisioning, bad drinking water, lying out, loss of sleep, exhausting marches, exposure, excitement and anxiety, it may be that the white soldiers would be worn down worse than the yellow soldiers" (vi). The better man, in short, might not always win, if circumstances are unfavourable.

The problem is a quintessentially biopolitical one not only in its demarcation of race as an index of population fitness but in its measurement of fitness in terms of the ability to subsist in a particular environment. Foucault describes this extended locus of biopolitical concern as:

> control over relations between the human race, or human beings insofar as they are a species, insofar as they are living beings, and their environment, the milieu in which they live. This includes the direct effects of the geographical, climatic, or hydrographic environment: the problem, for instance, of swamps, and of epidemics linked to the existence of swamps throughout the first half of the nineteenth century. And also the problem of the environment to the extent that it is not a natural environment, that it has been created by the population and therefore has effects on that population. (2003, 245)

For Ross, the challenge for Anglo-Americans is this: "It is a case of a man fitted to get the most out of good conditions refusing to yield his place to a weaker man able to withstand bad conditions" (Wang 1999, vi). The dilemma is clear: the Anglo-American is intransigent; he refuses to yield his place (we can hear echoes of this in Halls's assurance "we know they will succeed"), but he may yet fail because he is not equipped for "bad conditions." Hardiness is not just a property of individuals, it is a measure of adaptability.

Adaptability has gained currency throughout the twentieth and twenty-first centuries in tandem with the worry that the likelihood of encountering "bad" conditions of unpredictable nature, scope, and duration is no longer contained to one part of the world but has become generalized. A key preoccupation amongst educators is a determination to equip students with the risk-management skills they need for the future. Sean Dunne, deputy head of Wycliffe College, Gloucestershire, writes in *Independent School Parent* magazine, "Today, more than at any other time in our society, we need to teach our children resilience. If we cannot prepare them for certainty then we must then prepare them for uncertainty" (2014). The rhetoric of preparedness and forward-looking resolve is shot through with nostalgia for less turbulent times. Like many educators, Dominic Randolph, the principal of New York City's Riverdale Country School, speaks to the need to cultivate qualities that will help students navigate the challenges of the future – qualities that are rooted (like old-fashioned fun) in the past. Randolph looks to "essential traits of mind and habit that were drilled into him in boarding school in England and that also have deep roots in American history" (Tough 2011, 2). Echoing Skenazy's reference to "slow rusty steamers to the New World" (2009, xii), Randolph offers some specific examples: "Whether it's the pioneer in the Conestoga wagon or someone coming here in the 1920s from southern Italy, there was this idea in America that if you worked hard and you showed real grit, that you could be successful … Strangely, we've now forgotten that" (Tough 2011, 2).

The moral values Randolph seeks to reinvigorate are rooted in Anglo-American mythology, from a time when those countries held places of unquestioned dominance.[19] But one doesn't need to go as far back as the nineteenth century, or even 1969, as a touchstone for a better time: Headmaster Halls wistfully recalls the relative security and certainty of the late twentieth century:

> The pupils I taught thirty years ago easily understood the idea that the century they inhabited was one of global catastrophe. World wars were part of their families' memories, and part of their own Cold War inheritance; any self-respecting "wild child" daughter could join the Greenham Common women's peace camp; famines were televised and Live Aid offered hope to the starving and a palliative to the western conscience. But these issues were by and large external ones – great, world-sweeping affairs that did not call into

> question the tiny and fragile world of the individual self. On the contrary, they helped promote a belief in the power of the individual to change things for the better. Without a doubt, this reached its climax in the fall of the Berlin Wall. This defining moment of 1989 proved to the world that individuals not only mattered, they could win the battle against apparently invulnerable and oppressive regimes. (2014b)

Faith in the power of the individual has eroded for young people today, Halls argues, and the principal culprit is technology. The solution, for Halls, is to help students to recover a sense of their power as individuals: "'True grit' and resilience training is as much as anything a means of celebrating the miracle of human life, and the vast potential of every person to change things both within them and around them for the better" (2014b). In a subsequent blog post, Halls again locates these values in the 1980s: "It was the decade of Band Aid optimism and purpose, and young people felt they really could make things better for other people ... Individuals really seemed to have a voice, and we need to recreate that sense of personal meaning in the 21st century" (2014a).

Several elements are notable in these odes to a mythologized recent past. First, they reduce complex geopolitical contexts to individual morality tales (note "individuals," not collectives, gathered to fight injustice). Second, they assume a perspective that is outside and impervious to catastrophe. British subjects are hailed as dispassionate observers and charitable helpers (with a nod to "wild child" activists) in events like the Cold War and the 1981 Ethiopian famine. Missing is a sense of history and global interconnectedness that would acknowledge the complexity of the events mentioned, including the complicity of Britain and the US in supporting policies and practices that contribute to hunger in Africa and to the arms race. Missing too is an acknowledgment of the vast numbers of youth for whom these "great, world-sweeping affairs" were *not* "by and large external ones" but part of their everyday lives. This provincial, apparently unconscious, assumption of privilege might explain the bizarre transition from talking about global catastrophe to seizing on the Internet as the culprit in modern students' unhappiness. The premise of Halls's position seems to be that students' internal locus of control has been surrendered to an external one – a position shared by psychologists like Levine (2006) and Gray (2010).

Another way of reading it is that the world has intruded on their personal space, in the form of looser financial markets, climate change, terrorism, global pandemics, and ethnic conflict – all of which bear the imprint of the capitalist and colonialist systems from which Britain and the US, until relatively recently, reaped only benefits.

Nowhere, arguably, have the indignities of these changes been more acutely felt than in the British boarding school and its epigones throughout the English-speaking world – institutions that style themselves as the inheritors of proud tradition and the breeding grounds for the next generation of leaders. While the concerns these educators express are not unique to private schools, there is a sense that the stakes are higher here, that the possibility of a diminished capacity to navigate, let alone command, change cannot be countenanced. The predicament facing the independent school community recalls American worries of a century ago but in a changed geopolitical landscape in which the terms of engagement are less legible and more volatile. The principal of Lakeside School offers this advice: "The good news on the subject of resilience is that this character trait can be developed in our students. The challenging news is that comfort is the enemy of resilience and that for independent school students, both campus and family environments are often too comfortable and failure averse" (Noe 2013).

One solution is to create an environment in which students are allowed, even encouraged, to take risks and to learn from failure. Some schools have adopted the idea of character education – an idea that doesn't just echo but overlaps in substantial ways with approaches used in military training, such as the $145 million US Comprehensive Soldier Fitness program, "a preventive program that seeks to enhance psychological resilience among all members of the Army community" (Casey 2011, 1). This focus represents a shift away from traditional conceptions of the good soldier based on the ideal of moral fortitude and towards what Pat O'Malley describes as a "new kind of 'warrior' subject, more entrepreneurial, flexible and adaptive, more relational and active than is consistent with subjects distinguished by fortitude alone" (2010, 502). These qualities, it turns out, also resonate with the kind of leadership abilities independent schools seek to inculcate in their students. Neither hardwired personality attributes nor moral code, these traits represent, rather, habits of mind whose cultivation enables individuals to thrive in the face of challenge (Peterson and Seligman 2004). O'Malley describes the difference between these and earlier conceptions of virtue this way: "Elements formerly identified as human 'attributes,' such as courage, willpower, fortitude and character, have been reconfigured as 'coping strategies' or 'skills' that can be learned by anyone. In turn, these attributes no longer appear as adamantine elements deeply inscribed in the moral soul. Rather they appear as readily acquired, scientifically tested and mutable cognitive manoeuvres appropriate to the governance of the self in conditions of uncertainty" (2010, 489). The argument that these "maneouvres" are teachable is critical to the meritocratic principles on which private schools stake their claim to contemporary legitimacy.

Analogous to the shift in what is understood to constitute a good solider, beyond the measurable indices of resilience like "honesty" and "prudence" that would be familiar to a nineteenth-century moral educator, others in this list speak to the contemporary context in which adaptability has come to supplement (though significantly not replace) deference as a key survival strategy; these include "vitality" and "humour." A quality that the authors, psychologists Christopher Peterson and Martin Seligman, acknowledge as being "as much a property of the body as it is of the mind," vitality describes "feeling alive, being full of zest, and displaying enthusiasm for any and all activities" (2004, 209). It is also associated with the capacity for fun, which Peterson and Seligman suggest is a quality that is universally recognized as a hallmark of moral value. They explain, "When we describe people as fun, we may or may not mean they are funny, but we certainly mean that they have twinkling eyes and approach ongoing life with gusto and relish" (210). Peterson and Seligman are careful to point out that "vitality, as we conceive it is not the same thing as hyperactivity, nervous energy, tension, or mania. Rather, vitality is zest that is experienced as volitional and fulfilling as it is brought to bear on life's worthy activities" (209).[20] The definition of humour is at once vague and specific: "We define the humorous individual as one who is skilled at laughing and gentle teasing, at bringing smiles to the faces of others, at seeing the light side, and at making (not necessarily telling) jokes" (530). By way of clarification, they explain that "humorous people may well tell jokes, or pass them on via e-mail, but jokes are but one part of humor. Indeed, a highly playful person may never tell a single joke but still inject humor into a situation by choosing the right moment to raise an eyebrow or make a wry comment" (530). More than a confirmation of the truism that comedy is all about timing, this characterization of humour classifies it as a key part of the arsenal of responsivity and preparedness, a tool capable of leveraging circumstances to enhance and amplify the landscape of social possibility. "Good" humour, Peterson and Seligman assert, is inclusive, in contrast to "evil" humour that works at someone else's expense:[21] "Sharing a joke or a laugh is one of the best ways to feel close to someone else, even a stranger, because it is a sign that we have something in common. The USO does not send Shakespearean actors overseas to entertain troops by reciting lines from Hamlet; it sends comedians" (531).

The last observation is significant, and not only because the "character strengths and virtues" are the basis of Comprehensive Soldier Fitness: a sense of humour is considered vital for soldiers in part because, in concert with other traits like "hope," it enables them to extract the good from bad situations. What is particularly interesting about the nod to the military uses of humour is its juxtaposition with the previous sentence, which alludes to the putatively universal character of humour: it allows us to "feel close to someone else, even a stranger." There is an obvious limit to this closeness, one defined by borders of the liberal democracy that it is the business of troops to defend. The enemy, we can presume, is a legitimate target of humour but incapable of possessing it. With this distinction we can unravel a little the conundrum identified by Ross regarding the Chinese labourers who were hardier than Anglo-Americans but with "less of the martial spirit" (Wang 1999, vi) – a quality that Peterson and Seligman now allow us precisely to quantify.

The problem of Chinese hardiness finds echoes in military observations about the frustrating resilience of modern-day enemies: Al Qaeda, and later ISIS, proved surprisingly adaptable in the face of the superior weaponry and resources of the US and its allies. This can be attributed to organizational factors: a light decentralized structure, enabling the scaling up or down of operations in response to changing circumstances (Zolli and Healy 2012, 65–7), and the capacity for "hybridized warfare," which uses elements from different styles of war, "leveraging them selectively and integrating them" to adjust to evolving conditions (McFate 2015, 17), confound the scale and hierarchy of the traditional army. But analysts also identify another source of ISIS resilience, which is ideological: "The *takfiri* jihadist ideology of ISIS has roots reaching back to the early days of Islam. Accordingly, the enduring appeal of this ideology to some Muslims will likely prove difficult, if not impossible, to expunge – at least in the short term. Furthermore, ISIS's supporters reject the authority of establishment religious scholars, making the movement difficult to delegitimize on religious grounds" (Eisenstadt 2014, 1). Conforming to mainstream characterizations of radical Islam, this analysis is also oddly contradictory: on the one hand, the ideology derives strength from its historical roots; on the other, its strength is attributed to its renegade nature, its indifference and even opposition to established authority. We can make sense of this contradiction if we read it not for its anthropological accuracy but for its orientalist strategy of shoring up Western legitimacy. By characterizing ISIS adherents as simultaneously fundamentalists and insurgents, we assert our own liberal individualism, a freedom that is secured by our "superior" civilization.

We can therefore begin to see the mythological underpinnings of the "science" of resilience as it is pegged to character. While global change is increasingly understood, in the military and beyond, in terms of systems thinking and complexity theory – approaches that often appear in discussions of resilience – character education uncritically holds up the individual as the locus of consciousness and agency. The thinking seems to go something like this: The world has become more complicated and unpredictable, a circumstance that is exacerbated by the media, especially digital media. But contemporary risks remain intelligible to and manageable by the principles of (neo)liberal democracy, which also, and not coincidentally, help to secure the conservation of privilege in the hands of the dominant Anglo-American class – at least for now. The nostalgia and anxiety that this chapter has documented is warded off by a belief that resilience – the kind that was nurtured on the playing fields of Eton and the woods of New England – persists and can be fortified. Here, the focus on the individual is paramount. Although Seligman and Peterson's list of character's strengths and virtues boasts its multicultural credentials – or perhaps *because* it boasts these credentials (Seligman 2011, 104) – it takes no account of the structures and dynamics of power like race, gender, and class that shape behaviour. The ideal character that emerges from their list of virtues looks a lot like the typical private school student: confident and optimistic about their place in a world that unfolds before them as a landscape of infinite possibility.[22]

The Final Frontier of Fun

An implicit, if not explicit, corollary of settler-colonial resilience is the capacity to challenge known limits, courting the thrill and danger of encountering new worlds. In *Last Child in the Woods*, Louv (2005) describes the closing of the first two American frontiers and the imminent approach of a third. The first, described by Frederick Jackson Turner, marked the wilderness uninhabited by (civilized) men that disappeared with the settlement of the West; the second corresponded to the period of celebrating nature, defined by Roosevelt's presidency (see Haraway 1985) and the rise of the Boy Scouts. The third frontier entails a "rapid slide from the real to the virtual, from the mountain to the Matrix" (Louv 2005, 4), a decline that can be addressed only by reclaiming nature. A different vision of the next frontier – one that retains the ideas of freedom, risk, and fun – can be found in Ridley Scott's 2015 film *The Martian*.[23] Based on Andy Weir's 2011 novel of the same name, the film encapsulates the popular embrace of resilience as a settler-colonial (in this case overtly US American) virtue, embodied in the exemplary "guyness" (Karabel 2006) of Matt Damon as astronaut Mark Watney.

Watney is notable – and cheer-on-able – not only for his remarkable persistence and ingenuity when accidentally abandoned alone on Mars for days, but for his vitality (summed up succinctly in the instructions he gives a colleague to tell his parents, in the event of his death, "that I loved my job, and I was good at it" [Scott 2015]) and, most notably, the humour with which he approaches his plight. Humour was a key element in Andy Weir's novel, as well, but it assumes particular significance in the film through its expression in Watney's character, which is inseparable from the acting persona of Matt Damon.[24] Damon's myriad roles, ranging from *Good Will Hunting* (1997) to the *Bourne* series, epitomize a model of modern masculinity: a good looking white guy, athletic but smart, with a healthy mix of sensitivity and bad-assedness. Humour is essential to his storylines, to relieve the awfulness of the situations he encounters ("Fuck you, Mars!"; "Things didn't go exactly as planned, but I'm not dead, so it's a win" [Scott, 2015]) but also to temper what otherwise might come across as unbearable arrogance. This function of humour is especially important in *The Martian*, which, for all its billing as "a love letter to science" (Hassan 2015), is also a legitimation of an American-led mission to colonize space.[25] Preoccupied with the business of survival, Watney doesn't often allude to the world-making project he is engaged in, but when he does, his comments are leavened with humour. For example, of his successful effort to grow potatoes fertilized with human feces (an instance of ingenuity that's also an occasion for jokes), Watney muses, "They say once you grow crops somewhere, you have officially colonized it. So, technically, I colonized Mars. In your face, Neil Armstrong!" (Scott 2015). Later, as he makes his way across the planet to access the ship he will use to meet his former crew for a fly-by rescue, he comments:

> I've been thinking about laws on Mars. There's an international treaty saying that no country can lay claim to anything that's not on Earth. By another treaty, if you're not in any country's territory, maritime law applies. So Mars is international waters. Now, NASA is an American nonmilitary organization, it owns the Hab. But the second I walk outside, I'm in international waters. So here's the cool part: I'm about to leave for the Schiaparelli Crater where I'm going to commandeer the Ares IV lander. Nobody explicitly gave me permission to do this, and they can't until I'm on board the Ares IV. So I'm going to be taking a craft over in international waters without permission, which by definition ... makes me a pirate. Mark Watney: Space Pirate. (Scott 2015)

Focusing on the character of Watney as an audacious, rule-defying smartass, his comments deflect questions of the legal and political implications of space colonization. At least they almost do – with one exception. The reference to the status of NASA as a civilian agency is key to the film's message that the (US-led) exploration of space is not a militarized, state-building project but a peaceful enterprise for the benefit of all humankind. This clarification of NASA's role is important for framing the cooperation of the US and Chinese space agencies in Watney's rescue. The Chinese happen to have a booster of the calibre needed to launch the ship that will send Watney the supplies he needs to carry him until the next mission arrives to bring him home. It is in the feel-good spirit of the movie that China offers this booster to the Americans – even though it will scuttle their next planned mission. This cooperation is not a foregone conclusion, however, and we're not initially sure it is going to happen. When we first see employees of the China National Space Administration, they're conducting a briefing in clipped, urgent tones about the state of the American mission. From the appearance of the subtitled conversation – its pointed, serious nature in contrast to the looser, sometimes funny, exchanges between the US scientists – and the unsmiling, formal appearance of the officials, who, unlike their casually dressed American counterparts, are all wearing conservative business attire, it is unclear whether the outcome will be a statement of satisfaction that the Americans will have their comeuppance or even a declaration of aggression. When the senior official (president?) determines that they will give the booster to the Americans, the audience breathes a sign of relief. But let there be no mistake: the Chinese are willingly assuming a subordinate role in their venture with the Americans. They have the technology, but the Americans possess the superior leadership skills, moral authority, and – it can't be discounted – a sense of humour.[26]

In this way, the film resolves US anxieties about globalization (which contain echoes of Edward Ross's worried 1911 observations of hardy Chinese labourers) not by representing a US triumph over other countries but by representing those countries' – China is the obvious exemplar – willing accession to a subservient role in a US-led mission to colonize space for all humankind.[27] Cementing the relationship, and future trajectory of the mission, are the scenes at the end of the Ares V mission to Mars, which includes a Chinese astronaut. Watney has become an instructor for new astronauts, establishing his experience, wisdom, and character as the template for future space travel. In an interview about his role in *The Martian*, Damon says, "It's a really optimistic and hopeful movie – and sometimes that's our job, to put something like this out in the middle of really tough times" (Hassan 2015). Reflection upon this geopolitical subplot of the film highlights the role played by globalization in producing "tough times" and precisely reveals where the "hope" of the movie lies: in the continued dominance of the US, amidst fears of global turbulence and uncertainty epitomized by China's growing strength.

It might seem incongruous to conclude a discussion of "old-fashioned fun" with a story about space travel. However, a central objective of this chapter has been to highlight a contradiction at the heart of resilience thinking between an embrace of risk – by definition a forward-looking activity that is open to the possibility of transformation – and a conservative retreat to an imagined past. Both the anticipatory and nostalgic structures of feeling focus on freedom of movement, a freedom that has been the hallmark of a particular mode of white Anglo-American privilege that is felt to be under threat by other nations and nonwhite populations within the US/Canada. Anxiety about the loss or curtailment of that freedom finds expression in a preoccupation with the resilience of children and young adults. This preoccupation emerges in distinct but overlapping conversations about declining engagement with nature and the outdoors, the spread of technology, and the erosion of character (expressed in phenomena like the weakening of sportsmanship—gender specificity intended—and the rise of "entitlement culture"). What has been lost, and what must be secured in the future, is an ease of movement that is the hallmark of white Anglo-American dominance. Enhancing resilience will shore up the "martial spirit" (Wang 1999, vi) for which "old-fashioned fun" means, among other things, the right to move freely in the world (and beyond it), to explore, and to lay claim to whatever opportunities it offers.

2

Today, Tomorrow, Together

WHEN THE IDEA OF RESILIENCE gets enlisted in defence of the restoration of "old-fashioned fun," it's attached to enhancing both the capacity and the freedom to navigate risk. In other words, it is not, or not only, about security but about the maximization of opportunity and scope to take informed risks, to make choices about where and how to move around in the world. I've suggested that this emphasis on movement and engaging with one's environment (sometimes represented as a positive experience of being in nature) aligns with implicit settler-colonial beliefs about the right to occupy the land and exploit its resources into the future. Though its dominant framework is psychosocial, the concept of fostering (or restoring) resilience in kids gestures to the social-ecological in its invocation of nature and the outdoors, the space or field in which resilient individuals are assumed to flourish. This chapter addresses a valency of resilience that starts at the scale of the social-ecological: the resilient cities movement. Taking as its focus the resilience strategies of Melbourne and Toronto, developed as part of the Rockefeller Foundation's 100 Resilient Cities (100RC) Project, in this chapter, I consider how the idea of resilience works to support and extend the role of cities as engines of settler colonialism and racial capitalism.

Cities played a crucial role in colonial expansion, serving both as hubs for exchange and wealth generation and the imaginary apex of the implantation of European civilization into the so-called new world. At the beginning of the twenty-first century, the physical and imaginary infrastructures of settler-colonial cities is beginning to wear out in the face not just of age and neglect but a range of new threats, ranging from chronic poverty and homelessness to climate change and pandemics. Urban resilience strategies promise to help cities come up with ways to weather the coming challenges, not only by designing smart transit systems and efficient buildings but also by renovating the policies of exclusion, segregation, and the conquest of nature that, while integral to the establishment of settler-colonial cities, are now understood as impediments to their function. By embracing the values of settler-Indigenous reconciliation, equity, diversity, and inclusion and the rehabilitation of nature, the resilience strategies of Toronto and Melbourne work not to undermine the foundations of settler colonialism but to foster the conditions for its sustainability into the future. As creator and funder of 100RC, the Rockefeller Foundation is an important author of the settler-colonial urban resilience narrative that inspires Melbourne's and Toronto's Resilience Strategies. Through a close reading of those strategies, I identify how the concepts of social-ecological and psychosocial resilience, shot through with philanthrocapitalist energy, create a blueprint for settler-colonial futurity. But I am also interested in where the blueprint gets blurry, in the places where the promise of resilience falters and the glimmer of other possible storylines emerge. Those other storylines are the subject of subsequent chapters. For now, the focus is on the Rockefeller Foundation's mission to help usher cities safely into a dangerous future that they may have helped to create but are not equipped to survive.

100RC

In operation from 2013–2019, 100RC marked an unprecedented initiative to incorporate resilience into urban planning on a global scale (Fitzgibbon and Mitchell 2019, 648). Launched in 2013 to mark the Rockefeller Foundation's hundreth anniversary, 100RC sought to help local governments plan for disasters, or "shocks," as well as to cope with long-standing environmental, social, and economic problems, or "stresses" (Berkowitz 2017). The Rockefeller Foundation provided participating cities, chosen by competition, with funding, including money to hire a chief resilience officer (CRO), as well as access to technical and networking support to help design and implement a resilience strategy. While the chief areas of focus were the interconnected challenges of urbanization, globalization, and climate change, its ambit remained broad: "A city became 'resilient,'" as one commentator put it, "by identifying virtually any social and infrastructural fault line that a shock might expose" (Bliss 2019).[1] The project wound up in 2019, though the Rockefeller Foundation continued to fund some of its initiatives, including CROs in the one hundred participating cities. In 2020, two new organizations emerged to take over some of the activities the Rockefeller Foundation had launched: Resilient Cities Catalyst, launched by former 100RC president Michael Berkowitz and former Rockefeller Foundation president Judith Rodin, draws funding from Facebook and the Conrad N. Hilton Foundation; and the Global Resilient Cities Network, led by CROs from the original hundred cities, is in partnership with companies ranging from Visa to the Nature Conservancy. The goal of the GRCN, articulated by Acting Executive Director, Lauren Sorkin, is to "build[…] on the legacy of 100 Resilient Cites, transitioning the network to a city-led impact focused organisation that will become independent and financially sustainable" (Carey 2020). The emphasis on financial sustainability, a conspicuous addition to the "resilient city" criteria laid out in the 100RC, might have bearing on the project's abrupt termination in 2019 – a possibility explored at the end of this chapter.

The 100RC project was a product of its time. By 2013, resilience had become a key concept, perhaps *the* key concept, guiding modern life in volatile times. A 2011 *Guardian* article predicted that resilience would be the word of the new year, replacing guiding values like conservation and sustainability as societies confront the "need to deal with inevitable major shocks, including those which are impossible to predict" (Juniper 2011, 2). The last decades of the twentieth century saw the infusion of resilience into the field of development (Duffield 2007, 18), with initiatives targeted at countries and regions in the global South. Resilience thinking also found a home in cities for reasons that are in some senses self-evident: as urbanization increases the size and complexity of cities, they become more vulnerable to risk, ranging from climate change and terrorism to pandemics. With dense concentrations of human, technological, and economic capital, cities are also places from which solutions to complex global problems are likely to emerge.[2] A growing body of literature addresses the importance of cultivating urban resilience to address these threats (Goh 2021; Zhang and Li 2017; Kelbaugh 2019; Coaffee and Lee 2016; Sharifi and Yamagata 2016; Vale and Campanella 2005). The 100 Resilient Cities project also makes sense for less obvious reasons having to do with the confluence of resilience thinking with philanthrocapitalism, settler colonialism, and the city.

Together with the Carnegie Foundation, the Rockefeller Foundation exemplifies a movement in early twentieth-century America to direct the triumphs of settler-colonial industrialization (railways and oil respectively) towards humanitarian ends. Founded in 1913 by Standard Oil cofounder John D. Rockefeller, with the goals of ending energy poverty, achieving health for all, nourishing the world, and expanding economic opportunity, the Rockefeller Foundation promoted a vision of the world as a complex system best managed by the combined energies of science and capitalism (The Rockefeller Foundation 2020). This vision helped to generate the phenomenon of global public health managed as a private enterprise, spawning campaigns to eradicate hookworm, malaria, and yellow fever, which had the less publicized side effect of boosting American capitalist interests in the global South.[3] More than this, historians have highlighted the role of the Rockefeller Foundation in advancing public health as part of an overtly imperialist agenda. The campaign to eradicate hookworm, for example, owed a lot to hookworm's reputation as the "germ of laziness" due to the erosion (by anemia) of the productivity of poor workers in the American South and tropical countries in the global South where the foundation had investments (Brown 1976, 898). Internal communications praise the extension of the hookworm campaign overseas "on account of the direct physical and economic benefits resulting from the eradication of the disease and also on account of the usefulness of this work as a means of creating and promoting influences" (Brown 1976, 899).

In short, as E. Richard Brown argues, the Rockefeller Foundation's public health campaigns "were blatantly intended, first, to raise the productivity of the workers in under-developed countries, second, to reduce the cultural autonomy of these agrarian peoples and make them amenable to being formed into an industrial workforce, and third, to assuage hostility to the U.S. and undermine goals of national economic and political independence" (1976, 900). The Rockefeller Foundation also played a central role in the Green Revolution, which began in Mexico in the 1950s and spread from Latin America to India. Celebrated by proponents for developing strains of wheat and rice that dramatically increased crop yields, the Green Revolution is also cited by environmentalists such as Vandana Shiva (2016) as one of the principal instruments of the destruction of biodiversity in the global South. Billed as a solution to global hunger, the Green Revolution served the foundation's geopolitical ambitions of forwarding American modernization (Mueller 2013, 132).

In its history as a global wealth-generating distributor of social goods, built on the foundations of resource plundering, the Rockefeller is a quintessential settler-colonial success story. That success informs the message of then foundation president Judith Rodin's 2014 book, *The Resilience Dividend*, which uses the language of business finance (peppered with exhortations to personal responsibility) to make the case for resilience as the capacity that will allow us to "adapt and grow from disruptive experience" (4). In her account, the values of resilience are inseparable from those of philanthrocapitalism wherein the history of colonialism dissolves into a narrative of inexorable turbulence from which smart, agile, and liberal-minded entrepreneurs can reap profit and extend charity.[4] This is the vision that inspires 100RC.

Settler-Colonial Cities

The 100RC project extended to a wide variety of cities in dozens of different countries. But the phenomena it sought to intervene in, including urbanization and globalization, along with the tensions that the idea of resilience aims to manage – between nature and culture, identity and diversity, continuity and change – are most acutely present in settler-colonial cities, which make up about a third of the 100RC (Hofman 2021, 6–7).[5] As geographer Jane M. Jacobs notes, settler-colonial cities, which began as outposts, are key nodes in "the anxious articulations of imperial authority" (1996, 159). It was through cities that "the spatial order of imperial imaginings was rapidly and deftly realized [and] resources of colonized lands were harnessed and reconnected to cities in imperial heartlands" (4). But cities are not bastions of order. On the contrary, Jacobs suggests, "The hold of imperialist regimes of power is tied to the very uncertainty they face in their manifestation on the ground: in their encounter with the unpredictability of the Other and the inconsistency of the Self. In the face of this uncertainty imperialism must always reinscribe its frames of power and difference and this is what helps to give it its tenacity" (159).[6] In the course of time, "postcolonial" cities in Australia, the focus of Jacobs's research, and also in Canada, become increasingly heterogeneous without becoming more equitable or democratic.[7] As Jacobs points out, "People connected by imperial histories are thrust together in assemblages barely predicted, and often guarded against, during the inaugural phases of colonialism. Often enough this is a meeting not simply augmented by imperialism but still regulated by its constructs of difference and privilege" (4). Thus, "'Post'colonial politics in Australia is practiced within a nation-state which joyously moves towards multiculturalism" (23) at the same time as the nation's cities are riven with inequality and racist policing.

Urban settler-colonial resilience also reflects moves simultaneously to replace and profit from Indigenous peoples. Patrick Wolfe puts it succinctly: "On the one hand, settler society required the practical elimination of the natives in order to establish itself on their territory. On the symbolic level, however, settler society subsequently sought to recuperate Indigeneity in order express its difference – and, accordingly, its independence – from the mother country" (2006, 387). The figure of the native also mediates the paradoxical place of nature as simultaneously an ideal outside and a commodity within capitalism – a phenomenon Jacobs examines in Brisbane's ecotourism centre, whose brand conjoins Aboriginal culture and Australia's (now endangered) national symbol, the koala, in "a marketable image of how the Aboriginal culture has co-existed with the natural environment for several thousand years" (Jacobs 1996, 132). Jacobs explains the bait-and-switch of this gesture in which the centring of Aboriginal culture is used to bolster the settler-colonial urban economy: "Indigenous peoples are placed back in First Nature, they have become the First People of the world, and then are reabsorbed into a global chronology of planetary survival, which begins with 'them' but ends with an environmentally sound 'us'" (1997, 137). As discussed below, this dynamic is evident in both the Melbourne and Toronto Resilience strategies, which have each become essential toolkits in what Jacobs succinctly terms "the ongoing struggle within settler societies around property and propriety" (146). Put differently, resilience strategies work to manage risks to settler-colonial occupation of land and define and guide the terms of occupation, including how urban life should be organized to optimize sustainable growth.

Within the 100RC project, resilience was defined as "the capacity of individuals, communities, institutions, businesses, and systems within a city to survive, adapt, and grow no matter what kinds of chronic stresses and acute shocks they experience" (Berkowitz, 2017). The inclusion of growth signals an expansive definition of resilience whereby one not only survives but flourishes through disruption (the idea of bouncing *forward* rather than back [Manyena et al. 2011]) as well as the foundational significance of capital and capitalism to the 100RC project. In what follows, I read the resilience strategies from Melbourne and Toronto as documents of settler-colonial placemaking.[8] In doing so, I follow Jacobs's (1996) assertion that ideas and physical processes are co-constitutive in the construction of the postcolonial city. Or, as Emily Potter puts it, "Place-making and story-telling go hand in hand" (2012, 132). Toronto's and Melbourne's resilience strategies tell stories about specific places.

They are also templates of the "urban resilience complex" (Webber, Leitner, and Sheppard 2021, 346),[9] whose meaning and legibility are determined by a global rubric, generated by the Rockefeller Foundation. The selection process for the competition by which cities were selected for inclusion in the program emphasized "innovative mayors, a recent catalyst for change, a history of building partnerships and an ability to work with a wide range of stakeholders" – criteria geared towards the likelihood of delivering a "reliable return on the Foundation's philanthropic investment, or what 100RC calls a 'Resilience Dividend'" (Fitzgibbon and Mitchell 2019, 650, 653).[10] The nod to local stakeholders alongside the prioritization of corporate interests that goes by the name of "building partnerships" reflects what Malini Ranganathan and Eve Bratman observe in the different but related context of disaster response programs in the US in which "the main beneficiaries are private contractors, consultants, architects, designers, and the financial and corporate executives who profit from federal resilience-related contracts. Meanwhile, affected residents are forced to act as entrepreneurs to receive funds, while city agencies rubber-stamp community 'participation' as part of their sustainable city planning" (2021, 6).

The neoliberal tilt of this distribution of risk/gain is reinforced by the scalar slipperiness of resilience thinking, which vacillates between validations of local knowledge and of global expertise. In the case of 100RC, beyond the pragmatic recognition that cities might lack necessary resources to address the magnitude of the problems they were facing, the project's promotion of global communication networks reflects the systems focus of resilience thinking. In emphasizing the opportunities and risks presented by enhanced connectivity, the resilience thinking that guided the project downplayed interscalar power relations, including the foundation's specific role as a dominant player in the landscape of philanthrocapitalism.

The resilience strategies that comprise the case studies for this chapter are from Melbourne, part of the "first wave" of thirty-two cities selected for the 100RC in 2014, and Toronto, one of the final thirty-seven cities selected in the third and final competition in 2016. Rather than analyzing the strategies in sequence to illuminate the particularities of each city, I discuss them together, with a focus on their common thematics as they relate to settler-colonial time and space. The words, "Today, Tomorrow and Together" (City of Melbourne 2016, ii, 5, 55),[11] which together and separately form a refrain throughout the Melbourne strategy, organize the discussion.

Today

The 100RC resilience strategies are an odd mix of boosterism ("here's how we're great!"), town hall-style consultation ("who are we?"), and scenario plans that are equal parts vision ("how will we grow?) and risk management ("how do we survive disaster?"). Though the normative concept of resilience is necessarily oriented towards the future, it's predicated on an understanding of a past and present subject that has endured, that should be preserved. The temporal confusion of the idea of the resilient city is visible in an aerial photo that appears in the introduction of the Melbourne strategy with the title "Our changing city" (City of Melbourne 2016, 8–9). The logic of the title depends on a transposition of scales in which the spatial variety that characterizes the snapshot of the city, stretching off towards the horizon in a tapestry of high rises, residential neighbourhoods, green spaces, and the Yarra River, stands in for temporal movement – diversity equals change. This rhetorical sleight-of-hand gives form to a narrative that grants the city visibility by fixing it in place, establishing roots from which growth and change are projected as inevitable. The aerial photo gives visual expression to the implicit assumption that the resilient city occupies a space – comprising what the strategy elsewhere calls "our shared places" (42) – whose expanse and boundaries (and ownership) are incontrovertible.

The strategies from both Melbourne and Toronto legitimize the perspective of "today" by grounding it in the history of settlement that acknowledges Indigenous origins. The Melbourne document begins with an Acknowledgment of Country: "Resilient Melbourne acknowledges the Traditional Owners of the Land, and their strength, resilience and pride as the oldest continuous culture in the world" (2). Toronto's Land Acknowledgment is more detailed, noting that "this strategy was developed on the traditional territory of many nations including the Mississaugas of the Credit, the Anishnabeg, the Chippewa, the Haudenosaunee and the Wendat peoples and is now home to many diverse First Nations, Inuit and Métis. We also acknowledge that Toronto is covered by Treaty 13, signed with the Mississaugas of the Credit, and the Williams Treaties signed with multiple Anishnabeg Nations" (City of Toronto 2019, 2). Though both statements gesture to the continuity of Indigenous presence, it's in the space between the "traditional" past and today where things get murky.

Both strategies contain a historical sketch that makes brief reference to colonialism. In the Melbourne strategy, a colourful timeline traces the shape of the Yarra River, beginning at the top of a page with a roughly sketched circle labelled "30,000 years ago." Radiating out of the circle are a series of dotted lines, presumably meant to evoke Aboriginal dot painting, encasing the words "Kulin Nation inhabit the area now known as Melbourne" (City of Melbourne 16). There follow, nestled in the bends of the river, four other circles in which the roughly sketched quality is replaced by clean lines, designating other time periods, beginning with "1800s" and culminating in "Melbourne Tomorrow 2051." A series of unbroken lines radiates out from each circle, identifying dates – "1847 – Melbourne officially becomes a city"; "1851 – Gold rush in Victoria, large-scale migration, mostly from Britain, Europe, China and USA"; "1919 – Spanish Flu pandemic reaches Melbourne"; "1962 – Commonwealth Electoral Act amended, allowing all Aboriginal Australians to vote in Federal election," etc. Moving forward along the timeline, there is an increasing emphasis on climate change: "2009 – Black Sunday bushfires – 173 deaths, 2133 homes destroyed, 370 deaths from heat"; "2014 – Major heatwave – 97% increase in cardiac emergencies compared to 2013"; and, radiating out from the circle "Melbourne Today," "Bushfires," "Floods," and "Heatwaves." Scanning the record of milestones, triumphs, and disasters, it's easy to miss the huge chunk of time missing between "30,000 years ago" and "1800s," during which, presumably, nothing happened. Though it could be argued that that span of time has to be left blank because there's no written record, the impression, which naturalizes the existence of Melbourne "today," is of a long period of stasis, which required the arrival of Europeans to get things moving. The impression gains reinforcement from the design of the timeline in which the first, roughly drawn circle and colourful dots gives way in the 1800s to the smooth lines of modern culture, implying through the harmonious visual transition both a homology between Aboriginal and European cultures and the natural replacement of the former by the latter.

The Toronto resilience strategy offers a similarly potted history that simultaneously acknowledges and conceals the continuous presence of Indigenous people in the space now known as Toronto (from the Mohawk Tkarón:to, meaning "the place in the water where the trees are standing" [2]). "For thousands of years before colonization," the strategy reads, "[Toronto] was a place where many Indigenous communities would meet to trade, exchange ideas, and solve resilience challenges; today, Toronto continues to be a place for creating innovative solutions to resilience challenges" (12). As with the Melbourne timeline, this history locates Indigenous peoples in a precolonial past *and* represents their activities as seamlessly morphing into the business, communications, and resilience strategizing of today, obscuring the historical dispossession of Indigenous peoples from urban space.[12] In this account, Indigenous practices – and indeed Indigenous peoples – figure as a kind of prototype or precursor to be superseded by the innovations (and innovators) of today. The image of continuity between past and present elides the history of colonialism that has severely compromised, and continues to compromise, the resilience of Indigenous peoples.

Both strategies struggle to reconcile their representation of Indigenous peoples with the rhetoric of resilience. Noting that Aboriginal peoples have "lived, cared for country, and maintained their distinctive culture, for at least 30,000 years," the Melbourne strategy goes on to comment that "this longevity alone demonstrates [their] resilience" (City of Melbourne 2016, 18). Twice commended for their resilience, Aboriginal peoples barely rate a mention in the rest of the document, except to note that "in 2013, average weekly disposable incomes of Melbourne's Indigenous population were $135 less than the incomes of non-Indigenous Melburnians" (21). The Toronto strategy follows a similar pattern: vague tributes to the "essential, far-reaching knowledge and practices" (City of Toronto 2019, 137) that make Indigenous people ideal guides to resilience give way to data. For example: "Indigenous people are overrepresented in the homeless population that sleep outdoors" (24, 60). The ability to sleep rough is clearly not the kind of resilience to which either the Toronto or the Melbourne document aspires; in fact, both strategies represent the living conditions of Indigenous and other vulnerable people as impeding not only their own life chances but the resilience of the city as a whole, a point to which I return below (the contradictions in how resilience discourse represents Aboriginal peoples in Australia – as exemplars of both resilience and its failure – are explored in detail in chapter 6).

The strategies tiptoe delicately around the dynamics of settler colonialism. Noting that "traditional Aboriginal cultures and communities were severely and irrevocably harmed by the arrival of Europeans" (City of Melbourne 2016, 18), the Melbourne strategy goes on to say that "repercussions" of "actions of explorers, whalers, sealers and settlers ... are still felt today" (18) – an acknowledgment that places colonialism in the past, suggesting it exists today only in the form of lingering aftereffects. The Toronto strategy refers to "the major shock of colonization, including the Residential School system, which has created ongoing stresses around language and culture loss, child removal, racism, poverty, inequity and displacement" from which it infers that "Indigenous communities are experts in long-term resilience" (City of Toronto 2019, 137). An ungenerous reading would take this observation to imply that the shock of colonization actually did Indigenous people a favour in making them more resilient. The Toronto resilience strategy does recognize Indigenous peoples' quest for "reconciliation and a restoration of the health, wellness, self-determination and sovereignty, which were eroded through historical and ongoing colonization" (23)[13] and emphasizes the goal of "healing from intergenerational trauma" (Indigenous Climate Action Report on Indigenous Knowledge and Climate Action, quoted in City of Toronto 2019, 52). The strategy also acknowledges the colonial history of Toronto itself, which includes the 1787 purchase by the British Crown from the Mississaugas of the Credit River, which was later acknowledged to be illegitimate and settled in 2010 with a $145 million payment from the Canadian government (City of Toronto 2019, 48). By recording the settlement without providing any context,[14] the strategy represents colonialism as a completed transaction, dodgy at first then finally made right. There is no space in this narrative to acknowledge the inadequacy of the settlement (Edwards 2010), ongoing obligations to Indigenous peoples, or continued infringements on their sovereignty.[15]

As Libby Porter and Oren Yiftachel note (2019), the settler-colonial imaginary has defined the city "as a place not Indigenous, profoundly spatially and temporally disconnected from Indigenous histories and geographies, despite the obvious fact in settler-colonial societies that most cities and settlements sit on unceded territories" (177). The Toronto and Melbourne resilience strategies conform to this pattern in the story they tell of an Indigenous past giving way to hoped-for reconciliation within (and to) a settler-colonial present and future. It is in keeping with that spirit of reconciliation that the Toronto resilience strategy states that it is guided by a commitment to an "'all my relations' Indigenous worldview" as defined by Thomas King (24),[16] a perspective that extends beyond human beings to encompass "the web of kinship to animals, to the birds, to the fish, to the plants, to all the animate and inanimate forms that can be seen or imagined. More than that, 'all my relations' is an encouragement for us to accept the responsibilities we have within the universal family by living our lives in a harmonious and moral manner" (King 1990, ix, quoted in City of Toronto 2019, 24).

The reference to "all my relations" thinking does double duty in the strategy, signalling a commitment not just to reconciliation but also to nature, which is a key component of urban resilience. Nature features in the Toronto strategy in the form of the aspiration that the city might become "a place where we each feel connected to the natural world" (City of Toronto 2019, 65), as well as more concrete "nature-based solutions" to specific problems (43), such as rejuvenating shoreline vegetation to reduce the risk of flooding. The latter is an example of "green and blue infrastructure – sometimes called natural or resilient infrastructure – [which] refers to the use of nature as infrastructure to meet specific goals and service targets" (105). The nature-as-infrastructure concept draws inspiration from Melbourne, whose resilience strategy designers collaborated with Earth Economics on a 2018 document, "Building Urban Resilience with Nature: A Practitioner's Guide to Action." The guide notes the typical failure of urban policy to regard nature as "an asset or resource to meet challenges arising from urbanization, globalization, and climate change" (United Nations 2018, 9) and promises to help urban leaders "leverage nature and natural infrastructure to build city resilience" (4). The idea of "leverage[ing] nature" as an "asset" and a "resource" follows the familiar "win-win" logic of green capitalism whereby the valuation of nature produces environmental benefits along with new economic opportunities. It is hard to square this rhetoric with the affective and ethical bonds of kinship that "all my relations" thinking encompasses. This incongruency characterizes the presence of Indigenous peoples in the strategy more generally. At the same time as they stress their consultative approach, explaining that "we work with the Indigenous community in Toronto to incorporate Indigenous worldviews into our approach to environment" (54), the strategy's authors acknowledge that "Indigenous views of the world do not have a separate category for the environment or the climate" (138). Thus, in a move that echoes the selective take-up of Traditional Ecological Knowledge (TEK) by Western science (Nadasy 1999; Birch 2016; Doxtater 2004), Indigenous knowledge is simultaneously celebrated, picked over for its catchy bits, and relegated to a secondary category of "tradition," which is understood to be peripherally relevant to the process of modern urban planning.

The persistent dynamics of colonialism in urban spaces like Melbourne and Toronto have resisted scholarly scrutiny until relatively recently, perhaps because the forms of "predatory expansion" (Hugill 2017, 3), intensive industrialization, and segregation that characterized earlier forms of the colonial city have morphed into more fluid and ostensibly democratic dynamics of displacement.[17] This shift finds expression in a new urban planning vocabulary centred around the concept of "liveability," a feature of both Toronto and Melbourne strategies.[18] Defined simply as "suitable for living in or habitable" (Gurstein 2018, 138), the concept of liveability emerged in Dutch planning literature in the 1950s, solidifying over the next several decades into a keyword through which to "frame urban problems, select and order concepts and build narratives that shape policy action" (McArthur and Robin 2019, 1712) as well as a metric through which cities could compete for infrastructure and investment. Melbourne and Toronto both ranked in the top ten of the Economist Intelligence Unit's Global Liveability Index in 2019, along with Adelaide, Vancouver, and Sydney, meaning that Australia and Canada account for 60 per cent of the top ten cities.[19] The association of liveability with settler colonialism is not a coincidence, as critics of the concept have argued (McArthur and Robin 2019; Ruth and Franklin 2014; Ansfield 2015; Gurstein 2018; Mohamud 2020a) and as analysis of the Toronto and Melbourne resilience strategies demonstrates.

"Today," the Melbourne strategy proclaims, "Melbourne is a Liveable City." It elaborates, "Melbourne is a stable and cohesive society, with many residents enjoying a high standard of living and quality of life, supported by ready access to education and healthcare" (City of Melbourne 2016, 20). Toronto's strategy is more effusive, noting in an introduction by Michael Berkowitz, the president of 100 Resilient Cities, that "Toronto is an important and dynamic city, the largest in Canada and the 4th largest in North America. The city has been consistently recognized as one of the world's most livable cities, in part because of its vibrant arts and cultural scene, beautiful neighbourhoods, safe communities, stable economy, and presence of world-leading companies" (City of Toronto 2019, 11).

Liveability is distinguishable from previous metrics, focused largely on economic criteria, in its emphasis on the environment – it is often linked to sustainability (Ruth and Franklin 2014, 18) – culture, and health or, as Mohamad Kashef puts it, a concern for "optimizing the performance and the integrity of human life" (2016, 240).[20] While the rankings differ somewhat in their metrics,[21] liveability indices share an emphasis on initiatives that simultaneously address the objectives of population health, environmental sustainability, and cost savings. Consistent with this focus, two of Melbourne's three "flagship actions" are an urban forest strategy (City of Melbourne 2016, 62) and a cycling network (112) (the third is an "emergency management community resilience approach" for the state of Victoria [90], about which I say more below).[22] Toronto's resilience strategy also features a cycling network and walking strategy alongside a move towards "complete streets" (City of Toronto 2019, 122). Both Toronto and Melbourne strategies temper their promotion of the cities' touted liveability with acknowledgments that their advantages are not universally shared. The global rankings, the Melbourne strategy notes, "do not consider factors such as housing affordability or account for inequality across [the city]" (20). The Toronto strategy similarly identifies "unequal access to resources, funding and opportunities" and aims to promote "equitable life outcomes ... increased access and shared prosperity" (52). In appending equity and inclusion to their discussions of liveability, the resilience strategies don't just subordinate these values, implying that equity is not a precondition for urban liveability, they also leave unquestioned the metric of liveability itself, failing to consider how these metrics themselves exacerbate inequality.

In explicitly framing urban priorities around quality of life, liveability discourse obscures the partiality of its perspective, which skews towards the preferences of a wealthy, well-educated, mobile class (McArthur and Robin 2019, 1720). Mobility, though less obvious perhaps than the other class markers, is implicit in the apparatus of ranking; as McArthur and Robin note, "The notion that liveability can be meaningfully reflected through a global ranking implicitly assumes that the reader is globally mobile. If not, it is of little utility or even reassurance that a city is more 'liveable' than another" (1720). The cosmopolitan underpinnings of liveability discourse inflects its understanding of environment in terms of natural capital. In addition to its function as infrastructure, discussed above, nature, abstractly defined, fuels liveability, "providing our communities and economy with valuable co-benefits that build community resilience and support individual well-being. From improved health outcomes to lowered crime rates, the integration of natural spaces in the urban environment ... improves the daily lives of a diverse and growing urban population" (United Nations Office for Disaster and Risk Reduction 2018, 9). More specifically, "research has repeatedly shown that greener cities have lower levels of obesity and other chronic illnesses, higher levels of physical activity, and improved mental health" (City of Melbourne 65). In highlighting nature's usefulness for boosting liveability, 100RC twists Indigenous spiritual conceptions of the elementality of land and place into fungible benefits for an abstractly conceived human life. Moreover, design elements that aim to maximize particular modes of engagement with outdoor space that are seen as universally desirable (pedestrian-friendly streets, for example) carry assumptions about whose conception of liveability – and ultimately whose lives – matter.

As a clear example of the exclusivity and even hostility of these conceptions, Black urban planners have noted that open streets – a concept embraced by many cities during the COVID-19 pandemic as a way to maximize physical distancing for pedestrians – tend to proceed without consultation with communities for whom walking around in public is associated not with enhanced health but increased exposure to surveillance and violence. "Every week in America," scholar, antiracist activist, and self-proclaimed "unurbanist" Destiny Thomas notes, "people like Ahmaud Arbery and George Floyd have their lives stolen because their visibility in public space goes against the ways we've come to understand who should have access to 'outside' and how they should be allowed to access it. Without a plan to include and protect Black, Brown, Indigenous, trans and disabled people, or a plan to address anti-Black vigilantism and police brutality, these open streets are set up to fail" (2020b, 3). Key aspects of liveability, in other words, don't just obscure but exacerbate the conditions of racial inequality that promote some lives at the cost of others. Jamilla Mohamud highlights the jarring irony of Toronto's celebration of its "livability" in the face of the unmet demands of Black Lives Matter Toronto (BLMTO): "In rejecting the long-standing claim that Toronto is one of the most livable cities in the world, BLMTO is engaging in an act of Black refusal that asserts that this city has not been planned to be livable for Black lives" (2020a, 1).

The emphasis on *planning* is critical here. Both Toronto and Melbourne resilience strategies address the problem of inequity largely in terms of access: to jobs, transit, education, services, retail, information, financing (City of Toronto 2019, 62, 75, 80, 88). These inequities break down by neighbourhood, with implications for opportunity – neighbourhoods outside the downtown core have less access to transportation and, by extension, options – and for resilience: "Communities that experience historic underinvestment, high levels of food insecurity, concentrated poverty, and a lack of social infrastructure are hardest hit by extreme weather and other shocks" (84). Racialized and immigrant populations make up a significant part of these communities, contributing to what the Toronto strategy calls "the problem of socio-economic segregation" (120).[23] This representation of inequality treats the racialization of urban geography as a spatial/ distribution problem that can be significantly ameliorated by "investment" (variations on the word "invest"/"investment" appear a total of forty-nine times in the Toronto strategy), rather than as the consequence of deliberate planning strategies shaped around the priorities of racial capitalism and settler colonialism. "Municipal placemaking has long been an active effort to displace and erase Black people," Thomas argues (2020a, 1).

Historian Bench Ansfield draws on the work of Sylvia Wynter and Katherine McKittrick to create a detailed picture of this process, linking the kind of anxiety about "concentrated poverty" evident in the Toronto strategy (City of Toronto 2019, 84) to colonial urban planning practices that relegated Black and Indigenous populations to marginal spaces, then condemned those spaces as "unlivable" and ripe for reform, the better to be incorporated into "the teleological parade known as urban redevelopment and renewal" (Ansfield 2015, 124, 126). In research focused primarily on post-Katrina New Orleans, Ansfield identifies redevelopment efforts there as reflecting dominant views (on the left and the right) of the evils of concentrated poverty in which tropes of contaminated spaces have come to stand in for the pathologized bodies that inhabit them (134). The Melbourne strategy uses the poverty-pathology equation in its discussion of a correlation between high unemployment, "the stresses caused by economic inequality and geographic disadvantage," and alcoholism, family violence, and obesity. A map showing the "Distribution of Obesity and Economic Prosperity" helpfully highlights the danger zones of concentrated poverty and pathology, whose inhabitants place "significant strains on [the city's] healthcare system" (City of Melbourne 2016, 32).The language of contamination may have been scrubbed clean of references to race (the concentration of Black/Brown people in low-income neighbourhoods is observed as a demographic accident to be remedied by the extension of liveability initiatives rather than an inherent part of them); however, it springs directly from the white supremacist geographical logic that, as Wynter has shown, ties together "notions of habitability and gauges of humanness" (Ansfield 2015, 125). Ansfield goes on to explain, "Because space attains meaning from body, and body from space, the widespread engagement of discourses on behavioral pathology complements the liberal/ humanitarian concern for spatial unlivability, thus reinscribing the naturalness of both and, in so doing, creating the requisite ontological atmosphere for the reproduction of bioevolutionary narratives that render low-capital black subjects genetically inferior, deviant, and other" (133). Once the ideological backdrop of bioevolutionary progress comes into view, it becomes easier to understand why the dominant discourse of liveability is hostile to Black lives. Liveability is not just a measure of current forms of enjoyment, it's also a biopolitical index of future prospects, framed by racist narratives of human progress – narratives that strongly inflect the idea of resilience.

Tomorrow

In the 100RC project and beyond, discourses of liveability and resilience are complexly intertwined. Copenhagen's city plan is exemplary in its aim to "make the city liveable, so all aspects of citizens' lives are taken into consideration in an inclusive strategy of urban planning, making cities and inhabitants more resilient to shock and stress" (City of Copenhagen 2018, 30). It isn't necessarily clear, here, whether resilience aims to preserve qualities of livebility or if liveability, defined by metrics of "healthy behaviors" and "neighborhood revitalization," are valued because they are understood biopolitically as indices of futurity. Biopolitics is a revealing lens through which to read the strategies' framing of racialized inequality. In support of the claim for the city's liveability, the Melbourne strategy boasts about the city's stability and cohesion – features that are predicated on the satisfaction of the needs of "many" of its residents. However, the claim that lots of people enjoy a high standard of living and excellent education and health care requires a qualifying note: "In Melbourne, a challenge for our resilience is maintaining these advantages and making them available to everybody" (20). The temporality of this representation of the city is worth noting: *today*, the unequal distribution of resources, if less than ideal, is tolerable; that some sectors of the population do not enjoy a high standard of living and quality of life or ready access to education and health care does not threaten stability or cohesion: "Today, Melbourne is a liveable city" (20). *Tomorrow* is another question.

One of four "action areas" in the Melbourne strategy, "Survive," describes the goal of "withstand[ing] disruption and bounc[ing] back better than before" (City of Melbourne 2016, 55). Toronto's strategy is similarly geared towards "prepar[ing] for the future" (City of Toronto 2019, 40), with an emphasis on disaster preparation. Resilience Officer Elliott Capell explains that "we can either prepare ahead of the storm or we can prepare after the storm," concurring with interviewer Steve Paikin that "the storm is inevitable" (Cappell 2017). The orientation towards a future replete with (paradoxically expected) surprises underlies repeated references to "challenges" and "opportunities" (or, in the preferred formulation of resilience thinking, "challenges *and* opportunities," as though the two are always conjoined, or the right kind of thinking turns challenges into opportunities [City of Toronto 2019, 121, emphasis added]). Both Toronto and Melbourne strategies identify one of the main challenges to the smooth translation of challenges into opportunities as inequity. As the Melbourne strategy explains, inequity "impacts the entire city's resilience. When certain groups are at higher risk to shocks and stresses or are more vulnerable, the entire system is stressed because those groups experience more shocks and stresses, and experience them with greater intensity. Deep inequities polarize a city, making residents more segregated, less trusting of each other and of government, and less able to agree on solutions to the biggest challenges" (City of Melbourne 2016, 24). When seen through the lens of resilience, inequity signifies not as the consequence of persistent systems of colonialism or racialized capitalism – or even as a measure of direct harm to those who live with poverty and precarity – but as a metric to be factored into the calculation of systemic risk for the city as a whole.

The concepts of social-ecological and psychosocial resilience bleed into one another in the neoliberal tilt of proposed solutions to inequality and other social problems, including mental health crises. Mental health – defined as "the capacity to be autonomous, regulate one's emotions, have self-confidence and empathy, and solve problems" (City of Melbourne 2016, 111) – is the focus of Melbourne's Young and Resilient Living Labs (126), where "young people will be helped to design, create and test out their own technology-based strategies to tackle stresses and shocks affecting youth mental health" (127). The Young and Resilient Living Labs typifies initiatives favoured by the resilience strategies in its reading of interconnected structural problems including unemployment, family violence, and alcohol and drug abuse (127) as systemic "stresses" amenable to individual strategic fixes. Charging young people with the task of coming up with tech-based strategies to address their own suffering (which is significantly not the same as enfranchising them in processes of democratic social transformation) ticks a number of boxes, including the provision of "diverse local employment opportunities that support an adaptable workforce that is ready for the jobs of the future" (39) and "empower[ing] communities to take active responsibility for their own and each other's wellbeing, safety and health" (127). Both Melbourne and Toronto strategies emphasize self- and community reliance, personal responsibility, and capacity-building (City of Melbourne 2016, 41; City of Toronto 2019, 85) on the understanding that "all too frequently we deliver services in ways that lead to dependence, rather than fostering capacity and empowering our citizens" (City of Melbourne 2016, 41). In a tone at once paternalistic and dismissive, the Melbourne strategy elaborates, "We are fortunate to have governments that are able to respond to disaster events. However, this is contributing to a common perception that our safety and preparedness are someone else's responsibility, and that governments can always be relied upon to come to the aid of those who do not plan ahead. We need our communities to be better able to recognise the hazards they fact, to plan to manage risks and their consequences for themselves and their broader communities, supported by certainty that governments will always help the most vulnerable and those who are simply unfortunate" (41). In this push towards responsibilization, there is a clear line being drawn here between the "unfortunate" – a small, identifiable group deemed to be suffering through no fault of their own – and "those who do not plan ahead" (i.e., those who, by not buying robust insurance policies, have no one but themselves to blame when disaster strikes [41]). This division is crosscut by another opposition between "communities" and "governments."[24] When it comes to surviving the "inevitable" storms of the future, both Toronto and Melbourne strategies place hope – and responsibility – on communities.

The emphasis on community, discussed in detail in the section below, is a foundational principle of resilience, which is also a point of tension. If the nominal objective of resilience strategies – urban and otherwise – is moving confidently into the future (the word "change" appears forty times in the Melbourne strategy and eighty-three times in the Toronto strategy), resilience is in one sense interested less in change or disruption than in what survives in the face of it. Explicitly or not, resilience strategists are committed to preserving the essence of something that is understood to have roots in the past and that continues to exist, perhaps precariously, in the present. In the case of both Toronto and Melbourne, at the core of what is at risk, what resilience strategies aim to preserve, is settler colonialism.

Together

The conservative function of resilience, implicitly tied to settler colonialism, informs the Toronto resilience strategy's interest not in decolonization (or even social transformation writ large) but in fostering "meaningful relationships," with, for example, "Indigenous leaders, Elders and Knowledge Keepers, and community members" that are "based on mutual respect and trust" (City of Toronto 2019, 138). The focus on building trust reflects a common emphasis in organizational resilience scholarship (Strycharczyk and Elvin 2014; Longstaff and Yang 2008). It also aligns with the neoliberal downloading of responsibility to individuals. Focusing on the presence or absence of trust shifts attention away from institutional problems such as inadequate social welfare programs, colonial dispossession, or racist policing to focus on personal relationships, the maintenance of which is understood to be the equal responsibility of everyone. In functionalist terms, trust operates in a similar way to "community" in resilience discourse, as a marker of organizational integrity that tends, as Debra Davidson has noted, to assume a harmonious convergence of community residents' interests and actions that are in reality "enormously diverse" (2013, 23).

Diversity is not inimical to resilience thinking; indeed, it is often cited as one of the hallmarks of a resilient community. In Canada, diversity is part of the Liberal Party brand, frequently touted by Prime Minister Justin Trudeau as key to the nation's economic flourishing. At a 2019 tech conference, for example, he pointed to Canada's nominally open immigration policies, arguing, "It's not just a moral, right thing to do; it's the smart thing to do. Diversity and resilience go together" (Lindzon 2019).[25] In the Toronto strategy, the word "diversity" appears in relation to civic engagement (City of Toronto 2019, 19, 128, 129), multiculturalism (3, 8), wetlands (95), and parkettes (105). Making the case for a link between cultural diversity and community resilience in the Australia context, Michelle Grossman draws on the work of environmental geographer Neil Adger to argue that diverse communities enhance social memory, produced through "the diversity of individuals and institutions that draw on reservoirs of practices, knowledge, values, and world views crucial for preparing [a] system for change, building resilience, and for coping with surprise" (Grossman 2013, 4). The presumed moral and practical virtue of diversity in late liberalism gains scientific credibility through ecological resilience thinking. Carl Folke, Johan Coldings, and Fikret Berkes argue that diversity ensures a rich repertoire of ways of dealing with change, both in terms of accumulated experience, or what they call memory, and adaptability to change: "Diversity of memories provides the potential for alternative ways to maintain functioning when faced with change" (2003, 376). This functionalist rationale, rather than a concern for democratic representation, arguably informs the emphasis in both Toronto and Melbourne resilience strategies on "empower[ing] a broad range of stakeholders" (City of Melbourne 2016, 43) and implementing plans through "multi-stakeholder working groups" (City of Toronto 2018, 144).[26]

Ethnic and cultural diversity are a central feature in the cities selected for inclusion in 100RC. The Melbourne resilience strategy describes the city as "proudly multicultural and diverse" – evidence for which can be seen, it is suggested, in the fact that "the surname Nguyen is our second most common surname, after Smith" (City of Melbourne 2016, 24; it is clear that "Smith" is the presumed norm against which diversity, metonymically represented by "Nguyen," is measured). The celebration of diversity is qualified by an uncomfortable fact: "Unfortunately," the city's most multicultural municipalities of Greater Dandenong and Brimbank "also rank first and third in Victoria on the Socio-Economic Indexes for Areas measure of disadvantage, indicating that establishing a prosperous life in Melbourne can be difficult for many people arriving from overseas" (25). Similarly, in Toronto, "segregation ... by race and income has worsened, even as diversity has increased" (City of Toronto 2019, 52). As noted above, Toronto's nonwhite residents are disproportionately concentrated in low-income neighbourhoods. In the Melbourne strategy, the word "unfortunately" signals a regrettable and inexplicable deviation from an otherwise positive set of circumstances. While the strategy gestures to "problems, including racial intolerance," there immediately follows the assurance that such problems are "at comparatively low levels compared to some parts of the world" (City of Melbourne 2016, 25).

The failure of diversity to correlate with or translate into equality is not surprising given the institutional history of the concept as a tool for managing difference. Numerous critics have interrogated the progressive claims of institutional diversity policies (Ahmed 2012; Walcott 2019; Bannerji 2000; Diaz et al. 2019), which normalize whiteness as the centre of a constellation of others to whom it offers token recognition for the price of conformity. "Diversity," as Ahmed notes, works as a "containment strategy" (2012, 53). So it goes in resilience rhetoric in which, celebrations of diversity notwithstanding, survival is understood to rest ultimately on strategies that prioritize the "integration" (City of Melbourne 2016, 25, 98; City of Toronto 2019, 106) of those populations euphemistically labelled "diverse" into a unified (and trusting) community. The Melbourne strategy cautions that "to be truly resilient, our city must also be cohesive, to avoid the stresses caused by disunity, and to be able to act as one when shocks do strike" (24). The Melbourne document makes explicit what other champions of resilience assume: the value of diversity is subject to an overarching principle of unity: it is essential that the resilient city, country, system, or organization must "be able to act as one" (24). "Community inclusion" (111), "community connectedness" (118) and "community identity" (117) are stressed throughout the Melbourne strategy as critical to resilience. A pillar of both resilience strategies (it appears in the Melbourne strategy 161 times and in the Toronto strategy 137), the word "community" proves hard to define. Toronto's resilience strategy, for example, refers to community in both a descriptive way, "Indigenous community" (54), "low-income community" (27), and a normative way, as in "people's commitment to community" (56) and "shared community vision" (64). Like trust, the idea of community in its normative aspect expresses the conjunction of ecological and ethical models of relationality; it does not sit comfortably with the dynamic of political struggle.

The kind of social order resilience thinking imagines, which is simultaneously progressive and conservative, holistic and hierarchical, also emerges in the way the cities' resilience strategies prioritize leadership. When residents were consulted about their vision of a resilient Toronto, they talked about a city that is "led by brave and caring leaders who reflect the communities they serve" (City of Toronto 2019, 7). The words "leader(s)" and "leadership" appear sixty-four times in the strategy, referring to individuals, organizations, and sometimes the city itself (as in "Toronto is a global leader"). Though it is suggested that leadership should be transparent (56) and represent the diversity of the community (65), there is no discussion of how leaders emerge. The words "democratic" and "democracy" do not appear in the strategy. While the concept of resilience that informs 100RC proceeds from the premise that cities are social-ecological systems, the emphasis on leadership reflects a broader preoccupation, in resilience thinking as well as late liberalism more generally, on exemplary individuals (an emphasis that is discussed in detail in the introduction). Suggesting that any of us can display the "bravery" that characterizes our best leaders by navigating our circumstances competently and confidently, the Toronto resilience strategy celebrates "inspirational and profound" stories of resilient individuals (City of Toronto 2018) in the form of stories submitted by residents via videos and on postcards using the hashtag #MyResilientStory.

One video linked in the strategy, *Resilient People: Joe, Husam and Keosh* (Regis 2019), features three such stories, focusing on individuals whose first-person accounts offer quintessential resilience stories: they all navigate landscapes strewn with challenges (alcoholism, lack of employment opportunity, unaffordable housing, racism) and find their way, fortified by a combination of personal grit, entrepreneurial energy, and community resources, to a liveable life. Not coincidentally, the three all come from racialized communities: a middle-aged Indigenous man, a young Muslim man, and a Black woman. The stories all describe linear, upward trajectories from struggle to resilience, if not triumph. Framed as a set, Joe's, Husam's, and Keosha's stories appear to confirm the principle of strength in diversity, their efforts simultaneously consolidating and transforming the resilient city. The stories are framed by a voiceover, accompanied by a swelling orchestral score, that begins by describing Toronto as "the city of growth and opportunities that are here for the taking. The city of diversity, with talent that has greatness in the making. The city that is fierce and persistent. But most important, the city that is resilient" (Regis 2019). The inclusion of Joe's, Husam's, and Keosha's narratives in the Toronto resilience strategy represents the integration of psychosocial and social-ecological models of resilience. Their stories work – at least superficially – to harness the genre of personal biography to serve the design of the strategic plan. They all evoke the past as something to be overcome on the way to a successful present and promising future. Their scalar focus moves between the individual and the city (signified, in between close-ups of the three subjects, by shots of Lake Ontario, a high-rise apartment building, the downtown skyline dominated by the CN tower, a playground, a library, the subway, an Indigenous health centre). In this exemplary model of resilience policy, stories of individual struggle and triumph work to complement the systems thinking that informs the vision of the city, articulating a dynamic of unity-through-difference and preservation-through-change, in aid of a blueprint for settler futurity. However, closer attention to Joe's, Husam's, and Keosha's stories reveals some cracks in the resilient people/resilient city picture. These arise partly from distinctions between psychosocial and social-ecological models of resilience and between the (related) genres of recovery narrative and strategic plan.

The video begins with Joe, a grey-haired, soft-spoken Anishinaabe man, who tells a story of struggle with addiction. He cites alcoholism as the reason for his expulsion from school at age sixteen – "Just wasn't there, I never showed up" (Regis 2019), and subsequent homelessness: "Couldn't find a place because of my drinking, because of my addiction ... Because of my alcoholism, I couldn't hang onto a job, couldn't hang onto finances, couldn't hang on to relationships." Without lingering over the details of his recovery, he notes the date of his final drink, in October 1990. The story swerves briefly to describe the death of his brother – "a direct result of alcoholism" – before returning to Joe's upward trajectory: "Been through my struggle. Now I am in university," a transition illustrated by a shot of an application form for a scholarship for Indigenous students. He admits to not knowing where the degree will lead but affirms, "I just want to be able to help my own people, my own Anishinaabe people." He concludes by reflecting, "We are a resilient type, as myself we have been resilient people, resiliency through residential schools, 60s scoop and we are resilient and I am a resilient person because I came from my alcoholism into my sobriety, into my recovery and today I am celebrating 28 years of sobriety, is a lot for me, a person who couldn't stay sober, not even for a minute." Joe's story doesn't supply any details about the process and mechanism of his movement from addiction to sobriety: we can infer that it came about through strength of will that is either an example of ancestral resilience, "we are a resilient type," or an exception to it (his brother didn't make it).

What is left implicit in Joe's story is foregrounded in Husam's account, which begins with his growing up "isolated in marginalized communities" (Regis 2019), then describes his struggle with unemployment, depression, and suicidal ideation before announcing a turn: "To get a grip on my life I knew something had to be changed. I knew I had to move forward." Husam moves to Toronto, which doesn't solve his problems immediately but marks a turning point on the road to employment and wellness. Keosha similarly describes growing up in a "marginalized neighbourhood" and experiencing the intersecting oppressions of racism and sexism, whose effects she also saw on the women around her, including her mother and her siblings. "I knew I wanted to do something that changed this narrative of what Black women are like," she explains, "but as well as change the narrative of what all women are like." In self-help narratives, insight leads to action; accordingly, she goes on to say: "I founded a community organization called Our Women's Voices ... a platform for women to share their experiences, their stories and their art in order to empower other women around the world."[27] Keosha perhaps offers the best embodiment of the message that the "Resilient People" video is trying to convey, which is to say that it not only offers a story of resilience, but it advances the concept of storytelling *as* resilience, serving at once as instrument and proof.

While the stories of Joe, Husam, and Keosha work on one level to support the resilient Toronto strategy, attending to their formal construction reveals an underlying dissonance. The social-ecological model of urban resilience strategies understands the city as a site of "interwoven processes" and "heightened complexity, harbouring diverse social and ecological realities and imaginative potential" (Beilin and Wilkinson 2015). Both Melbourne and Toronto strategies lean into the concepts of complexity and connectedness. "All *Resilient Melbourne* objectives are interdependent," the Melbourne strategy announces (City of Melbourne 2016, 39), recognizing that "issues are complex, difficult to understand and interconnected" (151). Systems thinking informs the strategies as a whole, as well as their engagement with particular areas of concern. A "systems approach" is required, for example, to understand the "complex web of interactions and networks" of food in Toronto (City of Toronto 2019, 106), whose resilience strategy also stresses a need for "collaborative, cross-division dialogue ... to identify interdependencies" when it comes to flood mitigation (99). With the aim of "seeing the bigger picture" (City of Toronto 2019, 107), Toronto and Melbourne strategies both demand what the Melbourne strategy identifies as "an interdisciplinary focus ... breaking out of narrower, more traditional structures such as 'society, economy and environment'" (City of Melbourne 2016, 55).[28]

Individual resilience stories are an awkward fit with this "big picture" focus. Unlike the systems within which their lives are presumably enmeshed – systems made up of governance structures and policies, physical infrastructure, nongovernmental agencies and institutions, all experiencing while also influencing the effects of a changing climate, Joe, Husam, and Keosha are represented as autonomous agents, the primary if not the sole authors of their own successes.[29] There is no interdisciplinary lens here – no expert lens at all, to identify "interdependencies," "interactions," or "networks"; the meaning of the stories of "resilient people" are presumed to be self-evident, containing lessons for all of us. The awkward fit between the "Resilient People" video and the Toronto resilience strategy that frames it reflects a tension between different models of resilience. It is also a generic tension. The stories featured in the video conform in many ways to the genre of the classic recovery narrative, whose principal ingredient is its framing of "the individual as the agent of her own story" (Woods, Hart, and Spandler 2019, 13). A hallmark of this approach is its propensity for "disregarding the social relations in which we are embedded, and deflecting attention from systemic inequalities and social injustice, such as racial and socio-economic discrimination" (7).[30]

Joe's story painfully embodies this individualist focus. Except for the historical reference to residential schools and the 60s scoop, which testify to the resilience of his people, Joe's story contains no social context to complicate its focus on him as the sole owner of agency and responsibility: he had a problem and overcame it. His story also has "an obvious beginning, middle and end," criteria emphasized, along with qualities such as "accessibility," in "Sharing your Story" guides produced by mental health charities in the UK, US, and Canada as key to the success of a recovery narrative (Woods, Hart, and Spandler 2019, 8).[31] Its tenor is also clearly inspirational, meant to encourage others along the same journey. Husam's and Keosha's stories aren't recovery narratives per se, though grappling with mental illness is part of Husam's narrative; however, they do offer analogous stories of persevering through difficulty, with success represented not through abstention or cure but through their arrival as successful entrepreneurs. The conclusion of Husam's story is emblematic: "Now, although I'm a little bit struggling still, I am truly humbled and blessed that I am living in City of Toronto, doing the things that matter to me" (Regis 2019). The visual conclusion of the video, in which shots of the speakers are replaced with more scenes of streets and subway tunnels, is at odds with the voiceover, which sticks with the personal: "You've seen their stories, you've seen how they've thrived on the road to glory. They've survived challenges, adapted to unpredictable situations, overcame personal complications, most importantly, remained persistent. That's how we'll all stay resilient." Joe's, Husam's, and Keosha's resilience stories play an important role in the Toronto resilience strategy, lending support to the idea that, to be both credible and useful, "Toronto's strategy needs to be informed by lived experience and integrate the voices and perspectives of diverse stakeholders" (City of Toronto 2018, 32). However, the voices and perspectives represented in the video, which centre the values of autonomy and individual agency, do not neatly align with the message of the strategy, which, while equally oriented to the future, emphasizes interdependence and complexity. With its focus on systems and infrastructure, the strategy is arguably indifferent to their testimonies even as it relies on them as resources – just as the city relies on human capital for its resilience.

Joe's, Husam's, and Keosha's are not the only testimonies included in the Toronto resilience strategy. Along with videos, the framers of the strategy invited residents to submit their stories via postcards, using the hashtag #MyResilientStory (City of Toronto 2018, 26). While all the videos are available on the website, only two of the two hundred plus submitted postcards are featured in the strategy, with a few others decorating the cover page. Because they are arranged collage-style, the postcards are not easily legible; however, on reading them we can perhaps understand why more of them are not included more prominently. Many of the recipients heeded the instructions to document challenges while ignoring the question about "resources, assets or networks ... you draw on to help you cope with the challenges." Taken together, the postcards speak not as much to resilience, except indirectly, as to coping and to struggle: "Housing wait time is too long. I have been waiting for too long and til now I haven't heard [obscured]"; "I recently started working and I fear it will be hard to balance my school grades along with my work"; "I am facing about immigration problems [*sic*]. I am trying to bring my parents to Canada. I had many refusal because I have big family [*sic*]. not enough income" (City of Toronto 2018, 1). The postcards are nicely integrated into the design of the strategy; presenting them on the front page supports the principle of consultation, the idea that the resilience strategy is something created "together," as the Melbourne strategy puts it, with all the residents of the city. Their content tells another story, though, one that doesn't sit well with the vision of Toronto as "the city of growth and opportunities that are here for the taking," whose residents have "thrived on the road to glory" (Regis 2019).[32]

"Public Parks Are Not Places People Can Legally, Safely or in a Healthy Way Live"

When the 100 Resilient Cities program was terminated in April 2019, it caught many people by surprise, including program staff, who had expected the program to continue "in perpetuity" (Anzilotti 2019, 3), and city officials, who had come to depend on its funding: "Against climate change's hydra-headed environmental and social catastrophes ... local governments on six continents had come to rely on the resources and pull of 100RC to steady themselves" (Bliss 2019). By way of explanation, the Rockefeller Foundation noted that it was in keeping with the institution's history to serve as an incubator for projects that would then become self-sustaining – with the implication that the 100RC would follow this route (Anzilotti 2019). Foundation leaders later explained to staff that "as it existed, 100RC had grown too costly, and its model no longer aligned with Rockefeller's goals" (Bliss 2019).[33] Internal emails showed that 100RC faced pressure from the Rockefeller Foundation "to identify 'marketable evidence' of their impact" (Bliss 2019). Some observers suggested that the termination of 100RC highlighted the risks of privatizing the urgent work of disaster planning: "The public should not allow itself to be fooled by philanthropic promises," noted Lucy Bernholz, a senior research scholar at Stanford's Center on Philanthropy and Civil Society: "foundation dollars will always move on" (Bliss 2019, 100). The general tenor of responses to the termination of 100RC reflected agreement that 100 RC was "not a failure" (Cappell 2019); it had a positive impact both at the level of individual urban initiatives and the development of global networks. Its demise was widely seen as a surprise, a regrettable outcome to many, but to others an inevitable part of a funding cycle: cities would need (ironically) to be resilient against the loss of their resilience funding.

Looked at another way, based on two limited case studies, 100RC was a failure from its inception, rooted in the fundamental incoherencies of the concept of resilience on which it was based – one which sought to preserve the structures of racial capitalism and settler colonialism while managing the crises they engendered, including the "stresses" of racial inequity and the "shocks" of climate change. To better understand that failure, we can look at two moments in the aftermath of the publication of Melbourne's and Toronto's resilience strategies in which the cities' respective responses to crises illuminated their investment in the continued disenfranchisement of poor and racialized residents.

In Melbourne, on 4 July 2020, in response to a rise in COVID-19 infections in the city, police advanced on nine public housing towers without warning, surrounding them and detaining their more than three thousand residents for five days. The low-income, mostly immigrant residents of the towers described the experience of police swarming the buildings as traumatic, particularly for those who had fled countries where human rights were routinely abused (Boseley 2020, 4). In her report commissioned after the lockdown, Victorian ombudsman Deborah Glass described a scene of chaos in its early days: "People found themselves without food, medication and other essential supports. Information was confused, incomprehensible or simply lacking ... No access to fresh air and outdoor exercise was provided for over a week. In a particularly unfortunate act, temporary fencing for an exercise area was erected one night, surrounded by police, and, although quickly taken down, reinforced the residents' sense of being imprisoned" (2020, 4).

Glass determined that, while a lockdown may have been warranted to prevent the spread of the virus, its preemptory imposition had not been based on medical advice and had breached residents' human rights

(2020, 4). In response to the report's recommendation that the Victorian government issue an apology to residents, the government argued that their actions were justified in the name of "prioritis[ing] the protection of human life" (Boseley 2020, 3). Housing Minister Richard Wynne argued that the government "had to act and act immediately because of the viciousness of the virus" (BBC 2020) and asserted, "We make no apology for saving human lives ... The primary objective of government is to protect the community'" (Boseley 2020, 3). Commenting on government documents related to the lockdown that described the towers as "a hotbed of criminality and non-compliance,"[34] Glass noted, "It is unimaginable that such stereotypical assumptions, leading to the 'theatre of policing' that followed, would have accompanied the response to an outbreak of COVID-19 in a luxury apartment block" (2020, 5). The treatment of the rise in COVID infections as a security rather than a health emergency, citing fears of "criminality," raises questions about who is seen to merit protection from whom/what.

A year later, a similar scene unfolded in Toronto in response to a different crisis. On 21 July 2021, Toronto police and security officers violently broke up an encampment of unhoused people and their supporters at Lamport Stadium. The camp was one of many that had been set up around the city as the overlapping emergencies of homelessness and COVID-19 stretched the capacity and safety of the city's inadequate shelter system to a breaking point. It was the third such violent police action in less than a month. When pressed on the heavy-handed tactics of the police, which included tearing down tents and throwing out the belongings of encampment residents and beating, pepper spraying, and kettling protesters, then mayor John Tory defended their actions, describing police as "compassionate [and] professional" and arguing that the city is trying to assert the principle "that public parks are not places people can legally, safely or in a healthy way live and that everybody is entitled to the use of those parks" (Tory 2021). That the substance of Tory's comment is difficult to parse through his tortured syntax is perhaps not incidental but indicative of the contradictions of an urban policy whose vision of collective well-being is framed by the principles of colonial capitalism.[35]

Toronto's resilience strategy, which was crafted during Tory's tenure as mayor, aims to manage the crises of poverty, inequity, homelessness, decaying infrastructure, and climate change within the framework of the city as a place of opportunities "there for the taking" (Tory 2021). Tory's take on encampment residents is shorthand for the incoherency of that vision. The distinction between legitimate and illegitimate uses of parks appears to hinge on the difference between *living* ("public parks are not places people can legally, safely or in a healthy way live") and *use* ("everybody is entitled to the use of those parks" [Tory 2021]). The relatively straightforward syntax of the second part of Tory's statement reflects its status as settler-colonial common sense; proper "use" of land is a cornerstone of settler colonialism, a rationale for taking land from Indigenous peoples, whose deep relations of belonging to place was illegible to European concepts of property. The concept of use continues to inform the Toronto resilience strategy, which understands parks as resources, in the service of either recreation (City of Melbourne 2016, 50) or "blue green infrastructure" (City of Toronto 2019, 105), and residents as rational users of those resources. The mangled syntax in the first part of Tory's statement, which inserts a bunch of bureaucratic qualifiers between "public parks" and "live," might reflect some unease about the too-obvious biopolitics that inspires the cruelty of the police action. As Azeezah Kanji and A.J. Withers note in an article that reads the park clearances as instances of colonial violence,[36] "Perversely, judges have rationalised encampment evictions in the name of preserving 'parks [as] public resources, intended to be available and used by everyone.' Encampment residents are expelled not only from parks, but from the human 'everyone' entitled to make use of them to fulfil their needs" (2021).

The Melbourne detention and the Toronto eviction might on the surface seem incompatible with or irrelevant to the two cities' resilience strategies. Instead, I would argue that they illustrate clearly what is implicit in the strategies, which is that liveability for "everybody" is predicated on the disposability of certain lives. COVID-19 is a clear example of the kind of threat that resilience strategies are designed to address – a threat that is disproportionately borne by the poor, the unhoused, racialized immigrants, and Indigenous peoples. Police actions in which those populations are targeted not for care but for violent containment strip the veneer off the resilient city as an inclusive and equitable place for all its residents.[37] Today, tomorrow, together, Toronto and Melbourne demonstrate the resilience of settler colonialism and racial capitalism.

3

Antiresilience, or Learning to Die

CHAPTERS 1 AND 2 detailed the resonances of resilience thinking with settler colonialism. This chapter swerves from that argument to work through an important qualification: just because the idea of resilience has been enlisted in support of settler-colonial capitalism, it does not follow that critiques of resilience have an anticolonial thrust. I focus here on a particular strain of critique that goes beyond the excavation of resilience landscapes to the repudiation of resilience in favour of a cluster of values that we might provisionally call "antiresilience." Like resilience talk, antiresilience talk has come to assume a definitive narrative form with an identifiable protagonist. While dominant models of resilience find expression in the story of the plucky adventurer (recall the whitewater kayaker from the introduction, Mark Watney on Mars from chapter 1) who embodies the spirit of optimistic resourcefulness, antiresilience is a darker, brooding figure, more critical and cerebral than pragmatic. This figure might be who Rebecca Solnit had in mind, when, in 2012, she addressed a blog piece to her "dismal allies" on the left who are preoccupied by the failure of Democratic political leaders – particularly President Barack Obama – to live up to their stated ideals.

Solnit criticizes her dismal allies' emphasis on the crimes of the powerful instead of the struggles of ordinary people and speaks to the need for hope as well as creative thinking. She concludes by arguing that "to be hopeful means to be uncertain about the future, to be tender towards possibilities, to be dedicated to change all the way down to the bottom of your heart (2012, 5). The letter reflects the thesis of her 2009 book, *Paradise Built in Hell*, which takes issue with both prevailing images of victimage and with the right's emblematic image of looting following disasters, arguing that "the prevalent human nature in disaster is resilient, resourceful, generous, empathic and brave" (8). In championing the resilience of ordinary people to cope with devastating change, Solnit highlights a capacity for joy that she does not see in the traditional left: "The old figureheads … [whose] grumpiness is often the grumpiness of perfectionists who hold that anything less than total victory is failure, a premise that makes it easy to give up at the start, or to disparage the victories that are possible" (2016).

The university has its own version of that community, academic counterparts of those figureheads, whom we might call the "dismal scholarly left." In the introduction, I suggested that the idea of resilience finds an increasingly comfortable home in the interdisciplinary sciences, where its conceptual frameworks are applied to complex, "wicked" problems like those related to climate change. Antiresilience, by contrast, takes up residence in certain areas of the social sciences and the humanities, where it comes to stand in for the spirit of criticism, embodied in the figure of the lonely humanist who might be described (or might describe themselves) as speaking truth to power but who could equally be characterized as indulging in what Alexis Shotwell calls a "purity politics of despair" (2016, 195). The imaginary site of this politics, as Shotwell describes it, is "the catastrophic, crisis-laden sublime – that which signals a before and an after harm, and longs for a return to the state before" (195). The antiresilience stance that I'm describing converts that longing into a nihilistic embrace of the end of things.

In so characterizing – caricaturing, even – the attitude of a particular strand of critical theoretical opposition to resilience, I don't wish to dismiss entirely the intellectual foundations of arguments that I frequently draw on in my own efforts to get a handle on the meaning of resilience. However, I'm wary of the allure of a way of thinking that manages, by virtue of its armature of critical tools, to be exceptionally successful at concealing its own enabling conditions, interests, and histories. So, in this chapter, I want to tease out the foundations of a perspective that calls out resilience thinking for its positivism, its occlusion of the political, and its take on the world, which is simultaneously too local and too global. I want to focus on what is less explicit in this perspective: its infusion with the affective politics of left melancholy, which assumes a particular form in settler colonialism.

Left melancholy is a familiar affliction in the late twentieth and early twenty-first century humanities. Drawing on Stuart Hall's analysis of the late twentieth-century crisis of the left, Wendy Brown borrows the term "left melancholy" from Walter Benjamin, who used it to describe a condition of mournful attachment to a lost ideal of socialism as opposed to an engagement with contemporary conditions. Left melancholy, in Benjamin's and Brown's accounts "[represents] not only a refusal to come to terms with the particular character of the present, that is, a failure to understand history in terms other than 'empty time' or 'progress.' It signifies, as well, a certain narcissism with regard to one's past political attachments and identity that exceeds any contemporary investment in political mobilization, alliance, or transformation" (Brown 1999, 20).

While acknowledging that the political left has many concrete losses to mourn, including the disintegration of a coherent movement, the diminished currency of labour and class as terms of analysis, and the waning of actual and imagined alternatives to capitalism, Brown highlights Freud's theorization of melancholia as more complex than mourning in its partly unconscious character. In Freud's analysis, "the melancholic subject will often not know precisely what about the object has been loved and lost ... The loss precipitating melancholia is more often than not unavowed and unavowable" (Brown 1999, 20). Left melancholia therefore has another interesting – and paradoxical – quality: for all its putative weddedness to materialism, its melancholic attachments are to thoughts and feelings, which become reified as goods. The left melancholic, in Benjamin's formulation: "takes as much pride in the traces of former spiritual goods as the bourgeois do in their material goods" (Brown 1999, 21). Brown elaborates, "We come to love our left passions and reasons, our left analyses and convictions, more than we love the existing world that we presumably seek to alter with these terms or the future that would be aligned with them" (21). In setting out the terms of left melancholia, I do not mean to suggest – as Brown does not suggest – that these passions, analyses, and convictions are without worth; rather, that their disavowed form, *as* passion, *as* a particular kind of intellectual exercise, invites critical scrutiny.

Twenty years after the publication of Brown's article, left melancholy persists, with slight mutations in expression. In Freud's formulation, in dealing with the loss of the unrecoverable (unidentifiable) love object, the melancholic imagination takes a self-destructive turn, which it projects on substitutive objects. For the melancholy leftist, Brown suggests, hate is directed in two places: first, towards cultural/identity politics, which is seen as driving a wedge into the solidarity of leftist resistance, and second, towards poststructuralism, whose theoretical manoeuvres derail and deny the materiality of history (to this we might add postmodernism, of which I say more below) (23). Supplementing and even supplanting this list today is the idea of resilience, whose focus on adaptation blunts the force of resistance and mitigates against utopian (or dystopian) imagination. A related problem, aesthetic as much as political, is the resolute cheeriness of resilience thinking, along with its favouring of pragmatism over principle, which is connected to its high tolerance for mess. Cecilia Åsberg links resilience to the conceptual and corporeal "trouble" favoured by Donna Haraway, suggesting that resilience can most productively be understood "as trouble, as cyborg, as monster" (Åsberg 2013, 2), "moving away from Universal Man as the pinnacle of world order and civilization" (3).

I have linked left melancholy with settler colonialism. To explain this, it is useful to employ the framework of "settler sense" described by Mark Rifkin as "the ways the legal and political structures that enable non-Native access to Indigenous territories come to be lived as given, as simply the unmarked, generic conditions of possibility for occupancy, association, history, and personhood" (2013, 322–3). Leftist politics that cite "capitalism" and "neoliberalism" as default explanations for inequity and exploitation without acknowledging colonialism is one iteration of settler sense. In the Canadian context, settler mourning for the lost welfare state is in direct contradiction with the qualified hope of Indigenous resurgence. Similar to the elision of slavery and white supremacy that critical race theorists point to in class-based analyses of power (Robinson 1983; Harris 1993), what gets left out of the narrative of the neoliberal unravelling of political collectivity is that that collectivity was built on the displacement, attempted elimination, and selective incorporation of Indigenous people. I have suggested in earlier chapters that the idea of resilience has worked in service of that project. More specifically, I've argued that resilience thinking assuages anxieties about the waning power of the West in the context of globalization, which, along with decolonial and antiracist movements, has led to a loss of confidence in the capacity of white, Euro-American subjects to navigate an increasingly unruly world/planet. But the rejection of resilience in favour of a Marxian model of revolution may express an equally defensive reaction.

How is it that both resilience and antiresilience can work in the service of the same Western fantasy/nostalgia? Mark Rifkin has shown that settler sense, as a dominant iteration of that fantasy comprising "a shifting assemblage of ordinary actions, occupancies, ethics, aspirations, dispositions, and sensations" (2013, 327), is an extremely capacious vehicle, encompassing diverse and even contradictory affective strands. Settler sense need not – in fact, in its everyday ideological form, generally does not – consciously refer to settler-Indigenous relations, state practices, or land rights. Instead, it operates to confirm "the unreflexive, generic, given conditions of personhood, occupancy, and belonging," claims that "may not be identical or congruent with each other, inasmuch as multiple histories of state action that inhabit, orient, and stimulate the present 'impress' in ways that might produce different (even incommensurate) forms of engagement" (331).

Rifkin illustrates the diffuse operation of settler sense through the example of *Walden*, a text in which Thoreau derives from Nature "a sense of his own autonomous embodiment and a related set of ethical resources that enable him to reject the demands of contemporary political economy" (2013, 322). Of course, that sense of possibility is enabled precisely by the policies, interests, and imperatives of the burgeoning state, or, as Rifkin puts it more precisely, "The particular kinds of inhabitance made possible through Indian policy and the Indian wars" (334). The ability not to think about conditions of inhabitance is what characterizes settler sense. In this way, even though Thoreau's experiment at Walden Pond constituted a rejection of capitalist practices and values, its assertion of freedom and the possibility of an unmediated immersion in nature expressed the unarticulated logic of settler colonialism. As Rifkin puts it: "Thoreauvian inclination toward 'nature' as a space of escape from the extant regime of property ownership, comfort in the (Lockean) privatized autonomy of one's home(stead), and immersion in the obscure anonymities of urban dwelling do not resemble each other and arise out of disparate affective

– and perhaps ethical – commitments, but all iterate, to varied effects, the geopolitical self-evidence and security of the state whose unquestioned endurance anchors and animates them" (331). There is a sense in which, in seeking to escape the more obvious, middle-class forms of security and entitlement, Thoreau simply attains a purer version of them. His experiment at Walden Pond expresses a confident sense of his right of occupation, understood as a relation of "immersion in the wilderness rather than extraction from it" (335).

The attachment to the woods as a "natural" site for old-fashioned fun that is the focus of chapter 1 is one modern iteration of this settler sense. A darker mode of thought that is equally expressive of twenty-first-century attachments to a settler-colonial conception of the world replaces the fantasy of an unmediated connection with nature with resignation to its – and our – total destruction. In this vision, human activity has exhausted the plenitude of nature, confronting us with the spectre of our own imminent extinction. This perspective conditions *anti*resilience thinking, a bleak neo-Thoreauvian refusal to submit to the "quiet desperation" (Rifkin 2013) that lurks beneath the façade of cheerful adaptation to a life of constant adversity.

In the introduction, I suggested that the kayaker in the rapids serves as one exemplary figure for representing the idea of resilience as it is invoked in relation to the individual; Matt Damon scooting across Mars in a jury-rigged rover in *The Martian*, discussed in chapter 1, is another. These images – both redolent of colonial adventurism – work through the concealment of the supporting frameworks, material and ideological, that enable their production. But they don't work entirely; that is to say, they perhaps work *too well*, to the point of conforming perfectly to the demands of the present. Each presents a model of individual striving that is focused not on transcending or changing his circumstances but, rather, on adapting to their extremity: white water figures in resilience morality tales for the turbulent circumstances that define everyday life, while Mars operates literally and symbolically as a site on which we can continue to exercise our capacity to adapt and grow after the resources of earth have been exhausted. Mark Watney and the kayaker both model the capacity to survive amidst conditions of constant danger. Neither, though, is able to escape those conditions, to imagine a different world to that of the swollen rapids or inhospitable Martian climate.

The Martian is a clear example both of how contemporary resilience thinking works and of what antiresilience critics hate about it, even if *The Martian* isn't on their radar as a piece of resilience propaganda. In addition to foregrounding the bravery and humour of the resilient individual, the film that's billed as "a love letter to science" celebrates the enlistment of tools of measurement and forecast to the aims of a biopolitical regime that has been extended to the biosphere. *The Martian* encapsulates an idealized image of how knowledge is produced in the interests of world management and expansion, if not world-making. Watney's survival depends on an interdisciplinary array of calculations, encompassing math, botany, and astrophysics, and a sophisticated digital communications network; all of these tools work to optimize the chances of Watney's survival in the short term and, in the long term, to enable the continuation of the space program. The movie is a celebration of a way of thinking focused on understanding how things are, and how they might continue to be, based on mathematically derived predictive models. Its imagination is focused on figuring out modes of action within predetermined limits – not questioning and moving beyond them. These become the self-appointed tasks of antiresilience, which does not reject the model of the solitary hero but takes it farther, beyond the limits defined by the scientific imagination and the entertainment industry, into the realm of pure critique.

The mission is a metaphysical one, for which the philosopher is uniquely equipped by a discipline that is focused on the task of learning how to die. In the remainder of this chapter, I draw on Roy Scranton's *Learning to Die in the Anthropocene* (2015a) and Brad Evans and Julian Reid's *Resilient Life: The Art of Living Dangerously* (2014) to sketch out a vision of antiresilience. Both texts condemn the oppressive futility of an ethic of adaptation to intolerable circumstances and call instead for a mode of negation or rejection that involves a mode, material or symbolic, of death. While Evans and Reid use critical theory and Scranton takes a more traditional humanist approach, both texts indict a culture whose promotion of a certain vision of the good life, they argue, only entrenches our domination. They suggest that the problem for us is not, as it was for the scholars of the Frankfurt School, that we are caught in the Enlightenment dream of progress and mastery of nature; rather, it is that as that dream – the dream of liberalism – plays itself out, it has morphed into a nightmare of imminent danger and chronic crisis in which our domination – of nature, and then, ultimately, by nature – is complete. Resilience thinking, in teaching us how to survive, if not enjoy, our subordination to planetary forces, represents a new form of governmentality that we must teach ourselves to reject. This rejection constitutes a practice or technology of the self, as Foucault might put it, that demands the renunciation of life as it is presented to us.

Each of these critiques incisively highlight some of the problems of resilience thinking, including its enlistment in the neoliberal project of demanding that we adapt to capitalism rather than challenge it. Each of them rejects the contemporary politics of resilience because of its foreclosure of the possibility of radical social transformation. But there is another aspect of resilience that leads these scholars to recoil against it, an aspect that is not incidental to its disciplinary alignment. In seeking to model social and ecological dynamics in all their complexity, resilience confounds a constellation of principles that animates traditional modes of humanities and social science scholarship: human exceptionalism, individual autonomy, and a hierarchical division between reason and corporeality. These principles have their own politics, which traditional humanists and social scientists have been less willing to subject to scrutiny. At the very least, they embody a conservatism that belies their claims to take us beyond conventional ways of thinking. I'd like to suggest, therefore, that there is a sense in which we might read the antiresilience program that purports to teach us how to die as a call to preserve the right to inhabit a space of autonomous reflection, a space that, for all its claims to newness and speculative inchoateness, is infused with a nostalgic conception of the University (Evans and Reid employ the capital "U") as a refuge for the solitary, not incidentally masculine, scholar engaged in radical thought.

In the face of this image, amidst ubiquitous narratives (from the right and the left) of decline, it is worth noting that the university has always played a crucial role in the power-knowledge nexus of social regulation, the exclusion of women and racialized minorities was not accidental but integral to its state-sanctioned role of nation-building,[1] and that the opportunities for inquiry and discovery that can be found within it have always been small and unevenly distributed. We need to keep this history in mind as we survey calls to fight resilience issued in the name of a mythologized radical scholar who, at best, is struggling to discover and articulate difficult truths and, at worst, is trying to fight off an imaginary team of climate scientists who are trying to take over his office.

What does antiresilience look like? It's important, first, to distinguish the spirit of rejection called for by settler scholars like Evans and Reid from Indigenous people's refusal of the demand that they adapt to the conditions of the settler settler-colonial state. Ana María Fraile-Marcos elaborates the difference in this way, "Refusal of victimhood and of the frameworks set up by settler states to manage Indigenous existence is ... an important aspect of radical resurgence and clearly differs from Evan's and Reid's use of the term. Whereas for them, the call for refusal entails the rejection of the naturalization of the neoliberal idea of resilience, the refusal envisioned as the foundation of Indigenous resurgence is deeply grounded in Indigenous thinking, geographies, and temporalities. Indigenous refusal is also rooted in anticolonial and decolonial struggles, which are firmly interconnected with the land and, therefore, attached to the specificity of place" (2019, 8). This mode of Indigenous refusal/resurgence is discussed in chapter 5. The mode of refusal under consideration here is predicated not on an attachment to the more-than-human world but on assertion of independence from it.

The first element of this brand of antiresilience, the one around which this chapter is loosely organized, is death, a refusal of the biopolitical life that it is the business of resilience to preserve. Evans and Reid and Scranton, in different ways, invoke death as an antidote to unbearable life, in support of the preservation of ideals of human exceptionalism, individual autonomy, and – here the spectre of Thoreau looms into view – the figure of the radical philosopher/poet. All these elements of not-resilience work, I suggest, to support a vision not of the future but of an embattled present seen through a lens whose critical acuity is blurred by nostalgia. The call for death, issued from deep in the centre of the Western academy, rings weirdly (badly) at a time when antiracist activists are demanding acknowledgment that Black Lives Matter and Indigenous people are rising up globally in movements of resurgence against past and continuing regimes of displacement and elimination. We will return to that later. For the moment, let's think about the story of antiresilience, a story of radical refusal in which the challenge of learning to live in the woods has morphed into the task of learning to die in the Anthropocene.

The Case for Death

"Individuals die, populations disappear, and species become extinct. That is one view of the world. But another view of the world concentrates not so much on presence or absence as upon the numbers of organisms and the degree of constancy of their numbers" (Holling 1973, 1). The first sentence of C.S. Holling's article "Resilience and Stability of Ecological Systems" (1973) – the article that resilience scholars often cite as an origin for resilience ecology – invites a shift in thinking away from absolute limits, that is, the distinction between life and death, towards modulation, shifting norms, and thresholds of potential or vulnerability.[2] Inaugurating an illuminating paradigm shift in forest biology for the study of populations within an ecosystem, this aspect of resilience thinking also resonates with Foucauldian models of biopolitical security that emerged in the mid-eighteenth century with the aim of regulating life within specific milieus (Foucault 2003). "While the preceding regime focused on preventing scarcity, from the middle of the eighteenth century, with the physiocrats as well as many other economists, there was the attempt to find a point of support in the processes of scarcity themselves, in the kind of quantitative fluctuation that sometimes produced abundance and sometimes scarcity: finding support in the reality of the phenomenon, and instead of trying to prevent it, making other elements of reality function in relation to it in such a way that the phenomenon is cancelled out, as it were" (Foucault 2009, 87). Foucault cites the example of smallpox variolation, "which did not try to prevent smallpox so much as to provoke it in inoculated individuals" (88), on the principle that embracing a small danger might forestall a larger one. Institutionalizing the practice of inoculation in modern medical practice is part of a larger shift away from thinking in terms of limits – sickness and health, danger and safety, life and death – towards tolerable thresholds. Instead of disciplinary distinctions between normal and abnormal, there is a move towards "establishing an interplay between ... different distributions of normality and [in] acting to bring the most unfavorable in line with the more favorable" (91). As an ecological theory that focuses on the capacity for systems to function with and through disruption, resilience resonates with this model of security – a model that has become more deeply entrenched as states struggle to deal with the effects of climate change (Cooper 2010).

Among the political implications of this social-ecological model are (1) an acceptance of danger not as an extrinsic threat against which we must be secured but an endemic condition of life; (2) a disavowal of death in favour of an emphasis – imaginary and technological – on managing life, which is always-already compromised by its implication in landscapes of risk; and (3) an orientation to the future framed by the sustainability, more or less, of current modes of life. Informed by the dynamic of adaptation by which systems persist, resilience thinking cannot envision an end to the current order of things. In sidelining death, it also forecloses the possibility of radical change. Scranton and Evans and Reid call on us to embrace that possibility, rejecting the demand, implicit in dominant modes of resilience thinking, that we attempt to ride out a life of perpetual crisis – what Eric Cazdyn evocatively calls "the dull soreness of a meantime with no end" (2012, 14).[3]

Resilience catches us up in the embrace of this "meantime" by promising, if not deliverance from danger, then careful management of it. This management extends, in contemporary regimes of global governance, from species to planetary life. The environment in this process becomes, as Evans and Reid put it, "properly bio-politicized and bio-capitalized as a moral source for human welfare and setting the conditions for emancipation" (2014, 35). In effect, we are increasingly subject to what they describe as "the ecologization of the political" (162) in which the desire and will to change withers in the face of the imperative to protect life. "Life," in this formulation, "is speciated according to the usefulness, irrelevance or threat it represents for the infrastructural and biospheric systems necessary for capitalism's widening cycles of reproduction, consumption and accumulation" (Duffield 2011, 14, quoted in Evans and Reid 2014, 20). An adjunct of the biopolitical imperative to "make live" (Foucault 2003, 241) is a regime of management focused on adaptation – biological, ecological, and social – to naturalized conditions of terminal turbulence.

Evans and Reid reject the terms of a regime of ecological/biological management that, in exchange for our submission to a condition of permanent danger, offers us just a bit more life: "The promise, at most, is that the human, understood in terms of its species existence, may go on living, a little longer, and that other species and living systems, including the biosphere itself, may also be granted more and longer life, all the while dying off" (2014, 15). While they accept that our circumstances are dire, Evans and Reid do not counsel adaptation or offer coping strategies; rather, they advise us to confront the darkness and embrace what comes next: "If it is an end, and if it is true that there is no turning back from this tipping point of extinction time," they ask, "why are we choosing to live out that end by adapting to the conditions of our own demise, rather than with experimenting with other ways of living less attached to preserving our life as such, and more attuned to the inevitability of death and extinction as realities that can contribute to the intensity of our experience of worldly living for the finite time that we are left with as a species already fated to extinction in the end? (154). Embracing death produces an "intensity" of experience that soars above "the dull soreness of a meantime with no end" (Cazdyn 2012, 14). Scranton shares this perspective, going beyond it to suggest that "our choice is a clear one. We can continue acting as if tomorrow will be just like yesterday ... [as we become] more and more desperately invested in a life we can't sustain. Or we can learn to see each day as the death of what came before, freeing ourselves to deal with whatever problems the present offers without attachment or fear. If we want to learn to live in the Anthropocene, we must first learn how to die" (2015a, 27).

This is the hallmark of antiresilience: it is not just a critique of biopolitical constructions of "life" but an attempt to get beyond them, to restore the possibility of transcendence through the cultivation of radical autonomy. If resilience thinking approaches the problem of how to live with others (human and nonhuman) in ecologically precarious times by discovering or imagining formulas that balance the imperatives of identity and change, antiresilience rejects the terms of the problem, shifting the terrain of the debate to a "higher" metaphysical level. In doing so, antiresilience declares its allegiance to a traditional conception of humanist scholarship defined by withdrawal from the world of abject things into a realm of pure possibility, a stance of rejection that is elevated by its metaphorical representation as a kind of death.

"We need," Evans and Reid argue, "to focus more clearly on the affirmative and poetic qualities of existence that are by their very nature 'irreducible to life'" (2014, 175). A key concern in their text is the reduction, in a culture that is preoccupied with problems of physical adaptation and sustainability, of the status of the human as a being uniquely endowed with the capacity for metaphysical thought. In the new ecological dispensation, they lament that we have lost a sense of "the human subject's lone capacity for reason, along with the ability to connect language with thought" (62). In short, "human life is no longer understood as distinct from any other life form. Neither can it think itself greater or lesser than the complex structuring of the universe most broadly conceived" (7). Evans and Reid do not dismiss the validity of biological or ecological understanding out of hand – an issue to which we will return – rather, their key objection is the extension of the purview of these disciplines to the human realm. Admitting that "a political scientist is not necessarily well positioned to question knowledge and laws deriving from the life sciences as they are applied to the study of the interface between biological species and the ecological systems with which they are said to co-evolve," they hasten to add, "What concerns us, however, is what happens when such frameworks are transferred to the human world of peoples" (62). The urgency of that concern emerges in the curiously redundant phrase "human world of peoples," which serves to reinforce the sanctity of its subject, drawing a double line around the realm that claims exemption from what are identified as otherwise (*possibly*) legitimate laws of biology and ecology. Human exceptionalism must not be surrendered.

Scranton concurs, noting in a 2015 *New York Times* opinion piece that extends his thesis on the need to learn how to die that "scientific materialism, taken to its extreme, threatens us with meaninglessness; if consciousness is reducible to the brain and our actions are determined not by will but by causes, then our values and beliefs are merely rationalizations for the things we were going to do anyway. Most people find this view of human life repugnant, if not incomprehensible" (2015b). For Scranton, however, the divide between the social and the biological – even the geological – is not exactly straightforward. Where Evans and Reid regard Anthropocene thinking warily,[4] Scranton adopts its temporal perspective, through which he relates the story of human "civilization" in the context of a larger narrative of planetary history. The ruling metaphor in this narrative is "energy: energy production and social energetics" (2015a, 56), which allows for the following formulation of human society: "Just as a beehive is structured around the production of honey, so are human societies structured around labor, horses, wheat, coal, and oil. How bodies harvest, produce, organize, and distribute energy determines how power flows, shaping the political arrangements of a given collective organism behind whatever ideologies the ruling classes may use to manufacture consent, obscure the mechanisms of control, or convince themselves of their infallible omniscience" (56). The energy metaphor is a provocative one, appearing to open the possibility of imagining ways of living, working, and communicating in a more-than-human world – a possibility that finds support in Scranton's evocative suggestion that "politics, whether for bees or for humans, is the energetic distribution of bodies in systems" (55–6). But then, a funny thing happens to the hive metaphor in the course of the book. While the passage just quoted uses the image of the hive to place humans within a broader evolutionary and ecological framework, later in the book the same metaphor symbolizes a form of dangerous collectivity from which we need urgently to detach ourselves: "The enemy isn't out there somewhere – the enemy is ourselves. Not as individuals but as a collective. A system. A hive" (84). In case the hazards of this way of life aren't clear, Scranton amps up the metaphor, asking, "How do we stop ourselves from fulfilling our fates as suicidally productive drones in a carbon-addicted hive, destroying ourselves in some kind of psychopathic colony collapse disorder?" (86). The logic of Scranton's argument rests on the contradictory invocation and rejection of nature. We are *of* nature insofar as ecology establishes a framework for thinking the human in species – that is, universal – terms. But we are also *above* nature, in that we are able, through philosophical reflection, to assert our autonomy, to resist subjection to our fearful and desiring animal instincts.

One of the ways Scranton sees these instincts activated, via the "hive mind," is through the circulation of "constant messages of apprehension and danger," which agitate the "deep lizard brain" (2015a, 78). In response to these messages, Scranton suggests, we try "to dampen the vibrations by searching out positive reinforcements … We buy something. We eat food. We pop a pill. We fuck … In either passing on the vibration or reacting against it, we let the fear short circuit our own autonomous desires, diverting our goals and loading ever more emotional static into our daily cognitive processing" (78–9). Salvation depends on extracting ourselves from the "emotional static" that leads us to the distracting and, it is implied, empty pleasures of eating and sex, which are represented as contrary to our "autonomous desires." The electricity metaphor that underwrites the representation of corporeal activity that is subject to "short circuit[ing]" and "static" appears to grant the materiality of human existence. However, this materiality ultimately gives way, in the final chapter, to the concept of "A New Enlightenment," in which humans' putatively unique capacity for "cognitive processing" – that is, reason – succeeds in banishing our animal selves.

As an alternative to the bad habits of biological life, Scranton calls for the "daily cultivation of detachment" (2015a, 92), which will allow us to realize "a divestment from *this* life in favor of deeper investments in a life beyond ourselves" (91). Evans and Reid similarly enjoin us to resist instinctual, emotional attachments, reminding us that "life continually desires that which it should find oppressive ... Life also shamefully compromises with power to the subjugation of both the self and others" (2014, 174).[5] For Evans and Reid, moving past our animal attachment to "life" to embrace the specifically human capacity "to transcend each and every boundary, each and every limit, and lose all sense of its own finitude and that of the world itself" (195) means resisting the base emotional pulls of *ressentiment* (116–7) and sentimentality. They stress, "We do not accept the idea so widely propounded by others that the most urgent question of our time is how better to relieve human suffering, or that of any other form of life defined by tales of survival. We are, it appears, or ought to be at least, exhausted by the discourse and aesthetic practice of suffering" (177). Determining that "tired people are tiresome in their suffering" (177), they celebrate in the place of tiredness the paradoxically more vigorous (or at least more aesthetically satisfying) state of radical exhaustion that finds compelling embodiment in Beckett's dramas. The characters in those dramas "in seeing the end, do not fear it," in a theatre that "beyond the possible, ... posits the question of absolute freedom" (178).

Human Exceptionalism/Exceptional Humans

In addition to – in fact, bound up with – human exceptionalism in both texts is a sense of strong, if embattled, individual autonomy. Evans and Reid, though critical of the biopolitical dynamic of liberalism, remain wedded to the liberal ideal of the autonomous subject, specifying, "By autonomous, we mean a subject defined by its disconnection from other human beings, and a certain non-adaptivity or resistance to the will of others" (2014, 58). In the light of this value, they reject resilience, which, to the extent that it is "all about thriving in complex systems which promote radical connectivity and accept radical uncertainty," (62) is fatal to the "affirmative potential of the autonomous subject" (174). Digital connectedness is singled out for particular condemnation. Citing Heidegger, Evans and Reid argue that digital technology is being used to reshape humans and "secur[e] a technologized order of things" (54). Specifically, they note that "the information technologies that enable us to connect more and better, be they mobile phones, laptop computers, or iPods, are ... far from neutral in operation. They are all enfolded within desiring frames which, rather than being used by humans to increase natural propensities, are deployed by liberal regimes of power to constitute humans with specific tendencies and habits" (54). The "tendencies and habits" that "liberal regimes of power" seek to cultivate are presumably those that will enhance resilience. Interestingly, "liberal regimes" and the digital technology they purportedly command are the same targets singled out by those seeking to *restore* resilience through a return to nature (see chapter 1).

Nature, invoked in the form of "natural propensities," plays an ambiguous role for Evans and Reid. While it serves in this instance to describe a normative set of human desires and capacities, "nature" elsewhere refers to a squalid realm of physical necessity that it is our human right and obligation to transcend. Scranton's treatment of nature is similarly incoherent, as we have already noted with respect to his bee analogy. What begins as an acknowledgment of humans' ecological being, with politics understood as "the energetic distribution of bodies in systems" (2015a, 55–6), morphs into a strained metaphor highlighting the need for independence. Drawing on Peter Sloterdijk's conception of the philosopher as an "interrupter" (Scranton 2015a, 86), Scranton describes the philosopher's role in "the human swarm" as one of "an aberrant anti-drone slow-dancing to its own rhythm, neither attuned to the collective beat but continually self-immunizing against the waves of social energy we live in and amongst by perpetually interrupting its own connection to collective life" (87). This final flourish of bee imagery accomplishes the significant task of using nature to bolster the idea of the postnatural human. The metaphor retains the formal authority of evolutionary biology while it abandons anything resembling the actual behaviour of bees.

The image of the "aberrant" "slow-dancing" bee vs the madness of the hive informs Scranton's critique of digital culture. Like Evans and Reid, Scranton is dismissive of what he calls "social media vibrations, products of cultural technologies that we have interpolated into our lives" (2015a, 78). But he is equally critical of what he sees as social media's real-life counterpart: organized political protest. He describes the 2014 People's Climate March as "little more than an orgy of democratic emotion, an activist-themed street fair, a real-world analogue to Twitter hashtag campaigns: something that gives you a nice feeling, says you belong in a certain group, and is completely divorced from actual legislation and governance" (62). The indictment of digital media and organized action merges in Scranton's observation that "in a perverse irony, one of the main things that connected the disparate parties at the United Nations, Flood Wall Street, the IETA, and the People's Climate March was a system of cultural technology that is silently burning up masses of carbon while shunting activist outrage into impotent feedback loops. The most common sight at all the events that week was people on their iPhones and Androids, checking email, tweeting and taking pictures. The global information and communications ecosystem that they were plugged into is now estimated to use about 10 percent of the world's electricity" (68). This observation echoes standard right-wing indictments of environmentalists who use some form of (presumably carbon-emitting) transportation to get to meetings and demonstrations in its implication that (a) anything that entails contradiction or compromise is "perversely ironic" and (b) activists don't recognize this "irony" because they are guided not by thoughtful deliberation but self-righteous emotion. Evans and Reid are similarly contemptuous of the "card-carrying Leftists of Occupy Wall Street [who] still bleat like lambs" that "'another world is possible'" (2014, 188). The implication for both is that we need to emancipate ourselves from the animalistic hive/herd and the "emotional static" it generates – including commitments to collective action – to realize our full, rational, autonomous humanity.

For Evans and Reid, that realization mandates detachment from base emotional entanglements to embrace an "original love for the Other – a poetic connection that allows one to have confidence in their communion, that all subsequent bonds based upon a sense of vulnerability and endangerment would be superfluous" (2014, 193).[6] Scranton similarly advocates for a practice of "philosophical humanism," which, in its most radical practice, is the disciplined interruption of somatic and social flows, the detachment of consciousness from impulse, and the condensation of conceptual truths out of the granular data of experience. It is the study of "dying and being dead," a divestment from this life in favour of deeper investments in a life beyond ourselves. In recognizing the dominion of death and the transience of individual existences, we affirm a web of being that connects past to future, them to us, me to you (2015a, 90). In exchanging the "social excitation" (108) of the hive for the abstraction of the "web of being," Scranton, like Evans and Reid, suggests that the renunciation of a world of others is a necessary precondition for achieving communion with the Other.[7] Because such an engagement entails the merging of the self into an abstract realm of negativity/possibility rather than the concrete obligations of mundane relations with others, it confirms (and ethically affirms) the status of the autonomous subject.

The Poet Warrior

In each case, the stance is a heroic and embattled one, pitting truth against power through whatever means necessary. In contrast to the cringing posture of adaptation, the figure that Evans and Reid call "*The Poetic Subject*" (2014, 136, italics in original) is determined to "live through these uncertain times, and view the troubled waters in a new, more exhilarating and aesthetically enriching light of day" (155). The poetic commitment is characterized by fidelity not to life but to "political truth," which "demands an affirmation of the conflict between worlds, a breaking through without due care for what the implications will be for the world we inhabit and believe we somehow possess" (198). The substance of political truth and the authority of the poetic subject reciprocally affirm one another: "Political truths are told by subjects that risk life, their own, that of others, and the world itself, in telling the truths which they do. They respect not the truth of biological life which Kant insists on, it being a phenomenon of finitude and vulnerability, but the life of truth" (198). Thus, the antiresilient hero emerges as a revolutionary whose commitment to transformation puts to shame the resilient subject, who "surrender[s] ... to the mercies of the world" (xv).

In Scranton's case, the heroic figure is literally a warrior. His book begins by recounting his 2003 experience serving with the US military in Iraq, an experience he uses to symbolize the devastated and dangerous landscape of the Anthropocene. Scranton describes his initial fear of the future embodied by that landscape (a symbolic move I discuss in more detail below) and his eventual acceptance, which is conditioned by the experience of war and the reading of "an old book: Yamamoto Tsunetomo's 18th-century Samurai manual, the *Hagakure*," which counsels daily meditation on death (2015a, 21). "To survive as a soldier," he concludes, "I had to learn to accept the inevitability of my own death. For humanity to survive in the Anthropocene, we need to learn to live with, and through the end of our current civilization" (22). Philosophy, exemplified in the Samurai manual, is the bridge that enables the individual/soldier to stand in for civilization as a whole: "These two ways of learning how to die come together in the role of the humanist thinker: the one who is willing to stop and ask troublesome questions, the one who is willing to interrupt, the one who resonates on other channels and with slower, deeper rhythms" (24). Scranton, along with Evans and Reid, reads the acceptance of death as a confrontation with truth.

No less important in both accounts is the connection between death, thus construed, and the revival of a certain mode of life – that of the traditional poet-philosopher. As its title suggests, *Learning to Die in the Anthropocene* offers a hybrid memoir-guide take on living in difficult times. But it also has powerful subtheme, which is a defence of a particular vision of the humanities. "The greatest challenge the Anthropocene poses," Scranton suggests, "isn't how the Department of Defense should plan for resource wars, whether we should put up sea walls to protect Manhattan, or when we should abandon Miami. It won't be addressed by buying a Prius, turning off the air conditioning, or signing a treaty. The greatest challenge we face is a philosophical one: understanding that this civilization is already dead" (2015a, 23).

In place of small-scale, practical problem-solving efforts, Scranton outlines a larger, existential project, one designed not to protect physical infrastructure, but to let it go, "to let our old way of life die while protecting, sustaining, and reworking our collective stores of cultural technology" (2015a, 23). The humanities scholar plays a special role in this task by virtue of having cultivated the skills and disciplined commitment to the arts of "contemplation, philosophical debate, and posing impertinent questions" (108). These arts must be urgently directed to the project of recognizing and curating the ideas that best exemplify our universal humanity – a condition that he implies we have lost touch with through a well-meaning but now unhelpful focus on difference. To attain a properly humanist perspective, Scranton suggests, we need "to draw from our immense heritage of intellectual production, living and dead, exotic and close at hand: from the Iñupiat and from Islam, from Heraclitus and Zhuangzi, from the Torah and from the Buddha, from the *Federalist Papers* and from the *Communist Manifesto*. Carbon-fueled capitalism has given rise to a truly marvelous liberal multiculturalism, but if we are to survive its death throes, tolerance must mature into conservation and synthesis, grounded in a faith in human community existing beyond any parochial identity, local time, or single place" (24). In another weird echo of the resilience-in-nature advocates discussed in chapter 1 (recall Richard Louv's complaints about the summer camp turn to "race-relations"), Scranton gives a condescending nod to "multiculturalism" and "tolerance" while implying they have served their purpose and are inadequate to the challenges of the present.[8] The task of moving past them falls to the traditional humanist scholar who rises above not only physical or applied disciplines, whose purview is confined by the limits of the material world, but also those branches of human or social scientific inquiry (e.g., feminism, postcolonialism, ecocriticism, critical race studies) that employ a materialist or political – or even a critical theoretical – lens in their approach to the human. In place of those "parochial" approaches, Scranton calls for a "new humanism" (19), one that we might read as an extension of Matthew Arnold's nineteenth-century proposal to unite a fractured Britain using "the best that has been thought and known in the world" to a planetary level.

Evans and Reid also invoke a history of thought, but in a spirit less of conservation than romantic refusal. While Scranton calls for "the patient nurturing of the roots and heirloom varietals of human symbolic life" (2014, 98), Evans and Reid place more emphasis on exemplary thinkers and artists. They cite a select group of philosophers (Nietzche, Foucault, Arendt, Deleuze, and Derrida) – "allies with those who we continually collaborate with *in absentia*" (xiv) and creative writers (Franz Kafka, Ingmar Bergman, Bertolt Brecht, Lewis Carroll, George Orwell, Samuel Beckett, Francis Bacon, and Philip K. Dick) as "the real revolutionary figures – the poetic subjects of our historical present, who continue to shape our existence in the most creative, compelling and affirmative ways" (2014, xv). While the principles of inclusion in this revolutionary group are not exactly clear (though it is distinguished by a dearth of women and people of colour), the stakes of the battle are high and the enemy powerful in its blandness. Against "the one-dimensional personalities of seasoned experts" (xiv), it is the task of the *Poetic Subject* to counter "the greying of existence by those who demand that we surrender ourselves to the mercies of the world" (xv).

As already noted, the physical sciences come in for criticism from both Scranton and Evans and Reid. The latter regard with suspicion "increased collaboration between the physical, natural and social sciences, such that previous distinctions between the natural and social worlds have been largely erased. Human life is no longer understood as distinct from any other life form. Neither can it think itself greater or lesser than the complex structuring of the universe most broadly conceived" (2014, 7). The problem with this collaboration in their view is not just one of incommensurability between disciplinary methodologies or epistemologies but of a shrinking of the horizon of possibility for the humanist poet. It is not just the sciences that are responsible for these diminished circumstances but, more generally, "the intellectual realities of the times," which are characterized by "the power of conformity and the seduction of mediocrity" (xvi). More darkly, they note, "Both of us can personally relate to encounters with previous colleagues who appeared more like 'thought police' as they preferred to suffocate or diminish the force of our ideas instead of celebrating intellectual differences, in these testing times" (xiv). These comments point to a significant subtheme of Evans and Reid's book: it is not only the autonomous subject who is imperilled by resilience but also the radical scholar, and indeed, "the meaning of the University as such" (xiv). Against the attacks of "disingenuous careerists," they praise the efforts of "intellectuals worthy of the term, who still believe that the essential function of the University is to continue to hold power to account" (xiv). Leaving aside the question of whether this is (or ever has been) the university's "essential function," it is worth noting the temporality of the characterization. The use of the words "still" and "continue" – along with a stated commitment to "*reclaiming* the meaning of the University as such" (xiv, italics added) – imply that the *traditional* role of the university, and its capacity to provide a home for a certain kind of scholarship, is in danger of being lost.

Left Melancholy

These words sound a powerful note of conservatism in an argument that is otherwise cloaked in the language of revolution and has the stated aim of producing and cultivating the kind of political project that will "excite our imagination to compel us to live our lives differently" (Evans and Reid 2014, xi). Indeed, repeated gestures to "hope of a new time to come" (xv) do not quell a mood Evans and Reid's book conveys of nostalgia for a world of confident liberal humanism and the attendant politics of masculine individualism. This feeling ruffles an argument that on the surface takes a Foucauldian genealogical view of the liberal project – a view in which the current biopolitical resilience-focused regime is not a departure from the liberal security apparatus that dominated modernity but a natural evolution of it – "as liberalism now faces the reality of its finitude, haunted in fact by the very logic of infinite potentiality that its contemporary bio-philosophy of life equally promotes, the turn to resilience becomes inevitable" (29). But while the dominant thrust of Evans and Reid's argument appears to be critical of liberalism, the critique does not sufficiently quell the wistful sense that something has been lost. Punctuating their nuanced analysis of biopolitics are undisguised laments for its earlier incarnation in the form of the "social state" that "has been under attack for over three decades" (44). In keeping with the demise of the social state, it is not surprising to find that "universal aspirations are all but abandoned, along with any natural claims to promote all life as a self-endowed subject with inalienable rights" (30). Permeating these complaints is a mood of liberal melancholia, directed primarily (as such moods frequently are) at a mythical institution – the capital "U" University – that is seen to have abandoned its revolutionary mission and the soldiers/scholars who are still committed to carrying it out.

On the face of it, Scranton's prescription for learning to die in the Anthropocene seems more resolutely forward-looking. His book opens with an account of his arrival as an American soldier in Baghdad in 2003. Burning oil towers, broken bridges, and ruined buildings combined to create an experience that "felt like driving into the future" (2015a, 13). The full horror is realized a couple of years later when Scranton gets home from Iraq and witnesses a similar scene of chaos and wreckage following Hurricane Katrina: "The grim future I'd seen in Baghdad had come home: not terrorism, not WMDs, but the machinery of civilization breaking down, unable to recuperate from shocks to its system" (14). The conclusion? "We're fucked. The only questions are how soon and how badly" (16). The reality of climate change, identified by US Admiral J. Locklear III as "the greatest threat the United States faced" (14), means that "the future's not going away" (14). The stated goal of Scranton's book is to enjoin us to face that future. But a close reading reveals that the futurity of Scranton's vision has deep roots in the past, specifically the imaginary of settler colonialism.

Iraq plays a central role in the story Scranton is telling as a symbolic site for the rise and fall of civilization. It is the stage for the exemplary figure of the soldier, who must now show us how to navigate that fall. The American occupation of Iraq is not so much ignored as it is taken as a given, the most recent chapter in the story of humanity, a chapter driven by oil. Though they don't actually appear in Scranton's account, the role of present-day Iraqi people in the story presumably mirrors that of the landscape: their plight is not the material consequence of American invasion but the symbolic harbinger of a universal future. If the Indian, in an earlier strain of settler thinking, represented a figure of primordial life now tragically but inevitably superseded by progress, then Iraq is subject in Anthropocenic thinking to a different kind of temporal disjunction Cheryl Lousley has termed the "gothic future" (2015) and Jennifer Wenzel a "projected future inferior" (2014). In both instances, the recent and ongoing history of dispossession disappears, giving way to a fantasized spectacle of the non-Western other, projected into a romanticized past in the first instance, and, in the second, a fearful future humanity (read: Western humanity) must courageously confront.

Like Evans and Reid, Scranton is relating what purports to be a universal story, one that "works ... to create a sense of collective humanity that exists beyond any one place, life, or time. The story this book tells is of the human soul coming to know itself in its mortality" (2015a, 25). This actually is the synthesis of two stories. One is the physical history of life on earth. The other is a story of the philosopher hero who achieves fulfillment through detached meditation. These interwoven stories contain echoes of Thoreau's account of the solitary life in nature. For each narrator-protagonist, the misguided priorities of the societies in which he lives obstruct a truth that can only be understood (that only he can understand) through detached reflection. While Walden signifies as a microcosm of the natural world with which, Thoreau's experiment suggested, it was possible to live in harmony, Iraq symbolizes the failure of that experiment. Both stories, in reconciling the soul and the world, leave out geopolitics and, more specifically, the history of colonialism that underwrites the ability of colonizers and settlers to project their own experience as universal. For Scranton, "Accepting this emptiness, letting go of my self, was only the first step in coming to understand my responsibility to and participation in a larger collective self, a kind of human existence transcending any particular place or time, going back to our first moments in Africa 200,000 years ago, and living on in the dim, fraught future of the Anthropocene. We are humanity. We are the dead. They have become us, as we will become the dead of future generations" (93–4). Though the story is about renunciation, it has the ring of triumph about it. Having seen the tedious futility of grappling with the conflicts of a "particular place or time," the protagonist of this story transcends place and time to become one with the universe.

In his embrace of death, Scranton, like Evans and Reid, claims to be facing head-on a future that no one else wants to recognize. They both indict the dominant mood of resilience thinking that encourages adaptation to the changing conditions of a stressed biosphere. Each holds instead to a view of the autonomous individual who is able, by virtue of his uniquely human capacity for critical and creative thought, to refuse the biopolitically regulated terms of nature and life itself. However, rather than opening out into something new, this model of heroic transcendence remains deeply rooted in a Western humanist tradition – one that has turned out to be not only ethically flawed but ecologically unsustainable. The tradition rests on a contradictory abstraction whereby Nature sanctions the exceptionality of the human from the physical constraints of nature. Philosophy and poetry offer a guide to dying, which is understood not so much in a physical sense, by the corporeal processes of suffering and decay, as in a metaphysical sense, defined by the liberation of the soul. Thus, the staging of death becomes a stealth project of self-preservation. In defending the autonomy of human thought and creativity, Evans and Reid and Scranton are also defending a particular kind of scholarship, for which the figure of the poet-philosopher is the self-appointed guardian. In other words, it is not just that the idea of resilience threatens the human but that its currency, extending to the development of new academic centres, funded research, and even extracurricular programming, threatens a way of thinking about the human and those who are invested in that way of thinking.

The critical theoretical hostility directed at resilience thinking recalls the hostility that was once directed at cultural studies, whose interest in articulating a "politics in which you are already complicit with the violence in which you are trying to struggle against" (Hall 2018, 896) undermined the integrity of the humanist (anti)hero. In her 1994 defence of cultural studies and the contaminated stream of postmodernism that fed it, Angela McRobbie expressed no nostalgia for the loss of that figure, wryly noting, "The obvious question to ask is which social subjects have had the privilege of being whole, or 'healthy,' and thus fully inscribed in history and in culture?" (1994, 4). The decline of metanarratives of emancipation is something less than tragic for those who were never granted a role in them to begin with. And as we lament the weakening of Enlightenment concepts of "reason, humanity and even equality," we cannot lose sight of the history of their deployments such that, as McRobbie puts it, "to enlighten some was to regulate many others" (8).

More than two decades prior to the publication of Scranton's and Evans and Reid's books, McRobbie wrote against a backdrop that she dubbed "the years of living dangerously" (1994, 6). While life in the 1990s might look relatively calm from the vantage point of our crisis-ridden present, the reference to danger signposts the real stakes of losing the certainties of modernity "as an enabling structure" (7). As a feminist, McRobbie acknowledges a certain fidelity to this structure and its centrality to the women's movement as she and many of her contemporaries understood it. But McRobbie demands that we attend to the exclusions that sustained these comfortable institutions and patterns of thought. With respect to the latter, McRobbie draws on Jane Flax's 1992 essay, "The End of Innocence," to suggest that "the failure to face up to the limits of reason, truth and knowledge, is predicated on a fearfulness of letting go. Go on, [Flax] says. And I would agree. Not to live with fear and danger is to block out so much of daily lived experience. If postmodernism forces uncertainty on to the agenda, if we have to look beyond reason, then at least we are forewarned. Our politics can begin to reflect the multiple realities of social insecurity" (9). To which we can add environmental security. I cite McRobbie's comments not to contrast the dangers of twenty years ago with the bigger ones of today but to highlight the differences in response to them. While Evans and Reid and Scranton decamp for the elevated terrain of metaphysics, where reason still holds supreme, McRobbie dwells with the dangers of daily lived experience, looking for ways to live through them.[9]

The "everyday life" that cultural studies elevates is not the same as the ecological life that is the purview of resilience theory. What the two approaches have in common is an interest in life, which does merit some critical scrutiny.[10] Evans and Reid and Scranton help us to see how "life" is the ultimate trap of resilience thinking, our attachment to which helps to enlist us in our own enslavement to late modernity. However, their proposed antidote – death – is arguably a product of that same modernity. More than this, I suggest, the mode of romantic refusal that these critics endorse can be read as a nostalgic return to an outmoded model of (white, academic) leftist politics embodied in the figure of the masculine revolutionary subject. For this figure, death preserves the possibility of heroic transcendence against a life of subjection to more-than-human others – what Kyo Maclear evocatively calls the "mosh pit of relational coexistence and care that challenges the telos of our good intentions" (2018).

I have also suggested that, in its rejection of the mosh pit for the heady altitude of solitary reflection (what Evans and Reid call "an atmospheric politics that counters a fascistic earth" [2014, 137]), antiresilience contains traces of the settler-colonialist logic Mark Rifkin (2013) identifies in Thoreau. It is easy, Rifkin suggests, to proclaim one's independence from the squalid business of what Wordsworth derisively called "getting and spending" when the conditions of one's inhabitation of a place are already secure. And when, as a result of the combined dangers of the twenty-first century, those conditions appear to be getting a bit less secure, the call to abandon them entirely in favour of death offers a way to avoid acknowledging the historical violence that determines their still wildly unequal terms. Put another way, issuing a universal call to death seems like a way to conveniently avoid confronting the selective practices of elimination that has undergirded white Western (particularly North American) privilege. It also ignores the voices of those who have endured – who continue to endure – those practices.

"It's Been the End of the World for Somebody All Along"

In 1930, some seventy-five years before Roy Scranton saw the "grim future" as he drove into Baghdad, Chief Plenty Coups – the last hereditary chief of the Crow Indian nation – gave an account of a different time of devastation. In a note at the end of Plenty Coup's autobiography, ethnographer and transcriber Frank Linderman recounts a conversation about events not included in the main account – the near extinction of the buffalo and the confinement of the Crow to a reserve. Plenty Coups explains, "When the buffalo went away the hearts of my people fell to the ground, and they could not lift them up again. After this nothing happened" (1962, 169).

Settler scholars have struggled to make sense of this succinct testimony to the events that precipitated the end of the world. Philosopher Jonathan Lear uses Plenty Coup's words as the centrepiece of his book, *Radical Hope: Ethics in the Face of Cultural Devastation* (2008), which explores the question of "what happens to the subject when the possibility of living according to its associated ideals collapses" (44). Lear wonders: "if *our* way of life collapsed, things would cease to happen. What could this mean?" (6, emphasis added). He explains: "I am not primarily concerned with what actually happened to the Crow tribe or to any other group. I am concerned rather with the field of possibilities in which all human endeavors gain meaning" (7). Environmental historian William Cronon approaches Plenty Coups's words more sympathetically, reading them as a corrective to dominant narratives of the Dust Bowl in which the Plains Indians are relegated to a footnote. Cronon laments Plenty Coups's emphasis on ending, which Cronon reads as mirroring the "classic imperialist myths of the frontier" that feature the figure of the disappearing Indian (1992, 1366). But there is something that Lear and Cronon both miss in Plenty Coups's precise description of the end of the world, precipitated by the destruction of a vital thread in the fabric of Crow life. It is not an example of what *could* happen to "us"; nor is it only a historical event, "the tragedy of an older Indian generation," whose "shadow" looms over present generations (Cronon 1992, 1366). Rather, it is an on-the-ground account of an ongoing process of devastation from which Plenty Coup wrests meaning in the face of its impossibility.

Chief Plenty Coup's account of the disappearance of the buffalo is an unsettling resilience story, told against the dominant narrative of settler-colonial resilience, which tells the story of the successful adaptation of intrepid pioneers to a landscape rife with dangers: arid soil, unpredictable climate, uncivilized Indians – the story to whose unwinding Scranton and Evans and Reid are bearing uneasy witness. In the traditional narrative, the conquest of Indigenous people testifies to the resilience of the settlers, whose colonization – historical and ongoing – of the land becomes part of the larger story of the evolution of Man outlined by Sylvia Wynter (2003). Plenty Coups's narrative offers a different version of events, one in which the European domestication of the Great Plains figures not as a moment of challenge met and overcome on the way to the consolidation of the America but as the end of "happenings": the destruction of the world. At the same time, the chief's straightforward narration of the cataclysm that has already happened (continues to happen) confounds the call for heroic refusal – for antiresilience – in the face of the Anthropocene.

Plenty Coup's story confirms what many Indigenous scholars have pointed out: to comprehend Indigenous history, as Anishinaabe scholar Lawrence W. Gross argues, it is necessary to "correctly name the experience Native Americans have suffered and which they continue to endure to this day. To put it in a word, Native Americans have seen the end of their respective worlds. Using vocabulary from the study of religion, this should be correctly termed an apocalypse" (2014, 33). However, "just as importantly," he goes on to say, "Indians survived the apocalypse. This raises the further question, then, of what happens to a society that has gone through an apocalyptic event? The effects of the apocalypse linger on and the history of apocalypse continues to be the current-day reality for many Native Americans" (33). And, lest settlers indulge in the hubristic shame of the belief our people are the only authors of apocalypse,[11] it's worth noting that ends-of-worlds are already understood by Indigenous creation stories. As Mohawk scholar Amber Meadow Adams puts it, "We know [the apocalypse] is not a moment, but a process that shudders along a broad time scale. The Haudenosaunee story of Earth's creation is about total ecological collapse, the terror of free-fall, and what it takes to remake a world that will always be fragile" (2020a). What does it mean to live on *through* apocalypse? Plenty Coups's account doesn't fit the template of a dominant resilience narrative, but neither does it support settler renunciations of resilience that call for a heroic embrace of an imminent end. Instead, it offers a paradoxical account of resilience in the midst of the ongoing destruction of the world.

At the risk of overburdening a few words with too many layers of analysis, there are two elements of Plenty Coups's account of the disappearance of the buffalo that are remarkable for the challenge they pose to Anthropocenic thinking in general and antiresilience in particular. First, in speaking from within the shattered world, after the point at which anything happened, after the point at which anything could be said, Plenty Coups's words upend the frame of linear thinking, according to which death is always "to come" rather than an event that has already happened, is continuing to happen. Second, for all that they appear poetically to register a situation of impossibility, undercutting the ground of their own utterance, Plenty Coups's words are not metaphysical but situated, in a particular place, to which they are accountable. Their reference point is not the individual (or the system) but a set of more-than-human relations: the Crow people and the buffalo. And in centring those relations, they emphasize neither life nor death but loss, registering a grief whose magnitude is world-shattering.

Another element of Plenty Coups's story is worth commenting on. Though he is framed by Linderman and has been historically celebrated as the hero of it, his story undercuts the importance of what Scranton refers to as "our own autonomous desires" (2015a, 79) and Evans and Reid call "the affirmative potential of the autonomous subject" (2014, 174). In fact, Plenty Coups's story is shot through with entanglements and compromise. As the Crow chief, he formed an alliance with settlers against the Sioux and Cheyenne, traditional enemies of the Crow. On the reservation to which Crow were subsequently relegated (close to their traditional lands in Montana, a dubious reward for their cooperation), Plenty Coups took up farming, participated in intertribal networks to defend the land against further encroachment, and encouraged his people to embrace education as a "powerful weapon" against colonialism (Heidenreich 2016). He continued to practice traditional Crow religion while also being baptized into the Catholic Church. He was honoured (or mourned, depending on how you look at it) by the Crow as their last traditional chief. In contrast to the contemporary scholars who adopt a heroic posture of pure negation, Plenty Coups presents an awkward story of resilience in which he fights off the assaults of settler colonialism while also adapting to and ultimately being transformed by them.

In contrast to the contemporary scholars who adopt a heroic posture of pure negation, Plenty Coups presents an awkward story of resilience. It's awkward not only because of the high price he paid to ensure the survival of his people but because of the context of its telling. Though the story is nominally his, as Jasmine Spencer succinctly outlines:

> Unlike an "authentic" first-person statement of confession or of witness, Plenty Coups's book is really the product of an amanuensis who could not understand the language in which Plenty Coups told his life story and of an interpreter whom the amanuensis does not represent in very respectful terms. In other words, this book is complicated by the fact that it was told in Crow or Apsálooke and in Plains Indian Sign Language (PISL), interpreted by an interculturally positioned Apsáalooke interpreter, and then rendered into English from memory and mnemonic field notes by a European American writer who understood PISL – which is a regional, cross-linguistic semiotic system not specific to Apsálooke – but who did not understand Apsálooke. (2019, 169)

Spencer describes the generic untidiness of Plenty Coups's story in support of a compelling argument for reading it, not as autobiography, but "as a multispecies, multivocal text composed of many voices and viewpoints, both human and more-than-human, including buffalo, chickadees, and eagles, and true dreams of the same" (169).

The multivocality of Plenty Coups's text, embedding it in a threatened but still thriving world, places it in stark contrast with the solitary voices of reason rising up against the Anthropocene.

I began this chapter by describing the condition of left melancholia that infuses some academic circles, of which antiresilience is one symptom. In turning to Plenty Coups's story, I want to place that feeling in the context of settler colonialism, to which I think it offers a confused reaction. Antiresilience, theorized in relation to the history of liberalism, civilization, and the Anthropocene, seems completely oblivious to colonialism. A slightly more complicated (generous?) reading would attribute it to the perpetrator of violence who, confronted with the consequences of their abuse, throws up their hands and says, "OK, I'm guilty. We're all guilty. We've made a mess of everything so let's tear it up and start again." Which is a lot easier than listening to those who have been harmed, sitting with the words, and figuring out how to move forward. It is in this spirit that white settler scholars might, as an alternative to learning "how to die" (or rather, to model the critical theoretical posture of rejecting the deteriorating conditions of life on earth and our implicatedness in that deterioration), begin to reckon with the resilience of those who have dwelled in the moment after which "nothing happened" and created newness in the foundry of loss. "I think that the impetus to act and to change and to transform, for me, exists whether or not this is the end of the world," Leanne Simpson attests. "If a river is threatened, it's the end of the world for those fish. It's been the end of the world for somebody all along" (2013a).

Stories of Decolonial Resilience and Refusal

The first three chapters of this book analyzed the dominant narratives of resilience and antiresilience that, in different ways (though drawing from the same radical individualist playbook) help to sustain the projects of racial capitalism and settler colonialism in the face of planetary destruction. The remaining chapters look to fiction to find alternative models of flourishing through and beyond those violent systems.[12] To turn to literature in this way is to reject the posture of anti-instrumentality that Caroline Levine has identified as the hallmark of contemporary literary criticism, which may be the place where the dismal scholarly left has found the most hospitable home. Levine notes that literary criticism has long professed a preference for "open-endedness" (2021, 227–8) and critique in place of any gesture that smacks of usefulness or looks like it could be harnessed to a progressive end.[13] In its embrace of radical critique over practical problem solving, Levine suggests, literary criticism retreats (along with its melancholic brethren in other disciplines) to "withdrawal, inaction, and mourning" when it should be addressing itself to the "the vast and urgent project of sustaining collective life over generations" (233). As a model of what this might look like, Levine cites Potawatomi scholar Kyle Powys Whyte's concept of collective continuance (Whyte 2018) – the framework for Indigenous futurity defined around interdependence and responsibility – as a model for *good* instrumentality. Collective continuance is, in Levine's words, "a capacitating end, a crucial means of affording a range of other ends" (234).

This book subscribes to the tenet of good instrumentality in literary criticism against the lure of left melancholia. It also engages, as Levine does, with Whyte's theorization of collective continuance (see the introduction and chapter 5) while at the same time holding in mind another key part of Whyte's argument: that the goal of settler colonialism is to undermine the collective continuance of Indigenous societies, to replace Indigenous ecologies with settler ecologies (Whyte 2018, 134–5). And, qualifying without invalidating Whyte's point, that those ecologies are racialized; the "settlers" whose "aspirations are to transform Indigenous homelands into settler homelands" (135) are predominantly white, their aspirations both exclusive of and dependent on Black and Brown others. This book, a work of white settler literary criticism, has to reckon with these facts in the process of warding off the academic edgelords of antiresilience and thinking its way instrumentally towards a new conception of continuance. That conception must, in its essence, be decolonial before it is resilient.

The works of Chariandy, Simpson, and Wright that are the focus of the final three chapters refuse the dominant idea of resilience. They offer in its place stories that speak to what a liveable world might look like for Black and Indigenous people and others rendered disposable by racial capitalism and settler colonialism. In so doing, they support Robyn Maynard's observation, in a letter to Leanne Simpson in their 2022 collaboration *Rehearsals for Living*, that "world-ending and world-making can occur, are occurring, have always occurred, simultaneously" (2022, 26) and that "we and ours have been building livable worlds all along, despite and against forces aligned to steal our light, and ... we will continue to do so no matter what comes our way" (28). There is hope in that statement. I also choose to read in it an invitation to white settlers to dismantle the unliveable structures "we and ours" have made as part of the process of making new worlds.

4

Somehow, a City

THE IDEA OF SOCIAL-ECOLOGICAL RESILIENCE is all about the successful functioning of complex adaptive systems. That is the premise of urban resilience strategies, which were the focus of chapter 2. Urban resilience rests on a delicate dance between diversity and unity, equity, and market forces. The exclusion of certain neighbourhoods, made up largely of racialized residents and newcomers, is understood to compromise the resilience of the city as a whole. *Toronto's First Resilience Strategy* therefore places special emphasis on ways to eliminate barriers to inclusion, such as improving access to employment (2019, 89), strengthening civic engagement (128), and investing in communities (85). The problem, the strategy suggests, is not only that some people have been excluded from the city's growth and prosperity, that their community "is not fully resourced or equitably integrated into the city" (58), it is that they embody the risk to which the very idea of the city – "the system" – must become resilient. This fact supports the argument in chapter 2 that racism is a not a bug but a feature of the resilient city.

It is against the backdrop of that formulation of resilient Toronto that this chapter analyzes David Chariandy's 2017 novel, *Brother*. In Chariandy's words, "The story represents communities that have often been misrepresented and people in them who have often been misrepresented. I wanted to take care to represent those very same communities and people in ways that drew attention to the resilience, the imagination, the sheer intelligence of individuals in Scarborough" (Chariandy 2017c). Set in a fictional

Scarborough neighbourhood called the Park, *Brother* illuminates and celebrates a part of the city that figures in Toronto's resilience strategy largely in terms of lack. At the same time, the novel, which centres around the police killing of a Black teenager, documents the racism and police violence that play a defining role in the resilient city. In doing so, it offers a truer, fuller story of a place and people who are not well served by the dominant model of urban resilience. More than this, though, and crucially for the purposes of this chapter, it unearths the racial capitalist foundations of that model and the concepts of opportunity, character, mobility, family, and futurity that are its pillars. This work is tied to the story's function as fiction, which works not to just to reproduce but to creatively remediate the world as it presents itself to us, unearthing buried histories, grieving their losses, and giving voice to their unrealized possibilities. *Brother* explicitly explores the capacity and the limits of different forms of art, including writing and music, to amplify what is absent from *Toronto's First Resilience Strategy*, what Rinaldo Walcott and Idil Abdillahi call BlackLife (2020).[1]

Part of the discussion in chapter 2 focused on how the form of the strategy worked or didn't work to carry its message about resilience – for example, by including the voices of residents invited to bring "their personal stories to identify the city's vulnerabilities, and to propose ambitious but practical actions" (City of Toronto 2019, 11). Some personal stories, like the *Resilient People* video analyzed in chapter 2, sync up neatly with the vulnerability/action, challenge/opportunity balance that the strategy aims to strike. Others resonate less comfortably with the message, such as the comments of a Kingston-Galloway-Orton Park resident, presented without context in a full-page text box: "Being black is a struggle on a day to day to survive because there is so much stigma attached to the colour of your skin and living in a neighbourhood that has been labeled as a high risk neighborhood for things such as gun violence and poverty. As a mother of black children, it is something that I have to live with every day knowing that my kids are been [*sic*] stigmatized by police, the very people that should be protecting them, abusing them because they have power, knowing that they will get away with it because they are in control and the system will back them" (City of Toronto, 2019, 29). While the comment speaks to a kind of resilience, it is not the aspirational model that the strategy celebrates. In fact, the experience the comments describe, of racism that doesn't just stick to a person, enclosing their neighbourhood and entrapping their family, but also animating the institutions that are meant to protect them, exposes the contradictions in the idea of the resilient city. In spite of being included in the Toronto resilience strategy as one of the "voices and perspectives of diverse stakeholders" (32), the Kingston-Galloway-Orton Park resident holds no stake in the power structure that defines the resilient city. Their position in the city is mirrored by the place of their testimony in the text. Enlisted in the interests of equity and inclusion, the experience the testimony describes cannot be accommodated by the disciplinary or generic conventions of the urban resilience strategy. Like other conventional representations of resilience, shaped through the logic of complex adaptive systems and individual *bildungs*, the strategy cannot conceptualize the still-unfolding history of racism; nor can it imagine what it means to live on through that history. The Kingston-Galloway-Orton Park resident's testimony, indexical of the Toronto resilience strategy's stated commitment to diversity and inclusivity, also emblematizes the inhospitality of resilience discourse to stories of BlackLife. Where those stories appear at all, they remain segregated via text box, untranslatable into the future imagined by the strategy. *Brother* shifts the focus and also the trajectory of the story, writing a story of BlackLife embedded in the future of a place – Scarborough – that is part of Toronto but not tethered to the discourse of the resilient city.

Resilient Kids, or "the Running Challenge of Opportunity"

Brother doesn't only dismantle the ideal of the city embodied in *Toronto's First Resilience Strategy*, it also undoes the nostalgic fiction of the resilient (white) child explored in chapter 1 of this book. With resonances that reach into the themes of this chapter, that implicit racial coding informed a 2013 talk at a school in Hamilton, Ontario, by Toronto psychologist Alex Russell, coauthor of *Drop the Worry Ball: How to Parent in the Age of Entitlement* (Russell and Falconer 2014), about kids and the police. In support of his argument that children must be allowed to experience and work through anxiety, Russell cited the incident of his seventeen-year-old son's "first brush with the police" (Phillips 2013), shortly after getting his driver's licence. The point of the story was not the event itself, about which Russell does not offer many details (such as: what happened during the interaction? Were charges laid? Or was it just a "routine stop" to check his identification?), but its aftermath: after the "run-in," Russell's son "became somewhat anxious about the police and traffic laws and became a more cautious driver – a clear consequence of what Russell terms 'good anxiety'" (Phillips 2013). Among the other details conspicuously missing from the story is Russell's son's race. His whiteness can be inferred by the way that Russell (who presents as white) interprets the "brush with the police" as a fortuitous bump on the road to growing up. The story does not square with the experience of Black youth, who are routinely stopped by police for no reason, face disproportionate consequences for minor breaches of the law, and are frequently subjected to arbitrary violence (Maynard 2017, 84). In its implicit veneration of the police, Russell's anecdote describes a risk landscape that doesn't just accidentally leave out Black youth; rather, it depends on their violent containment for the preservation of white resilience.

This risk landscape is where one strand of thought about resilience and childhood ends and another picks up. Beyond the enclaves where overly attentive parents dote on too-comfortable children, the landscape of this second way of talking about resilience focuses on economic disadvantage, conflict, and family stress. A corresponding emphasis on *un*resilience is concentrated in "priority neighbourhoods" like those discussed in Toronto's resilience strategy. In this literature, poverty figures as one element in a cluster of adverse circumstances, including parental divorce and genetic vulnerability to mental illness, that are defined, as Christopher Denny and Jennifer Henderson point out, as "essentially immutable risks" against "a normative obligation to embrace individual and family responsibility for meeting those risks" (2015, 2). As in the free-range childhood resilience literature, there is stress on the role of family. But while the former calls for the removal of restrictions and regulations, the latter tends to favour various forms of voluntary and involuntary state intervention (Hoffman 2010). The other key difference between the two ways of talking about resilience and children concerns race, which rarely comes up in conversations about old-fashioned fun, which are invisibly organized around and in defence of whiteness. The at-risk child, on the other hand, is, more often than not, Black, Indigenous, or otherwise racialized (Park, Crath, and Jeffrey 2020, 4).[2]

Two resilience imaginaries, one aspirational and one monitory; one (implicitly) white, the other explicitly not. Where they converge in their approach to youth is in the moralization of life chances, which are tied, implicitly or explicitly, to race.

Articulating a space that exists in the shadows of these dominant stories about (un)resilient children, *Brother* illuminates the historical, systemic violence that presses in on Black suburban youth, along with modes of survival and flourishing that are firmly rooted in place. The story is narrated by Michael, the son of Trinidadian immigrants, growing up in Scarborough and struggling with the aftermath of the murder of his brother, Francis, by police. In contrast to the forward movement of conventional stories in which coming-of-age corresponds to the honing of resilience, Michael's narrative moves back and forth between his memory of his childhood and the present, in which he and his mother grapple with the loss of Francis. There is a tonal shift in the two different periods, between an environment of anxious striving in the early part, dominated by Michael's mother's (and in a different way, Francis's) determination to rise above their circumstances, and the atmosphere of roiling grief that follows Francis's death. Neither atmosphere is unequivocally one thing: in the childhood period, when Michael is struggling to survive in a world he increasingly understands to be inhospitable to his existence, there are also moments of discovery, friendship, and love. The potential of these moments becomes clearer in the period after Francis's death, when the drive for mobility and success gives way to feeling and reflection. A different kind of resilience is revealed in Michael's account of this period and in the construction of the novel itself. It is not a knitting together of Michael's broken self but an exploration in both theme and form of the particularities of his brokenness, its history, its pain, and its susceptibility to healing through love and creative production.

From the start, in *Brother*, Michael's family tries and conspicuously fails to live up to conventional standards of resilience. This is true even as he and Francis in some ways embody the kind of free-range childhood that some parenting experts tout (Skenazy 2009). Far from being excessively "supervised and programmed" – the supposed ills of modern parenting – the boys are mostly left to their own devices to roam around the neighbourhood, encountering the "risk, misadventure, conflict and failure" that resilience advocates deem necessary for "healthy development" (Simmonds and

White 2018, 12). But their lives, even before Francis's death, don't exactly correspond to the celebrated model of "natural" childhood. As children of a poor, Black, single mother, living in a suburb with a high concentration of poverty, recent immigrants, and racialized residents, the boys resemble much more closely the profiles of "vulnerable communities" described in Toronto's resilience strategy. In the eyes of their neighbours, the boys are not "free-range" but "feral" (Chariandy 2017a, 13), not vulnerable but sneaky and dangerous, "'hooligans' up to no good 'gallivanting,'" "oiled creatures of mongoose cunning" (13). Their mode of movement in the world doesn't correspond to the form of mobility stressed in resilience discourses, which is oriented towards recognizing and seizing "opportunity." "Opportunity" is understood to help youth "face life and its challenges" (Paterson, Tyler, and Lexmond 2014, 6) to "realise their full potential" (4).

The moral climate Michael grows up in in *Brother* is thick with these platitudes. For example, he faces constant admonitions from his boss, Manny, at the Easy Buy supermarket "about people pulling themselves up by their bootstraps and saving money and not expecting handouts. It's about attitude. It's about possessing the right mindset" (Chariandy 2017a, 2). Manny warns Michael against associating with local youth – "criminals, degenerates" (93) – and asks (rhetorically): "You ever actually think about your future?" (93). To be resilient, in the mode Manny celebrates, is to discount the present in favour of imagined prospects and to cultivate individual strength by severing ties with "degenerate" others (Black youth like him). Manny's exhortations echo those of Michael's mother, who reminds the boys at every turn of "the running challenge of what [she] called 'opportunity'" (10). She is herself a model of finding and seizing opportunity: "If a job suddenly arose in some distant part of the city but held the promise of future opportunities, or if, just as suddenly, the opportunity for time-and-a-half beckoned, she would accept the work, though it meant leaving her two young boys alone at home" (10). In addition to its orientation towards the future, a notable element of "opportunity" is its predication on mobility.

Manny attributes his own success to moving away to "what he braggingly calls the good neighbourhood of Port Junction" (Chariandy 2017a, 41–2). The Park is seen as a place of squalor and criminality, when its existence is registered at all. At night, Michael is "haunted by the sight" of darkened windows in the apartment towers: "As if through magic a whole neighbourhood had been made to disappear. As if a power existed to do such a thing" (27). The power is not just metaphorical. In the aftermath of a shooting in the neighbourhood, Michael notices that, when they are "illuminated" by the lights on a police car, "the buildings I had known all my life were changed. The stucco of a low-rise looked like the sole of an unwashed child; the rust on the balcony railings and fire exits of an apartment building looked ugly and contagious, a bubbling rash. Even the ordinary clothes that people hung to dry on laundry lines suddenly looked suspicious. Conspiracies in the open hanging of slacks and saris, in headless baby jumpers" (31). The scene demonstrates powerfully the speed with which the lens of indifference can suddenly harden into surveillance. It also shows, via the projection of impurity, disease, and criminality onto clothing and living spaces, the effects of racist geography (discussed in some detail in chapter 2). And finally, it shows Michael seeing these things, understanding and internalizing what it means to be the opposite of resilient: the embodiment of risk, a threat to the resilience of the city as a whole. In recognition of what the Park represents, Michael recalls his neighbours writing fake addresses on job applications (39), a tactic that resonates with the testimony of a "Scarborough Resident" in Toronto's resilience strategy: "Once they hear Malvern [a Scarborough neighbourhood] it's a block. I know someone that had to get a PO Box to get a job so the [employer] didn't know they lived in Malvern" (City of Toronto 2019, 59). The resilience strategy acknowledges that "the physical fabric of the city as well as the planning and design of civic infrastructure act to proliferate the current systems and structures of inequity, allowing some people to access high-income neighbourhoods, jobs and civic amenities, while keeping others out" (120). This stops short of recognizing the extent to which racism is baked into urban planning, obscuring the dynamics that lock neighbourhoods like the Park into patterns of underinvestment and overpolicing.

Racial capitalism also systematically regulates the kind of mobility that's necessary to seize "opportunity." "Opportunity" is what Christina Sharpe describes as the dream that drove millions of Black people, including her own parents (like Chariandy's parents), to move to the suburbs, as it drives millions of Black people to migrate from the South to the North in the US, and from various places in Africa and the Caribbean to the metropolitan centres of North American and Europe (2016, 3–4). Many ended up discovering, as Sharpe's parents did, "that things [are] not better in this 'new world': the subjections of constant and overt racism and isolation continued ... Precarity and more than precarity remained" (2016, 4). The Park exemplifies the geography of disappointment described by Sharpe. It is a place where "new people are always arriving ... And they often come under challenging circumstances, from the Caribbean, from South Asia and Africa and the Middle East from places like Jaffna and Mogadishu" (Chariandy 2017a, 36). But while the idea of the Toronto suburb promises, if not arrival, exactly, then at least a staging ground from which it is possible to find or make a good life, it turns out to be the opposite: a physical and metaphorical enclosure whose residents are consigned to suffer simultaneously indifference and surveillance from the rest of the city.

If a crucial part of resilience is finding a way to get by in a place that's not conducive to your thriving, then Michael's mother is in one sense a pillar of resilience. She is "one of *those* black mothers, unwilling to either seek or accept help from others. Unwilling to suffer any small blow to her sense of independence or her vision of eventual arrival" (Chariandy 2017a, 10). His use of italics signals Michael's awareness of his mother's embodiment of a stereotype that is nevertheless a source of pride,[3] at least in one sense, at least at first. When Michael worries about the effect Francis's leaving home might have on their mother, Francis reminds him, "She's strong. She's survived stuff we don't even know about" (26). The context and the costs of his mother's survival become clearer to Michael as he becomes aware of his place in the world, learning as a teenager to "spot the threat that is not only about young men with weapons, about 'gangs' and 'predators,' but also the threat that is slow and somehow very old. A mother lecturing you about arrival and opportunity while her breath stinks of the tooth she can't just for the moment afford the time or money to fix" (22). Michael's mother exemplifies what Jane Eilliott terms "suffering agency," the predicament of life under neoliberalism in which the dilemmas is not so much lack of choice as it is a compulsion to choose among different kinds of awfulness, to make "a choice that is unfairly constructed but still meaningful, imposed upon [them] but still [theirs] alone" (2013, 84). Michael's mother's determination to support herself and her family means that she has to leave her children unsupervised. In fulfilling the neoliberal ideals of self-reliance and flexibility – both understood to be essential qualities of resilience – she necessarily compromises another neoliberal ideal of family (read: maternal) responsibility. Both the context and the consequences of her choice are conditioned by racism and by the flipside of being seen as "one of *those* Black mothers" (10).

Conventional resilience studies tell us that "poor parenting" predicts a range of negative outcomes, including disruptive behaviour, low emotional adaptivity, and academic failure (Prevatt 2003, 471). And "poor parenting" is generally code for "bad mothering,"[4] a charge to which the boys' mother becomes susceptible when Francis drops out of school and leaves home. Their absent father fails in a different register. When Michael asks his mother what his father studied in school, she answers dismissively, "He *was* studying to be a man … but then the bitch dropped out" (Chariandy 2017a, 82). Alongside, and in complicated tension with, the suffering endurance Michael's mother exemplifies is a mode of conventional Black masculine resilience characterized by tough insouciance. Francis tries to instill this quality in Michael, telling him, "You've got to work on things … Like always looking so unsure. You've got to be cooler about things" (81). Francis himself is a model of confident ease, his "a name a toughened kid might boast of knowing" (8). He is so widely admired for his success with girls that it takes Michael a long time to realize that Francis is queer.[5] The elusive secret to successful masculinity is tied up for both boys in their absent father, in whose mystery lies a "special *opportunity* … Our father could be anything" (82, emphasis added). When Francis thinks he has figured out where their father lives, he takes a reluctant Michael to try and find him, chiding his brother for "not trying stuff, not believing" (83), insisting "you never know when your break is coming" (82). After they have been rebuffed by a man who may or may not have been their father, Francis says to Michael, sitting silently in the car, "Why do you always have to be such a pussy?" (87).

"Too, Too Harden"

Reflecting on the experience of boyhood that he tried to convey in *Brother*, Chariandy observes, "My sense is that, too often, in multiple ways, black people are denied childhoods. They are expected to 'toughen up' – *harden*

– quickly, are erroneously but also notably 'prematurely' read as threats and thugs and sexually active. They are oftentimes hastily treated as adults in the everyday and also, devastatingly, in the criminal justice system. For me, the concerted recollection and representation of the everyday joys specific to black childhood and youth – while vulnerable to the charge of being 'nostalgic' and definitely never a purely innocent endeavor – nevertheless works to contest a dangerous social myth of maturation" (Chariandy 2019, 2–3). We will come to the "joy" part in time. But first, it is important to explore the novel's depiction of the devastating consequences of that social myth and its connection to the idea of resilience.

By many of the conventional measures of masculine resilience – toughness, confidence, optimism, and the willingness to seize opportunity – Michael is a failure. Francis is a failure, too, but in a different way. Like Michael, he is put into the "basic" stream at school, in spite of being a proficient reader and writer (Chariandy 2017a, 24). After telling a teacher to fuck off, he leaves school, never to return (24), throwing away, in his mother's words, "your one and only chance" (24). His imperviousness to education confirms his mother's worries about a "lack of ... plain civilization" in Francis (24). Using Trinidadian creole to name her gravest concerns, she reads lapses of manners – "a spot of food on our shirts or a crust of toothpaste around our mouths" (165) – as signs of fatal intractability, shouting: "You all is *harden*! Too too *harden*" (165). In Trinidadian, "harden" is an adjective that refers to stubbornness and disobedience. "'Harden,'" as Mark V. Campbell explains it, "captures in one succinct term the impact of antiblackness on Caribbean youth in diasporic homes ... Francis is harden. Michael is not harden enough. And their mother laments their hardening – yet she herself is harden" (2019, 1). The concept of "harden" resonates strongly with the ways resilience discourse both interpellates and excludes Black people, especially Black youth. Together with the other fear voiced by his mother, that Francis lacks civilization, "harden" evokes the myth of young Black male invulnerability – the dark side of "grit," which is a staple ingredient in dominant understandings of psychosocial resilience. While Francis's mother's optimism for what education would give him might have been overblown, her anxiety that his exclusion from one institution foretold his violent capture by another – a fatally foreshortened version of the "school-to-prison pipeline" (Maynard 2017, 220) – was well placed. And her worries that he is "harden" – or, maybe even worse, that he is *seen*, as a Black teenager, to be "harden" – are legitimate.

As chapter 1 noted, the rollout of resilience programming in schools highlights a racist tangle of ideas about the character trait of "grit." This racism plays out in the stark difference between programs for affluent white students who are seen to be deficient in grit but successful in every other measure and those designed for poor, racialized students who are thought to have grit in abundance but insufficient discipline and self-control. A private school featured in Paul Tough's book on resilience education (2012) employs a flexible approach to discipline, reasoning that, as the guidance counsellor explains, definitions of self-control need to be calibrated to school populations: "If you're showing self-control at [the predominantly Black and Latinx Bronx middle school], for example, you sit up straight and you track the teachers," she explained. At the private school, by contrast, "you can sit in a ball in your chair and no one cares. We don't care if you lie on the floor" (89). She continues: "It's almost like, we assume our kids already have manners here, so if they need to sit funny in their chair, that's okay. Whereas at [the Bronx middle school], it's like, No, no, no, everyone has to conform, because the conformity is supposed to help them succeed" (90). In this example, described uncritically by Tough, Black and other racialized students are cast as simultaneously too resilient and not resilient enough – a contradiction that matters in the face of the broader belief that having just the right amount of grit or resilience is an index not only of adaptability but of evolutionary fitness.

This belief, racist at its core, has a long history. Nineteenth-century racial science is riddled with assumptions about essential physiological differences, including assertions that Black people's "thicker skulls" and "less sensitive nervous systems" made them impervious to pain – myths that justified both slavery and inhumane medical treatment, including covert experiments (Hoffman et al. 2015, 3). Beliefs that "the black body is biologically different – and in many cases stronger – than the white body" (Hoffman et al. 2015, 2) flourished alongside beliefs about their relative *in*capacity in other registers of fitness. For example, until well into the twenty-first century, physicians using a spirometer were trained to use a different set of metrics for Black patients based on the belief in a *natural* deficiency in Black lung capacity (Braun 2014).[6] These beliefs – that Black people are essentially stronger *and* weaker than white people – inform contemporary studies, such as the one that finds that Black Americans experience better mental health than white Americans in spite of "higher levels of exposure to a wide range of stressors" and greater morbidity in general (Assari and Lankarani 2016, 350). The finding that "although white Americans are, on average, the 'healthiest group,' they are also, on average, far less 'resilient' than black Americans" and the corollary observation that "it seems that vulnerability is a cost of privilege, and resilience comes as a result of adversity" rests on a bizarre separation of resilience and health. The idea that, as one scholar breezily puts it, "What does not kill you makes you stronger" (Assari 2016) – at least when "you" are Black – supports the continued withholding of health care from Black people, ranging from the undertreatment of pain to substandard pre- and postnatal care for Black mothers and babies (Knox et al. 2000' Nelson 2002; Freedman et al. 2020; Liu et al. 2019).

That idea also plays out in brutal ways in policing. The excessive resilience or "grit" projected onto Black people warrants violent intervention. Simultaneously, their failure to be resilient enough, whether measured in a lack of "vital capacity" represented in lung function or by the absence of will required to seize opportunities, normalizes their premature death (even or maybe especially when that death occurs in the course of a well-intentioned violent intervention, understood as part of the risk management necessary to sustain community resilience). The incoherent stew of beliefs about Black (un)resilience converge around a fundamental tenet of racism: that Black people are less than human. Dehumanization offers a pretext for "moral exclusion" (Goff et al. 2014, 527), which provides the ultimate justification for the killing of unarmed Black people by police.[7] This formula does not spare Black children; routinely perceived as both older and "less innocent" than their white peers (Maynard 2017, 210; Goff et al. 2014, 529, 532), they are seen to merit the withdrawal of the basic protections usually afforded to children and subjected to harsh discipline (528).

The labels applied to Michael and Francis in *Brother* – "feral children," "oiled creatures of mongoose cunning" (Chariandy 2017a, 13), then later, "thug youths ... Predators. *Criminals*" (50), carry the insinuation of animality and an invincibility bordering on dangerousness. The process of dehumanization is at work in media coverage of the shooting death of Anton, a small-time drug dealer in the neighbourhood, in an altercation with some other youth. Anton, pictured in "one of those high school photos that for so many of us always seem to go wrong" (73), is identified in the news simply as "both known to police and deceased" (73). The two descriptors buttress each other: because he was "known to police," Anton's death is not surprising, maybe even expected, maybe even deserved. It is therefore not surprising when, later, in the police interview following Francis's murder, Michael is asked, "Would you agree that Francis had a bit of a reputation? Did he sometimes exhibit unpredictable moods? Would you agree, Michael, that your brother possessed a history of violence?" (169).

Being asked to implicate his brother in a pattern, not of criminality per se, but of disordered affect and orientation to the world is a variation on the imperative in resilience thinking to psychosocial surveillance.[8] Contained in both institutional settings like school and extra-institutional resilience discourses like the narrative of opportunity that depends on "possessing the right *mind set*" (Chariandy 2017a, 42, italics in original), is a mandate for self-monitoring, a complement to the external interventions aimed at "at-risk" youth.[9] The mandate and the implications of self-scrutiny are particularly heavy and particularly harmful for Black youth, who are obliged minutely to monitor and manage their conduct within a framework that defines them as always-already lacking. *Brother* illuminates this process clearly through Michael's recollection of how he and Francis learned from an early age to read their own bodies through the lens of racism, as when they look into a newspaper box "to read a headline about the latest terror and ca[tch] in the glass the reflection of our own faces" (16). The boys are manifestly not, like the youth described in chapter 1 or imagined in Alex Russell's story about the fortuitous "brush with police," riding a "powerful wave of entitlement – entitlement to life, entitlement to health and entitlement to complete safety" (Russell and Falconer 2014, 34), which compromises their development of resilience. In fact, they are manifestly *unsafe*, not because they are excluded from the dominant resilience narrative but because of the complicated ways they are interpellated and demonized by it.

Michael explains the aura of fear that pervades their childhood: "What scares two boys aged ten and eleven? Sometimes, in the midst of our play, a siren would cut the air and cars with flashing lights would brake screeching on the avenue, a neighbourhood kid soon cuffed on the sidewalk, his face turned away from us in shame" (Chariandy 2017a, 16). The scene of the boy on the ground conjures not only the many ways that Michael and Francis could be considered "at risk" – of poverty, crime/criminalization, and violence, including police violence – but also the way that all of those risks are shot through with shame. If resilience describes the possibility of self-preservation in a landscape of danger, it founders on the racist contradiction that, for children like Francis and Michael, the danger they are taught to fear is themselves. This message pervades the security footage replayed in the media following a violent convenience store robbery in their neighbourhood, which depicts "murder reduced to three indistinguishable dark faces, haunting the city" (150). It also haunts their trip to the mall the day after the convenience store shooting, when they are hassled by security guards and assaulted by a group of white boys. That night, when neither of them can sleep, Francis leads Michael to his mother's room and tells her "He's afraid" (154). She asks what he is afraid of:

> "I don't know. Maybe the black murderers."
> "The … *who*?"
> "The murderers. In the news. The black men …"
> She closed her eyes, pressed her temples. She recovered. "The *criminals*, Francis. The criminals will be caught by the police and punished. They do not stand a chance. Please try to understand. We're very lucky here. We're very safe."
> "He doesn't believe we're very safe."
> "We *are*, Francis."
> "We're not. We never were." (155)

These events crystallize Michael's recognition that he lives in a dangerous world. The danger is located not in the murderers but the "*black* murderers" (155, emphasis added). The feeling follows them everywhere: "You caught in the eyes of strangers the suspicion or outright fear. You sensed the halo of menace above your head, glimpsed the turbulence swirling behind as you walked" (98). Both in and of the turbulence, Black youth become the targets of police violence.

Complicated Grief

The tendency for the idea of resilience to arise in connection with youth is connected to its orientation towards the future. Resilience, or the ability to stay afloat amidst the turbulence, matters because it seems to promise survival and even growth through dangerous times. Its affective dimension is hope, which might be better described in the world of *Brother* as what Lauren Berlant (2011) calls "cruel optimism." Even as they are manifestly excluded from its promise and, worse than that, cast in the role of threat to its realization, as a risk to the resilience of their community, Michael and Francis are caught up in its pull. The pressure to move forward remains even after Francis's death. Michael explains, "I've kept to a minimum all discomforting talk about the past. I've given away things belonging to Francis that might remind and disturb" (33). He does so in the hopes that it will give him and his mother "both the time and space to reckon with loss" (33). In understanding loss as something to be reckoned with, Michael understands mourning to be a process of settling up accounts, after which it will be possible to move forward. Ten years after Francis's death, he believes that his mother is well on her way in that process. Recalling that she was unable to work at first, he notes approvingly that "in the past couple years she's grown increasingly independent," offering "proof that those who have suffered enormous loss can also endure" (34). The ideal of resilience survives even Francis's murder.

At least it looks that way, until Michael's friend, Aisha, who has come home to the Park to mourn the death of her own father, implores him to look again at his mother: "You know she's not well, right, Michael? The way she drifts. The way she wanders. Yesterday, when you were at work, we were talking about the old neighbours, and she excused herself to start searching for something she couldn't describe to me. She ended up wandering outside, still searching. I watched her cross the avenue without even looking. I had to shout for her to turn and wait" (Chariandy 2017a, 65). His mother is like this, Aisha tells Michael, "because she's still mourning. Or else she's unable to mourn. It's been ten years and she still can't accept. She's stuck" (65). "Complicated grief" (175) is the name Michael has learned from doctors to describe this condition in which a person is "mire[d] in mourning, ... prevent[ing] them from moving forward by making sense of the past" (66). Complicated grief affects movement both literally and metaphorically. It is clearly implicated in the accident in which Michael's mother wanders into traffic and is hit by a car. The collision (like the police bullet that killed Francis) is not an isolated blow – the kind to which resilience is meant to inure a person; rather, it is a concentration of circumstances: of exhausted, maybe even suicidal grief; of an urban environment that favours automobility and speed; and of the racist geography of the city that limited housing options for Michael's family to an arterial road, "exposed to the constant hiss of tires on asphalt" (5).

Many things come together in this moment so that, when a nurse at the hospital asks Michael for some background information, Michael struggles for words. She encourages him: "I know it's a lot to process at once. Let's just start from the beginning" (138). The directive to "just start from the beginning" is one of several rhetorical devices in the novel that reminds us that this is a narrative, subject, like all narratives, to conventions of storytelling. The conventions of the personal resilience narrative, evident, for example, in the *Resilient People* videos referenced in Toronto's resilience strategy (City of Toronto 2019), locate the beginning in the risk landscape of childhood, out of which the protagonist carves a self-determined path in search of opportunity. *Brother*'s departure from, its explicit resistance to, this trajectory is evident in the way it responds to the cue to "start from the beginning," which comes at the end of chapter 5. Chapter 6 begins in this way: "Once, when we were very young, Mother took us back to the place where she was born" (Chariandy 2017a, 139). In Trinidad, the boys have glimpses of the world of their mother's childhood, the sense of community, the poverty, and the segregation of white tourists from the locals. They also intuit another reality that lies beneath this life and their lives back in Scarborough. On the first night, Michael recalls, "I remember feeling afraid, though of what I did not know. Something old and unburied in the darkness, something closer to us now than ever before. I remember lying awake with Francis and hearing for the first time the scream of a rooster, my brother's hand pressed hard in mine" (142–3). Only much later does Michael gain some insight into the source of the fear, in the history of slavery and indenture (143). That history – barely traceable in the modern landscape of abandoned cane fields, the airport, and white-sand beaches reserved for tourists and the small, rocky beach he visits with his mother's family, still polluted by an oil spill from years ago – becomes part of the story of Francis's death and Michael and his mother's struggle to recover from it. It provides the contours of a narrative of finding resilience "in the wake" (Sharpe 2016).

Living "in the wake" in Sharpe's formulation describes a Black project of learning "to survive (and more) the afterlife of property," of finding "a mode of inhabiting and rupturing this episteme with our known lived and un/imaginable lives" (Sharpe 2016, 18). In *In the Wake*, slavery is the backdrop against which Sharpe memorializes the individual deaths of Black people, her own family members as well as those of well-known murder victims such as Trayvon Martin and Michael Brown, while also tracing the broad landscape of Black mortality. "The wake" has multiple valences in this remembering, ranging from the word's most obvious association with the aftermath of a death – "*Wake: a watch or vigil held beside the body of someone who has died, sometimes accompanied by ritual observances including eating and drinking*" (10, italics in original) – to a more generalized historical conjuncture defined by environmental disturbance: "*Wake: the track left on the water's surface by a ship; the disturbance caused by a body swimming or moved, in water; it is the air currents behind a body in flight; a region of disturbed flow*" (3, italics in original). This meaning evokes not just the slave ships but also the disrupted hydrological, meteorological, and geographical systems that Black bodies continue to navigate.

Framing the directive to "just start at the beginning" within the forcefield of the wake unsettles psychosocial resilience narratives by locating "the beginning" beyond and prior to the individual biography, beyond Michael's story, beyond even his mother's story. It also challenges the systems thinking that informs urban resilience discourse, which is particularly concerned with the "shocks" and "stresses" of climate change (City of Toronto 2018, 91). The metaphor of the wake connotes not just the idea of the aftermath of an event but also its materiality: the wake is a physical medium, a disruption in a current through which bodies struggle or flow. It works alongside, in connection with, the more concrete metaphors in Sharpe's book – "the ship" and "the hold" – as well as the more diffuse but no less substantial metaphor of "weather," whose meaning Sharpe extends to encompass "the totality of our environments; the weather is the total climate; and that climate is antiblack" (104).[10]

Though it isn't coded in any obvious way as a climate change novel, the weather is an insistent presence in *Brother*, encompassing a collection of forces that vary in intensity but are frequently inhospitable and even inimical to life. When Michael meets Aisha on a winter's night, ten years after Francis's death, her first comment to him is, "You're not dressed for this weather" (Chariandy 2017a, 3). The issue of insufficient protection from weather comes to assume a larger significance as "bullets of slush" hit the windows of Michael's house while he, Aisha, and his mother are sleeping (7), recalling the instance from his childhood when lies awake, haunted by images "of those wanted men, their formless dark faces. Outside the trees were clawed with ice and the wind blew and rattled the window and brushed sleet on the panes" (154). The harshness of the winter is matched by the fierceness of summer in which heat is a "physical oppression from which none could escape. Nature carrying on like the sort of thug you only hear about" (25). It would show up in the morning, Michael recalls, as "a menacing red haze. By the afternoon it was a syrup misery in the air, suffocating your will, making even breathing difficult. Even at night there was no relief, and the heat cooked up all day within our homes made staying there unbearable" (25). The tension is not just metaphorical but metonymical, the excruciating heat contributing to the tension that enwraps the neighbourhood. On the morning after a night of violence, "the temperature ... rising by the minute" (50), the menace pervades the bus stop where the boys are waiting alongside "[women] in cleaning uniforms, men in thick jeans and safety boots, everyone's clothes already darkening with sweat around necks and underarms" (49). The racist insults directed at the boys combine with the heat that is "carrying on like [a] ... thug" (25) to produce in Michael a "deep-gut sickness, dizziness" (50). His experience illuminates the concrete, physical precarity of life in an anti-Black climate, "living in and with terror" such that "Black people become the carriers of terror, terror's embodiment, and not the primary objects of terror's multiple enactments" (Sharpe 2016, 15).

One place in the novel that offers physical and mental respite from the heat is the library, in whose "air-conditioned cool" (58) Michael and Aisha's friendship begins. There are different ways of looking at the library in a novel that evokes so strongly the history of colonialism. One is to see it as an apparatus of the state, whose air conditioning (which, of course, as it makes the weather more bearable, will contribute to making the climate worse) signals its segregation from the world, a division that's heightened by the presence of a metal detector on the way in. But it is also a public space, for rest, and for chance encounters that turn into friendships. It is a place of refuge, where Michael goes when there's nowhere else to go,[11] and for learning to read the world differently than the way it has been read. Learning to read and interpret the world points to another meaning of "wake" relating to the stirring of consciousness (Sharpe 2016, 4), a recognition of dynamics that have driven, that continue to drive, premature and often violent Black deaths, as well as the celebration of "the largeness that is Black life, Black life insisted from death" (17). Drawing the different definitions of "wake" together, Sharpe explains that she wants "to think and argue for one aspect of Black being in the wake as consciousness and to propose that to be in the wake is to occupy and be occupied by the continuous and changing present of slavery's as yet unresolved unfolding" (14). Consciousness obviously refers to one connotation of the word "wake"/"woke," but it also refers to the consciousness Sharpe brings to the word itself, to the significance of the work of metaphor, employed deliberately and self-reflexively, to illuminate what cannot otherwise be seen. Thus, in addition to interrogating "current quotidian disasters in order to ask what, if anything, survives this insistent Black exclusion, this ontological negation," Sharpe's project is interested in how creative work, including literature, "observe[s] and mediate[s] the modes of 'un/survival' that emerge in the wake" (14). What does it mean to think about *Brother* in this vein, as an observation and mediation of "un/survival" that is conscious of its own status as art?

The first part of this chapter reads *Brother* as a story about the inability of Black youth to become resilient. Put differently, it describes *Brother*'s illustration of the failure of conventional ideas of resilience adequately to convey the dangers and possibilities of young Black lives. This failure is not merely incidental, the novel shows, as the qualities associated with the dominant view of resilience – an optimistic orientation to the future, self-control, a facility for intelligent risk-taking – are associated with the reproduction of white, neoliberal society. That society "produces and requires Black exclusion and death as normative" (James and Costa Vargas, quoted in Sharpe 2016, 7). The language of resilience forms a support structure around that bio- and necropolitical process: Black people die because they are not resilient (i.e., they lack fitness) and/or Black people die because they are *too* resilient (i.e., they are wild forces of nature that need to be violently suppressed). Another way of reading *Brother* is as a story about how Black youth can make lives in spite of the mandate for their death. It is a story about finding and fashioning resilience against the dominant model in which white thriving is premised on Black abjection. This version of resilience is animated by memory and grief, by intergenerational collectivity, by a felt connection to the more-than-human world, and a mode of consciousness that is part critical literacy, part creativity.

To "occupy and be occupied by the continuous and changing present of slavery's as yet unresolved unfolding" (Sharpe 2016, 14) is an act of memory, a combination of grieving the lives of the recently dead and becoming conscious of the history that gives shape to the present loss, not in the manner of linear cause and effect but of continuous inhabitation. Wake work is akin to the mode of reckoning with loss that David L. Eng and David Kazanjian connect both to Freudian melancholia and to Walter Benjamin's mode of historical materialism – a mode of mourning that is distinctly different from the left melancholia that is the subject of chapter 2. Melancholia, in their account, "might be said to constitute, as Benjamin would describe it, an ongoing and open relationship with the past – bringing its ghosts and specters, its flaring and fleeting images, into the present" (2003, 3–4). This process performs a kind of political work to the extent that "the past is brought to bear witness to the present – as a flash of emergence, an instant of emergency, and a moment of production" (5). It's an emergency in the plain sense of the word, when Michael's mother is hit by the car and ends up in the ER, that precipitates the flashback, the trip to her birthplace in Trinidad that brought Michael up against "something old and unburied in the darkness" (Chariandy 2017a, 142) that he only later learns to give a name to. The traces of what Sharpe describes as "slavery's as yet unresolved unfolding" (14) are present in the deliberate violence that killed Francis and also in the accidental violence that befell his mother in a neighbourhood where Black and Brown workers, the labour force of the city, precariously, separately, reside (5). The diagnosis of "complicated grief" (175) Michael's mother is given is focalized on her son's death but not reducible to it. Reckoning with that irreducibility is the substance of the novel, part of its wake work.

Place, Ecology, and Belonging

Tied to the polyvalence of the metaphor, the multiscalar dimension of wake work means that the reckoning isn't just historical, coming to terms with the past, but also geographical. Michael's childhood visit to Trinidad affords him a glimpse into the past that has shaped his family life; it also enlarges his understanding of the place he comes from. In Trinidad he sees not just history, but also contemporary connections to the geographies that segregate Black life in Scarborough.[12] Recognizing those geographies entails a form of awakening that changes Michael's relationship to his environment. Analyzing oppressive geographies works to denaturalize them, as Katherine McKittrick has shown, "mak[ing] visible social lives which are often displaced, rendered ungeographic" (2006, x). Highlighting the active process of place- and space-making – including local forms of inhabitation, knowledge, and representation that have been eclipsed by colonialism – exerts a resistant force; "openings are made possible for envisioning an interpretive alterable world rather than a transparent and knowable world" (xiii). This practice of critical geography, of learning to recognize, and then to *un*read, the ways of seeing that underlie Black subjugation, finds expression in Michael's story. But even as the novel champions critical awareness and attention to historical and geographical details obscured by dominant understandings of the present, it also documents the impossibility of mastery, based on the inescapability of circumstance (and concurrent vulnerability to danger) alongside the bonds of kin and friendship that are bound up with place.

Against the image of a neighbourhood illuminated by the lights of a police car, which makes the things of everyday life – laundry on a clothesline, rust on a railing – look malignant (Chariandy 2017a, 31), *Brother* explores through Michael's narrative the places where life happens, places of momentary solace and belonging, where vulnerability coexists with possibilities for flourishing. One such place is Desirea's barbershop, where Francis hangs out with his friends. Desirea's is where they go after he is beaten up and also the place where, shortly afterwards, the police arrive and shoot him. Just before the shooting, Michael recalls surveying the group and making the following recognition: "We were losers and neighbourhood schemers. We were the children of the help, without futures. We were, none of us, what our parents wanted us to be. We were not what any other adults wanted us to be. We were nobodies, or else, somehow, a city" (Chariandy 2017a, 157).

In highlighting the places where Black youths congregate – places of sanctuary that are also places of risk (and places of risk *because* they offer sanctuary for Black youth), *Brother* makes visible not just the lines of racial geography but the relations and processes through which it is generated – and, maybe, re- or degenerated.[13] Seen from the perspective of the "unitary vantage point" of the dominant society (McKittrick 2006, x), which Michael's mother and boss both strive to adopt, Desirea's is a hangout for "*lowlifes*" (Chariandy 2017a, 92, italics in original), "criminals," "degenerates" (93), and "boys known to police" (24). For Francis and his friends, it is something else: "In Desirea's, you postured but you also played. You showed up every one of your dictated roles and fates … in Desirea's different styles and kinships were possible. You found new language, you caught the gestures, you kept the meanings close as skin" (101). Skin is the membrane between private and public life, inflamed by race but also the site of connection and desire, especially as they are expressed in the intimacy between Francis and Jelly that Michael sees for the first time at Desirea's. The multivalence of "skin" extends to the novel's title, *Brother*, whose most obvious reference is to Francis, his childhood bond with Michael expressed in "the shoulder pressed against me bare and warm, that body always just a skin away" (8). As Michael Bucknor highlights (2019), *Brother* also insistently highlights bonds of Black male homosocial connection that the conventional model of resilience (white, heteronormative, individual-focused) suppresses.

Belonging in *Brother* extends from human to more-than-human connectedness. It is not natural, in the sense advocated by outdoor resilience enthusiasts, but it is ecological, in a way that Sharpe's work elucidates through her discussion of weather. As "the atmospheric condition of time and place," the weather, in Sharpe's analysis, "produces new ecologies. *Ecology: the branch of biology that deals with the relations of organisms to one another and to their physical surroundings; the political movement that seeks to protect the environment, especially from pollution*" (2016, 106, italics in original). This conception of ecology differs markedly from the "nature" that is associated with childhood resilience as discussed in chapter 1. Resilience in that latter sense is understood to emerge in the course of "natural" development, defined as a relatively unrestricted engagement with the world. To the extent that this engagement involves periodic confrontation with, and successful management of, risk and surprise, it is seen to strengthen evolutionary fitness. Following from the first point, which emphasizes the value of self-direction outside the bounds of parental, state, or technological regulation, resilience is associated with the experience of being outdoors, connected to the "natural" world. Thought together, both resonances of "nature" combine to describe a sense of security and ease of movement through the world. This could involve wilderness camping or it might just take the form of messing around on a yoga ball (the privilege that is extended to the white students of the prep school described by Tough [2012] while their Black students learn to sit up straight and track the teacher). The ecological approach Sharpe takes, also evident in *Brother*, dispels the myth of nature – an undifferentiated zone of freedom and belonging – in favour of a nuanced exploration of relationships, including the networks, flows, and blockages that sustain white dominance.

Like the human inhabitants of the Park, the plants and animals who live there, and even its geological formations, have been subject to abuse and neglect; they also find ways of thriving. The Rouge Valley is "a wound in the earth. A scar of green running through our neighbourhood, hundreds of feet deep in some places, a glacial valley that existed long before anything called Scarborough" (Chariandy 2017a, 18–19). The valley not only preexists human geography, it also confounds it, "cutting its own way through the suburb, heedless of manmade grids" (5). And it serves as home and habitat; as Michael explains: "The Rouge was not 'nature,' not that untouched land you could watch on wildlife shows or read about in history books. The Rouge wasn't the sort of place you could pretend to have discovered, nor imagine empty and now your own. But it was the place we knew, and the place, even as we grew older, we kept returning to (20).[14] The Rouge provides sustenance of a different sort than that described by the back-to-nature, old-fashioned fun advocates described in chapter 1, as illustrated in a passage that is worth quoting at length. "When we were very young," Michael recalls:

> we'd build forts and hideaways in the brush, using branches but also cardboard and broken pieces of furniture occasionally dumped here. We'd race twigs in the creek, spot the little speckled fish swimming together in the blowing current, hunt for the other small lives that had managed to survive in the park unnoticed. The tracks in the mud of a muskrat or a racoon or maybe a turtle. One summer we used a stick to corner a crayfish, blue-red and mottled, and Francis explained shiveringly how it grew by cracking its own body open. One fall we piled the stuff of this land over our bodies like blankets. Coloured leaves and pine needles, branches and the barbed wire of thistles. Also plastic bags and foil drifting down from the fast-food joints above. Our hair camouflaged with mashed drinking straws and rushes. Our faces already the colour of earth. (19)

Several features of this scene are crucial to the ecology *Brother* illuminates and the kind of resilience it thereby imagines. First, it features the integration of organic life (branches, fish, muskrats, and crayfish) and inorganic matter (cardboard, broken furniture, plastic bags, and foil) – garbage in fact – all of which is subject to the "blowing current." Second, it highlights the vulnerability of the lives in the valley who, like the boys, strive to "survive ... unnoticed" (19) and are subject to random violence. The crayfish cracking its body open signals the potential for life to emerge out of brokenness. Finally, the image of the boys buried in leaves and trash, their faces "already the colour of earth" (19), signals their dehumanization, the condition of dispossession that links them and the detritus (living and nonliving) of urban life, but also the possibility that, in this place of rejection, they can find comfort and solidarity.

As noted in chapter 1, the naturalness of nature is produced and maintained by the displacement of Indigenous people and the exclusion of Black people and people of colour. Black Caribbean immigrants experience a double alienation from the physical environment: estranged from the land of their origins by the brutality of colonialism, which broke both land and people and determined that the only bond that could form between them was defined by forced labour, they are also barred by racism (and transportation) from forming a connection to wild nature in their new homes. In

Brother, Chariandy describes the experience of making a home not so much *in* as *with* nature, recalling the process Dionne Brand describes in *Land to Light On* (1997) and *thirsty* (2002) that Cheryl Lousley describes as "claiming ... place while resisting territorialization" (2015, 50). Brand's poetry, Lousley suggests, "intertwines diasporic experience and the plight of nature" (51), finding relation between the conditions of not-at-homeness and a physical world that is suffering, degraded, yet still beautiful and worthy of love. *Brother* articulates similar connections, focalized around Michael's mother, who was the brothers' first guide to the valley: "Always, for our mother, there was the hidden life to point out for us in the Rouge. The monarchs she explained had crossed whole lands to be here" (Chariandy 2017a, 148). The emphasis on "hidden life" insists that the butterflies in the valley are not just metaphors for migrating humans but fellow travellers and potential allies. Michael's questions about his mother's relationship to nature – "What was the hope or philosophy in these excursions? What is a mother's dream of land?" (148) – gesture, perhaps explicitly, to the same complexity Brand describes in *Land to Light On* (1997) and *Map to the Door of No Return* (2001) wherein the speaker grapples, against a history of displacement both symbolic and literal, to find sustenance in a new dwelling place. Attending to nonhuman lives in the Rouge with gentleness and curiosity might be the kind of resistant placemaking McKittrick describes in which the inhabitants of a place undo the geographies of colonialism and capitalism, "envisioning an interpretive alterable world rather than a transparent and knowable world" (2006, xiii).

This mode of being with more-than-human others also defies the dominant temporality of opportunistic, risk-laden futurity by following a different set of rhythms: as Michael recalls, "We'd spend whole seasons of time down there" (Chariandy 2017a, 147). These rhythms inform the healing power of the valley. It is where Michael's mother goes when she is beside herself with grief, where Michael finds her clutching a bunch of blue flowers "an unnameable pretty colour. Singular" (68) – the same flowers (forget-me-nots) that Aisha later brings to her in the hospital following her car accident (176). It is also the place where, after Michael's mother is released from the hospital, the three of them go with Francis's friends, a place for mourning and new collective possibility.

"As If with New Ears"

The generation of a sustaining relationship with the life of the Rouge Valley does not come about naturally; it is a process of learning how to read it. For example, Michael's mother draws the boys' attention to moths that look like little bits of paper: "A scattered and wasted alphabet. Without any meaning at all ... 'But look closer,' she said, eyes still closed. 'Cup your hand and feel the proof of them against you. They're not trash. They're living things. And they're flying'" (149). In this moment, the contrasting meanings – trash vs. living things – corresponds to different modalities of reading: traditional, alphabetic textual reading and another more sensuous form of paying attention. Mastery of the first, conventionally recognized form of literacy proves vital to the boys' capacity to decipher the codes that shape their lives (even if it doesn't gain them entry into the academic stream at school); however, its limitations as a tool of resilience emerge in a scene where Francis, who is just learning to read, looks at the newspaper the day after the convenience store murder and robbery. As he studies the words that accompany the newspaper images of the faces of the three Black suspects, Francis begins to understand "what is executed every day in language" (150).

The use of a metaphor that manages to combine both violence and the aura of official decree highlights the determinative force of words, as well as their limited value for sense-making or survival. The treachery of words changes (if it doesn't totally undermine) the significance of learning to read; it also adds a layer of complication to memory as a form of self-preservation. Not simply a matter of bringing to light a history that is customarily suppressed, the act of decolonial, antiracist "memorying" requires illuminating, highlighting, and reworking the forms (words, tropes, narratives, styles) through which memory appears. In this process, the line between memory and creation blurs; there is a sense in which the two movements are interdependent. The structure of the novel highlights this interdependence. It complicates the dominant conception of resilience by challenging the conventions of time and subjectivity on which it rests. The narrative proceeds via movement back and forth between the present (rendered in the present tense) and the boys' childhood, leading up to the moment of Francis's death. In this way, the present is never fully or only the present but saturated with history. The temporal rhythm of the story also complicates the progressive development of the narrator, who both is and is not the story's protagonist; as the title suggests, the narrative is less a *bildungsroman*, in the sense of a conventional coming-of-age novel, than it is a "reclamation, preservation, and remembrance" of place (McKittrick and Woods 2007, 5) and a "gathering," to use Aisha's words, that draws together Michael's immediate family, their Caribbean relatives, friends, and the more-than-human denizens of the Rouge Valley (Chariandy 2017a, 64). "Not trash. They're living things. And they're flying."

The movement of the novel to revive and transform "what is executed every day in language" echoes another mode of resignification rooted in Black history and instrumental to Black resilience (150). Life in Desirea's barbershop revolves around the turntables on which Francis's boyfriend, Jelly, mixes music. The centrality of this activity to the lives of the boys in the novel reflects the vital place of DJing, and hip-hop more generally, in contemporary Black culture. In Katherine McKittrick's words, "Loving and sharing and hearing and listening and grooving to black music is a rebellious political act that is entwined with neurological pleasure and the melodic pronouncement of black life" (2016, 81). Jelly's DJing recalls the music of the past, not to nostalgically return to a sound of imagined purity but to make the past live in the present, a mode of simultaneous grounding and defamiliarization: the boys "heard, as if with new ears, the music of our parents, the lost arts of funk especially, but also ska and soul, blues and jazz ... We listened patiently to Satchmo and Aretha Franklin, Marley and Harry Belafonte, stuff too sweetly familiar from TV commercials and movie soundtracks. But Francis and Jelly stole it all back for us, the dead and the living, made it ours to listen to (Chariandy 2017a, 102–3). The turntable becomes Jelly's accomplice in a practice of restoration and unauthorized resignification, of creation and revolt. Jelly's name evokes the art of the West African *djeli*, "as in a griot. A storyteller with memory" (111);[15] he is also, as his friend Raj puts it, a "*metaphysician*" (103, italics in original) who both illuminates and messes with the nature of reality. In this sense, he performs what music critic and DJ Mark Campbell suggests may be the critical "role of the DJ in our lives" – that of "br[inging] together, into new relationships, those things we previously imagined to be separate" (2019, 1).

Jelly's art works alchemically in the novel, "overla[ying] voices on top of one another, mess[ing] with time, and ma[king] a man sound like a woman and a woman like a man, the truer feeling and meaning of a song suddenly emerging through the work of his hands" (Chariandy 2017a, 127). Through this creative labour, the categories that violently contain and separate the boys' world come undone, unleashing moments of possibility and mobility. Writing about the role of music in *Brother* specifically, Campbell highlights the importance of remixes as "intergenerational, genre-defying sonic innovations that disrupt copyright regimes and put nostalgia and familiarity to work in the excavation and reimagining of buried sonic subjectivities" (2019, 2). Their movement momentarily interrupts the individualistic and forward-looking thrust of the narratives of opportunity and resilience that permeate the world outside the barbershop.

Music is an accompaniment to and a vehicle for Francis and Jelly's love. Michael describes the scene: "I saw Francis sitting next to Jelly as his man switched up the music, knitting together two completely different tracks, old and new, Caribbean and American and now African soul, and then a cheer rising from the crowd. Francis calling out 'Volume!' and others joining the call ... Every voice in the place together. *Volume!*" (Chariandy 2017a, 114–15). The power of the music is, significantly, not just emotional or even, in its amplification, political. "As a culture," Campbell argues, "hip hop expresses a holistic modality; it is invested in stimulating and engaging all the human senses ... it is also dispersed across a number of life's spheres. The oral, sonic, visual and physical are ways in which hip hop engages the human and operates to refute the foundational mind/body split in Eurocentric thought" (2015, 4). In *Brother*, this refutation facilitates a rebellion against "what is executed every day in language" (Chariandy 2017a, 150): the codes that determine who counts as human and which lives must be sacrificed to preserve the current social order. But music also goes beyond this deconstructive function to offer a mode of living on and living differently.[16] It arguably represents the surest movement in the novel towards a mode of Black resilience. This role is consistent with what McKittrick, drawing on Sylvia Wynter's unpublished manuscript *Black Metamorphosis*, describes as an "affirmation of black life [that] includes, but is not restricted to, the repurposing of multiethnic traces and phantasies – not as vestiges of nostalgic idealization but as adaptive social innovations" (2016, 84). It is not only that record collections provide what Brian Cross describes as "soundtracks for urban survival" (1993, 64); more than this, as Paul Miller/Dj Spooky puts it, "It's music that says 'there could be another way'" (2004, 20).

Music's power in the novel – and its limitations – lie not only in the sound and listening experience but also in the broader conditions of its production. As one of the boys, nicknamed the Professa, explains, rap has gone mainstream and, in the process, "suddenly all ears were on MCs. In the moneyed rush for the next big voice, the DJ was abandoned, his work onstage easily replaced by pre-recorded tracks and engineers working in studios. But as a result, something else became possible. The DJ, now fired from his day job as backup for the mike, was free to return to the origins, to the *materials* ... a new generation of innovators was left to experiment on their own" (Chariandy 2017a, 102). DJing becomes an instrument of cultural resilience in which exclusion facilitates new forms of attention and creativity and disenfranchisement becomes a source of unexpected opportunity. But the power of DJing (and art more generally) as an instrument of emancipation is precarious, as the events preceding Francis's shooting demonstrate. Following months of preparation, the boys show up at an audition for a possible record deal with a hip-hop producer where they wait in a long line behind a group of middle-class white boys. When Jelly finally gets his turn, he performs briefly before being perfunctorily cut off by the promoter who is running the auditions. Reluctant to believe what has become clear as the auditions proceeded – Jelly does not have, never did have, a chance in the competition, which appeared to have been conducted purely for show – Francis tries to return to talk to the promoter but is stopped by bouncers, who taunt the boys with racist slurs. A fight breaks out, and Francis is badly injured. He returns in this condition to Desirea's where he is shot and killed by police. Both the shooting and the beating that precedes it highlight the material conditions of the boys' lives, which lie beyond the redemptive power of art (musical or literary). These conditions delimit what art can do by determining the places and terms of its circulation.

Resilient Whiteness

At whatever scale it is invoked, resilience describes the capacity of something or someone – a system, an organization, a community, a person – to cope with external disruption. That is to say, the idea of resilience depends on a relatively firm distinction between inside and outside whereby resilience is the property of an autonomous object or being in relation to the world. Even in theories of resilience psychology that attend to circumstances in an individual's environment (family, community, and education, for instance) there is an element of narrowness to the analysis such that a dynamic like poverty is read as a singular risk factor affecting certain people rather than an inherent and pervasive part of a broader social system. Many critics have pointed out the tendency in resilience scholarship to celebrate local autonomy without regard for the constraining force of the larger systems in which individuals, organizations, communities, and places operate. For example, Danny MacKinnon and Kate Driscoll Derickson critique the "internalist conception" of resilience thinking, "which locates the sources of resilience as lying within the particular scale in question" (2012, 3), arguing for a broader perspective that takes into account the determining force of capitalism. By this reckoning, poverty is not a challenge that an individual encounters haphazardly in the course of their lives that they can overcome through resilience; rather, resilience is, along with poverty, a constitutive element in the dynamic of inequality through which capitalism operates. As MacKinnon and Derickson put it, "resilient spaces are precisely what capitalism needs – spaces that are periodically reinvented to meet the changing demands of capital accumulation in an increasingly globalized economy. From this perspective, both the sources of resilience and the forces generating disruption and crisis are internal to the capitalist 'system.' Crucially, the resilience of capitalism is achieved at the expense of certain social groups and regions that bear the costs of periodic waves of adaptation and restructuring (2012, 3). Considered in this light, the relation between the art of DJing and resilience assumes a different meaning. Vitally dependent on the work of the "new generation of innovators … left to experiment on their own" (Chariandy 2017a, 102), the music industry also requires the sacrifice of the innovators themselves. Jelly's talents might be real, but his dreams of a possible music career founder at the borders of a commercial landscape in which the concert venue, like the shopping mall, is no place for young Black men. The dynamics of his exclusion demonstrate that racism is a fundamental element in the resilience of capitalism that MacKinnon and Derickson illuminate.

As noted above, conventional definitions of resilience exclude Black youth by deeming them at once too resilient (tough, unrefined) and not resilient enough (lacking character and discipline, insufficiently adaptable). The problem with this exclusion is not that it rests on contradictions: resilience is a complicated capacity, dependent on counteractive functions of solidity and flexibility, identity and openness to change. Where the problem arises is in the figures or metaphors through which proponents of resilience imagine the resolution of these tensions. For school principal Dominick Randolph, cited in the resilience education research explored in chapter 1, the resilience he wants to instill in his students recalls the "traits of mind and habit" he acquired in boarding school in England, traits he also identifies in American history in figures such as "the pioneer in the Conestoga wagon" (Tough 2012, 56). That is to say, bound as this definition of resilience is to a (white, masculinist) colonial history, no demonstration of the right balance of strength and adaptability would be sufficient to extend it to Black youth. Part of what *Brother* does, in the story it tells and the way it tells it, is to counterpose this image of resilience with a different one in which human and nonhuman connections with place, nurtured by memory, constitute tools for surviving into the future. This latter form of resilience does not work in opposition to vulnerability, in the conventional way conveyed by Francis's mother's exhortation to him to "be a man" (Chariandy 2017a, 119), or Michael's boss's lectures about "people pulling themselves up by their bootstraps" (42), or Francis's advice to Michael about how to not "be such a pussy" (87). Rather, it describes a way of living through and with "complicated grief," recognizing that "some deaths ... will never simply be 'gotten over.' Some mourners will never quite again 'be themselves.'" (175). And while the book's nominal focus is on Black masculinity, the model of alliance and kinship it portrays is broadly inclusive and preeminently feminine;[17] it is Aisha who precipitates the reunion of those who loved Francis ten years after his death. Against Michael's strong desire to maintain his and his mother's autonomy and freedom from reminders of the past, Aisha proposes the get-together – "just a gathering, really, with food and music, maybe a few words spoken about the people we've lost" (64) – that forms the base for a recovered and rejuvenated community.

Resilience in the Wake

This mode of resilience "in the wake" (Sharpe 2016) comes into focus in the final scene of the book, which takes place in Michael's house. His mother has just been discharged from hospital following the car accident, and Francis's friends have shown up, uninvited. Michael notes, "They're precisely the sort to ignore a command to go away. They are exactly what my mother would call *harden*" (Chariandy 2017a, 176). In this instance, the term of insubordination and intransigence signals not irredeemability but, rather, strength and steadfastness. Everyone returns to the house where they cook, listen to music, and make plans to go down into the valley, with a wheelchair if necessary.

This scene of frailty, sadness, sustenance, and togetherness contrasts starkly with the first scene of the book, a prologue that gestures to a more conventional vision of resilience. In that scene, Michael recounts a memory of Francis leading him to his "place in the sky" – a "hydro pole in a parking lot all weed-broke and abandoned" (Chariandy 2017a, 1). It is a climbing structure that is fraught with hazards: "step badly on a line, touch your hand to the wrong metal part while you're brushing up against another, and you'd burn. Hang scarecrow-stiff and smoking in the air, dead black sight for all" (1). However, as Francis explained, "if you made it to the top ... you were good. All that free air and seeing. The streets below suddenly patterns you could read" (1). The description of the climb up the hydro pole, of Francis as "a kid reaching brave in the skull hum of power" (1), reads like an extreme, almost stereotypically urban version of the stories of climbing trees or shooting rapids that dominate the old-fashioned fun strain of resilience thinking. In this case, the image of the height and the danger of dying, becoming a black corpse, evokes a racialized Icarus, punished (murdered) for the effrontery of climbing so high, of trying to access the detached "unitary vantage point" (McKittrick 2006, x) from which geography makes sense and the world feels graspable. As the book's prologue, this scene plays a significant, if not defining, role in shaping the meaning of the narrative. Since Michael presumably climbed the pole without getting electrocuted, we might expect the novel to unfold from the perspective of his view from the top, his resilience demonstrated by his successful climb and new-found capacity to decipher the "pattern" of streets below. But that is not how the story plays out. An important part of the dynamic of the story is Michael's attention to Francis:

"You had to watch your older brother and follow close his moves. You had to think back on every step before you took it. Remembering hard the whole way up. He taught me that, my older brother. Memory's got nothing to do with the old and grey and faraway gone. Memory's the muscle sting of now. A kid reaching brave in the skull hum of power. 'And if you can't memory right,' he said, 'you lose'" (1). One way of reading this statement, in light of Francis's subsequent death, is that he must have "memoried" wrong. Another way of reading it is through the recognition that Francis offers this piece of advice without knowing what is going to happen. Though the relationship between the brothers is shaped by Francis's superior experience and knowledge, it is Michael – the younger, less cool, and apparently more fragile brother – who has to grapple with the aftermath of Francis's death, a violent event in which the calculus of memory, of individual agency, and of "winning" and "losing" does not hold.

Francis's advice to Michael, "If you can't memory right ... you lose," is sound in its assertion of the importance of memory but wrong in its attribution of responsibility for bad outcomes, in its understanding of the relationship between individual action and resilience. The opening scene is saturated with an atmosphere of danger, the ever-present prospect of making a fatally wrong move against the hope of safely reaching the top.[18] The final scene focuses not on strategies for averting future risk but on reckoning with tragedy that has already happened. The scene in which, in Michael's words, "we have eaten together, and there is music low on the record player, and we are here and for the moment together" (177) also resonates with Sharpe's representation of Black life "in the wake" in another sense: "*Wake: grief, celebration, memory, and those among the living who, through ritual, mourn their passing and celebrate their life in particular the watching of relatives and friends beside the body of the dead person from death to burial and the drinking, feasting, and other observances incidental to this*" (2016, 11, italics in original). The novel ends with Jelly selecting a record from Michael's mother's collection: "He cues it up, and when the low voice of a woman cuts the silence, Mother frowns slightly, as if in pain. Jelly fumbles to dial it down, but Mother shakes her head. Gestures upward. 'Volume,' she says" (177).

This moment, which recalls the scene of Francis playing in Desirea's barbershop, bears on the novel's take on Black resilience in many ways. First, the scene is at odds with the model of the resilient individual that is represented in different ways by the interpellation/exclusion of Black youth and the effort to escape that process that is represented in the hydro pole scene. The sense of empowerment afforded by the prospect of arrival at the top – "The streets below suddenly patterns you could read" (1) – does not insulate the boys from the dangers of the world they live in, including the risk of racist violence. In contrast with the landscape of opportunity and risk associated with the height of the pole, the end of the novel finds Michael not only close to the earth (about to walk down to the valley) but also differently oriented to the world. The act of listening to music, here as at Desirea's barbershop, commands a particular kind of attention, not detached surveillance but affective, collective, corporeal immersion, not mastery but surrender.

Michael's mother's call for "Volume!" is especially significant to the mode of Black resilience the novel evokes. "Volume" denotes "quantity, strength or power, combined mass of sound"[19] as well as "a quantity or mass (esp. a large one) regarded as matter occupying space" (OED n.d.). *Brother* is a story of the unacceptable risk of living as a Black youth, a risk that is conducive not to strengthened resilience but to violence, death, and loss. It is also an exploration of what it means, in Sharpe's words, to "survive (and more) the afterlife of property" (2016, 18) and an expression of "the largeness that is Black life, Black life insisted from death" (17). The verb "insisted" is instructive: contrary to the claims of (white) resilience advocates that resilience emerges "naturally" in the course of a childhood left to its own devices, Black resilience is a matter of active nurturing, advocacy, and activism. It is also, crucially, not just a measure of the "human capital" of youth, a resource for the future. It is Michael's mother, finally, a character from an older generation who has all but lost her voice through much of the novel, who turns out to embody more than "bare endurance and sacrifice" (Chariandy 2017a, 147),[20] who surprises Michael and Francis's friends by calling for the music to be turned not down but up (177). In an interview with Catherine Hernandez, whose 2017 novel, *Scarborough*, also carves out a space against the vision of resilient Toronto, Chariandy explains that part of what he wanted to explore in the novel's depiction of Black life was "the ability to be loud, to be embodied, and to enact desire" (Chariandy and Hernandez 2017, 4). If this isn't a testament to Black resilience, it is a call for it, a call for amplitude, for gathering, and for the insistent inhabitation of the space/time of the wake.

5

The Ocean and the IKEA Couch

IN HIS MEMOIR, *A History of my Brief Body*, Cree writer Billy Ray Belcourt asks, "How do a people who have been subject to some of the country's most programmatic and legal forms of oppression continue to gather on the side of life?" (2020, 9). The question is both rhetorical – "how have we survived?" – and practical, asking, "How *will* we survive, in the face of a culture that is predicated on our death?" The necropolitics of colonialism encompasses the prevalence of suicide in Indigenous communities, which "emerges as a political response to structurally manufactured sorrow where joy has been shut out of everyday life for a long time" (133). Within the logic of those oppressive structures, suicide is simultaneously stigmatized and unsurprising, almost expected; living is an act of collective and joyful defiance. The question of how to "gather on the side of life" is the subject of Leanne Simpson's "it takes an ocean not to break," which is a story about not committing suicide (2013b). In pointed contrast to Roy Scranton's meditation on "learning to die" in the face of the Anthropocene, discussed in chapter 3, Simpson's story is about learning how to live in the shadow of colonialism and its genocidal machinery.

"it takes an ocean not to break" unfolds against the backdrop of suicide – the suicide attempt of the person to whom the narrative is addressed and the suicidal ideation of the narrator herself. The story recounts an imaginary conversation between the narrator and an unnamed young person interspersed with her account of therapy sessions in which a white therapist is trying to get her to become more resilient by cultivating self-sufficiency, optimism and, by extension, the willingness to put the past behind her. In the words addressed to her absent friend, another, more complex, version of resilience emerges in ambivalent opposition to the first one. The second kind of resilience challenges the conventional therapeutic approach that strives to create clear divisions between the present and the past, reality and imagination, and self and world. It encompasses – though is significantly not reducible to – the process of working through trauma, which is understood to be collective and ongoing, encompassing body and spirit, and inseparable from colonialism. To persist in spite of trauma is not a matter of morality or reason, of positive thinking or making smart choices. Rather, the story ends up expressing and advocating a form of persistence that is rooted in what Simpson, following Junot Díaz (2012), calls "decolonial love." Other stories in the collection reinforce the entwined significance of land, movement, and story in fostering decolonial resilience. I discuss these stories briefly at the end of this chapter but focus primarily on "it takes an ocean not to break" for its illumination of both the snares of settler-colonial resilience thinking and the possibility of escape.

Decolonial Resilience Stories

"it takes an ocean not to break" stages the difficult emergence of an Indigenous resilience story against the official narrative of psychological resilience. The official narrative, signified by the use of regular ("normal") font, informs efforts of "therapy-lady" to lead the narrator out of the shadow of past trauma to develop the trust and coping skills to confront the present and move forward: "therapy-lady liked to compare my life to refugees from war-torn countries who hid their kids in closets when airplanes flew over their houses. this was her limit of understanding on colonized intimacy" (Simpson 2013b, 80). Therapy-lady takes a cognitive behavioural therapy approach to the narrator's pain, framing trauma as a momentary flare up of painful memories that can be overcome by a realistic view of present circumstances. Implying, with an oblique reference to residential schools, that Indigenous children are no longer in danger, she encourages the narrator to recognize the relative safety she enjoys in the present, from which she can move confidently into the future.

The counternarrative offers a different perspective on living through trauma, and on the relation between past, present, and future. The story begins with the words: *"i knew you were going to try and kill yourself before you did it"* (Simpson 2013b, 79).[1] Framing therapy-lady's narrative, set off by italics, the narrator's words establish a different temporality in which danger is not safely relegated to the past but is present and imminent and not confined within the psyche of a single, troubled individual. The narrator acknowledges the appeal of the official, future-oriented resilience narrative. She recalls the hope she once had that *"finally we had given birth to a generation that didn't have to spend their adult lives recovering from their childhoods"* (79) before learning that her young friend's mother was dying, that *"there was a diagnosed train wreck coming [their] way"* (79). It is unclear – deliberately so – whether the train wreck refers to the mother's death or the suicide attempt, described at one point as "the accident" (79). In this narrative, grief is communal, both historical and present, and tied to the trauma of losing mothers. The narrator's friend's personal loss, anticipated and shared by the narrator, is tangled up in the history of residential schools that therapy-lady delicately invokes, part of "colonized intimacy" that must work through the destruction of intergenerational connection.

The relation between the narrator and white therapy-lady is also part of that colonized intimacy, which the narrator struggles to navigate. She explains, "lucy says I made a critical mistake on my first day of therapy. 'you have to lay all of your indian shit out on the first day, drug abuse, suicide attempts, all the times you got beat up, all of that shit, then you sit back and watch how they react, then you'll know if they can deal or not.' lucy had a social work degree but she didn't buy it, which is always useful" (Simpson 2013b, 80). The narrator's conflicted conception of therapy – she keeps going in spite of deep skepticism; "i was two years invested in therapy-lady" (81), but also, "i was there so I didn't commit suicide" (80) – mirrors Lucy's ambivalence about her social work degree. As Simpson's story shows, the therapeutic profession is deeply infused with settler-colonial thinking, even when it isn't inextricably tied to the settler-colonial state. The story lays out the script for recovery/resilience, which consigns the Indigenous subject to a complicated performance of *patience*, both as obedient patient and patient handler of white fragility. It also enacts the narrator's struggle with and eventual refusal of that role. Part of therapy-lady's goal, reflecting her deep misunderstanding of "colonized intimacy," is to get the narrator to examine, and eventually escape, her compulsion to rehash the subject of suicide with her distraught friend. After giving several "incorrect" answers to therapy-lady's question, "what's in it for you?" (82), the narrator tells her "love. and that is all" (83). The story ends with the narrator's decision to leave the therapist's office, pick up her friend, and drive to the coast – a course of action that offers nothing more certain than love, and a refusal of the prescribed therapeutic journey towards self-consolidation and the definitive affirmation of life.

"Ready to Start Again"

Alluded to in Simpson's story, the residential school experience is the starting point – and in some cases the end point – of considerable psychological research focused on Indigenous people. As the devastating effects of that system finally began, in the last decades of the twentieth century, to be recognized by Canadian society, attention and research dollars turned to the theme of resilience. The question of what qualities enabled some individuals to overcome their childhood trauma and achieve some measure of fulfillment compelled researchers in Indigenous studies as well as those interested in cross-cultural determinants of psychological resilience. Between and even within resilience studies we can detect conflicting impulses, ranging from an implicitly assimilationist agenda to an emphasis on the necessary connection between resilience and decolonization.

The latter focus reflects the recognition that traditional Indigenous conceptions of adaptation and persistence anticipate and complicate elements of dominant resilience thinking in significant ways. Many Indigenous cultures identify concepts that describe the capacity for individuals to endure change, as discussed below. However, these ideas of resilience exceed psychological definitions in their focus on collective, rather than individual, thriving, the fundamental interconnectedness of natural and cultural realms, and an emphasis on story as an embodiment of these connections. The disciplinary wall that still notionally marks a distinction between theories of psychological and ecological resilience in Western science does not exist in Indigenous thought. That is not to say that Indigenous understandings of resilience simply combine the two Western approaches, which focus on the adaptive capacities of individuals and systems respectively; Indigenous resilience is at once more expansive in its cosmological scope and more grounded. Inhering in places and those who live in them, it is expressed not through timeless abstraction but through stories that implicate tellers and their listeners in a relationship with the world in which the story is told. As Simpson's story highlights, Indigenous resilience stories struggle to emerge and be heard against the clamour of settler-colonial resilience narratives.

In his opening statement in the Truth and Reconciliation Commission's (TRC) final report, commission chair, Judge Murray Sinclair, observes, "That any Indigenous person survived the culturally crushing experience of the schools is a testament to their resilience, and to the determination of those members of their families and communities who struggled to maintain and pass on to them what remained of their diminishing languages and traditions" (Sinclair 2015, vii). The report contains numerous references to resilience, alongside values of "humour [and] perseverance" (Truth and Reconciliation Commission of Canada 2015, 23), "vision" (207), "courage and ... resistance" (273), whose invocation helps to strike a balance between exposing the magnitude of violence that children suffered in residential schools and celebrating their endurance. The report acknowledges that the Truth and Reconciliation process evoked "contradictory feelings" (283). Characterized in this list by its contrast with a set of crippling emotional obstacles, resilience serves in the document as a whole to signal Indigenous strength; to commend and marvel at the capacity for Indigenous people to "continue to gather on the side of life" (Belcourt 2020, 9). The report makes clear that that gathering also entails an intimacy with death.

Read through the lens of dominant resilience thinking, though, the invocation of resilience as one half of a set of positive attributes, arrayed against "loss," "anger," and "shame," can be harnessed to a narrative of successful overcoming. This reading legitimates nonaction on the part of the Canadian government on TRC recommendations, illustrating what Marjo Lindroth and Heidi Sinevaara-Niskanen have identified as an upshot of the global move to celebrate Indigenouos people's resilience: "The promise of resilience –

as it is all about the future – not only assumes that one will overlook the past but also purports that those victimised by history will transform their own conditions" (2019, 243). The flipside of this promise is the legitimation of contempt and indifference towards those Indigenous people who fail and/or refuse to move on, who fail to be resilient. Resilience is part of a prescribed emotional journey tantamount to "moving on," and as such, comes to carry the weight of a moral imperative.

The moralization of resilience informs the reception of residential school survivors' stories in settler Canada. We can see an example of this dynamic at work in settler scholar David Carpenter's account of why he decided to help an elderly Cree man struggling with alcoholism to write his 2015 residential school memoir. In his introduction to *The Education of Augie Merasty*,[2] Carpenter explains that he was reluctant at first but made the decision to help after receiving a letter from Merasty recounting heartbreak and the struggle to stay sober: "What resilience, I remember musing. I thought we had lost Augie to despair and worse, and here he was at age seventy-two, ready to start again. From his earliest days at St. Therese he demonstrated this resilience in the face of terrifying and degrading attacks. When I began to connect the resilient, oppressed child with the alcoholic, love-spurned old man, my feelings for Augie began to climb up the moral ladder from abhorrence to pity to sympathy to empathy. I just had to meet this guy face to face" (xvii). In Carpenter's use of the word, resilience is a character virtue, linked to courage in the face of external threats and the willingness to leave the past behind. Though the "alcoholic, love-spurned" old man inspires revulsion, presumably because his situation looks like the product of bad choices mingled with self-pity, he becomes more sympathetic when Carpenter superimposes present-day Augie with the much more appealing image of the brave and innocent child. The resilience invoked by an "oppressed child" offers Carpenter a pathway from disgust to empathy, pity to sympathy.

In Carpenter's view, which reflects prevailing settler Canadian perceptions of residential school survivors, horror at the brutality visited on Indigenous children is mixed with, and leavened by, celebrations of the resilience of those who lived to tell the tale of suffering overcome. As suggested in Carpenter's framing (and de facto authorization) of Augie Merasty's narrative, which echoes *Toronto's First Resilience Strategy*'s (2019) framing of Joe's story, discussed in chapter 2, the ability to tell a story that conforms to conventional conceptions of thriving – or at least coping – in the face of trauma itself constitutes a demonstration of resilience. These views, of resilience and the value of personal resilience stories, inform scholarly studies of Indigenous resilience in Canada, which seek to identify factors associated with positive adaptation and to draw on this information to foster resilience in others. Both Simpson's story, in which the narrator acknowledges her initial belief in conventional happy endings, and Merasty's memoir, which is overshadowed by Carpenter's patronizing introduction, highlight the difficulty – even for Indigenous writers – of pushing back against hegemonic settler resilience narratives and the institutions they undergird.

The Mandate to Heal

A 2003 study authored by Madeleine Dion Stout and Gregory Kipling titled "Aboriginal People, Resilience and the Residential School Legacy" exemplifies the discursive challenge of articulating a model of Indigenous resilience outside the dominant settler-colonial sense of the term. The report was produced under the auspices of the Aboriginal Healing Foundation (AHF), a nonprofit organization established by the Canadian government in 1998 in response to a recommendation by the Royal Commission on Aboriginal People. Run by Indigenous people ("a Native who's who in health, social work and recovery," in the words of Tanana Athabascan scholar Dian Million [2013, 103]), at arms-length from the government, the foundation was given a mandate to "encourage and support Aboriginal people in building and reinforcing sustainable healing processes that address the legacy of physical abuse and sexual abuse in the Residential School System, including intergenerational impacts" (Spear 2014, 130). The governing framework of the foundation imposed strict limits on what it could study and recommend. The centrality of "reconciliation" in the foundation's mandate sets out its goals with reference not only to the health of survivors and their families but also the relationship between Indigenous people and the settler-colonial state. Stout and Kipling's report is bound by the terms of the AHF while attempting to articulate experiences and knowledge that exceeds them. As a registered nurse, professor in Canadian Studies, and founding director of the Centre for Aboriginal Education, Research and Culture at Carleton University, Cree elder and scholar Madeleine Stout is well placed to employ an interdisciplinary perspective that is also attentive to Indigenous perspectives on resilience.[3] However, the framework of "healing" circumscribes the concept of resilience to a medical, primarily psychological, model, precluding a more expansive or multifaceted approach.

The report proceeds from the premise that "understanding resilience can serve as a basis upon which to plan interventions to foster greater resilience among Aboriginal residential school Survivors" (Truth and Reconciliation Commission of Canada 2015, 1). The report employs a standard psychiatric conception of resilience as "the capacity to be bent without breaking and the capacity, once bent, to spring back" (Vaillant 2002, 284, quoted in Stout and Kipling 2003, 5), specifying that "a resilient person is someone who manages to have a good life outcome (for example, a steady job, long-term marriage and overall well-being) despite being exposed to situations that carry a high risk of emotional, mental or physical distress" (5). For each aspect of resilience they identify, Stout and Kipling draw on existing literature, which they then apply to the population of residential school survivors. In each instance, the standard criteria fit awkwardly with – and are sometimes confounded by – survivors' experience. Thus, "Aboriginal People, Resilience and the Residential School Legacy" gestures, implicitly in places and sometimes explicitly, towards the inadequacy of dominant models of resilience and to the limits of their mandate for addressing the ongoing realities of settler colonialism. These occasions of questioning punctuate an account that generally upholds the dominant psychiatric models.

A notable element of the report, reflecting the AHF's emphasis on reconciliation, is a definition of resilience that emphasizes its timeless and universal quality. Stout and Kipling contextualize their focus on resilience by observing "stories of marginalized individuals and groups, whose intelligence, perseverance and good humour allowed them to achieve success or win a great victory despite all the odds being stacked against them, have always fascinated people. Examples of such stories can be found in the mythologies of Aboriginal nations across the country, as well as in the popular culture of Canadian society" (2003, 5). The reference to Indigenous history gestures towards the important point that resilience already has a basis in Indigenous culture; however, the juxtaposition of "Aboriginal myth" and "Canadian popular culture" risks invoking the stereotypical image of an Indigenous past giving way to a Canadian future, folklore melding into modern culture. This risk is compounded by the real-life example that follows of "one individual [who] despite a childhood marked by poverty, tuberculosis and relocation far from home in a residential school ... went on to gain notoriety in politics and become one of the most important Aboriginal political leaders in the country" (5).[4] Stout and Kipling go on to note, "If this individual [Elijah Harper] is one example of someone who was able to rebound in the face of serious life difficulties, there are many others who have been unable to do so, instead finding their hopes and aspirations shattered by alcohol, criminality or dysfunctional relationships," asking the ultimate question: "How can one explain the difference in outcome?" (5). The answer: resilience.

When it comes to determining what constitutes resilience for residential school survivors, Stout and Kipling's report both reflects and complicates the conventional psychological criteria. For example, while identifying a spouse as a factor in many individuals' capacity to thrive, Stout and Kipling also cite studies that suggest Elders and other family members, as well as organizations such as AA, can also provide necessary support (Stout and Kipling 2003, 48). Other factors associated with resilience, including friendship, humour, and education, reflect standard resilience literature but with important qualifications. "Education," for example, has a decidedly ambiguous significance for residential school survivors. For many survivors, Stout and Kipling note, healing depends on undoing the effects of early experiences with so-called "educational" institutions by seeking out different learning opportunities, often focused on becoming (re)acquainted with their own language and culture (49). Spirituality, another factor commonly associated with resilience, also has a fraught significance for residential school survivors, given the putative spiritual mission of the schools. Some survivors derive strength from the Indigenous belief systems that the school attempted to dismantle; others come to embrace Christianity, making a distinction between the institution, represented by the church and the "schools," and spirituality more broadly (50).

Stout and Kipling's report acknowledges pervasive institutional impediments to resilience. For example, they note the impact of "systemic racism, [which] influences individual self-perception and interaction with others, heightening vulnerability to a range of negative outcomes" (9). However, consistent with conventional models of psychological resilience, the report plays down structural factors in favour of an emphasis on individual resources. The report notes that "researchers have found that resilient people cope by engaging in 'flexible, problem-solving, and help-seeking behaviors rather than through brittle and rigid responses to adversities'" (14), placing the onus on individuals to adapt to circumstances and to ask for help without accounting for the accessibility and quality of "help" (a question Simpson's story clearly illuminates).

Personal narratives of overcoming form an important part of the report. In the case of a young Métis man named James Tyman, for example, "rampant discrimination" is cited as part of the cause of a "downward spiral of violence, incarceration and substance abuse" (Stout and Kipling 2003, 9); however the negative effects of racism are qualified by a happy outcome for Tyman, who was "in the end, able to turn his life around, enrolling in university and feeling pride in his Métis identity" (10). Tyman's success is attributed to a combination of "coping strategies" and "protective factors," the latter of which include such "individual" traits as "good genetics," "easy temperament," and "optimism regarding future events"; "family" characteristics (e.g., "quality parenting" and "mother's education") and "environment[al]" factors (e.g., "participation in extra-curricular activities" and "church involvement") (Mangham, McGrath, Stewart, and Reid, 1995, quoted in Stout and Kipling 2003, 10). Stout and Kipling point out the role of residential schools in undermining many of these "protective factors" – for example, the ability to maintain close relationships (51); however, they do not take issue with the appropriateness of the criteria as such for evaluating the resilience of residential school survivors.

Significant emphasis is placed on the capacity of resilient individuals to move on from their trauma, shedding maladaptive coping mechanisms: "providing a break with the past and opening up new opportunities" (Stout and Kipling 2003, 15). Stout and Kipling cite psychiatrist Michael Rutter, who "refers to these breaks as 'turning points' and cites studies documenting the positive effects of military service or a harmonious marriage to a non-deviant spouse on individuals from disadvantaged backgrounds" (15). Resilience is associated with prosocial behaviour, with "social" defined according to conservative and nationalist settler-colonial norms. The emphasis on "optimism regarding future events," common in resilience psychology, not only asks Indigenous people to discount present struggle in favour of an imagined resolution of injustice but also implicitly reinforces a Christian-infused capitalist progress narrative to which Indigenous people must assent in order to be resilient.

The individualist focus of resilience psychology shapes how broad social determinants of well-being get interpreted. Stout and Kipling identify "culture" as an important component of resilience, in part because "manifestations of one's culture (for example, traditions, ceremonies and language) are often important sources of pride and self-esteem, serving to support individuals in their struggles against adversity" (2003, 23). The value of recovering traditional practices and teachings finds expression in another resilience story: "Ken Pateneau, a young First Nations man, spoke out against legislation that excludes him from gaining Indian status and, in the process, separating him from his mother in a hurtful way. However, even as he did so, he emphasized that the law would not prevent him from leading a good life" (Stout and Kipling 2003, 23–4). Read alongside examples of "the many others of Aboriginal children and youth who are growing long hair, assuming traditional names, dancing at pow wows and learning their Aboriginal language," Ken's story is cited to highlight "the degree to which individuals are making positive choices in their lives and entering into a dialogue about who they are" (24). The description of the legislation as "hurtful" risks understating the profound damage it does – *and is designed to do* – to collective Indigenous identity. By stressing Ken's determination to lead a good life in spite of the legislation, the example further emphasizes resilience as an individual character trait, one that operates largely independently of – and is therefore able to triumph over – social and political forces.

That the dominant concept of resilience used in Stout and Kipling's report fosters the individualization and depoliticization of those living with the legacy of residential schools is partly attributable to the framework of trauma/healing that governs the AHF, which is focused on the experiences of physical and sexual abuse in residential schools. By thus limiting the scope of the foundation, Elizabeth Fast and Delphine Collin-Vézina point out, the government "fails to take responsibility for the perverse nature of the schools in the first place," and for the trauma involved in wrenching children from their families (2010, 128).[5] As Dian Million points out, the emphasis on healing does not just absolve the government from historical responsibility; it also serves a contemporary neoliberal agenda represented by the devolution of responsibility for social welfare from states to individuals and communities, along with the expansion of the "psy" disciplines (17–20). Jennifer Henderson has shown the particularly pernicious form this agenda – of which vilification of government is a cardinal principle – takes in settler approaches to reconciliation that lay the ills of the residential school system and colonialism more broadly at the hands of a "paternalistic state of a former era that blocked the development of individual, family, and community capacities" (2023, 136). Detaching the mechanism of the state from Indigenous life – including federal, treaty-mandated responsibilites for financial support and social welfare – is coded as a win for Indigenous people; socioeconomic precarity with all responsibility downloaded to individuals "reinterpret[ed] ... as a new freedom from unnatural interference and enforced dependency" (137).

This model of resilience further reinforces settler colonialism by both under and overestimating the nature and extent of Indigenous trauma. First, by encouraging individuals to make "a break with the past" (Stout and Kipling 2003, 15), it disregards collective and ongoing suffering. Second, by personalizing and psychologizing the effects of domination – rendering colonization-decolonization as a dynamic of trauma-recovery, it sidesteps the reality of political struggle and the imperative of the restoration of sovereignty.[6] "The definitions of trauma and the meanings we make of it are historically constructed and defined," as Métis social worker Natalie Clark notes. They are "shaped by the intersection of structural factors, including our access to power and our experiences of oppression. Further, these contructions of trauma shape what we consider as violence, what kinds of violence are erased, and the kinds of supports and access to services that flow from this" (2014, 5). Numerous researchers have noted the inadequacy of traditional psychological definitions of trauma to addressing the "soul wound" of colonialism (Duran et al. 1998). Trauma, for Indigenous people, is not just individual but also historical (Fast and Collin-Vézina 2010;

Evans-Cambell 2008; Wesley-Esquimaux 2009; Wesley-Esquimaux and Smolewski 2004; Braveheart-Jordan and DeBruyn 1995), intergenerational (Menzies 2010; Duran and Duran 1995), and experienced at the level of culture and community (Erikson 1995; Gagné 1998). Everyday racism, in addition to singular instances of violence or discrimination, complicates the temporality of conventional trauma narratives in which trauma arises from a specific event whose effects can be overcome in the present (Williams et al. 2022). In Simpson's story, the narrator responds to therapy-lady's assurance that "none of us had to hide our kids anymore" (2013, 80) by noting, "we both knew that wasn't exactly true. I knew what every ndn knows: that vulnerability, forgiveness and acceptance were privileges. she made the assumption of a white person: they were readily available to all like the fresh produce at the grocery store" (80). The affective armature that is conventionally understood to undergird resilience – feelings like trust and optimism – contradict "what every ndn knows" about the dangers of the present.

Attending to these dangers is a critical task for trauma survivors that conventional therapy protocols do not acknowledge. These protocols, feminist psychotherapist Bonnie Burstow suggests, "see traumatized people as insufficiently trusting others as a result of the trauma and having a particularly distorted view of the world. Correspondingly, a fundamental therapeutic goal that they tend to posit and see as essential is survivors returning to a more 'normal' orientation in which they can once again trust in the goodness of others" (2003, 1297–8). To this end, patients are encouraged to recognize and challenge negative thought patterns that lead to a putatively distorted view of the world. In the words of Simpson's narrator: *"what's that crap that therapy-lady says? 'the feelings are real, but they are not reality.' yeah, that's it, your feelings are real, but they are not your reality. don't get tricked"* (2003, 82).

While acknowledging that trauma can sometimes produce distorted perceptions of things, Burstow refutes the idea that traumatized individuals need to recover a "normal" state of trust. Instead, she suggests that people who have *not* experienced trauma have a less complete picture of the world because they are able to "edit out" signs of their vulnerability (2003, 1298). Moreover, for large segments of the population, including "women, Blacks, natives, Arabs, and I would add, psychiatric survivors, the world is not a safe and benign place, and so mistrust is appropriate" (1299). In short, "For the most part, traumatized people experience the world as dangerous not because they have been rendered inadequate by the trauma and, therefore, have an essentially distorted worldview. They so experience it because events or conditions have brought home how very dangerous the world is and have precluded the editing out practices by which less traumatized people construct an essentially safe and benign world" (1304). Burstow's understanding of trauma supports the narrator's sense in "it takes an ocean" that trauma cannot be safely relegated to the past, that, given the ongoing reality of colonialism, her children's future, and her own, is still precarious. Hence her ambivalent response to her friend's suicide attempt: "*when it first happened, everyone was praying for you to live. i wanted to trust you. you saw what was laid out before you and you made a choice. shit. that's not what i'm supposed to say. i'm supposed to say i'm glad you're alive. i'm glad it didn't work. i'm supposed to look you in the eye and tell you that it's all going to be better, and when you don't believe me, i'm supposed to tell you to trust me*" (Simpson 2013b, 82, italics in original). The narrator's deep recognition of her friend's circumstances makes "trust" an uncertain proposition. She is "supposed" to convince them that life is worth living, when the evidence suggests otherwise.

Of the (white) therapeutic vision of the world, the narrator "*wonder[s] if these people had ever thought of driving their car off a bridge? had they ever felt an overwhelming need for release? had they ever experienced the kind of pain that makes bad choices utterly rational?*" (Simpson 2013b, 81). Having stripped away psychology's veneer of universal rationality and objectivity, the narrator can view the "truths" of therapy with a dispassionate scholarly interest; she can "interview therapy lady about happy people like I was an anthropologist. apparently happy people celebrate their birthdays. apparently happy people express their emotions as a way of processing experiences. apparently the ability to throw yourself in front of a bus and not get that hurt isn't something happy people strive for. if you're nish and you can't survive being dragged under the bus, you're not going to survive. period" (81). Resilience in a colonial state is an ambiguous proposition, the idea of trauma in this context a "psychological conundrum" (Burstow 2003, 1304), one that is "characterized by opposing pulls and directions ... Oftentimes ... the very coping strategy employed by traumatized people goes in opposing directions, with self-mutilation, for instance, both serving to numb people to unbearable psychological pain *and* to help them overcome the numbness" (1303). There is a fundamental incoherence here, but the source of that incoherence is not, crucially, the traumatized person but the situation in which she has lost – and is now being asked to find – herself.

The idea of resilience in settler-colonial society creates a double bind: when the idea of resilience is tied, in an ostensibly progressive way, to a model of character development based on education and the voluntary fortification of will, the failure to cultivate this version of resilience compounds Indigenous shame. In Simpson's story, the narrator's young friend compulsively apologizes for their attempted suicide, clear evidence of a failure of the will to resilience, to which the narrator responds: "*it wasn't you talking, it was your team of therapists as they tried to get you to accept responsibility for your 'bad choices' and the completely hellish reality those 'choices' delivered you to*" (Simpson 2013b, 80). Not only is the therapeutic discourse of settler-colonial society ineffective in addressing the kind of shame Simpson's story represents; it works to reinforce it. As Dian Million points out, even as white Euro-American citizens are typically enjoined to engage in projects of self-actualization, those colonized subjects, who are regarded as less advanced in the practice of freedom, have historically been seen to require more management and intervention (2013, 149).[7] More specifically, "as subjects of the medical diagnosis of addiction, of poor health, and of suspect willpower, Indigenous peoples are subjects of a concern for their ability to self-control, to be autonomous, to be happy, well-adjusted members of a free society where one monitors one's own behaviors" (151). Lisa Stevenson describes a similarly tangled legacy informing the objectives of state-sponsored care of Inuit people in the tuberculosis epidemics of the 1950s and the suicide epidemic of the early 2000. Noting the emphasis, consistent with biopolitics, on depersonalized, bureaucratic public health initiatives, Stevenson says, "The ultimate irony of such forms of anonymous care in the colonial/ postcolonial context is that caregivers exhort Inuit to live while simultaneously expecting them to die … The attempt to think colonialism and biopolitics together requires us, insofar as we are able, to account for the sense of expectancy that accompanies the indifference, the sense in which we, as bureaucrats and citizens of a bureaucratic regime, are also awaiting the death we are indifferently trying to prevent. Thus it happens that the death of the tubercular or the suicidal Inuk *comes as no surprise*" (2014, 7, italics in original)[8].

This perverse model of public health also influences the treatment of Indigenous trauma in settler-colonial society. Moreover, the concentration of government funding and attention on healing narrows the scope of inquiry, foreclosing an engagement with broader questions of remediation for Indigenous suffering that is exacerbated by, but not reducible to, residential schools. As psychologists Michel Tousignant and Nibisha Sioui (Wendat) put it, "Poverty, crowded and insufficient housing, lack of job opportunities, and security in the public and domestic spaces; all these factors are strong obstacles needing change. Healing can only do so much with regard to these basic needs" (2009, 57). These problems are – not accidentally – far beyond the scope of the AHF; however, the focus on healing can work to thwart further efforts towards decolonization. Not only are health and healing inadequate frameworks through which to articulate the complexity of transformation that must be undertaken; their primacy as ways of interpreting Indigenous people's experience comes to exert its own colonizing effect. As Million observes, "Healing from trauma begins to be narrated as a prerequisite to self-determination. If the Indigenous don't heal, they may not be able to self-govern; in any case, they would need to heal to be self-sufficient ... This healing would occur while capitalist development might still displace one or require one's land – a little like accepting being bandaged by your armed assailant while he is still ransacking your house" (2013, 105–6). The metaphor is a particularly resonant one given the yoking of health and reconciliation such that acceptance of help from the oppressor – as much as or more than the availability of bandages – becomes a key component of this vision of healing.

Of processes like the TRC, what she calls "trauma-based mobilizations" (2017, 238), Simpson acknowledges that they undoubtedly "bring healing and solace to some survivors and the families of those victimized" (238); however, she goes on to note that "Canada has become very good at responding to our pain by deploying the politics of grief: a set of tools focusing on individual trauma rather than collective, community, or nation-based loses [sic], by truncating historical injustices from the current structure and the ongoing functioning of settler colonialism, by avoiding discussions about substantive changes involving land and dispossession in favor of superficial status quo ones, and by turning to 'lifestyle choices' and victim blaming to further position the state as benevolent and caring" (238–9).

Stout and Kipling's report, along with the AHF more broadly, arguably facilitates these processes in spite of their best efforts to thwart them. At the same time, the report registers awareness of its limitations and gestures towards the magnitude of the problem to which the concept of psychological resilience is inadequate at best and at worst a contributing factor. Stout and Kipling acknowledge the reverberations of traumatic effects which, "like a pebble dropped in a pond, ... tend to ripple outward from victims to touch all those who surround them, including children and grandchildren" (2003, 50). More specifically, they complicate the emphasis on individual overcoming by highlighting the ongoing relations of exploitation that curtail it. They note that "steps taken to support healing and resilience enhancement at the individual level can only go so far if those involved are being re-traumatized on an ongoing basis. Thus, a commitment must be made to combat racism and discrimination in Canadian society, while supporting the efforts of Aboriginal people to achieve self-determination and resolution of outstanding land claims" (56). These statements, near the end of the report, push at the constraints of the mandate of the AHF by gesturing towards the broader social and political transformations that must occur for it to be fulfilled.

Going Forward

The AHF expresses the limitations of the economic, political, and ideological structures in which it operated. At the same time, it had the virtue of significant Indigenous control. In 2010, the Government of Canada announced a decision not to renew funding to the AHF, instead allocating $199 million to Health Canada to fund programs for residential school survivors and their families. The shift of responsibility for Indigenous mental health from the Aboriginal Healing Foundation to Health Canada saw a move towards a markedly more conservative, less nuanced embrace of the conventional psychological model of resilience, framed by the context of neoliberal state-building.[9]

Where the emphasis of the AHF was on healing from past trauma, the Health Canada perspective that replaced it was resolutely forward-looking and focused on Indigenous youth. These are youth that were supposed to be, as Simpson's narrator puts it, *"the generation that didn't have to spend their adult lives recovering from their childhoods"* (Simpson 2013b, 79). As it turns out, they are the generation who, from 2011–2016, died by suicide at a rate 6.3 times higher than non-Indigenous youth aged fifteen to twenty-four (Kumar and Tjepkema 2019). Framing resilience as a solution to the crisis, the 2013 report, "Acting on What We Know: Preventing Youth Suicide in First Nations," characterizes youth as "resources and assets to the community" and "encourages their active participation in the promotion of their health" (Health Canada, First Nations and Inuit Health Branch 2003, 91). In its conceptualization of youth as both forms of capital and as agents charged with the promotion of their own health, the report exemplifies a trend towards focusing on the figure of the child as a privileged site of resilience thinking. Jennifer Henderson and Keith Denny suggest that this trend supports the currency in "'progressive' political imaginaries" of "the figure of the developmental self" (2015, 4). The elevation of the child to a model of human social life, one that supersedes social structures and collectivities, "gives scientific credibility to the radical individualization in thinking about life chances that undergirds restructured social relations under neoliberal globalization" (4). Resilience, as Henderson and Denny describe it, "is a framework of knowledge and practice tied to the demand for growth. Populations are regulated through action that renders their elements into 'data' and makes them amenable to integration into a project of well-being for the sake of prosperity" (14).

"Acting on What We know" cites the Canadian Council on Social Development's declaration that "our future depends on the ability of our young people to meet the demands of a complex society and a volatile community," noting that "this view converges with the national goals for healthy child and youth development aimed at promoting and protecting their health and well-being through capacity-building and providing youth with meaningful opportunities for participation" (Health Canada, First Nations and Inuit Health Branch 2003, 80). "Opportunities" (a word whose baggage is examined in detail in chapter 4) include sports, expanded vocational training, and "economic development activities that enhance job prospects for First Nations youth" (90), which are meant to provide Indigenous youth with "a reason to be forward-looking in their outlook" and "develop their problem-solving skills" (90). The biopolitical language through which young people are characterized – "resources," "assets," "capacity building" – reflects an understanding of resilience defined by successful assimilation into the settler-colonial state.

Immersion in Indigenous culture is encouraged insofar as it serves the overarching objective of enhancing capacity: thus, the report favourably notes that "tak[ing] up traditional and modern legends, stories and songs ... mak[es] [First Nations Youth] feel more competent and useful as a result" (Health Canada, First Nations and Inuit Health Branch 2003, 91). Connections with the land are similarly cited as a factor associated with enhanced resilience. Defined as "a place or territory where family members reside and foster their unique cultures and livelihoods" and "a landscape made familiar by shared stories," the land also serves as a base for "educational experiences in country settings" (92). The youth who participate in "nation-gathering events, back-to-the-land rituals and survival training activities ... learn skills like responsible living, problem solving, team building and other traditional teachings, which may prevent suicide" (92). The land in this discussion is simultaneously instrumentalized (as a habitat, a "landscape," or "setting" for particular activities) and dematerialized, since histories of displacement and ongoing contests over sovereignty fall outside the normal definition of resilience. Though land is identified as part of culture, culture in turn is construed as separate from economics, leading to the absurd proposition that Indigenous people's resilience will be fostered by the land from which they continue to be displaced by colonization.[10] "The bottom line," Million observes, "is always land and resources. This is the adaptation that the Indigenous in North America are really asked to make" (2013, 159). To the extent that Indigeneity is rooted in the land (a relationship that is discussed in more detail below), resilience might be seen as predicated on the willingness to surrender everything.

The Health Canada report exemplifies the damaging model of suicide prevention that Jeffrey Ansloos and Shanna Peltier (2022) have in mind when they call for an Indigenous-studies approach to suicide and the larger problem of Indigenous liveability under settler colonialism. "In our context," they explain, "death by suicide is a question of justice, and perhaps, more than the prevention of suicide, so is the practice of promoting life in unlivable worlds" (105). Countering conventional associations of suicide with individualized mental health struggles, they argue against Health Canada and along with Billy Belcourt (2020; quoted earlier in this chapter) that "misery, and ultimately suicidality, are intentional, depathologized, and rational responses to the precarious nature of living under a colonial empire" (Ansloos and Peltier 2022, 106). They also follow Dian Million (2008) in calling for a shift away from risk assessment and surveillance towards attending to Indigenous people's felt knowledge (2022, 107). In what might be read as a direct rebuke of therapy lady's assertion in "it takes an ocean not to break" that "feelings are … not reality'" (Simpson 2013b, 82), they suggest, "Felt knowledge invites us to consider how Indigenous people are making sense of their life, amidst colonial suffering" (Ansloos and Peltier 2022, 107).

Ansloos and Peltier flesh out the backdrop to the therapist's office in Simpson's story, offering a detailed picture of "Indigenous peoples suffering and made suicidal under the weight of empire, while being surveilled, intervened upon to stay alive, denied the sovereignty to choose death, and asked to choose life in a social order that refuses to change" (2022, 110). Their remedy for change includes taking felt knowledge seriously, engaging in the kind of biosocial analysis that Belcourt offers, and returning insistently to the underlying issue of land relations. The hope they venture, that "if our 'why' for living is reoriented by decolonial desire, love, care, and an unwavering commitment to the dignity of persons and place, we may yet find healing beyond survival" (115) resonates with the longing in Simpson's collection (2013b). But the grip of "colonized intimacy" is not easy to shake in the search for that kind of healing, for that kind of resilience (Simpson 2013b, 80).

Already Resilient

Stout and Kipling's report, produced by Indigenous researchers as part of an Indigenous-led healing process, shows both the limits of settler-colonial resilience narratives and the difficulty of departing from those narratives

– a difficulty the narrator in Simpson's story also faces in her sessions with therapy-lady: "sometimes when she says things like [the world is a safe place], it's like i've never heard them before and so i ask if I can borrow her pen, so i write them down on my hand, and then I go back to worrying that my jeans are too dirty for her white ikea couch, and that maybe i'll leave a big grey stain of me on it" (2013, 83). Even as the therapy narrative is written on her body, though – even as she writes it herself – the narrator wrestles with another truth that is more historical and more personal. It isn't just that the therapy narrative is inadequate to this feeling; rather, its formula of optimistic, forward-looking self-sufficiency is part of the constellation of pain and shame that generates the feeling and compromises the narrator's resilience. The white ikea couch is stuffed with symbolic associations – to psychiatry, white supremacy, settler moves to purity and innocence, and the bourgeois life towards which the resilient subject is meant to aspire. The fear that her dirty jeans will get on the couch, leaving "a big grey stain of me on it," conveys the depths of the narrator's shame. That shame is not just a neurotic symptom to be gotten over, as therapy-lady would have it, but evidence of the successful internalization of settler-colonial racism that says her Indigenous body will always be "matter out of place," both in the sense anthropologist Mary Douglas (1966) meant by her structuralist account of cultural categories of cleanliness vs pollution, purity vs danger, but also in its connotations of leakiness and of *matter* – corporeality that resists incorporation into the cognitive resilience work that's meant to happen on the couch. The "stain of me" can also be read in another way, as a creative counter to the settler-colonial therapuetic script the narrator writes on her hand with the therapist's borrowed pen. It could be read as a form of what Michael Basseler calls "dirty resilience," the term he uses to describe "stories of resilience that complicate and critique the official narratives constructed by the government and mainstream media" (2019a, 25). But it also gestures in its physical embodiment to something else: a version of resilience that is informed by and accountable to Indigenous knowledge and experience and to the relationships and obligations that are barred from, and have been eclipsed by, the "white ikea couch."

Stout and Kipling's AHF report reflected in some significant ways the white ikea couch version of resilience. However, in contrast to Health Canada's approach, their method gestured to a different, Indigenous model of thriving. They note that a significant obstacle to articulating this model is a "tendency to ignore or pathologize Aboriginal children and youth's agency, while discounting their natural inclination to pursue best health and life-long healing strategies" (2003, 2) – a version of what Unangax̂ scholar Eve Tuck calls "'damage-centred' research" (2009, 409). Within the constraints of their mandate, Stout and Kipling work to free residential school survivors from a dominant narrative of Indigenous brokenness and from a "trauma industry" that works, as Clark puts it, to "create a colonial subject who requires intervention, support and saving" (2003, 2). Stout and Kipling go on to suggest that "because Aboriginal children, youth and adults are often reduced to mere victims of abuse, they are given no opportunity to act as key agents in their own health development and healing efforts. Often, their health beliefs, values and practices are dismissed by health professionals and others as superstitious and non-sensical" (Stout and Kipling 2003, 2–3). What Stout and Kipling's report gestures to without stating it explicitly is that those "beliefs, values and practices" are not just conducive to cultivating resilience; rather they define a model of specifically Indigenous resilience that is more capacious than the conventional psychological concept cited in the report.

An emerging body of Indigenous scholarship seeks to articulate this alternate concept of resilience, one that not only departs from the dominant psychological model but in large measure predates it. A growing body of pan-Indigenous scholarship attests that, as John G. Hansen (Opaskwayak Cree) and Rose Antsanen (Dene) put it, "resilience was a foundational part of Indigenous education; however, it has been undermined, or challenged by a history of colonialism and Eurocentrism" (2016, 1). Studies using participatory research methods suggest that resilience, defined from an Indigenous perspective, can be understood as a vital part of healing and decolonization. In their work with educators and social workers in Red Lake, Minnesota, for example, Iris HeavyRunner (Blackfeet) and Joann Sebastian Morris (Chippewa) note that

> Native prevention workers find the term resilience helpful. One participant said, "Now I have a word for what I have always known and struggled to explain to the children and adults I work with." Resilience helps us assist students in reconnecting with our cultural

> strength. Our work in Red Lake, Minnesota, has been resilience-based. We are pleased to see that a hopeful resilience message, well grounded in local cultural traditions, frees educators, social service providers and tribal community members to view future possibilities with excitement and energy. Our innate human capacity for transformation and change, our resilience, is ever present; like the circle of life it is unbroken and unending. (1997, 5)

Crucial to their project is participants' recognition that resilience is not a Western concept to be applied or adapted to Indigenous experience; rather, it describes *"what [they] have always known"* (Simpson 2017, 5). In other words: "The word [resilience] is new; the meaning is old" (HeavyRunner and Morris 1997, 2).

The interdisciplinary Roots of Resilience project, conducted by a team of settler and Indigenous scholars, similarly found a deep familiarity with the concept of resilience amongst its Indigenous participants. The mostly Indigenous researchers worked from the premise that conventional modes of understanding resilience in psychology and psychiatry "require systematic rethinking to address the distinctive cultures, geographic and social settings, and histories of adversity of indigenous peoples" (Kirmayer et al. 2011, 84). One part of the project, focused on Kahnawake, sought, through interviews and focus groups conducted from 2007–2009, to gather narratives of resilience to "understand resilience from the point of view of Kahnawakehró:non" (Phillips, Dandeneau, and Kirmayer 2012, 9). For the purposes of the study, researchers defined resilience as: "'The process of getting through challenges' in order to be well in life" (2012, 13). Though respondents identified aspects of personal resilience that conform to conventional definitions – "finding inner strength and courage" (22), for example, many conceptions of what it means to do well were at odds with the Western perspective. Among the sources of resilience identified by respondents across generations were "1. being Onkwehón:we, meaning "the original people"; 2. having a strong identity and connection to the land; 3. revitalizing and preserving language and culture; and 4. having the need and willingness to build stronger relationships and connections with each other" (23). Though anatomized for the purposes of the study, these "roots of resilience" are deeply enmeshed in and inseparable from the resilience of the land itself. The report notes, "Just as the riverbank has been eroded and separated from the heart of the community, people indicated that individualism and materialism are threatening their way of being Kanien'kehá:ka" (25). The phrasing here is instructive, with the words "just as" signalling not only a metaphorical connection between the community and the riverbank but also their material implication.

"Their way of being Kanien'kehá:ka" and resilience imply one another. The interconnection highlights that, far from being a recent gift from the psy- disciplines, resilience has long been a feature of Indigenous thought. The researchers in Kahnawake find that while "some people, especially elderly participants, were not familiar with the word 'resilience,' they were ... quite familiar with the concept of resilience" (6). The direct relation between resilience and "being Kanien'kehá:ka" further suggests that resilience is an intrinsic quality of life (not just human life) that everyone is born with. This idea resonates with HeavyRunner and Morris's finding that: "Resilience ... means coming to know how you think, who you are spiritually, where you come from, and where you are going. The key is learning how to utilize innate resilience, which is the birthright of every human being. It involves understanding our inner spirit and finding a sense of direction" (1997, 14). By this reckoning, resilience is not a measurable property that is possessed by individuals in varying degrees and evidenced by their differential capacity to overcome difficulty; it is something more basic to being itself, akin to the philosophical principle of conatus, or the "will to flourish" that is shared by all living things (Rose 2004, 7; see also chapter 6).

The meaning of resilience shifts in this formulation from a reactive to a more proactive, ongoing mode of being. Thus, while acknowledging the formative significance of challenge, epidemiologist Neil Andersson draws on research with different Indigenous groups throughout Canada to suggest that "Indigenous views of resilience ... include – indeed ... [are] based upon – a *positive* dimension. While the predominant (Western) 'survival in the face of adversity' view of resilience seems to hinge on a relationship with failure, we have come to understand Indigenous views of resilience to be closer to a sense of direction, wisdom, or common sense – all positive attributes" (2008, 4). While resilience from a Western perspective is always "resilience *to*" a potential impediment, Indigenous resilience deploys a different grammar. "Resilience *with*" comes closer to describing the relation of interdependence and communalism it describes.

From the perspective of Indigenous research partners in multiple locations, the Roots of Resilience project suggests that "much of what seems to promote resilience originates outside the individual ... Communities exist in an ecological balance with their surrounding environment. They require a moral economy regulated by ideas about coexistence" (Kirmayer et al. 2011, 89). It is within such a moral economy that the concepts of culture and land, and their centrality to Indigenous resilience, become intelligible. For Anishinaabe people, for example, "the term mino-bimaadiziwin or 'the good life' is a concept that relies centrally on the balanced relationship between one's own personal well-being (i.e., physical, mental, emotional, and spiritual), and their relationship to their family and wider community, including the natural and spirit world" (Big-Canoe and Richmond 2014, 128). This focus on relationship fundamentally challenges Western approaches to Indigenous resilience, where culture, community, spirituality, and the land are identified as autonomous "factors" that contribute to a conception of mental health that is itself based on a narrow definition of individual capacity. By contrast, "culture" features in Indigenous conceptions of resilience not as a single element that, combined with others, builds up an individual arsenal of resilience for taking on a world of risk; rather it is an inextricable part of a complex ecology encompassing community, spirituality, and land. Embeddedness *in* this whole, rather than the possession *of* one or more of its resources, is what determines an individual's resilience. Tousignant and Sioui expand on the premise of interdependence that lies at the heart of Indigenous resilience, a premise embodied in the importance of spirituality: "The spirit, contrary to the self-concept or self-esteem, is at the limit within the inside and the outside world, an entity one can identify with but also a presence one interacts with. This re-definition of resilience in Aboriginal terminology avoids the pitfalls of an academic solipsist psychology where the personal mind is the central concept" (2009, 47). The identification of spirit operating at the interface of inner and outer reality complicates conventional psychological ideas of agency while emphasizing and complexifying the ecological basis of Indigenous identity. Western conceptions of ecology, by contrast, are insensible to the existence and activity of the spiritual realm.

Moreover, as Health Canada's misconception of the significance of land discussed above highlighted, Western cosmologies rest on a distinction between human consciousness and the material world, while Indigenous conceptions of the world emphasize the priority of place. "Our truth," Anishinaabe and Hadenosaunee scholar Vanessa Watts explains, "conceives that we (humans) are made from the land; our flesh is literally an extension of soil" (2013, 28). The "literal" is critical here: while Western culture privileges a distinction between epistemology and ontology, Indigenous culture understands meaning to inhere in the material world, in place. "Place-Thought," Watts explains, "is based upon the premise that land is alive and thinking and that humans and non-humans derive agency through the extensions of these thoughts" (21). According to this formulation of agency, to be "well," to be resilient, is predicated on the resilience of the land, understood as "both context and process" (Simpson 2017, 150). This formulation resonates with a study in a Lake Superior Anishinaabe community that conceptualizes "the desire to maintain respectful relationships with the land, which has been central to Anishinaabe identity since creation, as resilience. In this sense, the act of being Anishinaabe is itself an act of resilience" (Tobias and Richmond 2014, 32). More than a "landscape," "habitat," or "base" for the development of skills and confidence (Health Canada, First Nations and Inuit Health Branch 2003), traditional lands are "part and parcel to the practice of Indigenous resiliency" (Tobias and Richmond 2014, 26); the health of the land is "inseparable from the health of those whose existence relies so indelibly on it" (Big-Canoe and Richmond 2014, 128). This relationship is irreducible to settler psychological conceptions of Indigenous resilience in which the land can never figure as more than an external factor, however strongly its significance is weighed.

Living on the land also demands a mode of temporal attunement. "Time is viewed as flowing and always with us," HeavyRunner and Morris explain. "We learn to follow nature's rhythm" (1997, 4). The seeming simplicity of HeavyRunner and Morris's explanation of Indigenous conceptions of time belies its complex embodiment, conjoining land and people, spirit and material worlds. This conception of time poses a significant challenge to Western linear thinking and to the future-oriented thinking of resilience psychology in particular. The exhortation to let go of the past and face the future with optimistic resolve reflects the biopolitical logic of resilience psychology, which is geared towards the entwined objectives of growth and the successful navigation of risk. Indigenous resilience, by contrast, is rooted: it flourishes when the individual is part of a land-based community that honours its ancestors and carries forward their teaching. Kanien'kehá:ka scholar Rod McCormick puts it this way: "The journey towards becoming a mentally healthy community is a difficult journey for Aboriginal communities, but it is one that we do not travel alone. Accompanying us on this journey are mother earth, sky father, grandmother moon, our brothers and sisters in the plant and animal regions and those who came before us and those not yet born" (2009, 6). Contrary to settler-colonial conceptions of Indigenous cultures' emphasis on ancestors and the cycles of nature as simplistic and/or regressive, Indigenous temporality, which is simultaneously fluid, polyvalent, and anchored to place, is more significantly more complex than the dominant settler-colonial perspective of linear time.[11]

The distinction between past, present, and future that characterizes Western thought is predicated on the extraction of time from space and materiality. Indigenous place-centred thought emphasizes the groundedness of time in the interconnected rhythms of nature, including processes of geological transformation, birth and death, seasonal change, and other cosmological cycles. The materiality of time can be seen in the Anishinaabemowin word *kobade*, which means, as Grace Dillon puts it, that "everything that's in the past and the future is also in the now" (Dillon and Marques 2021, 6). This sense of time infuses Simpson's description of the project of Indigenous resurgence as a "way of living [that] necessarily continually gives birth to ancient Indigenous futures in the present (2017, 21). The contemporaneity of what are understood as distinct temporalities in Western thought expresses a recognition of the endurance of history in the interwoven processes of being and becoming. Movement is fundamental to this conception of time, which informs an understanding of identity as comprising not only essence but also memory and transformation. Embedded in and nourished by an ever-changing universe, human identity cannot thus be understood in psychoanalytic terms as a structure comprised of different layers of consciousness; neither is it reducible to neurobiological systems and processes. A better way to understand it is through Indigenous conceptions of narrative.

Resilience and Narrative: The Power of Survivance

A major focus of the Roots of Resilience project is the predication of resilience for diverse Indigenous communities on "stories of identity and transformation at personal and collective levels" (Kirmayer et al. 2011, 85). The emphasis on collectivity is one way that Indigenous models of narrative as a gathering of consciousness from and into a moving world differ from the way narrative functions in Western models of psychosocial resilience, as an "expression of personal truth" (Fitzpatrick 2016, 271). In their capacity to convey continuity, relationality, and change, Indigenous stories may be vehicles of an alternative model of resilience. They can also be read another way, to highlight the insufficiency of the noun, resilience, to a world based on movement and complicate the idea of resilience as inherent in being.

In the Kanien'kéha (Mohawk) language, as Kanien'kehá:ka writer Amber Adams explains, "one cannot *be* resilient" (2023). It isn't only that the noun, resilience, is incommensurate with cognate words like "*ka'shatsténhsera*" ("Strong, rugged, durable, powerful, strict, rigid, demanding, brutal"); the words by themselves are not the point. "If verbs are the molecules of our understanding," Adams explains, "then stories are the matrices they join to make our law, government, families, ceremonies, and societies." To highlight something more/different than resilience, she invokes the Haudenosaunee Creation story in which a young woman, Yotsi'tsishon, recently married and pregnant, falls from "ne èneken" a "place above" and lands on the back of a Turtle. While the story goes on to describe her dancing across Turtle's back, spreading the mouthful of soil Anoyken (Muskrat) has brought up from the depths of the water, Adams draws our attention to the part that is missing from most surviving written accounts where, before she starts dancing, Yotsi'tsishon confronts the magnitude of her situation and has to decide what to do.[12] This moment recalls the beginning of the story, the part that happened in the world above, where, before she fell, Yotsi'tsishon lost everything: "her father, her mother, her home, her livelihood, her husband, her name, and the ground beneath her feet." After her fall, after the landing, she "weighs her grief against the fragile possibilities before her, and chooses to live." Adams goes on to note that "one of the primary themes of this story is *ka'shatsténhsera* – resilience at the most basic physical level – as a choice. Not a choice made once, but one that presses again and again and again, and which often presents the darkness of the void as the more seductive option." The decision is not moralized but contingent, enacted in a world that is in flux and that might at a different moment condition a different action. Adams's take on resilience complicates the Roots of Resilience view of resilience as intrinsic and emphasizes that the action of "gather[ing] on the side of life" is not given but must be set in motion again and again (Belcourt 2020, 9).[13]

The story of *Kayanerenhtserakó:wa*, the coming of the Great Law or Great Peace, is a vehicle for other Kanien'kéha concepts that are manifestly not "resilience": "*Skén:nen*," for example, which is "usually translated as 'peace' … describes frequency, a waveform that integrates the many waveforms of all beings into a single harmony" (Adam 2023). Another vital part of the story, a part that in a European story might emphasize victory, is the ceremony of Condolence, whose purpose is "to lift up the minds of people who have suffered profound loss." None of these words or concepts is reducible to resilience; neither does any of them offer an alternative. In offering these words, in a presentation to a group of settler scholars studying narratives of resilience, Adams highlighted the inextricability of each word to the stories that contained them, the land that embeds the stories, the relations they express – all of which have been battered by "three centuries of genocide … the staggering loss of global climate chaos and ecological catastrophe."

It is important to distinguish stories in Adams's formulation – the metanarratives that sustain Rotinonhsyón:ni life – from the way stories are routinely invoked in relation to Indigenous resilience. Settler accounts of the TRC understand stories as serving a process of bearing witness as well as offering a healing catharsis for both the teller and the listener. This process participates in a broader cultural economy of storytelling in which stories are understood to foster resilience. Autobiographical stories recounting suffering, followed by the harnessing of internal and external resources to cope with, and ultimately grow from, trauma, have come to be seen as a key part of the teller's recovery. Allison Hargreaves acknowledges the vital role of storytelling in the production of minoritized knowledges while also pointing to the "liberal *mise en discourse* that would 'capture' and recast the telling of trauma toward a manufactured moment of conciliatory closure" (2009, 108). Hargreaves critiques, in particular, the enlistment of stories of Indigenous women's trauma in a program of white sensitivity training within a broader program of storytelling as a route to organizational reform. She points to a glaring disconnect between the "institutionalized storytelling practices of dominant service agencies" that draw on white feminist conceptions of personal narratives as vehicles of healing and political empowerment (which reinforce stereotypical conceptions of Indigenous authenticity, expressed in stories of suffering) and "Indigenous epistemologies wherein story functions as a crucial site of memory, law and knowledge" (109–10).

These incommensurable conceptions of story emerge in "it takes an ocean" through the tension between the sections in which the narrator wrestles with the pressure to produce a particular kind of trauma narrative in conformity with the therapist's expectations and those in which she speaks to her friend's – and by extension, her own – pain. In the therapy narrative, "bringing up trauma from my life made therapy-lady cry, especially if it was 'aboriginal' themed. she said 'aboriginal' a lot, and I knew she was trying to be respectful so I planned on letting it slide until the breaking point and then I was going to let her have it one spiraling long manifesto" (Simpson 2013b, 80). In this scene, the narrator's story is elicited by and absorbed into a script in which she is not the central player. "therapy-lady," she tells us, "loves talking about anxiety. me the poor depressed indian. her the white fucking pathologizing savior. I tell her my anxiety and i are co-dependent, but in a lovely way" (82–3). One way of reading "it takes an ocean" is as the representation of an instance of storytelling failure. It is a failure not because of the content of the narrator's testimony in the therapeutic scene but because of the way the scene overdetermines its meaning, reifying her status as ndn at the same time as it demands that she adapt/conform to an impossible model of white resilience.

Traditional Nishnaabeg stories don't conform to the trauma-recovery model therapy-lady follows. In her research into her own culture, Simpson notes, "Although I found lots of stories ... about rebuilding, struggle, and self-determination, these were not crisis-based narratives, and they certainly were not victim-based narratives, nor were they about mere survival. These stories relied upon a return to self-determination and change from within rather than recognition from the outside" (2017, 22). The model of storytelling Simpson describes resonates with Gerald Vizenor's concept of survivance (1996), a principle of active being and becoming that is irreducible to mere individual survival. Survivance describes a narrative mode that works not in the sense of securing an autobiographical basis for individual identity but, rather, to recall Indigenous presence in a more-than-human world. "Native stories of survivance," Vizenor says, "are prompted by natural reason, by a consciousness and sense of incontestable presence that arises from experiences in the natural world, by the turn of seasons, by sudden storms, by migration of cranes, by the ventures of tender lady's slippers, by chance of moths overnight, by unruly mosquitoes, and by the favor of spirits in the water, rimey sumac, wild rice, thunder in the ice, bear, beaver, and faces in the stone" (2008, 11). The kinds of stories Vizenor describes are not just accounts of experiences in nature, though they may be that; rather, they are the laws and contingencies of nature playing themselves out formally through narrative. They embody collective processes of regeneration. More than and different from the survival narratives commonly associated with dominant concepts of resilience, survivance stories embody "an active resistance and repudiation of dominance, obtrusive themes of tragedy, nihilism, and victimry" (11). They also depart from the dominant therapeutic narrative formula of resilience, not only because its individualist focus and neoliberal economic frame are at odds with Indigenous concepts of resilience, but because the "trauma-based mobilizations" it serves (exemplified in the therapy session) enacts a dynamic of assimilation.

Survivance explicitly rejects that dynamic, along with the politics of recognition (Coulthard 2007), in its animation of what Jarret Martineau and Eric Ritskes call "decolonial ruptural forms" of Indigenous art. Such art "refuses the struggle for better or more inclusion and recognition ... and, instead, chooses refusal and flight as modes of freedom" (2014, iv). Dene scholar Glenn Coulthard (2007, 2014) and Kanien'kehá:ka scholar Audra Simpson (2014) have shown that a strong connection exists between decolonial resilience and refusal of the terms of settler recognition. While many commentators agree on the role of "spirituality, holism, resistance and forgiveness" in Indigenous resilience, Tousignant and Sioui note that "there is an aspect sometimes forgotten which is 'rebellion'" (2009, 46). Leanne Simpson concurs that, as a response to oppression, refusal is "always generative; that is, it is always the living alternative" (2017, 33). Elsewhere, she elaborates: "When colonization and colonial policy threatened our Indigenous ways of being, our peoples resisted, organized, and mobilized at every point in history – we were not passive victims of colonialism. Indigenous politics of contestation, dissent, and a mobilization spanning nearly five centuries in some nations are the very reason we have survived as *Indigenous* Peoples as we enter the twenty-first century" (2008, 13).

One clear example of this phenomenon is the 1990 Oka crisis, which galvanized Kanien'kehá:ka to embrace resistance as a vital source of resilience: "The mobilization of the community to oppose the appropriation of sacred land led to a renewed sense of political agency and engagement" (Kirmayer et al. 2011, 87).[14] The conjunction of resistance and conservation is a critical component of decolonial resilience. This dynamic is related, but not reducible, to the concept of adaptation that is central to dominant models of resilience. In the dominant model, resilience emerges through a process in which the individual learns to adapt to a harsh environment, characterized by random forces of disruption and violence. In Indigenous models, by contrast, the model of resilience that Kyle Powys Whyte calls "collective continuance" (2018) is innate, manifested in attunement to an ever mobile but fundamentally hospitable natural world, on whose own resilience human life depends. To maintain that adaptive relation means resisting the forces that threaten the land and humans' relationship with it.

Participants in Tobias and Richmond's study of the connection between land and resilience, for example, emphasized the importance of continuing their land-based practices, "even to the extent that doing so sometimes meant they were breaking the law, for example, during the middle part of the twentieth century when many ceremonial activities were made illegal, several community members continued to practice them" (2014, 31). Simpson's own experience fishing with her children echoes this association of land-based survival and resistance. Noting that they have become accustomed to settler surveillance, she comments, "They expect it. They also expect that we will be there anyway, in spite of environmental destruction, despite the violence of surveillance culture, because they were born into a centuries-old legacy of resistance, persistence, and profound love that ties our struggle to other Indigenous peoples in the Americas and throughout the world … Our presence is our weapon" (2017, 6). This formulation of resilience expresses an essential connection between Indigenous identity, commitment to the land, and resistance.

Decolonial resilience is not simply a matter of defying settler land use and property laws to revive traditional land-based practices; it also requires engagement with global processes of extraction and exploitation and with the associated brokenness of the land and people. Reckoning with that brokenness involves a dynamic of care that complicates the ethic of survivance, as Simpson acknowledges with the simple observation that "Indigenous bodies have to work very hard first to be alive and second to exist as Indigenous peoples" (2017, 42). This recognition informs "it takes an ocean not to break." At the same time as the story advocates for and embodies a spirit of militant refusal, it also dwells compassionately in the pain, shame, and uncertainty that make any movement at all, let alone resistance, so difficult. The story ends with the narrator's rejection of the therapy resilience script. She makes a crucial decision: "*i'm getting in the car right now, and i'm driving north to you … i want to pick you up, and i'm going to stitch every one of your broken bones back together with kisses, and then i'm going to drive us to the coast. i'm not sure which one, but i like the feeling of listening to music and driving and driving for days to get to somewhere different. i think you're going to like that feeling too*" (2013, 83).

With this ending, the narrator shifts her focus from the interiority of the therapeutic landscape to physical movement across the land to the water. Acknowledging that mobility signifies in complex ways for Indigenous people, including an association with "forced expulsion, relocation and diaspora," Simpson asserts, "I see mobility imbued with agency as resurgence" (2017, 196–7). This conception of mobility resonates with Whyte's emphasis on "migration" as a crucial aspect of the "collective continuance" of Indigenous cultures: "Migration suggests that relationships of interdependence and systems of responsibility are not grounded on stable or static relationships with the environment. Rather, these relationships arise from contexts of constant change and transformation" (129). The ending of the story speaks to this possibility of mobility and change; it also resonates with Martineau and Ritskes' concept of "refusal and flight as modes of freedom" (2014, iv).

Read another way, the story ends in a place of irresolution and uncertainty. The promise, *"i'm going to stitch every one of your broken bones back together with kisses"* (Simpson 2013b, 83), which echoes the narrator's earlier declaration, *"i want to suck the shame out of all forty-three of your broken bones"* (81) reads as a heartfelt but futile response to the magnitude of damage to which the story testifies. She is not sure where they will go. Where she does exert agency, it does not seem very consequential: she rejects the therapist's exhortation, "'the feelings are real but they are not reality'" (82), in favour of trusting her feelings – *i like the feeling of listening to music and driving and driving for days to get to somewhere different. i think you're going to like that feeling too."* The last sentence points towards a future that is both tenuous and insubstantial; it does not convey a strong sense of self-possession but more of a gentle reaching out, a conjecture moved by nothing but love.

"it takes an ocean not to break" recasts the kind of intimacy that therapy-lady might pejoratively label as "co-dependen[cy]" (83) within the frame of the collection's title: Junot Díaz's phrase, "islands of decolonial love." The "islands" are both metaphorical, atomized selves and fragile places of coalescence amidst the relentless waves of colonialism, and literal, referring to both the Caribbean islands and Turtle Island, which are the ground and the stakes of colonialism and decolonial struggle.[15] The resilience of both human and more-than-human islands emerges through the story's central dynamic: "love. and that is all" (83). A tension persists throughout the stories between the hope of restoring resilience through love and a legacy of damage that corrodes even the possibility of love. Moments of nurturing intimacy in the stories are interspersed between moments of defensive isolation that feel like self-preservation because, in the context of colonialism, "the skill set you need to survive is not the same skill set you need to love and be loved" (86). The persistence of a history that impedes intimacy clearly appears in the words that begin "buffalo on," the story that immediately follows "it takes an ocean": "right off the bat, let's just admit we're both from places that have been fucked up through no fault of our own in a thousand different ways for seven different generations and that takes a toll on how we treat each other. it just does" (85).

Resilience is a tenuous prospect in settler-colonial society, for both humans and more-than-human others. Nature has its own powers, on which human resilience depends. But those powers are contingent, subject to an infinite array of treaties between different parts of the system, including humans. Stories are one way treaties between humans and non-humans are honoured. "it takes an ocean not to break" is a resilience story, but not in the sense that it narrates the experience of someone who has learned to "knit positive experiences into the fabric of [their] life" (80), as therapy-lady encourages the narrator to do. It is a resilience story because, and not despite the fact that, its outcome remains open, predicated not on survival but on the love that leads the narrator to imagine she can stitch together her friend's broken bones with kisses.

Resilient Stories

Stories are vehicles of resilience in Indigenous culture, but it matters not only what stories are told but also what listeners/readers do with them. Storytelling demands of the listener a form of engagement that is "intense and intentional," in the words of Mohawk writer Beth Brant (1999, 98). As a practice, it embodies and affirms obligations between humans, the spirit world, and other living beings, along with other humans. Stories can be a way of restoring abused and neglected relationships. The kinds of stories that are told and the circumstances of their telling are therefore deeply consequential.

Although the stories in *Islands of Decolonial Love* don't follow any kind of linear progression, the positioning of "it takes an ocean" in the middle of the book makes it feel like a potential turning point towards the imagination of stronger storylines and more resilient futures. "gezhizhwazh," later in the collection, offers a contemporary take on gezhizhwazh, a warrior figure who sacrificed herself to the cannibalistic wiindigo to save the Anishinaabe people. In the story, set in the present, wiindigo have regrouped, their destructive power honed by "public relations experts," while gezhizhwazh has spent time working as a bureaucrat, a nuclear engineer, a hydro linesman, and a sex worker on Bay Street, with each role gaining a deeper understanding of the system, but still helpless to defeat it. Her lover (a male helper in traditional stories) advises her to "start at the beginning, even everywhere starts at the beginning. fix the beginning, gezh. maybe the rest will follow" (Simpson 2013b, 110). Reasoning that the wiindigo's stranglehold over the people begins with the patriarchal control of childbirth, gezhizhwazh harnesses her mothering power to become a bami ondaadiziike (doula), "foiling those interventions, protecting the circle" (111–2). The story itself offers further protection, as the introduction explains: "everyone always tells wiindigo stories when they should be telling gezhizhwazh stories. that's what this old one says" (105).

There is not a straightforward ending of gezhizhwazh's story. Having regained control over birthing, the old one explains, her battle with the wiindigo "was in its resurgence stage ... the light of gezhizhwazh's army of dancing eyes would change the world. just wait" (Simpson 2013b, 112). The complex significance of the ending, which enlists the listener as a participant, is conveyed in its unusual grammar, which moves from the past ("was") to the future-in-the-past ("would change") to the present ("wait"), and from third to second person. The listener in this story, "the young one," asks: *"just wait for what?"* (112), only to be told again, after an irritated exchange about what stories are supposed to do, *"you just wait. i already told you. and while you are waiting, get me some tea, and maybe something to eat. i'm hungry after all that storytelling"* (112). Bringing the action unambiguously into the present, this ending highlights the communal and the material character of storytelling: it takes energy and is inseparable from physical sustenance, relations of reciprocity, and care. Storytelling fosters resilience. "gezhizhwazh" also stages the emergence of story as a conflicted process: should we tell wiindigo or gezhizhwazh stories? But the conflict works itself out in the context of an affectionate intergenerational relationship and through an Indigenous frame of reference that the narrator in "it takes an ocean" cannot find in the overdetermined space of the therapist's office. The story ends in suspense ("just wait") but also with the confident sense that the necessary context for storytelling – a little food, a trusting relationship between listener and teller – has been established.

The end of "gezhizhwazh" sets the scene for the final story of the collection, "gwekaanimad" ("the wind changes direction" in Anishinaabemowin) In this story, the filter between the story the narrator wants to tell – a story of joyful resurgence – and the story of the disabling conditions for the emergence of that story is gone, or mostly gone. Rather than describing the scene of storytelling, "gwekaanimad" enacts it, using the second person to invite the reader in: "biindigen. namadin. oowah. good to see you" (Simpson 2013b, 135).[16] Story is still a tricky, elusive thing, but it has begun to take on a liveliness and warmth, as the narrator continues to set the scene: "i'll get the tea. watch your feet. don't let that one nip you in the toes. gotta watch your feet with that one. he bark too much too. I'll get the tea. that'll start the story off good. gotta start that story off in the right direction because you don't want it getting away from you ... don't want it to start thinking it is all kinds of a big deal, big shot, that one. tricky one, that story" (135). The story is haunted by the familiar colonial legacies of fear and shame, which are embodied in the narrator's eighty-year-old auntie, who is right about "some things" but "not so right about" others (135): "maybe not so right about all the hiding. all the scared. maybe not right about ... pretending all the time. telling her kids to pretend, so they could tell their kids. maybe not so right about that part. maybe not so right about wanting everything to be easy all the time either. drinking all that medicine so she floats all the time. floating. instead of walking (135–6).

"gwekaanimad" is primarily about walking, in the form of a parade to welcome the arrival of strawberries in June. Lots of people (including the old auntie) are skeptical about the parade; "only white people have parades ... they put up them metal fences so the watchers can't dance down the street too. they in the parade. we the watchers. they always gotta have watchers, white people" (Simpson 2013b, 136). But one nishanaabekwe (Anishinaabe woman) argues that the parade will "show we better. but it's not just about that. it's a party too, big party. big nishnaabeg party. big party celebrating big things. like we're still here" (137). The parade is full of people and animals – birds made by children and life-size puppets but also "those other ones ... the ones with wings and the ones with hooves and the ones with paws. they came and they lined that street ... just standing there. just still. just present" (139). All are there in response to the nishnaabekwe's call, "aambe! maajaada!" (come on! let's go!) (138), a call to gather, to stand up, to be present, to move, and to celebrate.

This account of collective movement challenges the familiar formula for survival that is embodied in the old auntie, who "keep safe her whole life. eighty years she kept safe that old auntie of mine" (Simpson 2013b,

136). Safety comes from playing a role, a recipe for self-preservation that, washed down with alcohol, carries her through her eighty years. Hers is a story of survival, but that's not what this is about. Recalling the narrator's words from "buffalo on": "the skill set you need to survive is not the same skill set you need to love and be loved" (86). This story is an account as well as a demonstration of that second skill set, resonant with survivance, in which participants, human, animal, and spirit, touch and look one another in the eye, surrendering to feeling: "something. something good. something that maybe you think you aren't suppose to feel, maybe something you didn't feel for a long time. and for that second you get all filled up with that special one. that one that makes you stay when you should go. full of potential. full of hope. full of love. and you fill yourself up with as much of that special as you can. and then you just keep walking. you just hold your head up high and you keep walking. walking instead of floating" (139).

The end of the story speaks to the importance of being present, touching the earth. It also entails giving in to the feeling "that makes you stay when you should go" (139) – an impulse counter to the lesson that feelings are "not reality" and that resilience comes from extracting oneself from painful relationships and moving forward independently. While "it takes an ocean" ends with refusal and flight, to escape the disciplinary apparatus of the ikea couch, "gwekaanimad" offers the space of choice and the invitation to stay. The space of choice is important, though not in the moralizing frame of the therapist's couch in "it takes an ocean." Instead, it resonates with the questions Amber Adams (2023) posits in connection with the Kanyen'kéha concept of *ka'shatsténhsera*: "Before gazing down the alternatives to choose a path, each person must know the ka'shatsténhsera of that self. Is it – am I – too tired to walk this path? Do I have the capacity to stay on it, once chosen? Can I find the will to stand, let alone move forward? Is the pain of walking it, of living it, so great that lying down here is better? Do I want to keep living?" Do I want to keep living? The answer to that question that is at the centre of "it takes an ocean" is affirmative, at least for now. The title of the story, "gwekaanimad," or "shifting wind," signifies a momentous change, in the environment, and the story that issues from it. It also, crucially, resists closure: the wind keeps on shifting, the walkers keep on walking, into an uncertain future.

As the last story in the collection, "gwekaanimad" is about what kinds of stories are conducive to survivance. Its beginning, in the second person, invites the reader in, manifesting a trust in the proper circumstances for storytelling that isn't there in the earlier stories. The inclusive address of the story resonates with the form of the parade in which, unlike white parades with their metal fences, "this party so big, there are no watchers. imagine that. a party with no watchers" (137). No watchers, only participants, who are collectively subject to and accountable for what happens next, as are the readers and listeners of the story.

6

Sitting Down in the Heat Now

WHEN IT COMES TO RESILIENCE, Indigenous people are objects of concern. Whether it's the crisis of youth suicide, poverty, or high rates of incarceration, the struggles of Indigenous populations in settler-colonial nations are often figured as resilience problems: Indigenous people are seen to lack resilience and this lack in turn threatens the resilience of the nation. At the same time, Indigenous people are often figured as the embodiment of resilience, their "strength, resilience and pride" corollaries of their survival as "the oldest continuous culture[s] in the world" (City of Melbourne 2016, 2). Settler cultures, by this reckoning, have a lot to learn from Indigenous cultures, especially when it comes to addressing environmental change (Rotarangi and Russell 2009, 209). Both of these perspectives – Indigenous people compromise national resilience, Indigenous people are the soul of resilience – inform the urban resilience strategies of Toronto and Melbourne, discussed in chapter 2. At a time of planetary crisis, both kinds of resilience talk get ratcheted up: the knowledge of Indigenous people has become an object of intense desire, even as they are targeted for interventions geared towards assimilation. Waanyi writer Alexis Wright's 2016 novel, *The Swan Book*, describes this landscape in which the concept of resilience is mobilized as an instrument simultaneously of appropriation and of discipline. The novel goes on to imagine a different model of resilience, rooted in the memory and creative energy of Country and the Indigenous lifeways it nourishes. It is offered not as a resource for settler-colonial futurity but as an invitation, a gesture of hospitality with conditions attached. For settlers, Wright's novel might offer a chance to learn how to be good guests on the land before it's too late.

The story centres around Oblivia, an Aboriginal girl who, at the start of the main narrative, is failing to thrive. This is a worry for her foster mother, Bella Donna, who is attempting to raise her with a few clear aims: "to get the girl to act normal: behave and sit up straight at the table and use a knife and fork properly, learn table manners, talk nicely, walk as a butterfly flies, dress like a normal person, learn something marvelous on a daily basis, and show some resilience" (Wright 2016, 21). But Oblivia does not talk nicely and she does not show resilience. Since Bella Donna discovered her in the hollow of a eucalyptus tree, where she had hidden for a decade following her gang rape by a bunch of boys high on petrol, Oblivia has not spoken. She remains impervious to Bella Donna's efforts to socialize her. A difficult child, she eventually becomes an indifferent wife before abandoning humans for the company of swans. And, as the central figure of the novel, Oblivia remains an undeveloped protagonist whose story never quite coheres around her. *The Swan Book* is the story of a failed model of liberal resilience in the ruins of which another, more viable form might emerge. Rooted in Waanyi cosmology, this mode of endurance emerges through a history of adaptation to almost impossible circumstances. Its survival is uncertain, though the novel creates some space for hope.

Set about a century from the present, *The Swan Book* knits Oblivia's story to the history of Australia as a settler-colonial state and the prospects of a planet devastated by climate change. The idea of resilience, if not the word itself, infuses the times and spaces of both of these histories. Whether it is focused on the problem of ensuring individuals – especially those identified as vulnerable – have the psychological resources to cope with turbulent times or on the adaptive capacities of social-ecological systems in the face of natural disaster, resilience conceptualizes and thereby goes some way to soothing the fear of living through dangerous times. In light of this current of resilience thinking, Oblivia's failure is at once disappointing and expected, fulfilling the settler-colonial belief that Australia's Indigenous people are unable to adapt to modern life. At the same time, the realities of climate change have precipitated a global crisis to which Indigenous cultures appear to provide possible solutions:

Indigenous knowledge, symbolized in the novel by Warren Finch, the first Aboriginal prime minister, comes to be seen as key to human survival on the planet. Oblivia's refusal to "show some resilience," either by assimilating to the norms of white Australia or by performing the national fantasy of Aboriginality/sustainability as Finch's wife, highlights the entanglement of both of these dominant narratives with the project of settler colonialism: the tenets of personal resilience – "act[ing] normal" (Wright 2016, 21) – to which Indigenous people fail to conform and those of ecological resilience, which Indigenous people are meant "naturally" to embody, come together in a way that supports the continued settler control of land. The novel represents the devastation that process has produced.

At the same time, without offering a consoling vision of a habitable future, Wright articulates an alternative model of resilience, one that, in contrast to the liberal ideal of individual thriving, starts with the land and draws together humans and animals, plants and rocks, wind and water. It also differs from the scientific concept of the ecosystem, with which it is superficially congruent, in the explicit infusion of the networks it describes with ethical, spiritual meaning. Like survivance (Vizenor 2008), discussed in the introduction and chapter 5, resilience in this way of thinking is inseparable from the modes of human expression (law, ceremony, story) that describe it. The form of resilience expressed in *The Swan Book* also differs from dominant versions in another important respect: it is tied to sovereignty. That is to say, in pointed contrast to dominant models of resilience that appeal to the laws of biology, psychology, or systems theory, Wright points out that the terms of flourishing are also – symbolically and materially – political: colonialism imperils the survival of not just Indigenous people but all of humanity, other species, and the network of existents that sustain them. Resilience, conversely, depends on decolonization. Wright describes her goals in writing this way: "I am interested in the reality of our social, political, economic and cultural in today's Australia as a consequence of the continued invasion and our ongoing war against genocide. However, I am also interested in our lives before the invasion, our culture in spite of the invasion, and I'm searching for the corners of the soil where joy can be found" (2016, 19). *The Swan Book* is a record of that search.

Keeping in mind the shaky reliability of the narrative, which follows a prelude in which Oblivia describes the struggle to "regain sovereignty over

[her] own brain" (Wright and Zable 2013, 4), a brief plot summary offers a way into *The Swan Book*. Following Oblivia's rescue from the eucalyptus tree, she and Bella Donna live on an abandoned war ship in a former lake, now a swamp, which is part of a detention camp for Indigenous people and others, some of whom have been displaced from elsewhere. Bella Donna is a refugee from the northern hemisphere, which has become uninhabitable due to freezing temperatures and frequent blizzards. Joining the human migrants is a flock of black swans, driven by drought from their home in the southeast and southwest. Oblivia, whose imagination has been captivated by the myths and poetry about white swans Bella Donna has recited to her, comes to love the black swans, forming a bond with them that strengthens over the course of the story. Following Bella Donna's death, Oblivia is taken from the swamp (which has come to be known as Swan Lake) by Warren Finch, who claims her as his promise bride. Finch has become an icon not just for the nation, but for the world, which is hungry for Indigenous wisdom that might help address the crisis of climate change. He is eventually assassinated and Oblivia flees the capital city along with a flock of swans who followed her there, travelling across the country back to the swamp. The novel ends with an image of Oblivia cradling a dying swan, followed by an epilogue, set in the future, in which an anonymous narrator locates the events we have just read in the terrain of myth: "a really deadly love story about a girl who has a virus lover living in some lolly pink prairie house in her brain ... but they say that she loved swans all the same" (334).

"A Future Humane World"

Many parts of *The Swan Book* – Oblivia's rescue from the tree; Warren Finch's identification as the "chosen one" and marriage to Oblivia, his "promise bride"; Oblivia's guardianship of the swan – have mythical resonances. The novel also represents variations on conventional resilience narratives, focused on individual and ecosystemic adaptability. These narratives coalesce around the figure of Finch, whose education has prepared him for a globe-trotting career as the "world's foremost environmentalist" (Wright 2016, 129). He is the emissary of his people, the Brolga, whose global recognition as a "showpiece of what a future humane world was all about" (106) spurs a successful bid for self-government. A key factor in their success is that "Brolga people had been opportunistic. They had made sure that they were in the right place at the right time" (105);[1] as a result, they "had grown prosperous with flukes of luck here and there called mining and saying yes, yes, yes to anything on offer – a bit of assimilation, a bit of integration, a bit of giving up your own sovereignty" (117). What might seem like contradictory moves – the celebration of Indigenous values and the exploitation of economic opportunity – fit together within a rubric of resilience that demands the marshalling of any and all resources in the service of adaptation to changing circumstance. This rubric supports and gives cover to the project of settler colonialism, which underpins a "heart-breaking trade-off" that lies at the centre of the Brolgas' success (105). They have won self-determination by sacrificing part of their nation: the territory of the swamp people is deleted from the land covered by the treaty and turned into a military dumping ground and target for aerial bombing practice. The exclusion of the swamp, which is separated by razor wire from "the decent people of mainstream civilization" (52), is not just incidental but fundamental to the success of the Brolga people, who regard themselves as "the antithesis of those other people, their over-the-hills so-called kinspeople in the swamp, mixed up, undone people and what have you, who … ended up having to be guarded night and day by the Army" (95–6). Whereas the Brolga people are seen as the key to a sustainable future, the swamp people are not only outside that future but a threat that must be contained. This dynamic highlights an important element of resilience: while it is defined by its normalization of change and corresponding positive emphasis on adaptability, it is implicitly tied to, if not secretly preoccupied with, the threat of a fatal transformation, of a disruption that will exceed the capacity for self-repair and cause an individual or a system to break down.

The Swan Book takes place against a backdrop of emergency. The Swan Lake detention conditions recall the 2007 Northern Territory National Emergency Response (NTNER), often referred to simply as the Intervention, when the military invaded Aboriginal communities in the Northern Territory to stem an alleged epidemic of child sexual abuse, an epidemic deemed to be "symptomatic of the breakdown of Aboriginal Culture and Society" (Howard 2007, 1).[2] Many commentators identified what anthropologist Melinda Hinkson has described as the "clear intent" in the government action: "to bring an end to the recognition of, and support for, Aboriginal people living in remote communities pursuing culturally distinctive ways of life" (2007, 5). The status of Northern Territory as a *territory*, with considerably less autonomy than states, eased the way for the government to take this action. The element of cultural distinctiveness that poses the greatest threat to the state is a relationship to Country.[3] Accordingly, one measure put into place during the Intervention was the institution of compulsory leases to the government, through which Aboriginal communities would surrender land in exchange for housing and health funds. This measure supports Pat Turner and Nicole Watson's characterization of the Intervention as "the Trojan horse to resume total control of our lands" (2007, 205). The Australian government did not deny that the resumption of Aboriginal land was a key goal for the Intervention. Then minister for Indigenous Affairs Mal Brough argued for the necessary disruption of kin-based and collective forms of ownership so as to provide economic opportunity: "If we get that balance right, people will flourish" (Hinkson 2007, 6). Hinkson points out that such statements make clear that "the NT intervention is aimed at nothing short of the production of a newly oriented, 'normalised' Aboriginal population, one whose concerns with custom, kin and land will give way to the individualistic aspirations of private home ownership, career and self-improvement" (6).

In *The Swan Book*, the demonizing of the swamp people happens concurrently with the praising of the Brolga, whose ecological vision offers a template for planetary sustainability that is conveniently detachable from place: Warren Finch is a global celebrity who "did not have it to be local ... [but] only thought of a moving world, which he epitomized by *imagine what you will*?" (2016, 134). Finch epitomizes the forward-thinking, flexible orientation that Oblivia and her people conspicuously fail to achieve. It is for this reason that, even though the Swan Lake residents reasonably reckon that they are among "the world's true environmentalists" who "could bet a million dollars that they were not using much of the world's resources" (129), their way of life is criminalized, while Warren is feted as the authority on global sustainability.

The apparently strange swings between recognition and repression of Aboriginal rights and culture mirrors shifts in Australian policy over the late twentieth and early twenty-first centuries. Decades before the Intervention, a series of federal government acts extended land rights to Aboriginal groups under limited conditions (unbroken ancestral ties to land and a conception of unbroken "tradition," narrowly defined – both impossibly, conveniently rare given the history of colonialism). Those acts, which were nullified by the Intervention, were passed during a time of liberal recognition in which the identification of Aboriginal knowledge as "valuable" coincided with the burgeoning of the global environmental movement in the 1970s and 1980s (Neale and Vincent 2016, 18). Since then, shifts in the global economy, including the growing Chinese market for raw minerals, have boosted the mining industry, which regards Indigenous control over land as a significant obstacle to its interests. The NTNER presented an opportunity to reverse the "mistake" of recognizing Aboriginal sovereignty (Povinelli 2017, 305). "Whereas traditions had once been good for the nation," Elizabeth Povinelli wryly observes, "now they were bad" (2017, 305). Or as Tanganekald, Meintangk Boandik legal scholar Irene Watson puts it, "Aboriginal culture and identity is more likely to be supported when it is not challenging development projects and when culture performs as a commodity" (2009, 50).

The Swan Book highlights continuities between the explicitly punitive Intervention and the more blandly biopolitical Closing the Gap policy, established in 2008 with the goal of reducing the statistical inequities between settler and Indigenous populations in the fields of health, education, employment, and housing. The phrase "close/closing the gap" appears repeatedly in the novel in the proclamation that "these were past times for kicking Aboriginal people around the head with more and more interventionist policies that were charmingly called Closing the Gap" (Wright 2016, 49). Resilience is an explicit focus of the Closing the Gap policy, which treads a delicate line between celebrating the "natural" adaptive capacity of Aboriginal people and calling them out for failing to successfully adapt to modern society. For example, the 2018 *Prime Minister's Report on Closing the Gap* begins by acknowledging the "extraordinary strength and resilience of Aboriginal and Torres Strait Islander people, [whose] endurance of human life and caring for country is both profound and inspiring (Turnbull 2018, 6), then proceeds to outline a government plan for a "prosperous future" (7), defined by assimilation to Australian norms of white settler education, employment, and private property.[4] Thus, two separate resilience narratives emerge in the report: against the story of the "profound and inspiring" resilience of Aboriginal people, rooted in the past, is a story of their present failure – their *un*resilience – for which the casting off of maladaptive cultural practices and integration into the mainstream is presented as a remedy. Underlying this paradox is another tension between "hope, optimism and purpose" (the report makes repeated reference to "high expectations" [7, 56] in a way that recalls the rhetoric of conservative parenting philosophies) and the consignment of Indigenous people to categories of failure, pathology, and crisis.

These contradictions define life in the swamp. For example, Bella Donna tells Oblivia that it was "lucky" she was found "in the nick of time: *Child! Minutes! Minutes! Otherwise it would have been a disaster,* what would normally be expected – You would have been dead" (Wright 2016, 88). Bound up with the spectre of barely averted disaster – an event of unanticipated and terrible magnitude – is the idea that such an occurrence would not be out of the ordinary; in fact, it would "normally be expected." This juxtaposition conforms with the discourse of colonial benevolence: the hope that Indigenous people can, with appropriate oversight, be saved and taught to be resilient coincides with the expectation of failure as the "normal" outcome.[5] Indigenous communities bear the marks of the hot and cold currents of settler-colonial paternalism: monuments to government largesse, such as an entertainment centre and football field – "grandness-emitting hyper rays of positivism to build muscle and brawn, sinew and bone, to breathe hot breath and punch the air" (84) – are erected behind the razor wire amidst the slums and garbage.[6] Elders in the community see through official exhortations to positivity to recognize what the swamp is: "a social-science experiment with a very big cemetery" (31). The swamp gives palpable shape to the irony that Watson identifies as characteristic of a long series of "'protectionist' policies ... [that] were in their time of operation also characterised as being of benefit to Aboriginal peoples" (Watson 2009, 47). Watson asks, "What was it/is it that Aboriginal people are being protected from?" (47), and "What is to be saved or transformed by the NT intervention, or what is likely to be achieved?" (50).

The Swan Book provides a stark answer to these questions through its portrayal of Warren Finch. Proceeding from the belief that "any view of a glitch in the modern world could be reshaped and resolved" (Wright 2016, 120), he arranges for the destruction of Swan Lake by a remote-controlled explosion. He explains to Oblivia: "*You have a future ahead of you now. They were doing nothing to change things by themselves for the future so they had given up the right of sovereignty over their lives*" (232, italics in original). The destruction of the Swan Lake detention camp is not a violation but rather an *extension* of "the mix of political theories and arguments about how to preserve and care for the world's environment and people" (47): the swamp people have failed to adapt to the modern world; their unresilience is a "glitch," which must be eliminated in the interests of national sustainability.

"Our Katrina"

Warren Finch's precipitous, extra-legal action to solve the problem of the swamp people parodies the logic of "emergency" that framed the real-life NTNER. The chairperson of the Northern Territory Emergency Task Force, Sue Gordon, told a Senate Hearing: "I appreciate people's concerns as to lack of consultation. But, as I have said on the radio in the Northern Territory ... very clearly this was an emergency. If you have an emergency like a tsunami or a cyclone, you do not have time to consult people in the initial phases" (quoted in Commonwealth of Australia 2007, 12). Gordon's framing mirrored then prime minister John Howard's characterization of the situation in Indigenous communities in the Northern Territory as Australia's "Hurricane Katrina." The metaphor of natural disaster depoliticizes the Intervention, defining it in terms of a humanitarian response to an extreme breakdown in the natural order of things.[7] Joanne Faulkner (2015) locates the Katrina metaphor, along with a reference to a "Hobbesian state of nature" in the same speech (Howard 2007), within a long history of settler-colonial representations of Aboriginal people as outside the realm of the human, part of nature. This conception underlays the doctrine of *terra nullius*, which justified European invasion and seizure of land. It continues to inform the idea that Aboriginal people are not only outside of history, but they also constitute a threat to its civilizing mission. Thus, as Faulkner notes, "The 'state of nature' that these remote communities comprehend, according to Howard, represents a danger not only to the women and children he purports to protect, but also to the sovereignty of the Australian nation itself, as a disorderliness that thwarts Australian law and threatens morality" (2015, 118). The threat warrants the suspension of rights – a process that, in *The Swan Book*, extends to the exclusion of the swamp people from the United Nations' Universal Declaration of Human Rights (Wright 2016, 48), laying the groundwork for their extermination.

The intervention, as Faulkner and others have pointed out, "reduces Aboriginal life to *bare* life, for which talk of equality or rights then seems inappropriate, even frivolous" (Faulkner 2015, 119).[8] The logic of bare life shapes the kinds of protection afforded to people in the wake of those events, like Katrina, that are categorized as "natural" disasters. As Faulkner observes: "Natural disaster ... reminds us of the struggle against nature that makes us human, but thereby also produces hierarchies within 'the human': distributing 'humanity' unevenly between those most exposed to the caprices of nature, and those in a position to offer them aid" (121). Those distributions are naturalized and moralized, such that those who do not succumb to disaster – those who are resilient – are credited with energy, foresight, and judgment; those who fail, by contrast, are seen as victims of a combination of bad luck, lack of capacity, and lack of will or moral fibre. This logic is made possible by what Faulkner identifies as "systemic ignorance of the far-reaching effects of colonization" (122). This ignorance leads settlers to perceive Indigenous disadvantage "as a result either of cultural backwardness or the cumulative failure of individual rationality, rather than as integrally tied to an ongoing process of dispossession of land, language, and culture" (122). As Faulkner goes on to note, this perception "allows non-Indigenous Australians to refuse a connection between 'their' history and 'ours,' 'our' situation and 'theirs.' Indigenous disadvantage can then be separated from white advantage – conceived not only as their own fault, but also as intrinsic to their nature" (122). Settler-colonial logic strategically misunderstands what is clear to the swamp people in *The Swan Book*: "It's not that shit happens as other people have said: it's the eternal reality of a legacy in brokenness that was the problem" (Wright 2016, 86).

Following Faulkner's insight into the significance of the use of natural disaster metaphors to justify the NTNER, we should not conclude that this was simply a mischaracterization, that the circumstances that precipitated the Intervention constituted a different kind of emergency. Given that, as Faulkner notes, "'natural' disasters" like Hurricane Katrina and responses to them are profoundly social and political (2015, 118), it makes sense not to quibble over the distinction between nature and society, but rather to consider what the discourses of disaster and emergency do, culturally: How do they work to anticipate, identify, and contain diverse forms of disorder? What kinds of "slow violence" do conventional discourses of disaster and emergency exclude (Nixon 2011)? And, of key relevance to the theme of resilience, what kinds of subjectivities do they make visible, bring into being, put under pressure, or cause to be erased?

The period of the NTNER coincided with the reorganization of federal government agencies with a focus on "all-hazards" planning (Commonwealth of Australia 2011, 1) and the protection of critical infrastructure. In 2007, the newly-created Department of Home Affairs centralized the functions of federal law enforcement, national and transport security, criminal justice, emergency management, multicultural affairs, and immigration and border-related functions – all "working together" as the website proclaims, "to keep Australia safe" (Commonwealth of Australia 2015).[9] Like the US Department of Homeland Security, with which it is frequently compared (Brew 2017), the Department of Home Affairs works on the principle of resilience thinking that it is not possible to "foresee, mitigate or prevent" all contingencies (Australian Government 2022). The concept of perpetual danger informs a "'culture'" of resilience that, as Jeremy Walker and Melinda Cooper explain, "turns crisis response into a strategy of permanent, open-ended responsiveness, integrating emergency preparedness into the infrastructures of everyday life and the psychology of citizens" (2011, 154). Moreover, "emergency preparedness," as defined by the Department of Home Affairs, blurs distinctions between civil, military, and environmental threats, with implications for the kinds of responses appropriate to each (Walker and Cooper 2011, 153). The comparison of the problem of sex abuse in the Northern Territory to a "tsunami" or a "cyclone" points to the prominence of weather-related disaster in the national risk imaginary – a focus seemingly backed up by Prime Minister Kevin Rudd's statement, a year later, identifying climate change as a "fundamental security challenge for our future" (Rudd 2008). However, to focus on the (shaky) emergence of climate change awareness is to risk overlooking the dominant framework of security and its governing narrative: the War on Terror.[10]

We don't need to look too far to see shades of 9/11 in the Northern Territory Intervention: while no supporter of the NTNER directly evoked the War on Terror, Marion Scrymgour, the deputy chief minister for the Northern Territory, who opposed the action, described it as a "shock and awe" operation (2014, 7) – a phrase that was subsequently picked up by other commentators (Grieves 2017, 87; Watson 2009, 46). Critics later observed that the Intervention "replayed many of the political themes and manoeuvres acted out on a global scale in the years since September 11, now projected into a domestic space" (Rundle 2007, 37). Describing the process by which discourses of evolutionary psychology, health, and security worked together to conflate difference with risk, Guy Rundle notes that the *Little Children are Sacred* report triggered "the right to portray Aboriginal society as implicitly pathological" (2007, 42).[11] This move made sense, he suggests, according to a broader post-9/11 culture wherein "any notion of cultural difference became not merely irrelevant but apparently potentially deadly" (42) and grounds for violent containment.

The segregation and ultimate destruction of the swamp community in *The Swan Book* illuminates this dynamic in which race operates as the key index of difference/danger. Even as refugees are interned along with Indigenous people, Bella Donna's whiteness makes her more Australian than Oblivia. While Bella Donna "liked talking about surviving, intervention, closing the gap, moving forward as the way to become re-empowered, learning 'lifestyle,' of aesthetically pleasing houses and gardens," proving to the swamp people that "she was really a local-bred redneck after all" (Wright 2016, 34), she warns Oblivia that her (Oblivia's) skin colour makes her liable to be identified as a terrorist. If she ever leaves the swamp, Bella Donna tells her, "they will say you are one of those faces kept in the Federal Government's *Book of Suspects* ... the place where they kept faces plucked from the World Wide Web by Army intelligence looking at computers all day long, searching for brown- and black-coloured criminals, un-assimilables, illegal immigrants, terrorists – all the undesirables; those kind of people" (Wright 2016, 54–5). The distinction is materialized when, during the flooding of the capital city, those fleeing are divided into categories: there are "the people with passports ... those who had passed the rigid nationality test for maintaining a high level of security in the country and could pay the tax that allowed them to pass through the numerous security checkpoints on the highways," and those who, like Oblivia, "were travelling incognito on unofficial and illegal crossings through the swamps" (304). The evacuation includes a third identifiable group, "navigators at the top of the line," who "claimed to be the policemen over this stretch of country, although in the real world, they were only a bunch of intergenerational environmentalists, turned greenies, turned ferals, turned strapped for cash to save a multitude of furry or feathered threatened species in international forums, or their favourite rare trees ... When the opportunity arose to make some money, who could blame them for becoming entrepreneurial? Human removalists they called themselves" (305).

The divisions that emerge in the course of the evacuation in the novel demonstrate that disaster does not just produce destruction and disorder, it also works productively to secure certain modes of being while negating others. In this case, the flood solidifies the vision of the future – one that marries conventional (white) environmentalism with entrepreneurial capitalism – for which the Brolga serve as convenient mascots.[12] As the emergency expands from the isolated case of Swan Lake to become a full-blown natural disaster, the racial elements of the vision don't disappear but deepen; the borders of the camp are extended, even as there is no land left to house it.

Resilience to What? Resilience for Whom?

Among the many questions that arose in the wake of the NTNER, Irene Watson's are particularly salient: "What was it/is it that Aboriginal people are being protected from? (2009, 47); "What is saved or rescued and at what cost?" (45). These questions resonate with those that have come to the fore in debates about resilience strategies: "resilience to what, and resilience for whom?" (Cutter 2016, 110), or, put slightly differently, "resilience from what, to what, and who gets to decide?" (Porter and Davoudi 2012, 331). These are real, not rhetorical, questions, taken up by policymakers who are concerned with problems of equity. They are also deceptively challenging because not only the answers but the questions themselves entail complex assumptions about identity, subjectivity, and security. These concepts are especially weighted in settler-colonial societies, where they are bound up in the problem of the continuity of (white) settlers' ability to safely enjoy unfettered access to land. As an impediment to that enjoyment, Indigenous people are subject to what Patrick Wolfe calls the settler-colonial "logic of elimination" (2006, 387). This is an ambivalent logic, Wolfe notes, as the settler colony also requires the spectre of Indigeneity to assert its distinctiveness and independence as a nation (389), a dynamic discussed in detail in chapter 2. Thus the "contradictory reappropriation of a foundationally disavowed Aboriginality" (389) helps to shape a national narrative in which a long Indigenous history on the land forms a foundation for (naturally gives way to) contemporary modes of inhabitation. Indigenous people are therefore in a sense both inside the system – the heart of it, even! – and outside it: the impediment to its flourishing. The contradictions deepen with the recognition of climate change as a different order of danger to life on the planet. In this instance, Indigenous people seem to present a kind of solution: both talismanic, as symbols of ecological harmony, and practical, as bearers of knowledge that can be taken up for the purposes of adaptation.[13] At the same time, the framing of climate change as a national and international security threat offers a rationale for extended and new forms of policing and colonial intervention.

Climate change presents an existential crisis in more than one sense. Not only does it threaten the viability of human and other lives, it also exposes and casts into doubt imaginary boundaries between inside and outside, human and more-than-human realms of being. It dismantles the concept of nature that has been, in Emily Potter's words, "crucial to the machinations of Western humanism and industrial capitalism, and to the assertion of human sovereignty on which these rest" (2012, 252). The principal casualty of this breakdown in meaning is the sovereign Western subject, "a subject that has relied on its others as its imaginary inverse, reflecting back, out of this supposed void, the certainties of modern selfhood and the Western liberal project" (253). Anxieties about this loss haunt the discourse of climate security, which wraps the work of strengthening social-ecological systems up in the broader mandate of securing the infrastructure of capitalism and settler colonialism against external threats. The central organizing concept of that project is "resilience," whose slippery and even contradictory resonances emerge in its application to Indigenous people.

The questions, "resilience to what, and resilience for whom," invite us to attend to a distinction based not only on a dynamic of antagonism (*for* vs *to*) but also on a subject/object distinction (*who* vs. *what*). Indigenous people in settler-colonial societies are assigned a shifting and indeterminate status as simultaneously failed (unresilient) subjects, falling beneath colonial measures of human fitness, and sources of capital, in the form of holders of ecological knowledge that may serve as a tool for coping with climate change (instruments of resilience). To the extent that the ideology of settler colonialism (white supremacy supported by economic growth based on resource extraction) informs resilience policies – that it is what those policies are designed to sustain – Indigenous communities who challenge those principles occupy a physical and symbolic sacrifice zone. Those policies are taken to a logical extreme in *The Swan Book*, with the deliberate destruction of Swan Lake that precedes the "natural" disaster of the flood that destroys the capital city. Wright suggests there is a fundamental connection between the two events: the root of climate change lies in the "catastrophic unnatural disaster" of colonialism (Dicken and Yumagolova 2016, 78), a dynamic that contemporary resilience politics works to sustain. The novel also plots an alternate model of resilience that engages the questions "resilience to what, resilience for whom?" not by asserting the humanity of Indigenous people but by undoing the colonial logic of the opposition between "from what" and "for whom."

Black Swan Thinking

Swans play a key role in this undoing. The literary tradition that Bella Donna celebrates is replete with images of white swans, while in Western philosophy black swans represented those things that could not possibly exist, as conveyed in the words of Roman poet Juvenal: "*Rara avis in terris nigroque simillima cygnus*" (a rare bird in the lands and very much like a black swan) (Wright 2016, 80). *The Swan Book* describes, then complicates, the primal encounter that cemented the place of the black swan in the narrative of Australia's colonization. Bella Donna recounts the moment when, in 1697, Dutch explorer Willem de Vlamingh recorded a sighting of a black swan, an event whose imagined conclusion represents the violent fallout of the encounter: "When the swans scattered, the sailors randomly ran down four swans, and once caught, they were taken on board the sailing ship. When they were taken out to sea, the swans became morose from their own stories being pulled away from them, but they were kept alive anyway, the birds of nightmare specimens in the hands of science, exhibits in Indonesia's old Batavia, where the devil swan feathers could be touched by anyone in order to defy their superstition" (81). The novel reorients the story of first encounter, emphasizing not the surprise of discovery or the amplification of European knowledge but the sorrow of the swans at the loss of the place-specific relationships and storylines that sustain them. There is a sense in which this story, which is recounted a third of the way into the novel, forms the back story of the whole narrative: the capture of the swans is an inaugural moment in the history of colonialism, which wrenches plants, minerals, and animals, human and nonhuman, from the networks that nurture them, converting them into capital for distant enterprises. As survivors of this process, the black swans who remain, who become central characters in *The Swan Book*, bear the pain of their ancestors both symbolically and literally, as climate change – the consequence of centuries of extractivism – drives them from their homes in search of new territory.

The representation of black swans as survivors of climate change clashes directly with another story that is a legacy of the narrative of colonial encounter. In the theory of scholar, former trader, and risk-analyst Nassim Nicholas Taleb (2007), black swans have come to serve as symbols for high-impact, low-probability events, outliers that surprise us through their sudden, jarring appearance on the horizon. These events are often experienced as disasters, though, according to Taleb, they can also, for those who adopt the right mindset, serve as opportunities.[14] Terrorism and climate change boosted concern about the increasing prevalence of black-swan events in the late twentieth and early twenty-first centuries. Recognizing the impossibility of preventing or securing against these events, resilience strategies were devised to cope with and even benefit from what otherwise might be catastrophic circumstances. Black swans in this formulation represent the outside of the known world, the invisible risks that loom on its horizon. Understood through the lens of colonial history, they become a different kind of figure, symbolizing the imperial logic that mistakes partial perspective for universal truth and regards the colonized world as a font of resources to be harnessed in support of that truth.

Importantly, in their fleshly incarnations, the black swans do not miraculously transform from shadowy figures on the outside of empire to avatars of Aboriginality. In discussing her inspiration for *The Swan Book*, Wright recalls that she kept hearing stories about black swans turning up in places they'd never been seen before in response to the drying up of their normal habitats. Someone tells her: "'I saw a swan out there and I didn't know if I should kill it or not. It's got no story up in our country.' So what do you do? What happens to a bird – or to anyone – who has no story for that country?" (Wright and Zable 2013, 3). The swans in the novel do not find a warm welcome in the swamp, where the local people "really feared any ancient business that was not easily translatable in the local environment" (Wright 2016, 88). Their status as outcasts shapes the swans' relationship with Oblivia, who, when the first one arrives at the swamp, "knew as a fact that [it] had been banished from wherever it should be singing its stories and was searching for its soul in her" (15). Oblivia is also without a story, "too unimaginable, unable to be recognized and named" (60). In different ways, Oblivia and the black swan are shadowy beings who lurk on the edge of settler-colonial resilience narratives. If Oblivia symbolizes a way of being that has failed to evolve, embodying, along with the swamp people, "the life of the overcome" (19), the black swan represents the geographical and temporal edge of the known world, the disruption against which the system must be guarded. Their collective story ends with the scene of Oblivia sitting in the burned-out hull with Stranger, the last surviving swan, in her lap. While the swan hopefully surveys the skies, looking for the rest of the flock, Oblivia tells him, "*They have all gone now and finished up, and none are coming back*" (332, italics in original). The swan, for his part, refuses to cooperate with her request that he fly up into the sky and make it rain: "Its belligerence was unbelievable. It was not interested in saving the world" (333). Like Oblivia, the black swan refuses to accept the role of symbolic agent of planetary resilience.

Neither the dark shadow on the edge of the system nor the hero at its centre, the black swan confounds the premise of conventional resilience thinking that asks, "resilience to what, resilience for whom?" If, as I am suggesting, the novel articulates a different vision of resilience, then it moves, following the swan, beyond the frame of who/what to articulate a mode of being that is nonoppositional, relational, and more-than-human. However, its realization is far from assured. The violence of the encounter between the swans and the Dutch sailors reverberates throughout the novel, echoed in repeated instances of abduction and displacement. And the damage is not only physical. The wrenching of the swans from their stories anticipates the plight of the contemporary birds who, displaced from their territory, wind up in the swamp: "So what do you do? What happens to a bird – or to anyone – who has no story for that country?" The question, which is central to *The Swan Book*, reveals resilience to be a problem not only of matter – how to survive when you are no longer in place, no longer, that is, yourself – but also of form: how to articulate the meaning of your existence? What kinds of stories can be remembered or invented to support suffering beings in times of profound change?

It is a truism in popular psychology that giving narrative shape to negative life experiences can help individuals to overcome trauma – a truism that reverberates in particularly damaging ways through settler-Indigenous relations. A corollary of this premise is the idea that the ability to give a coherent account of oneself may be read as a sign of resilience. Based on this conventional understanding, we can see a link between Oblivia's lack of speech and her failure to "show some resilience" (Wright 2016, 21). Warren Finch cajoles her: "Oh! Come on! Don't be a sooky baby. You have to be better than that ... You have a story to tell ... Tell everyone you have a few home truths to say to them" (100). As the exemplar of Indigeneity, Warren has obvious expectations for the kind of story Oblivia would tell, of traditional knowledge, of suffering overcome and hope for a bright future, reflecting the combined values of Indigenous wisdom and entrepreneurial capitalism. But Oblivia says nothing. Why is Oblivia unable to tell her story? The most obvious, immediate explanation is the trauma of her rape: "No sound comes out of her mouth since she had decided not to speak, that it was not worth speaking. She would rather be silent since the last word she had spoken when scared out of her wits, the day when her tongue had screeched to a halt with dust flying everywhere, and was left screaming *Ahhhhhh*! Throughout the bushland, when she fell down the hollow of the tree" (19). But her incapacity goes deeper than speech; she is unintelligible to herself, having been robbed of sovereignty over her own mind by the "virus" that has taken up residence in her brain (4).

Bush doctors diagnose the virus as "nostalgia for foreign things" (Wright 2016, 3), a disorder at least partly attributable to the love of European swan literature Bella Donna has gifted/poisoned her with. The white swan stories offer her equivocal consolation for the other stories she finds herself in, stories that swirl around the swamp about her: "Oblivia hears voices all the time, and thinks a lot about how stories are made, considering which words would be used down the centuries to describe herself, and representing what?" (82). She struggles to make sense of her life in terms of the words that enclose her, words like *Foetal Alcohol Spectrum Disorder* and *gang rape*, "pulling her head apart trying to remember what had happened to her, or perhaps whatever it was, it just happened to some other little girl that everyone was talking about and maybe it was not her either, or herself neither, but all girls" (82).[15] What can be deduced from Oblivia's predicament? At least three things: (1) Oblivia has been raped; (2) The rape is part of a wider dynamic of violence, encircling girls, other Indigenous people, refugees, animals, and country; and (3) The violence is physical and symbolic, including the colonization of speech and thought. It is therefore not just that Oblivia as a character cannot tell her story; rather, *The Swan Book* describes – formally as well as thematically – the struggle to produce a meaningful narrative in the context of colonial violence.

In thinking about this struggle, it is important to recognize some other dimensions of Oblivia's silence. First, it is at least partly voluntary. Though her cessation of speech follows her rape, her muteness is not only a symptom of brokenness: "No sound comes out of her mouth since *she had decided not to speak, that it was not worth speaking*" (Wright 2016, 19, italics added). Second, she is not entirely silent:

> Bella Donna knew that the girl would only manage to make certain sounds that did not even closely resemble vowels … The only sounds she heard emanating from the girl's mouth were of such low

> frequency that the old woman strained to distinguish what usually fell within the range of bushland humming, such as leaves caught up in gusts of wind, or the rustling of the *wiyarr* spinifex grasses in the surrounding landscape as the wind flew over them, or sometimes the flattened whine of distant bird song, or a raging bush-fire crackling and hissing from juju jungku bayungu, a long way off, which the old woman heard coming out of Oblivia's angry mouth. (20)

So, the problem is not that Oblivia does not communicate; it's that she communicates in a register that falls outside human comprehension. And, a third point, that she is not only hurt but angry: sometimes, "her guts … groaned and moaned while her stomach tried to shove a jumble of dog vomit words up her windpipe, although always in the nick of time, any of those screaming words that made it up to her mouth, crashed like rocks landing on enamel at the back of her clenched teeth" (Wright 2016, 38). Oblivia, then, is not without agency, thought, or language; her failure to "show some resilience" is to at least some degree a refusal.

It is in this light that we can consider the kind of resistance *The Swan Book* presents to expectations of a coherent and forward-moving – a resilient – narrative. It is common in reviews and critical articles on *The Swan Book* to comment on its difficult style.[16] One explanation for the generic unconventionality of the novel focuses on its representation of climate change, which challenges traditional narrative codes of space, time, and agency (Skeat 2016, 2; Gleeson-White 2017, 32). Another factor is the challenge of speaking truth in a form oversaturated with colonial power: the "virus" in Oblivia's brain infects the culture in which the novel was created and in which it is read. These problems are connected. As Emily Potter points out, coming to terms with climate change in Australia requires challenging the "over-invested paradigm" of the real by which settler-colonial humanism asserts its primacy, banishing nonwhite and nonhuman others to the realm of the unrepresentable (2012, 251). An exploration of that "over-invested paradigm" of the real reveals a historical connection to the idea of resilience as a way of managing the difficulties of those others.

As a genre, the novel is closely associated with realism. It also has a natural affinity with resilience, as Michael Basseler has shown (2019a,

2019b). The latter relationship arises partly through the modern novel's development in the environment of what sociologist Ulrich Beck termed "risk society." As Basseler observes (2019b, 169), Beck himself identified the novel as an ideal vehicle to attend to the turbulent conditions of industrial and postindustrial life: "The experiential dimension of risk – the discovery, the suffering, the prediction of the unpredictable, the fear, the desire, the surprise, the occasional anticipation of death, which risk smuggles into everyday life – all of this can be summarized in the (of course ironical and playful) assertion *I risk, therefore I am*. I venture, therefore I am. I suffer, therefore I am" (Beck 2007, 5). A chaotic world emerges from the background and instrument of character development; in this formulation, the novel becomes a journey of self-preservation in the face of unpredictable change.[17] Citing *Don Quixote* as an example of the novel's portrayal of life as a "never-ending adventure" (4) haunted by "the horror of ambiguity" (5), Beck draws an explicit connection between Cervantes and Descartes in the delineation of the modern hero as "thinking ego" who "defies the gods and a predestined future" (5). Against the mobile terrain of nonlinear, unpredictable events, the novel establishes the steady development of the protagonist and, by extension, the coherence and durability of human selfhood. "In a way," Basseler suggests ... the novel as a genre has always been concerned with resilience thinking, presenting its protagonists' experiences of risk and their adaptation to an ever-changing environment" (2019b, 171–2).[18]

The novel's facility for documenting risk and resilience is not incidental to its historical development as an instrument of European colonialism. As Edward Said put it in *Culture and Imperialism*, fictional colonial heroes "exhibit the restlessness and energy characteristic of the enterprising bourgeoisie, and they are permitted adventures in which their experiences reveal to them the limits of what they can aspire to, where they can go, what they can become" (1993, 71). The empire is a persistent presence in nineteenth- and early twentieth-century fiction, not only as a quietly dependable source of wealth but as a frequently disquieting realm of "far-flung and sometimes unknown spaces, with eccentric or unacceptable human beings, with fortune-enhancing or fantasized activities like emigration money-making, and sexual adventure" (65). Even in a novel like E.M. Forster's *A Passage to India* (1924), which uneasily registers "the impinging disturbance of resisting natives" (75), "the English presence [is] viewed as regulative and normative" (75); as its colonial possessions become more challenging, it remains resilient. One other aspect of that resilience is worth noting: "Almost all colonial schemes," Said notes, "begin with an assumption of native backwardness and general inadequacy to be independent, 'equal,' and fit" (80). The less-than-human status of the native helps to anchor the resilient humanity of the hero/colonizer. This is so even when that resilience is tested, as it is in a novel like Joseph Conrad's *Heart of Darkness* (1899), by the threat of degeneration posed by a too brutal, too heedlessly intimate, encounter with the colonized (23–4). Just as Kurtz offers a cautionary tale against which Marlowe's narrative authority holds, Belgium's misadventures in the Congo are an example of bad colonialism to be held up against Britain's morally justified – and resilient – empire.

To say the novel has historically worked as a vehicle of colonial resilience is not to suggest that it simply and confidently affirms the staunchness of the colonizer against a compliant, easily dominated colonized other. Postcolonial criticism has succeeded in exposing the foundations of the colonial edifice by what Said calls "contrapuntal reading" – the process of "giving emphasis and voice to what is silent or marginally present or ideologically represented" in the colonial novel (66–7). Basseler similarly describes the novel's capacity to highlight the fissures and margins in conventional resilience stories. Unlike popular resilience myths that cleave to the ideal of the neoliberal individual triumphing over circumstance, he notes, resilience fiction reflexively engages the "tension field between the necessity to tell empowering stories to overcome crisis and catastrophe in the global risk society, and the ideological pitfalls that such a project entails" (2019b, 172). Basseler highlights this potential in his discussion of resilience and the novel through an analysis of Jesmyn Ward's *Salvage the Bones* (2011), an example of what he calls, following Patricia Yaeger's concept of "dirty ecology," "dirty resilience" (2013, quoted in Basseler 2019a, 25). In this novel, conventional neoliberal conceptions of normative humanism, risk, and resilience unravel, pointing the way to something messier, more egalitarian, but also less certain.[19] In chapter 4, I made a similar argument for David Chariandy's *Brother*, a novel whose temporal and narrative form undo dominant models of individual resilience. With *The Swan Book*, that process of undoing goes farther, suggesting that the project of restoring

Indigenous imaginative sovereignty may exceed the adaptive capacity of the novel.

A central theme in *The Swan Book*, as noted by Artaud Barras, is "the importance of narratives in shaping identity and providing agency" (2016, 1). Identity and agency come together in Oblivia's struggle "to regain sovereignty over her own brain" (Wright 2016, 4). As Jane Gleeson-White puts it, "Oblivia's mind is both the realm of ancestral Country and of the novel itself; Country narrates through Oblivia" (2017, 31). Amidst the myriad conflicts the novel stages is that between a "capitalist realist" way of narrating the world (Fisher 2009) and the older, deeper, and more expansive frame rooted in Indigenous imagination that Wright calls "Aboriginal realism" (Ravenscroft 2010, 221, n. 26). The terrain of this cosmology is not unreal or "magical" realist but, as Emily Potter puts it, "multi-real," embracing "wider networks of more-than-human-life and power, in dynamic configurations of space and time" (2012, 254).[20]

One affront to capitalist realism comes in the form of ghosts, including the ghost of Bella Donna, who argues with her boyfriend/nemesis the Harbour Master (also possibly a ghost) about how Oblivia should conduct her new life as First Lady. Other characters flicker in and out of conventional embodiment, such as Finch's Aboriginal security guards, whom Oblivia recognizes as genies who have assumed human form (Wright 2016, 163). When they disappear, Bella Donna and the Harbour Master argue about whether they have been murdered, or if they ever existed (200–3). While the reader might be tempted to try and work out what actually happened – whether the genies, like the ghosts of Bella Donna and the Habour Master, are "real," or whether they are all figments of Oblivia's confused mind – the novel resists the impulse to certainty that the realist frame demands. When Oblivia is on the road with Warren and the genies, waking consciousness conveys one version of the world, while "the night spoke in dreams which took the wandering thinker far below the surface, to be jostled in a spirit sea populated with the salt-encrusted bodies of millions of grasshoppers, shoals of tiny fish bones, briny shrimps, larval fish like splinters of glass, colourless moths, seeds and stalks; grotesque bloated grunters, boney herrings, frogs, tadpoles and water birds that had perished in the increasingly saline waters, and been entombed when the water evaporated" (190–1). The truths of (more-than-human) dreams and imagination convey a multidimensional world while also speaking to deep, heterogeneous time. As Wright put it in her essay "The Politics of Writing," "All times are important ... No time has ended and all worlds are possible" (2002, 20). The juxtaposition of times explains why the dead persist among the living, looking to settle scores and offer advice.

In a broader sense, the novel's disruption of capitalist realist time inflects the throughline of Oblivia's story, from the indeterminate time of her rape and her discovery by Bella Donna to her final journey back to the swamp. Her untimeliness informs her unreadability by Bella Donna, who tells her, "*You child, are really peculiar.* She once told Oblivia that she was joined with the *undoable*. It was the principle, she said, of the haphazard way sanity and madness were reaped from her having been gang-raped physically, emotionally, psychologically, statistically, randomly, historically, so fully in fact: *Your time stands still*" (Wright 2016, 82, italics in original). This confusion shapes Oblivia's opacity to herself while also raising questions about how to read her: as a character in realist fiction? A symbol or allegory? A mythological figure? The novel refuses these distinctions by highlighting both the historical recurrence of violence and the continuity of the realm of myth, which extends to the distant past, with the ordinary everyday and the imagined future. As the narrator comments in the epilogue, "This might be the same story about some important person carrying a swan centuries ago, and it might be the same story in centuries to come when someone will carry a swan back to this ground where its story once lived" (333).

Wright's embrace of "all times" corresponds with new modes of apprehending and inhabiting the world. Probability, the governing logic of the world of ordinariness that is the terrain of the conventional novel, is tied to the concept of familiarity – both in the sense of what is known and what (or who) is familial, kin – as defined against the outside, unknown, and sometimes threatening world. Emergency provokes the shoring up of the familiar, the most basic aspect of which is the distinction of the human from the in/nonhuman. But another response is possible, embodied in Oblivia's connection with the swans but also prefigured by her time in the tree, when, though she was asleep, her fingers "were constantly moving, in slow swirls like music," writing words "dredged from the soup of primordial memory in these ancient lands" (Wright 2016, 7). Not just in tune with the physical world, Oblivia's imagination is coextensive with it, as Jean Skeat (2016) observes of the prelude, where Oblivia describes "the cut snake virus in its doll's house" in her brain – a space that also encompasses landscape: the "backwater swamp" and the "biggest slum of a *dirty* desert in one of the loneliest places in the world" (Wright 2016, 3). The entwinement of mind and Country extends beyond Oblivia as a character to imbue other-than-human beings, including the land itself, with subjectivity and agency. As Oblivia follows the swans back to the swamp, they are "caught in the winds of a ghost net dragged forward by the spirits of the country" (326) and awaken one morning to "land screaming with all of its life to the swans, '*Welcome to our world*'" (327).

Consciousness and voice also extend to nonorganic forms of being, ranging from the military junk that clogs the swamp at the beginning (9–11) to the drought that sweeps through it at the end (330–1). Contra the stereotypical construction of the Brolga as guardians of nature, the *The Swan Book* allocates meaning, substance, and value across different modes of existence in a way that does not separate life from not-life. What Povinelli calls the distinction between "the lively and the inert" (2016, 5) is a fundamental predicate of modern governance, based on the determination of what (nonlife) can be capitalized in support of what forms of flourishing. The distinction has been fundamental in settler-colonial nations, where resource industries operate by "sequestering certain forms of existents into the pure object realm" (114), and where the putative inability of Indigenous people to properly distinguish life from nonlife (i.e., by vesting meaning in land) is read as a mark of their prerationality and failure to adapt to modern existence. The politics of life/nonlife, which Povinelli calls "geontopower" (4), underpins biopolitics, its foundational solidity defined until recently by its invisibility. Now, faced with the existential and epistemological challenge of climate change and the attendant idea of the Anthropocene, late liberalism is striving to recalibrate while shoring up the foundations of geontology, reassuring us that "we can change and be the same, nay, even more of what we already are" (28–9). Resilience is the term we use to convey that reassurance, conveying the promise that, whatever else may be shaken, current relations of life (signified metaphorically if not literally by processes of growth, change, and adaptation) and nonlife will prevail.

Part of the logic of geontopower identified by Povinelli is its incorporation (uneven and incomplete) of the markedly different "analytics of existence" of Indigenous people (2011, 27). Mindful of the danger of reifying those analytics as an easily recuperable form of animism, Povinelli hesitantly sets out some principles of the worldview of her Indigenous colleagues and friends, which include the following: "1 Things exist through an effort of mutual attention ... 2 Things are neither born nor die, though they can turn away from each other and change states. 3 In turning away from each other, entities withdraw care for each other. Thus the earth is not dying. But the earth may be turning away from certain forms of existence" (28). These principles, which Povinelli offers as a rough guide or "dirty manifesto" of the Karrabing, the Indigenous media collective she is part of, also offer a way of thinking about being in *The Swan Book*, which is predicated not on identity but on situated relationality.

Among the many harms documented by the novel, one of the most significant is the destruction of bonds of kinship. Evidence of this is in the novel's iteration of the Intervention in which the government sought to correct what were deemed to be pathological family structures in Aboriginal communities and to "implement white ways of loving children as being better than theirs" (Wright 2016, 137). Colonialism creates and perpetuates a "legacy in brokenness" (86), which encompasses forms of violence that precede and follow Oblivia's rape. When Bella Donna eventually tracks down her parents, "now very old people with minds crippled by dementia," they are incapable of recognizing her: after a long grieving process, they have given up hope of seeing her again and are, moreover, "still fearful of welfare people like the Army coming back to plague them over their failure-to-thrive baby" (86). Human bonds are not the only ones that are broken. The tree where Oblivia hid is sacred to the community, a place where "all the stories of the swamp were stored like doctrines of Law left by the spiritual ancestors, of a place so sacred, it was unthinkable that it should be violated" (78). After Oblivia is found, the Army comes in and destroys the tree "on the premise that this nexus of dangerous beliefs had to be broken, to close the gap between Aboriginal people and white people" (79).

The state is mostly unsuccessful in this aim, as can be seen when Oblivia is "rescued" for the second time, by Warren Finch, from the community whose swamp he has just blown up. Unmoved by Warren's assurance, "*You have a future ahead of you now*" (Wright 2016, 232, italics in original), Oblivia is overcome not just by sadness or fear but by shame over what feels like her abandonment of the swans: "She sensed everything known to her had disappeared and blamed herself. Had she really negated her responsibility for the greater things in her care?" (162). This concern casts in a different light Oblivia's "failure" – as Bella Donna and Warren Finch see it – to "show some resilience." Against the model of entrepreneurial individualism to which Aboriginal people have conspicuously failed to conform, we can see in Oblivia, broken as she is, the glimmer of a different model of multispecies resilience, rooted in relationality and love.

Anthropologist Deborah Bird Rose has described this model of resilience as it has been taught to her by Aboriginal people from the Yarralin, Lingara, and Pigeon Hole communities in the Northern Territory. Predicated on "connectivity and commitment, it acknowledges the force, or desire, of living things to flourish, to be in connection, to find their mutually beneficial patterns, and to restore in the world the power of life which is always in delicate relationship with death" (2004, 49). Ethics is not just complementary with ecology in this conception of resilience but inseparable from it, as conveyed by the principles outlined by Kombumerri-Wakka Wakka philosopher Mary Graham: "The Land is the Law" and "You are not alone in the world" (Rose 2004, 186). Neither is ethics the exclusive property of humans any more than "self" is; rather, it describes the nexus of principles or Law that connect all beings, encompassing "'conatus,'" or the tendency to strive to persist and flourish, within dynamics of care that are bound to a particular place (7).[21] While it describes the systematic breaking of those relationships through the "bad history" of colonialism (Wright 2016, 1), *The Swan Book* offers glimpses of their recuperation,[22] most clearly in the connection between Oblivia and the swans. By the time they undertake their final journey back to the swamp, "they had found each other's heartbeat, the pulse humming through the land from one to the other, like the sound of distant clap sticks beating through ceremony, connecting together the spirits, people and place of all times into one. These were her swans from the swamp. There was no going back. She would follow them. They were heading north, on the way home" (303). In both its particular embodiment of girl-swan-home and its extension to encompass all beings and time, this configuration of being departs from conventional novelistic representations of the protagonist as "thinking ego" (Beck 2007, 5).

But *The Swan Book* confounds convention further in its dispersion of narrative voice. Following the prelude, narrated in the first person by Oblivia, the perspective shifts from a third-person omniscient narrator to a variety of voices, "which are variously anonymous and identified, singular and plural, living and non-living" (Daley 2016, 308). The passage describing the destruction of Oblivia's tree is notable in the vacillation of narration between third-person and first-person plural, explaining, "This ancestor was our oldest living friend for looking after the memories ... It made us strong and gave us hope that tree. The kinspeople of the tree had believed this since time immemorial" (Wright 2016, 79). This alternation in perspective is particularly effective in frustrating Western reading expectations for either the anthropological authority of the third-person narrator, describing beliefs of Indigenous people, or the confessional mode of the first-person serving as native informant. Separately, each of these perspectives allows the reader to experience the moral frisson of recognition from a position of comfortable detachment. Combined, they sow confusion, compromising the illusions of objectivity and authenticity with pathos and calls to acknowledge implication.

Black-swan theory operates on the presumption that all things are knowable from the perspective of a centre that is at once strong and infinitely malleable, that difference can be identified and transformed into a resource for resilience. *The Swan Book* counters the certainty implied by such a perspective in its assertion that stories are situated, deriving their meaning from their material contexts and in relation to one another. The stories in the novel, as well as the novel itself, represent the struggle to assemble meaning from fragments of people and country that have been overwritten by an alien master code. The struggle is dramatized by the plight of Oblivia, whose narrative incapacity proceeds not just metaphorically but literally from her rape, abduction, abandonment, and infection by the virus in her brain. Her complicated situation is evident in her name: "Oblivia" signals her virally induced disorientation, as well as her community's failure to remember her, while her last name, "Ethylene," denotes a naturally occurring plant hormone whose processed forms include fuel, plastic, and weapons. Oblivia is at once agent and victim, an embodiment of Country, and conduit for its pollution. A significant source of the poison that has corrupted Oblivia's mind is Bella Donna ("beautiful lady"/Deadly Nightshade), whose stories of the white swans of Europe simultaneously nourish Oblivia (Wright 2016, 89) and cultivate a "nostalgia for foreign things" (3).

However, lest we see black swans, embodiments of Indigeneity, as the obvious antidote to the white swans of English literature, Barras reminds us that the principle of relationality that informs the novel applies to stories, too. He points to paratextual elements of the book, which include the Robert Adamson epigraph *"A wild black swan in a cage/Puts all of heaven in a rage,"* as reminders of the danger of all attempts to confine identity, a danger that is political as well as hermeneutic, encompassing the complexity of lifeworlds and the polysemy of texts (which are themselves understood to be material entities) (Barras 2016, 6). The "Notes on Sources and Acknowledgments" at the end of the book give substance to this polysemy, highlighting the "relational meshwork" of literature from which Wright herself has found inspiration (6).[23] The meshwork comprises the narrative itself which, beginning in Oblivia's prelude, includes the "cut snake virus" (an allusion to the ancestral serpent that recurs in the story) as well as "wild Whistling Swan's easy wings sweeping over snow-capped mountains" (Wright 2016, 5, quoted in Barras 2016, 7). Thus, the activity of storytelling, which is fundamental to Aboriginal culture, is the mechanism that facilitates the integration of storytelling traditions and the articulation of the connection between Country and planet.

The imperative to illuminate planetary relationality is both ecological and ethical. With respect to the consequences of climate change, some already realized, some yet to unfold, Wright suggests—recalling her words quoted in the introduction—that "it is the work of the writer to try to imagine ... what the world might look like. It's not a simple thing like going out into the backyard and seeing a hornet's nest – it's describing the hornet's nest of the world" (Wright and Zable 2013). Through that process of imagination, ecology and ethics get caught up in the counterforce of poetics. Linda Daley draws on Gilles Deleuze and Félix Guattari's approach to literature in suggesting *The Swan Book* uses the deformation of the dominant social code to release the inhuman and untimely rhythms of the planet. That code is the "proper" use of English, associated with Bella Donna, whose speech is regarded by the swamp people as "*Very good English for sure, and would go far for the language betterment of Australia*" but useless in the swamp, "where all English language was spoken for political use only" (Wright 2016, 22). Daley highlights the places in the novel where Wright "makes the state language stutter or stammer, and by that means, finds another language within that language" (2016, 316). Read this way, the inclusion of Waanyi and Aboriginal English in the novel doesn't embody authentic Indigenous experience as much as it puts pressure on the presumption of singular truth, conveyed in the dominant language, while showing that Aboriginal people's relation to that language is "one of adaptation and inventiveness" (Daley 2016, 316). We can view in the same spirit the strange time in the life of the swamp when, influenced by Bella Donna's recitation of classical poetry, the people start speaking in Latin, "terminat[ing] their ability to speak good English anymore, and to teach their children to speak English properly so that the gap could be finally be closed between Aboriginal people and Australia" (Wright 2016, 80). The point here is not the appropriateness or authenticity of Latin to the life of the swamp, now imagined as "a colosseum," but rather the challenge it represents to the project of assimilating Aboriginal people into the rational mindset of white/English Australia. The narrator's take on the mixing of codes – "How bold to mix the Dreamings!" (81) – speaks to a project of uninscription, of working "to free a living, expressive material which speaks for itself and no longer needs to be formed" (Deleuze and Guattari 1983, 21). The effect is the opposite to the novel's generic imperative for realism, which serves as a vehicle for the resilience of the probable, refracted through the consciousness of the beleaguered but enduring human protagonist. The resilience *The Swan Book* articulates instead resides in the energies of the inhuman and the untimely that seep through the cracks of "*Very good English*" and the program of national "*betterment*" it describes (Wright 2016, 22, italics in original).

Becoming the Gatekeepers

But what does this resilience look like? Much of the preceding argument has hinged on a critique of the dominant idea of resilience, defined around the opposition contained in the question: "Resilience to what? Resilience for whom?" While the colonialist underpinnings of the who/what binary certainly merit suspicion, efforts to articulate an anticolonial alternative risk getting snagged on the broader implications of the argument, which favours openness and relationality over closure and identity. It is worth repeating a point that has been raised in previous chapters: the idea of resilience, from whatever perspective it is defined, depends on a distinction between identity and difference, inside and outside. Given this principle, it makes sense to shift our attention to the key questions of how these categories are defined and by whom and – of particular interest in a settler-colonial context – what happens in the interplay between them. The unsettling effects of climate change do not obviate these questions; they make them more urgent. To this end, even as we acknowledge the dynamics of relationality and planetarity, we need to turn to the problem of sovereignty. This assumes central importance in *The Swan Book*, beginning with the announcement in the prelude of Oblivia's "quest to regain sovereignty over [her] own brain" (Wright 2016, 4).

Sovereignty, as Emily Potter puts it, "means the ability to inhabit one's own reality" (2012, 255). Colonization is an assault on Indigenous sovereignty, imaginative and territorial; there is an unseverable link between these two, as Wright asserts, in a mode of "governance that is premised on the idea that *we do not own country, country owns us*" (2022, italics in original). In Australia, settler-colonial state law has overwritten the place and nation-specific laws that define Aboriginal sovereignty, in the process converting those laws into "custom" and stripping them of their power (van Rijswijk 2017, 130). Legal scholar Honni van Rijswijk reads *The Swan Book* as offering a legal "counter-archive" to that of state law, as manifested in the proliferation of laws the book enumerates. Not only do "swans ha[ve] law" (Wright 2016, 67); "law music" sings the country (187) and "law spirits" move through it, "keeping the balance" (187). In van Rijswijk's analysis, the novel shows "indigenous sovereignties continuing in spite of the white nation, and in spite, too, of state law's assertion of exclusive jurisdiction" (130). Climate change further unsettles sovereignty, as revealed in the plight of the swans, who have been displaced from their habitats to arrive at the swamp, "Law birds with no custodians in their rightful place" (68). Their situation mirrors that of displaced humans (including those internally displaced by colonialism), who, having lost their own places, learn more or less successfully to adapt to new ones.

Climate change mobilizes conventional concepts of resilience in different ways. In one context, already discussed in relation to the National Disaster Resilience Strategy, climate change is rolled into all-hazards planning that encompasses threats ranging from environmental disaster to terrorism under the umbrella of security. This strategy is consistent with, if not actually involved in, the enforcement of immigration policies that mandate the imprisonment of asylum seekers in offshore detention centres – including those fleeing conflicts related to climate change. In another context, international organizations ranging from the UN to the World Bank increasingly use the vocabulary of resilience to promote migration as a rational adaptive response to the contingencies of climate change. Thus, as Chris Methmann and Angela Oels put it, migrants are encouraged "to become entrepreneurs who are actively encouraged to shape their fate" (2015, 59), enlisting them in "a resilience discourse that couches loss and damage in the language of progress and transformation" (64). Among the problems Methmann and Oels identify with this discourse are the downloading of risk onto refugees in the absence of frameworks to secure their safety and legal rights and the representation of climate change as an "unavoidable reality" that is "naturalized and depoliticized" leaving no room to address its root causes or the political dynamics that impede steps to tackle it (62–3). Another problem that becomes especially salient in settler-colonial society is the normalization of global dislocation, following the logic that "migration has always been one of the ways in which people have chosen to adapt to changing environments" (Swing 2009, 5).

An affirmatory view of dislocation describes a Western orientation to the world embodied in *The Swan Book* by Bella Donna, who explains to the swamp people that she is "from many other countries equally and felt *not really here and not really there*" (Wright 2016, 24, italics in original). In this sense, her exile is not a tragedy; she says of herself and other climate change migrants, "*We wanted to relinquish our lands, their memories and stories, and after a little reflection ... we said we wanted to be exonerated from history*" (31, italics in original). As Gleeson-White notes, *The Swan Book* foregrounds an opposition between this orientation to the world, which inspires a Western history of travellers "searching for something to happen in their lives ... from the day their ancestors had been expelled from the Garden of Eden" (Wright 2016, 249), and an Aboriginal cosmology rooted in the land (Gleeson-White 2017, 32). For the original inhabitants of the swamp "sitting for all times in one place" (Wright 2016, 12), Bella Donna's situation is incomprehensible: *"Then, without country, imagine that?* Imagining! Can't imagine. For country never leaves its people" (26, italics in original). As Gleeson-White points out, the difference is not just between a local and a global orientation; rather, *The Swan Book* "attests that land – its nature, its stories, and humans' relations to it – is not just the question for postcolonial Australia, but also for the Earth itself in the face of climate change" (2017, 34). And the focus on land insistently returns to the question of sovereignty.

In ecological terms, as Rose notes, resilient systems are "self-organizing and self-repairing. In human terms, resilience has a similar meaning, referring to the capacity of groups of people to sustain themselves in flourishing relationships with their environment, to cope with catastrophe, and to find ways to continue" (2004, 7) – and implicitly, to create new relationships with new places as a response to dislocation. For Wright, who has a long history as an activist for Aboriginal land rights and self-determination, this theme is not just metaphorical but rather, as Philip Mead points out, bound up in questions of "fraught, real world constitutionalism and foundational questions of sovereignty" (2004, 1).

In an essay that is nominally focused on the politics of writing, Wright devotes a significant amount of time to these questions, asking: "What law gives the right of sovereignty to Australia? There is no legal agreement with the Indigenous people of this country" (2002, 15). She goes on to explain:

> Like any other culture in the world, we need to be able to take everything into account about ourselves, and to be able to plan for the future, and to be able to evolve in the way that we think is proper and viable for our particular family, clan, community or Aboriginal nation … This means, if we are able to heal ourselves of the colonial past and the failure of government policies, or free ourselves from being the fierce protectors of the small gains we have made in terms of our rights, we must become the gatekeepers of what is flowing in and out of our communities. This is the full meaning of the right of self determination and self management. (2002, 17)

Wright's reference to "gatekeepers" has special significance in the wake of the Intervention, one of whose provisions was the suspension of Aboriginal communities' right to bar entry to outsiders. The function of gatekeeping speaks to the complicated dynamic of resilience, which is predicated not on rigidly policed identities nor on unrestricted flows. Rather, self-organization, which is crucial to resilience, depends on the capacity to regulate the flow of things in and out of community.

We can see the dynamic process of that regulation in *The Swan Book* in the moment when, following an exhausting voyage across the sea, Bella Donna stepped ashore and "invaded Australia" (Wright 2016, 31). She headed into the bush.

> *"Anyone there?"* She called.
> A bullfrog sitting in the *janja*, the mud, a lone tiny creature guarding the closed-gap entrance to the security fence of government transparency erected by the Army around the entire swamp answered, *baji* – maybe. It was happy enough to grant her asylum when she asked for a look. (32)

The human response is later and more ambivalent:

> Two laws, one in the head and the other worthless on paper in the swamp, said she was an invader. But! What could you do? Poor Bella Donna of the Champions! The sight of her made you cry. She was like a big angel, who called herself the patroness of World Rejection … This was the place for rejection; there was no hotter topic in the mind than rejection in this swamp, so to prove that they were not assimilated into the Australian way of life, the ancient laws of good manners about welcoming strangers were bestowed – Here! Stay! Have a go! We don't mind. (Wright 2016, 32)

Bella Donna's acceptance depends on a collaborative (more-than-human) response, which must balance contradictory imperatives, including multiple and potentially conflicting laws, tradition, and sympathy. In the end, in pointed contrast to the "closed-door syndrome" that characterizes

Australia (3), the "ancient laws of good manners" prevail. The denizens of the swamp exercise their sovereignty and Bella Donna is allowed to stay.

Amidst its "strange panorama of toxic waste" (Wright 2016, 58), the swamp offers sanctuary to displaced Aborigines, black swans, and Bella Donna – even though she is a carrier of the "nostalgia for foreign things" that infects Oblivia (3). The swamp, it seems, is "bold" enough – resilient enough – to "mix the Dreamings" (81); its hospitality is directly linked to its contaminated status. The conditions that allow it to flourish as an "oasis of abandonment" are those that also might end up killing its residents (52). The swamp thus represents an instance of what Povinelli calls "toxic sovereignty," wherein "Indigenous sovereignty over space is reemerging in the space of utter state abandonment and total capital despoilment" (2016, 90). This paradoxical mode of intergenerational community, wherein the lives of current inhabitants are joined by their imminent deaths with their ancestors, evades capture by the liberal logics of assimilation or recognition. But its consequences are ambiguous: no one know what results from this truth – "that Indigenous sovereignty now thrives where Europeans have come, destroyed, and are fearful of returning, but to which [Indigenous groups] continue stubbornly to hold on. No one can foresee what forms of existence can be shaped in this milieu ... in this small pocket of corruption" (91). The naming of this toxic sovereignty gestures to the future, Povinelli suggests, "as a form of survivance in which survival does not quite fit into the picture" (90).

The Anishinaabe term "survivance" foregrounds imagination and remembrance (Vizenor 2008; see introduction and chapter 5), resonating with Wright's tribute to the Aboriginal poet Oodgeroo Noonuccal: "Oodgeroo absolutely understood the power of belief in the fight for sovereignty over this land – that if you succeed in keeping the basic architecture of how you think, then you owned the freedom of your mind, that unimpeded space to store hope and feed your ability to survive" (Wright 2008, 20).[24] Meditating on the *The Swan Book* a few years after its publication, Wright observes, "When I think about Oblivia now in terms of what the last Aboriginal person standing might be like, I see her as an ancestral traveling hero of extraordinary strength whom you might expect to find in the ancient law stories. It feels as though she is creating a new story track in the climate-changed world of a century from now, or perhaps she is following an old spiritual journey extending thousands of kilometers across the country. It is Oblivia's resilience that gets her home, back to traditional country" (2022). If there is hope to be found in *The Swan Book*, perhaps it lies in the anonymous narrator's words in the epilogue, addressing an unknown audience from the ruins of the swamp: *"Jungku ngamba, burrangkunu-barri. We're sitting down in the heat now"* (Wright 2016, 334, italics in original). Someone, in this vision of the future, has survived to tell the story of a traumatized Aboriginal girl and a flock of swans, and someone has survived to hear it. This is how the world will go on.

Epilogue/A Different Ending

Part of Oblivia's quest for mental sovereignty involves fighting infection by dominant resilience narratives, whether these focus on individual self-actualization or planetary sustainability, or even global political solidarity, "a sickness developed from channelling every scrap of energy towards an imaginary, ideal world with songs of solidarity, like We Shall Overcome" (Wright 2016, 3). Literary criticism can be a carrier of this sort of infection. Postcolonial and ecocriticism might be especially susceptible to the tendency to swoop in, Bella-Donna-like, and demand of stories of suffering that they "show some resilience" (Wright 2016, 21). This demand, like all such demands, is arguably less about the person or thing we're looking at than it is about a reader's desire for certainty, redemption, and hope in a dangerous time. *The Swan Book* tells us that the disaster we fear has already happened, that no existing resilience strategy or emergency management plan will save us. And to the extent that this hope is vested in the "discovery" of Indigenous stories, which promise reconciliation and redemption along with ecological vision, it participates in the same extractivist activity it purports to condemn. If *The Swan Book* offers an "unimpeded space to store hope and feed your ability to survive" (Wright 2008, 20), that space is neither infinitely nor universally accessible. Rooted in place and struggles for sovereignty, it cannot simply be scaled up to a model of planetary sustainability. It shows us a way of loving the "hornet's nest of the world" that is still here, that is not yet lost, that settlers might have time to learn and Indigenous people patience to teach us (Wright and Zable 2013, 2).

CONCLUSION

Resilience and/or …

WE ARE LIVING THROUGH TURBULENT TIMES. From this broad, seemingly self-evident idea, others follow: that our challenges are unfamiliar and unprecedented, and that we must as individuals and communities take steps to ensure our fitness to confront them, now and in the future. The idea of resilience works to support these common sense views of life in the early twenty-first century. In the years following its projection as the word of the year (Juniper 2011), "resilience" has continued to float steadily along in the mainstream. It no longer needs much of an introduction, nor the customary follow-up explanatory glosses touting its value as an essential capacity for navigating this extraordinarily risky moment. Resilience has largely been accepted as part of the basic toolkit of environmental, organizational, and personal maintenance.

A central aim of this book has been to try to unravel the blanket of common sense that shrouds the idea of resilience. Building on the work of scholars who have illuminated the alignment of resilience with neoliberalism (Cooper and Walker 2011; Joseph 2013; Evans and Reid 2014; Zebrowski 2015), one approach to this unravelling has been to historicize the growth of resilience thinking, to highlight its coincidence with a period of rising anxiety in the West. The narrative of endless progress, which had proved pliable enough to survive both its rebranding as sustainable development and the brief blossoming and long withering of the end-of-history fantasy, had begun, by the mid-1990s, unmistakably to sputter. Ulrich Beck's "risk society" thesis offers one way to read what was happening, as the externalities or "normal accidents" of modernity began to overwhelm its successes (Perrow 1999). Replace "modernity" with "colonialism" or "racial capitalism" and the end of the twentieth century marks the start of a time of increasingly frequent eruptions resulting from the West's failure to harness or subdue the energies of its others – human and more-than-human. In settler-colonial societies in particular, the containment strategies of multiculturalism, reconciliation, and sustainable growth were coming undone even as they retained their powerful narrative force. Resilience – the dominant version of it anyway – emerges as a promise that all the turmoil we see, and the greater turmoil we fear, in the form of climate catastrophe and its associated security threats, can be survived. Whether it's in service of a nostalgic attachment to white Western fantasies of childhood or plans to build cities for the future by buttressing them against threats from without and within, resilience helps to structure narratives of self-preservation in the face of confusing and frightening changes.

In these and other ways, resilience occupies a firm but flexible place in the settler-colonial imagination. Offering cover for the rationalization of prevailing hierarchies, the idea that the resilient will inherit – *deserve* to inherit – the earth, the concept of resilience builds on the evolutionary story of *homo economicus* and its founding principles of natural scarcity and survival of the fittest (Wynter and McKittrick 2015, 18). Enhancing the essentializing force of biology with the dynamics of adaptation and flexibility, resilience overlays the idea of natural inequality with the carrot and the stick of education: those who fail to be resilient are insufficiently flexible, or they lack discipline. Though it is billed as a natural capacity, it turns out that resilience is not for everyone. Built in to the very concept is the assumption of an outside, a source of ever-imminent disruption against which resilience must be mustered. The spectre of danger – natural disaster, terrorist attacks, epidemics – bolsters calls for community readiness, for population fitness. Implicitly and sometimes explicitly, this biopolitical imperative shores up the defences of white supremacy, even as it speaks the language of diversity, equity, inclusion, and reconciliation. Settler colonial resilience hails traditional Indigenous culture as a resource for environmental management at the same time as it casts Indigenous people as *un*resilient, a population at risk and by extension a risky population, one that must be managed to protect the health of the whole. Resilience upholds white supremacy in other ways. Held loosely together by the disciplinary threads of ecology and the psy-disciplines, vacillating between the poles of nature and morality, resilience promotes the ideals of white Western man as the index of human fitness. Black people are pathologized by this index, deemed both *too* resilient (lacking human refinement) and not resilient enough (lacking discipline). Settler colonial resilience discourse does not thereby just exclude those groups – IBPOC, 2SLGBTQIA+, people with disabilities – who do not fit the norm, it also subjects them to an array of surveillance and intervention mechanisms designed to manage the turbulent times "we" are living through.

In addition to exploring some of the ways resilience works, ambivalently, even contradictorily, to buttress colonialism, racism, white supremacy, and carceral violence, this book also addresses the critical theoretical appeal of *anti*resilience, a school of thought suffused in left melancholia that views resilience with suspicion for its lack of rigour and revolutionary fervour. *Anti*resilience, I suggest, does not disavow the racist, anthropocentric ideals of settler colonialism; rather, it harkens back to a Romantic ideal of human overcoming that pits solitary philosopher-heroes against a world of accumulating disorder and darkness. Though it disagrees about the stance that should be adopted towards that world, antiresilience shares with conventional resilience thinking the idea that we are living through times of unprecedented turmoil. It disregards the perspectives of those for whom the end of the world isn't a novel prospect to contemplate but an already-arrived-at reality from which it is possible – and urgent – to wrest life and meaning. The kind of resilience expressed, for example, in the opening words of African American poet Lucille Clifton's poem: "won't you celebrate with me / what i have shaped into / a kind of life?" The poem ends with an invitation to the reader to "come celebrate/ with me that everyday/ something has tried to kill me/ and has failed" (1993). Forgoing the prospect of learning to die in the Anthropocene (Scranton 2015a), this book has opted instead to take up that difficult invitation (difficult, for starters, because I don't think it's meant for me. Or maybe it is). The word "celebrate" is heavy with irony no matter who reads it, but for a white settler, it commands some recognition of complicity with the "something" that has tried to kill the speaker and failed – the thing against which she celebrates her resilience. It's an unsettling space to occupy, inside a gathering at which gratitude is tangled up with grief and anger, where one is not certain of finding welcome but is moved nevertheless to join in the complicated celebration.

Resilience Is a Metaphor

It is not to diminish the heft of the poem's call or the feelings it evokes to point out that it is a poem. One of the strands of this book focuses on the role of art – specifically, in this case, narrative fiction – in shaping visions of antiracist and decolonial resilience. I'm using the word "decolonial" cautiously, heeding Eve Tuck (Unangax̂) and K. Wayne Yang's warning that "decolonization is not a metaphor" (2012). In their much-cited essay of that name, Tuck and Yang call out "the ease with which the language of decolonization has been superficially adopted into education and other social sciences, supplanting prior ways of talking about social justice, critical methodologies, or approaches which decenter settler perspectives" (2012, 3). Decolonization, they assert, "is not a swappable term for other things we want to do to improve our societies and schools. Decolonization doesn't have a synonym" (2012, 3). Diluted of the specificity of the structure it calls out (colonialism) and the forms of justice it calls for – the return of "land/ water/ air/ subterranean earth," "land" for short (2012, 5) – decolonization-as-metaphor becomes a way for settlers to don the mantle of social justice advocacy and sidestep examination of their own complicity. It can also serve a stance of intellectual defensiveness, whereby literary and cultural scholars mis- or overstate the political impact of close reading. I'm mindful of that risk as I engage in a three-hundred-plus-page exercise in cultural and literary analysis. I also think it's worth attending to a minor casualty of broad readings of Tuck and Yang's essay: metaphor. In the way it is usually used, unconsciously as part of ordinary language, metaphor is banal, a bit thought-deadening but more or less benign. When it works surreptitiously to naturalize violence in the name of security (like "stopping the flow of illegal immigrants!"), metaphor can also be dangerous.[1] Metaphor can also be taken up consciously and creatively – as Christina

Sharpe does with "wake," for example – to rattle prevailing habits of mind, to activate latent memories and meanings, to make the strange familiar and the familiar strange. Engaging critically and imaginatively with metaphor is part of the process of unravelling the fabric of settler common sense. Metaphors of resilience make up a dominant thread in that fabric.

Of course, resilience as a concept is inescapably metaphorical, a fact that initially led to some scientific skepticism about its utility (Markusen 1999; Carpenter et al. 2001, Brand and Jax 2007). This book troubles some of the ways the term's conceptual elasticity has furnished settler-colonial imaginaries (think: the intrepid kayaker surfing the rapids) while seeing its figurative richness not as a liability but as a source of possibility for different, more transformative visions. More than just a word or a metaphor, resilience is also, as Michael Basseler has noted (2019a), inherently conducive to narrative.[2] Neoliberalism and settler colonialism have carved a road for resilience by privileging narratives in the vein of the "neoliberal worlding of a Eurocentric 'overrepresentation of Man,'" as Glynn and Cupples put it. However, as they go on to assert, resilience "does not originate with those narratives, nor is it reducible to them" (2022, 4). Like Glynn and Cupples, this book draws inspiration from Sylvia Wynter's conception of *homo narrans* in considering not only how resilience typically works but also how it *could* work and how it *has* worked otherwise as both frame and subject for humans' species being. Another way of saying this is that stories, including resilience stories, are key to human persistence – to resilience.

There is a fundamental recursiveness in this formulation that confounds how the relationship between storytelling or art and resilience often gets talked about. Social-ecological resilience advocates frequently tout the resilience-boosting value of art in terms of pedagogy or disruption. "Artistic expression has the power to synthesize complex stories and themes in ways that are immediately captivating," proclaims the catalogue for a 2019 World Bank exhibit "The Art of Resilience" (World Bank Group 2019). Art is thus valued for its capacity to convey in more accessible and engaging terms the truths of resilience science. A 2014 paper describing the role of art in fostering urban resilience and liveability ventures further to say, "Art can be disruptive. In this sense, artists are the outsiders: the powerful strangers who pose discomfiting questions to the self-satisfied, who speak truth to power. Resilience requires that we pay attention to what lies within and beyond the city gates of comfort and complacency. Artists are the ones who scan those horizons, who act as scouts and heralds of what is hidden and what is to come" (Musagetes et al. 2014). Confusingly, artists occupy two separate places in this vision, which confer different, mutually exclusive responsibilities: they are at once outsiders, charged with opening up a society to difference, and "scouts and heralds," enlisted as super-sensitive security guards charged with detecting and communicating imminent dangers. The contradiction makes a kind of accidental sense: societies are riven by tensions and incoherence, and artists may be especially attuned to pointing out the otherness that inhabits the most militant assertions of identity. But conventional resilience thinking does not acknowledge this contradiction, nor can it recognize the ambivalence at its heart. Nominally open to disruption and transformation, it is paranoically afraid of the shadows that lurk outside its borders. It does not want to know (it does not want art to show) what it doesn't already know.

Imagining Otherwise: Resilience and/or

Instead of thinking of how art or storymaking contributes to resilience, this book has argued that it's more useful to think about the converse: What models of resilience contribute to the sustaining practice of storymaking? We are living through turbulent times. To this broad, seemingly self-evident idea, resilience seems to offer a kind of solution: we need to learn how to live with it, to learn from and maybe even flourish through it. Rejecting the threads that tether that thought to the ideals of late liberalism and settler colonialism, this book has nevertheless found in resilience a capacious vehicle for representing "arts of living" through loss and danger (Baishya and Kumar 2022). It has also tried to keep in view the limits of resilience, not just in the concrete ecological sense that "the self-repairing capacity of ecosystems should no longer be taken for granted" (Folke et al. 2005, 558) but in its conceptual utility for thinking about change. Sarah Bracke suggests that resilience thinking "thwarts the developing of skills of imagining otherwise" (2016, 3), while MacKinnon and Derickson worry about its "evacuation of the political" (2012, 14), offering "resourcefulness" as an alternative concept that offers "a more productive means of challenging the hegemony of neoliberal capitalism" (14). The experience of COVID-19 intensified calls for "resistance, not resilience," as psychotherapist and Black Health Matters Lab principal investigator Roberta Timothy stresses: "It's not how much stuff we can take, how much violence we can choke off of, it has to be about how can we resist this, how do we dismantle this, how do we fight back ...?" (2021).

In the spirit of these challenges to the preeminence of resilience thinking, I asked students in a 2023 graduate class on resilience to engage in an exercise I called "Resilience and/or …." The assignment asked them "to propose supplements or alternatives to resilience to articulate conditions of human and planetary disruption, and/or to imagine things 'otherwise'" (O'Brien 2023). Of the fourteen thoughtful responses that were submitted, two were especially illuminating. Tayah Clarke offered the concept of *reworlding* which she defined, drawing on feminist abolitionist scholars Alisa Bierria, Jakeya Caruthers, and Brooke Lober, as "the process of 'burning down, shaking off, and building up'"; of "the everyday practice of willing an impossible future while resisting the deadly chaos of the present" (2022, 2, quoted in Clarke 2023, 1). Reworlding "centers liberation over adaptation, suggesting that we do not need to remain cyclically tied to the systems that inhibit life" (Clarke 2023, 2). Moreover, it emphasizes collectivity over individualism and dismantles colonial temporality, not only stretching forward into the future but "call[ing] on current generations to walk in the traditions and knowledges of those who lived in other worlds" (3). While Clarke called for the replacement of resilience, Zahra Tootonsab (2023) invited us to think about resilience alongside the concept of *sheltering*, understood in the context of her Bakhtiari nomad relatives in Iran. Against empty Western designations of Iranian women as resilient (or not resilient), Tootonsab outlines a Bakhtiari philosophy of "health, healing, and interdependency through migration" that operates in concert with "cycles of stability and change so that people can learn to survive and thrive with the land and all beings" (2). Describing traditional practices of weaving clothing, tents, beds, and blankets from cattle and local materials, she ventures, "I believe that one of the primary reasons Bakhtiari nomads have survived and adapted is their shelter-making skills, which were/are inspired and taught by Bakhtiari women" (2). Tootonsab offers these practices as metaphor and model for ways of addressing vulnerability in the present Iranian context of revolution.

The two concepts – reworlding and sheltering – expose the limits of resilience in different ways. Where resilience gathers around the status quo, reworlding demands better. Resilience describes a capacity; reworlding, by contrast, is an action, a radical political project, demanding movements of bold imagination and concrete praxis. Reworlding exposes the conservativism of resilience. By contrast, sheltering shows resilience to be indifferent to what's required, materially and imaginatively, for the conservation of human and more-than-human lifeways. Where resilience contains an imperative for toughness, sheltering as Tootonsab describes it engages the reality of vulnerability and shared responsibility for human and more-than-human protection from harm. It entails a specific kind of gendered labour, conducted in conversation with the ever-changing environment. Sheltering and reworlding are different, even incommensurable concepts that are nevertheless allied in their generative friction with resilience. Both contrast with its temporal inclination to the future, insisting on the incorporation of past traditions, past worlds into present-day imaginings. And in contrast to the universalist assertion of resilience, reworlding and sheltering are explicitly situated in specific histories and places. The idea of reworlding emerges from the distinct histories of the Black radical tradition and projects of decolonization from the global South, articulated in the "community education sessions, mutual aid networks, healing collectives, and protest mobilizations that were set in place during the 2020, 2016, and 2012 protests for racial justice" (Clarke 2023, 3). And the practice of sheltering, whether it is enacted in the mountains of Iran or in a Toronto park, is always necessarily embedded in the specificity of everyday practices, calibrated to the enabling conditions and dangers of local environments.

I am compelled by Tootonsab's and Clarke's, along with other scholars' and activists', imagination of alternatives to resilience. As this book has made clear, I think resilience still demands our attention, both as a vehicle of settler-colonial and white-supremacist ideology and as a tool for pre- and decolonial ideas of collective flourishing. In the latter mode, as we see in the literary works this book has explored, the dominant concept of resilience loses its swagger, its claims to self-evident virtue shaken by questions: Who or what counts as a being that can (or should) persist into the future? How did they get to be this way? What does persistence look like? What has been, what will be, lost in the process of becoming resilient? These questions resonate with Baishya and Kumar's assertion that "training the planetary imagination through modes of multiscalar thinking – both in terms of time and space – is the task incumbent upon us as we … envision ways of living otherwise (2022, 307). Thinking with resilience is not the end, but it can be part of that retraining.

Notes

INTRODUCTION

1 Nancy Fraser (2017) uses the term "progressive neoliberalism" to describe this cluster of ideas and policies, which Donald Trump's "reactionary populism" successfully countered in 2016.

2 This report elicited criticism from different quarters. Proponents of the free market bristled at the idea of fixed curbs on capitalist development and the implied requirement for governmental management (Lomborg 2012). From a radically different angle, Marxist critics and antipoverty activists challenged the antidevelopment agenda of the report, seeing in it a call for a "new corporate logic of planetary management" that would consolidate neocolonial relations between First and Third Worlds in the name of environmentalism (Ross 1994, 207).

3 Folke illustrates the metaphor through the example of a forest fire, which begins on the ground and then spreads to the crowns of trees and eventually the whole forest. The word "revolt" describes the reverberation of the disturbance across scales. "Remember" refers to the "accumulated experience and history of the system" embedded in the surviving seed bank and in surrounding structures and species (2006, 259).

4 The concept of a causal relationship between physical environment and social development, nourished by the pre-Darwinian evolutionary theories of Jean-Baptiste Lamarck and European explorers like Alexander von Humboldt, enjoyed wide circulation in the early twentieth century through the work of Anglo-American geographers such as Ellen Churchill Semple (1903). Of course, these anxieties largely ignored Europeans' own role as vectors of disease and destruction for Indigenous peoples and lands. The logic of environmental determinism has never fully fallen out of favour but persists in work such as Jared Diamond's popular 1997 book *Guns, Germs and Steel: The Fates of Human Societies*. See Peet (1985) for a comprehensive discussion of the evolution of environmental determinism.

5 In the years following the publication of Zolli and Healy's book (2012), Amin's story took an unhappy turn when he was found guilty of falsifying his finances in divorce proceedings with his wife and sentenced to four months in

jail (charges Amin denies). Amin noted that the judge in the trial repeatedly reminded potential jurors that he was Iranian "(the judge even pronounced it 'I-RAY-NIAN'), when in fact I am an American" (Amin 2019). When right-wing social media sites picked up the story, citing further reports that Amin had purchased guns following his conviction, an onslaught of comments ensued, questioning Amin's citizenship and identifying him as a Muslim terrorist (Walsh 2017). The point of mentioning these events is not to impugn Zolli and Healy's account of Amin's accomplishments as a scientist but to complicate the picture they sketch of a post 9/11 US as a complex adaptive system whose challenges are primarily infrastructural rather than sociopolitical.

6 Developed in the 1990s through the Beijer Institute for Ecological Economics, the Resilience Alliance comprises a group of physical and social scientists whose interdisciplinary work has significantly shaped the fields of environmental science and policy.

7 The premium Resilience Alliance members place on the ability to have fun is partly explainable by their practice of holding their nine-monthly weeklong workshops on various islands across the world (Parker and Hackett 2012, 26) – an unusual (enviable) mode of professional engagement that is itself worthy of scrutiny. Group rituals include limerick contests and induction into the Ralf Yourque Society. Ralf is a fictional creation, "a brilliant, challenging, cantankerous maverick scientist, much as RA members view themselves and their work as outside the march of normal science. He is the embodied spirit of the group, representing the fun and hard work occurring on islands; he is brought so much to life that some RA members refused to acknowledge him as fictional" (30).

8 Nikolas Rose notes a similar aspiration towards integration in the psy-disciplines, which "have been able to supply a whole variety of models of selfhood and recipes for action in relation to the government of persons by professionals in different locales" (1996, 139). Flourishing at the interface of the psy- and eco-disciplines, resilience thinking represents a perhaps inevitable confluence of two transdisciplinary tides.

9 Shell was one of the first corporations to formally incorporate the concept of resilience into its planning.

10 The "psy disciplines" describe fields of knowledge such as psychology, psychiatry, and psychoanalysis that are concerned with mental life and behaviour. The term originates in the work of Foucault, and is extended by critics such as Nikolas Rose, to emphasize the power-knowledge dynamics at work in these fields that "generate particular kinds of expert knowledge and have the capacity to produce politically expedient measures of normativity which can be harnessed to shape particular kinds of socially desirable individual" (McAvoy 2014, 1528).

11 A return to the essentialist blood-and-soil fantasy of national identity is evident in conservative movements worldwide. An exchange following a 2017

terrorist attack in London offers a clue to what this might mean for resilience thinking. Rejecting the response by officials that followed the usual liberal formula of expressing horror but rallying spirits with invocations of national resilience, Janet Albrechtsen in *The Australian* scoffed: "Surely Brits are tired of being resilient." Albrechtsen took London Mayor Sadiq Khan to task for failing to say that "defeating Islamist ideology is the greatest challenge of our time" (2017, 2). The comment, consistent with attitudes on the far right (since hardened and broadcast more unabashedly), rejects the delicacy of liberal/resilience thinking, countering its complex analysis with a simpler and older version of white supremacy.

12 Many scholars have highlighted the distinction between racial capitalism and settler colonialism, calling out the latter for its primary emphasis on land dispossession at the expense of (or sometimes implicitly conflated with) the dynamics of the white supremacist economic system that undergirded chattel slavery (Dorries, Hugill, and Tomiak 2022; King 2019; Garba and Sorentino 2020). Others highlight the inseparability of racism and settler colonialism: "The logics of white possession and the disavowal of Indigenous sovereignty are materially and discursively linked," Goenpul scholar Aileen Moreton-Robinson notes (2015, xiii), the dehumanization of Indigenous people a crucial rationale for their subjection to genocide and land theft. This book emphasizes the overlapping features of settler colonialism and racial capitalism while acknowledging that there are distinct differences in their formations and expressions.

13 The ideological work of narration, focused on describing the preservation of integrity through change, is particularly evident in psychosocial models of resilience, whether they focus on "trajectories of positive adjustment" for individuals following traumatic events (Bonanno and Diminich 2013, 379) or on a constellation of risk factors rather than a single adverse incident. In both cases, conventional psychosocial resilience stories highlight the achievement of particular milestones (e.g., school attendance, graduation, employment, marriage) based on normative developmental models – narratives of a successful life.

14 Latour (2004) uses the concept "matter of concern" to get past the usual critical theoretical impasse whereby the *objects* of critique dissolve into ideology while the *ground* of critique – where the critic stands – mysteriously retains the aura of fact. The emphasis shifts, in this formulation, from a world of fact and fantasy to the process of mattering, whereby a constellation of forces, feelings, knowledges, materials, and institutions emerges as sites of meaning.

15 The desire for such a ground might inform Jeremy Walker and Melinda Cooper's observation that resilience thinking "cannot be challenged from within the terms of complex systems theory but must be contested, if at all, on completely different terms, by a movement of thought that is truly counter-systemic" (2011, 157). N. Katherine Hayles suggests that it's possible

to get critical purchase on systems theory by putting it in a narrative frame, by thinking of it as a narrative emerging from, and attempting to organize particular historical contingencies. Narrative reveals "the exhilarating and chaotic space of constructions that are contingent on time and place, dependent on specific women and men making situated decisions" (2000, 137). She illustrates this point with a compelling narration of the formative influence of World War II on the work of scientists between 1946 and 1956 that led to creation of the theory of cybernetics (147). What this argument can't really take account of is how narrative can work alongside systems theory in a mutually reinforcing way, such as we see in the origin story of resilience ecology.

16 See O'Brien (2019) for a discussion of how settler-colonial cultures misapprehend the relationship between resilience and storytelling that many Indigenous cultures emphasize.

17 "The essence of an oral creation story," Vizenor explains, "was not absolute but deferred, and with respect to the tease and creative vision of another native storier" (2019, 2). He elaborates: "Native stories ... create elusive images of natural motion that are clearly more than the simulations of similitude and sincerity, more than the conventions of cultural intrigue, adventures, or petitions of commercial literary victimry. Native stories are not priestly liturgies. The stories of creation and the marvelous scenes of visionary motion or transmotion are related to visual memories, and without recitations, storyline structures, plot resolutions, shibboleths of character development, or the denouement of commercial literature" (40).

18 Both are evident in Sharpe's narration of the story of twelve-year old Mikia, who faced harsh disciplinary action for defacing a wall at school while her white friend only paid a fine. The events are the subject of a *New York Times* story in which Mikia appears only as a faintly drawn figure even though she is the nominal focus. Sharpe conveys Mikia's point of view by reproducing the text of the story with all the words redacted except hers: "Hi" – the word she wrote on the wall – "I only wrote one word, and I had to do all that," and "It isn't fair" (2016, 123). Those redactions call out, if they cannot overcome, the racist dynamic of narrative condemnation, while annotations deepen the resonances of the story, locating it in the larger history of slavery. This could be read as a decolonial resilience story.

19 "Shooting the Rapids" (Wack 1985a) and "Uncharted Waters Ahead" (1985b) are the titles of two articles in *Harvard Business Review* by a Royal Dutch Shell corporate planner focused on scenario planning as a tool of resilience. The same metaphor appears in Peter Schwartz's 2004 book, *Inevitable Surprises: Thinking Ahead in a Time of Turbulence*, where Schwartz explains, "The trick in navigating any set of rapids is being well prepared for all types of movement, and aware of the ways in which movement itself is changing. That's not an easy task, for rapids change all the time. The bottom of the river may only shift slowly, but the water level changes with the season and the weather. The

rapids in the late spring can be a raging torrent of white water, while in the late autumn they can vanish as the water level drops" (14).

20 Other resilience scholars use tamer water metaphors. In their *Resilience Thinking: Sustaining Ecosystems and People in a Changing World*, for example, Brian Walker and David Salt instruct the reader to "imagine you are on a boat docked in a calm harbor and you want to quickly carry a brim-full cup of water across a stateroom without spilling. Now imagine the same situation but with the boat in rough seas" (2006, x). Andrew Zolli and Ann Marie Healy counsel, "If we cannot control the volatile tides of change, we can learn to build better boats" (2012, 5). And the resonance many commentators have noted between resilience and neoliberalism is carried through a mutual propensity for hydrological metaphors: in his 1981 address to the London School of Economics, Friedrich Hayek described "multiple 'streams' of value, ebbing and flowing into a river of liquid capital, constantly readjusting the production process, coursing down an ever-changing river bed" (Walker and Cooper 2011, 149).

21 The differences between the concepts can also be traced to the moments of their respective emergence: survivance, which first appeared in Vizenor's work in the mid-nineties (see especially his 1996 *Manifest Manners: Postindian Warriors of Survivance*) is in dialogue with the then ambient discourses of post-structuralism and postmodernism, and Sharpe's "wake work" (2016) draws on insights from intersectional feminism and critical race studies.

22 Dionne Brand indicts this wish as a powerful refrain in media conversations about COVID, noting that "we are, in fact, still in that awful normal that is narrativized as minor injustices, or social ills that would get better if some of us waited, if we had the patience to bear it, if we had noticed and were grateful for the miniscule 'progress'" (2020).

23 The concept of Indigenous futurisms draws on Afrofuturism, whose conventional origin story (the white critic Mark Dery) Dillon counters (Dillon and Marques 2021), celebrating instead Alondra Nelson's 2002 *Social Text* special issue on that subject.

24 Dillon (Dillon and Marques 2021) notes that Gerald Vizenor and Cherokee writer Diane Glancy used the aeronautical term "slipstream," which describes the flowing together of space and time, to describe their writing in the 1970s, long before the word's conventionally recognized literary birth in the work of cyberpunk writer Bruce Sperling. Asserting this history, like the history of Afrofuturism, is vital, not just to remedy the perennial erasure of IBPOC innovation, but also, in the context of speculative or science fiction, to highlight that IBPOC writers have been forerunners in imagining the ends and beginnings of worlds.

25 Indigenous futurism is also an explicitly transnational endeavour. Dillon's 2012 edited collection, *Walking the Clouds: An Anthology of Indigenous Science Fiction*, contained work by writers from North America, the Caribbean, and

Australia. She later revised the term, inspired by Afrofuturism, to "Indigenous futurisms" to highlight its reflection of "the richness of Indigenous communities globally" (Dillon and Marques 2021, 6).

26 Dillon has identified Vizenor's concept of survivance as a "*sine qua non* of Indigenous futurisms" (2016).

27 As I argue in chapter 3, I am not suggesting that all critiques of resilience represent a failure of imagination. Taking decolonization and racial justice as the framework from which to imagine better futures, I am suggesting that both resilience and antiresilience can work against those aims or they can work towards them. The latter ideas are the ones I am suggesting merit more attention.

CHAPTER ONE

1 As critics have noted (see, for example, Heer 2010), the article does not distinguish between Canadian-born and international students, undermining the authors' claims that it is not about race.

2 This new obligation weighs especially heavily on mothers, who are told that "'a mother usually enjoys entering into her baby's play. Both of them enjoy the little games that mothers and babies have always played from time immemorial.' (This marking back to time immemorial is a way of skipping over the more recent past)" (Wolfenstein [1951] 1958, 91). This normalization of fun may lead, Wolfenstein notes, to a mother wondering what is wrong with her if she doesn't enjoy activities (e.g., nursing) that she is told she is meant to: "Her self-evaluation can no longer be based entirely on whether she is doing the right and necessary things, but becomes involved with nuances of feeling which are not under voluntary control. Fun has become not only permissible but required, and this requirement has a special quality different from the obligations of the older morality" (92).

3 Wolfenstein's essay is prescient in its identification of a tendency that would only increase in the decades since she wrote her article: the diffusion of fun into all aspects of life. She notes, for example, that "there has been a mutual penetration of work and play. Work tends to be permeated with behavior formerly confined to after work hours. Play conversely tends to be measured by standards of achievement previously applicable only to work. One asks onself not only in personal relations but now also at work: Did they like me? Did I make a good impression? And at play, no less than at work, one asks: Am I doing as well as I should?" ([1951] 1958, 93).

4 "The woods were my Ritalin," Louv says, expressing a common tendency to read ADHD (without citing any evidence) not as a neurological disorder but a metaphor for restlessness born of inactivity, too many video games, etc. (2016, 10).

5 Another caller puts his fears for the future even more bluntly: "As we try to idiot-proof the world we're going to produce idiots" (Goldman 2016).

6 First published in 2009, Skenazy's book was revised and expanded in 2021 with a different (more professional, less bloggy) subtitle. "Giving Our Children the Freedom We Had without Going Nuts with Worry" was replaced with "How Parents and Teachers Can Let Go and Let Grow."

7 "Commandment 3" for free-range parents: "Avoid Experts: Who Knew You Were Doing Everything Wrong? ... Them!" (2009, 21).

8 The identification of "bureaucracy" as the enabling structure for the litigation industry highlights a key element in these critiques: while many call out the commercial interests (read: greed) that they see as motivating both lawyers and clients, no one indicts capitalism. The implicit wish, rather, is for a return to an earlier, more straightfoward iteration of capitalism, an as-yet minimally financialized system that resonated more easily with the myth of rugged individualism.

9 In 1958, after the passing of laws prohibiting segregation on buses, eight African Americans in Montgomery, Alabama, filed a lawsuit demanding the integration of the city's public parks. The city responded by closing twelve of them "because 'this attempt poses grave problems involving the welfare and public safety of all the citizens of the City of Montgomery'" (Wolcott 2012, 162).

10 Wolcott cites the example of Shenandoah National Park in Virginia, which designated a separate campground for African Americans, along with separate bathrooms and other facilities, noting that (unsurprisingly) "few blacks ventured into the park until the 1970s" (2012, 170).

11 Given its centrality to his book, Louv's definition of nature is surprisingly amorphous. Citing Gary Snyder, who in turn channels John Milton, he summarizes, "For the purpose of this book, when I use the word 'nature' in a general way I mean natural wildness: biodiversity, abundance – related loose parts in a backyard or rugged mountain ridge. Most of all, nature is reflected in our capacity for wonder. *Nasci*. To be born" (2005, 8–9). Identified variously with an ecological property (wildness, biodiversity, abundance), particular places (yards, mountains), and a spiritual capacity (wonder), "nature" is both thing and quality, outside and within humans, determining our proper orientation to the world.

12 Foucault elaborates: "When I say 'killing,' I obviously do not mean simply murder as such, but also every form of indirect murder: the fact of exposing someone to death, increasing the risk of death for some people, or, quite simply, political death, expulsion, rejection, and so on" (2003, 256).

13 The article implies that it is these latter pursuits, rather than academic striving (note the contrasting language; the Asian students are "single-minded," while the white students are "building their lives"), that define the university's role as "oases of dialogue, mutual understanding, and diversity" (Findlay and Kohler 2010). "Diversity" will, presumably, inevitably flow into

"mutual understanding" – an assumption Ahmed (2012) takes to task in *On Being Included: Racism and Diversity in Institutional Life*, which extends her discussion of the hegemony of "happy multiculturalism" to the specific institutional context of the university.

14 Christakis also questioned its selectivity, citing the hypothetical example of Christian students being offended by "skin-revealing" costumes – a problem, she noted, that no one seemed to be worried about (Friedersdorf 2015).

15 The allusion to "bad names" is a specific reference to a female student who was upset at being called a "bitch" by her roommate. That the incident is framed in the article as an isolated (and trivial) event implies that this is how all instances of "bad" name-calling should be regarded – as one-off insults disconnected from broader social structures (Friedersdorf, 2015).

16 In his piece in *The Atlantic* about the student protests at Yale, Friedersdorf concurs, "If an email about Halloween costumes has them skipping class and suffering breakdowns, either they need help from mental-health professionals or they've been grievously ill-served by debilitating ideological notions they've acquired about what ought to cause them pain" (2015). In this effort to highlight the absurdity of the students' protests (which, by linking them to a single email, ignores the constellation of events that precipitated the protests including the blackface incident), it's not clear what point Friedersdorf seeks to advance in the reference to mental-health; in the context, it reads less like an acknowledgment of the possibility of genuine suffering than a lazily thrown together euphemism for "they're crazy!"

17 See O'Brien (2014) for an extended analysis of the currency of resilience in private education.

18 The school's website offers unambiguous assurance of student success with the following words from the headmaster: "King's College School is one of the most successful and prestigious schools in the UK. Founded by royal charter in 1829, it is a school whose exceptional academic standards sit easily beside great endeavour and success in a wide range of other activities. These qualities have helped King's reach the top of national league tables whilst enjoying one of the best records in sport, music and drama of any school in the country" (Halls n.d.).

19 While Randolph locates the value of grit in British boarding schools, a 2014 conference hosted by King's College School in the UK on the theme "True Grit: Developing Emotional Resilience" chose a different touchstone (Independent 2014): conference posters featured an image of John Wayne. Though the choice could be read as a jokey allusion to the actor's starring role in the 1969 film from which the conference took its title, there is nothing in the conference program that suggests it is meant to be read ironically. Titles of presentations, including "True Grit: Standing Up to the 21st-Century" and "Social Media, Gaming and Adolescence," and articles citing the conference, with titles such as "Don't Panic: Empower Your Child Online" and "Emotional Resilience: It's

the Armour You Need for Modern Life," convey a sense of collective alarm about contemporary life in which (again echoing free-range parents) concerns about technology loom large, part of a broader anxiety about globalization.

20 The definition raises some questions, such as whether "nervous energy" may not fuel a worthy activity or vitality an *un*worthy one, or what counts as worthy activity, and whether worthiness and vitality are meant to define each other in a circular (and, it must be pointed out, not very scientific) way. Peterson and Seligman do acknowledge that vitality, implied rather than identified in classical accounts of virtue, is one of the more difficult traits to define but is included in the list of positive character attributes because of evidence of its contribution to "the good life" (2004, 210).

21 Not all "evil" humour is equally bad, they point out: derogatory humour may be acceptable "when it calls attention to pomposity and pretentiousness. A wealthy businessman slipping on a banana peel as he hurries off to close a million-dollar deal is a lot funnier than a homeless mother taking the same fall on the way to a shelter" (2004, 531). Interestingly, the difference between the two situations is defined by inferred moral qualities rather than material circumstance, attention to which would muddy the argument for character as an independent variable. The question of what gauge should be used to determine who – by virtue of their dubious character – would be a legitimate target of humour is left unanswered.

22 Notwithstanding the epidemic of anxiety that is said to be afflicting the children of "aspirational families," it should not come as a surprise that it is these children who score highest on character tests. In Britain, the educational charity Sutton Trust conducted a survey that found extroversion (a measure of confidence according to Seligman and Peterson's list) is associated with both wealthier backgrounds and higher earnings: "Conscientiousness, self-discipline, efficiency and organisation are all, predictably, linked to higher-earning careers in the report. Adults from wealthier backgrounds, where parents had a professional job, were in addition 'significantly' more extrovert, displaying greater openness, imagination, aspiration and intellectual curiosity" (Weale 2016). Citing the teachability of character, the report calls on schools with a high population of disadvantaged students to concentrate on "wider skills as well as academic attainment" and to undertake "interventions to improve beneficial personality traits" (Baggini 2016).

23 Thanks to Simon Orpana and Jean Comaroff, who both pointed out to me what an excellent case study of resilience *The Martian* makes.

24 Numerous reviewers comment on the film's use of humour; see, for example, Travers (2015) and Truffaut-Wong (2015).

25 It is telling that some accounts quote screenwriter Drew Goddard as describing the movie as "a love letter to NASA" (McClintock 2015; McDonald 2015), raising the question of to what extent Goddard or his (mis)quoters see space exploration as science's ultimate goal.

26 Of the represented contrast between the American and Chinese space agencies, one reviewer has this to say, "There's some barely obscured propaganda, as well. The film goes out of its way to declare that, unlike the Chinese space program, NASA is a civilian agency, publicly funded and bound by laws regarding transparency and ethics. But, hey – just because it's propaganda doesn't mean it isn't true" (McDonald 2015). Other commentators have read the inclusion of the Chinese subplot as part of a wider move in Hollywood to gain a foothold in the lucrative Chinese market – a ploy that appears to have succeeded in the case of *The Martian*, which earned $50 million in its Chinese opening (Hoad 2015).

27 In the years since *The Martian*'s release, this scene has come to look increasingly implausible given China's increasing dominance in the field of space exploration and President Xi Jinping's stated ambition to make the country a "great space power" (Myers 2021).

CHAPTER TWO

1 In their study of the 100RC process in Washington, DC, Malini Ranganthan and Eve Bratman note that, in the process of establishing priorities for the resilient city, "everyday threats, such as gentrification or food insecurity, that do not fall under the categories of environment or climate per se tend to be ignored" (2021, 119).

2 Overlaying the material risks and opportunities of urban life is a history of ambivalent symbolism dating back to Enlightenment in which cities were seen to emblematize "an anarchic, indefinable, and uncontrollable mesh of bodies and structures" that was antithetical to nature: "toxic, human, degraded, fallen" (Ansfield 2015, 132). However, "even in its hazardous fluidity and unruly rapidity," as Bench Ansfield notes, "the city represented a fundamental achievement of Man: domination over an equally treacherous nature and implementation of human knowledge models onto a physical landscape" (2015, 132).

3 These projects resonate with the foundation's less publicized history of support for eugenicist projects in Nazi Germany (Schambra 2013).

4 The language of resilience seeps into the branding of the Rockefeller Foundation, portrayed on its website as "among the most respected and deep-rooted of American philanthropies," which is also characterized by its "fleet-footedness" and "reputation as a trailblazer that convenes unlikely partnerships and sparks innovations for transformative change" (The Rockefeller Foundation n.d.).

5 With the aim of achieving global coverage, the foundation divided the world into regions: Africa, Central and South America, Europe, Middle East, North America, Oceania, South Asia and Southeast Asia. Of the thirty-three cities selected in the first round, fourteen were located in North America, New

Zealand, and Australia (including Melbourne, one of the case studies in this chapter) (Rodin 2013).

6 Australian cities, Jacobs notes, "developed through an intensified variant of the more general spatial violence of settler colonialism ... proceed[ing] on the assumption of (re)settlement/dispossession. They were shrines to the colonial vision and imaginary of making productive land considered to be unproductive in European terms of property and utility. The territories over which Australian cities were built were secured by means (sometimes violent, sometimes merely tokenistic, and certainly unjust) that have not been able to sustain their legal and moral legitimacy into the present" (2012, 145). This illegitimacy forms part of the backdrop of vulnerability that fuels the urban resilience project.

7 Jacobs uses the term "postcolonial" in her 1996 study but with the qualifications and unease that – pressed by Indigenous scholars' objections to its clear misrepresentation of present-day realities – helped to generate the (still uneasy but more accurate) label "settler colonial" to describe those societies – Australia, Aotearoa New Zealand, Canada, the United States, and South Africa – in which the colonists "come to stay" (Wolfe 2006, 388).

8 The strategies are envisioned by the foundation as "living documents" and "holistic and actionable roadmaps to a resilient future" (Berkowitz, 2018).

9 Bohland, Davoudi, and Lawrence use the terms "machine" and "assemblage" to describe the operation of resilience in the urban context (2018). Sophie Webber, Helga Leitner, and Eric Sheppard prefer the term "complex" because of the presence of relatively immovable top down forces – including a network of organizations, metrics of assessment, techniques of institutionalization, and "experimental discourses and practices that seek to marketize urban resilience" (2021, 344).

10 Given the program's tilt towards the already somewhat resilient, it isn't surprising that "a disproportionate number (more than 75%) of participating cities in 100RC score 'high' or 'very high' on the Human Development Index (HDI), with the most vulnerable cities "effectively 'left behind'" (Fitzgibbon and Mitchell 2019, 653).

11 The phrase initially appears in a passage at the beginning of the document under the heading "People are at the Heart of All Cities," which reads: "A resilient Melbourne will draw on the strengths of our diverse communities and geographies, to pursue our shared interests, embrace our differences and be stronger together. We will help communities prepare for change and whatever the future may hold. We will work *today, tomorrow* and *together*, towards a viable, sustainable, liveable and prosperous Melbourne" (City of Melbourne 2016, ii, italics added).

12 In her analysis of urban reserves in Canada as sites of both colonialism and resistance, Julie Tomiak (2017) locates the emergence of these spaces within a history of Indigenous dispossession of lands occupied by the city.

13 Reconciliation is a prominent theme in the strategy: participants in the consultation process expressed the desire to live in a city where "residents know the history of Indigenous peoples and are committed to taking action for Truth and Reconciliation" (City of Toronto 2019, 7). Chapter 3 considers in more detail the tendency in resilience discourse focused on Indigenous people to employ the language of health vs politics.

14 See Laforme (2017) for a critical analysis of the initial "purchase" and subsequent settlement.

15 Carolyn King, the Mississaugas of the New Credit chief who launched the suit that culminated in the 2010 settlement, discusses these obligations in a 2017 interview (Weinberger 2017).

16 While it may be fair to say that "all my relations" thinking is shared by "many local Indigenous communities and communities across Canada" (City of Toronto 2018, 24), the prominence accorded to well-known Guelph-based Cherokee-Greek-German writer Thomas King draws attention to the relative absence of local Indigenous voices.

17 A growing body of research on settler colonial cities focuses on understanding how the violences of the past "have been recalibrated, recomposed, and transformed in ways that allow them to continue to shape relationships in the present" (Hugill 2022, 5). See also Tomiak (2017, 933) and the special issue of *Settler-Colonial Studies* edited by Libby Porter and Oren Yiftachel (2019).

18 While the Melbourne strategy uses the British spelling, "liveability," the Toronto strategy uses the American spelling: "livable." For the sake of consistency, except when quoting, I will use the British spelling.

19 The 2021 rankings show declining scores for Canada due to COVID-19 lockdowns (The Economist 2021). Sixty per cent of the top ten cities are in Australia and Aotearoa New Zealand, with Auckland ranked the most liveable city.

20 McArthur and Robin provide a representative sample of "liveability" statements from different cities, demonstrating similarities across regions that highlight the term's global currency and expression of international urban theory rather than local priorities (2019, 1714–5).

21 Several different formal ranking systems measure urban liveability, including the Economist Intelligence Unit's Global Liveability Index, the Mercer Quality of Living Survey, and the Organization for Economic Cooperation and Development Better Life Index. Among the indicators measured in liveability rankings are safety and security, crime, climate, transportation, infrastructure, health care, public policies and services, business environment, cost of living, recreational amenities, education, housing, gross domestic product (GDP) per capita, sanitation, culture, air quality, and natural capital, as well as qualitative measures focused on lifestyle, well-being, happiness, tolerance, and environmental aesthetics (Kashef 2016, 243).

22 Among the amenities the Melbourne strategy lists as contributing to liveability are a sporting precinct, art galleries, museums, libraries, and theatres, all of which support a "rich and diverse culture" and "economic opportunities." The strategy cites Melbourne's consistently high ranking for liveability as reflecting the city's "stability and security, access to healthcare, education and culture, advanced infrastructure and relatively clean environment" (City of Melbourne 2016, 20).

23 A map included in the Toronto strategy reveals that racialized residents are "overrepresented" in low income neighbourhoods "compared to their share of the city's population," with "visible minorities" comprising 68 per cent of residents in the city's poorest census tracts (City of Toronto 2019, 120).

24 While "government" is invoked negatively, the private sector is represented as a boon to community. The Melbourne strategy, for example, offers a proposal for "community-led neighbourhood renewal and development pilot projects" in which "property companies will trial new ways of putting residents at the heart of neighbourhood and local infrastructure planning and operations" (City of Melbourne 2016, 116–7). The possibility that the interests of property companies might not be aligned with neighbourhoods is not considered.

25 Canada's multicultural policy, which has been the subject of broad, trenchant criticism (Bannerji 2000; Mackey 2002; Thobani 2007), is frequently cited as a model for other nations, including Australia.

26 The Toronto strategy makes frequent references to "extensive public and stakeholder engagement" and "consultation" (City of Toronto 2019, 12, 64), raising questions about the distinction between the two groups: Which parts of the public would *not* have a stake in the outcome of the process of revisioning the city? Fitzgibbon and Mitchell highlight this distinction in their detailed analysis of (in)equity in 100RC and note that, while most of the cities' strategies (Toronto and Melbourne are not among those cited in the study) mention specific marginalized groups and outline actions to improve their circumstances, with a few exceptions, "the needs, priorities and portrayal of disempowered groups are being interpreted and communicated by actors that do not belong to those groups" (2019, 654).

27 In the years since the founding of Our Women's Voices, which still has an active presence on Instagram, Keosha Love has continued to focus on Black women's empowerment as an artist, activist, and educator, offering workshops on topics such as poetry, self-care, and racial equality. Her art and advocacy work have led to sponsorships with Nike, Footlocker, and Absolut Vodka. Her website describes Keosha as "a driven change-maker who has become a well-recognized voice that inspires others to use theirs" (Love n.d.).

28 The strategies go beyond identifying connections and complexities within Toronto and Melbourne to gesture towards the place of each city in global networks; the Melbourne strategy observes that cities are "increasingly in-

terdependent, meaning the effects of events in one place can be felt around the world" (City of Melbourne 2016, 11) and the Toronto strategy uses the image of a globe with cities connected via arrows to illustrate the theme of "Engagement in a Global Resilience Network" (City of Toronto 2018, 43).

29 Husam identifies "youth-oriented programs" such as "Youth Employment Services" and BITS (Business in the Streets – a non-profit program to support young, emerging underresourced entrepreneurs) in helping him to launch his career as a photographer. Neither Joe nor Keosha cite any city agencies or resources in describing their resilience journeys.

30 Psychiatric survivors and health studies scholars have called out the practice by which personal stories – once deployed as a radical empowerment strategy for survivors of addiction and mental illness – have been appropriated and shaped to the ends (fundraising, policymaking, and patient management) of mental health and addiction agencies (Woods, Hart, and Spandler 2019; McWade 2016.)

31 See also Howell and Veronka's (2012) discussion of the politics of resilience in mental health care.

32 The postcards also gesture to the scalar limits of the urban resilience strategy: immigration policies fall under federal, not municipal, jurisdiction. Suggesting that this kind of scalar "imprecision" is a common element in urban resilience strategies, MacKinnon and Derickson argue that "viewing cities and regions as self-organizing units is fundamentally misplaced, serving to divorce them from wider processes of capital accumulation and state regulation" (2012, 8). Urban resilience strategies take capitalism as a given, including the requirement it creates for cities and regions to compete for investment such that one city's resilience is predicated on capital flight from somewhere else (9).

33 References to the costliness of 100RC presumably pertain to the operating budgets of resilience initiatives, including the salaries of resilience officers appointed to each city, and not to efforts to broaden the philanthrocapitalist net through annual junkets that gathered tech entrepreneurs and venture capitalists in Italy where they were served "meals literally topped with edible gold leaves" (Cappell 2019).

34 According to the Department of Health and Human Services, the decision to involve police in the implementation of the lockdown arose partly from "broad public safety" concerns "including but not limited to child safety, sex offenders and family violence" (Glass 2020, 119). Later investigation revealed that the number of ongoing child protection cases and "persons of interest" in the towers – none of which were deemed to be high risk – were more or less in line with state-wide levels (119). The moral panic over child sex abuse recalls the 2007 Northern Territory Emergency response, which resulted in the severe curtailment of Aboriginal people's rights. Chapter 6 considers this event in some detail.

35 The mayor is known for his "dry and circumlocutionary speaking style," described by one critic as reflecting his approach to issues: "Within individual sentences, he searches for an agreeable balance on the issue at hand, and ideas and arguments often circle back on one another as clauses and subclauses nest within one another. These sentences ... contain the kind of lawyerly hedging that limits meaning and substance" (Park 2016).

36 They note that more than a third of displaced encampment residents are Indigenous (Kanji and Withers 2021, 3).

37 Unsurprisingly, resilience looms large in official and media reports of cities' responses to COVID-19. In July, 2021, *The Age* assessed the damage of the pandemic, acknowledging that "there are no easy answers here. But Melbourne and its people are resilient and adaptive, and if they display the same agility now as they did at the start of the pandemic, Melbourne can once again come alive and rank among the world's most liveable cities" ("Melbourne is" 2021).

CHAPTER THREE

1 Jeremy Gilbert sums up the changes of the last few decades this way:

> Almost everything I was afraid of happening over the past 30 years has happened. Everything my political mentors warned might happen, since I was a boy growing up on a poor council estate (that's a housing project, if you're American) in the North of England in the early 80s, or a high-school student reading denunciations of Thatcherism in the left press a few years later, has turned out just as badly as they said it would. And yet I don't wish I was living 40 years ago. The point seems to be: this is the world we were all afraid of; but it's also sort of the world we wanted. (2012)

2 See Métis/Michif scholar Max Liboiron's incisive analysis of the significance of the threshold concept to changing conceptions of pollution throughout the twentieth century (2021, 55–62).

3 Cazdyn also uses the phrase "the new chronic" to describe a temporal politics that "insists on maintaining the system and perpetually managing its constitutive crises, rather than confronting even a hint of the terminal, the system's (the body's, the planet's, capitalism's) own death (2012, 5). The new chronic forecloses the imagination of death or cure, along with their political counterpart: revolution. Though the thrust of Cazdyn's 2012 book, *The Already Dead: The New Time of Politics, Culture, and Illness*, coincides in some respects with Evans and Reid's antiresilience argument, there is an important distinction. While for Cazdyn, death and cure are imaginative horizons rooted in material experience, of illness and suffering under capitalism, Evans and Reid emphasize the philosophical – the critical theoretical – freedom that has been surrendered to the dreary and futile task of caring for life.

4 In what looks like an echo of that wariness but is more likely an accident of copyediting, the terms "Anthropocene" and "anthropocenic" (i.e., pertaining to the idea of the Anthropocene) are misspelled in different ways throughout the book, including "Anthropocence" (Evans and Reid 2014, 3, 11), "anthropocentric" (5, 7), and "anthropocentic" (11).

5 This argument recalls Berlant's (2011) concept of cruel optimism, but without the nuance and compassion that lead her to try and understand how attachments can be simultaneously harmful *and* sustaining – such that they cannot simply be abandoned. Scranton directly cites Berlant's "cruel optimism," which he attributes to "a system sustained by hopes that can never be fulfilled" (2015a, 79). This is a major oversimplification of Berlant's analysis, which seeks to understand the process by which an affect like hope is attached not to a specific object but to its own perpetuation. Scranton, like Evans and Reid, understands affect according to a simple calculus of positive – that is, geared towards the rational pursuit of freedom/aesthetic enrichment – or negative, leading towards subjugation. The indeterminate zone that Berlant clearly illuminates – that zone in which many, maybe even most, of us live, in which attachment and stuckness occasionally give way to positive change – is not part of the calculus.

6 Arguing that Judith Butler's call, in her 2004 book *Precarious Life: The Powers of Mourning and Violence*, to recognize vulnerability as a "shared condition" is complicit with the dominant power regime, Evans and Reid suggest that "Butler ... should be associated within the very tradition that the Left is forced to think against" (2014, 107).

7 As Carolyn Veldstra observes, Scranton's invocation of the Levinasian/Derridean uppercase "Other" connotes a meeting of two, rather than a complex interaction between many (Email message to author, 24 October 2016). Privileging the Other over others extends, in Evans and Reid's case, to a curious approach to the scholarly practice of acknowledgments. They begin by noting that "this book undeniably owes a tremendous personal debt to some remarkable colleagues with whom we have shared our ideas, thoughts and problems," and go on to say:

> Not that we hoped that they would respect some confidentiality pact – as if we could only impart our ideas to a select few who we believed wouldn't give the game away until it was ready for market so to speak. We have no fear for the sharing of ideas. Every one of us is a collaborator of multiple kinds. We maintain that friendships worthy of the name demand giving over the work to those who will offer a rigorous critique and infidelity to the prose. It is done so *with* confidence. And so it is to the critically minded in our midst, those who have the courage to speak truth to power that we begin our acknowledgments and offer our sincerest gratitude. Their names are sufficiently etched throughout this text for those who are intrigued

to know more about our sources of inspiration to be able to recognize. (2014, xiii)

While they go on to name names, this rambling meditation offers a muddled account of scholarship in which the gesture towards acknowledgment (subjection to others?) serves largely to elevate the idea of the exceptional individual scholar.

8 Implying multiculturalism and tolerance are shibboleths of the left, Scranton appears unaware of the vast body of scholarship pointing to the role of both in upholding white supremacy (Ahmed 2012; Hage 2000; Thobani 2007; Mackey 2002).

9 For McRobbie, the creativity of daily lived experience extends to the media culture that antipostmodern theorists decried in much the same way as antiresilience theorists do. Noting the tendency of Baudrillard and others to lament "the incursion of imagery and communication into those spaces that once were private – where the psyche previously had the chance at least to explore 'the other'; to explore, for example, alienation," McRobbie embraces the possibilities that are opened as "the frontiers of the self are effaced and transformed, [and] so too are the boundaries which mark out separate discourses and separate politics" (1994, 16). She stresses, "There is no going back. For populations transfixed on images which are themselves a reality, there is no return to a mode of representation which politicizes in a kind of straightforward 'worthwhile' way ... Social agency is employed in the activation of all meanings. Audiences of viewers, lookers or users are not simple-minded multitudes. As the media extends its sphere of influence, so also does it come under the critical surveillance *and* usage of its subjects" (22–3).

10 In the wake of Foucault, "life" has lost its innocence in Euro-American theory, becoming instead the vehicle by which power endlessly renews and strengthens itself under neoliberalism. Elizabeth Povinelli (2016) goes further to highlight the geontological life/not-life binary that precedes and underlies biopolitics as the foundation of late liberal/settler colonial sense. Lisa Stevenson's 2014 *Life Beside Itself: Imagining Care in the Canadian Arctic* (discussed in chapters 5 and 6) documents the violent effects of settler-colonial biopolitics on Inuit people, whose cosmology entails an understanding of being that confounds the Western secular life-death hierarchy.

11 In her exploration of the shame-pride nexus in Canadian settler reconciliation discourse, Sarah Kizuk describes the process whereby feeling bad about colonialism serves as an impetus not to listen but to avoid listening: feeling shame for settlers thus "becomes a way to love ourselves more but, as a failure of recognition, remains a mere optics of justice" (2020, 168).

12 I use the term "flourishing" not just as a nicer way of saying "resilience" but in a sense inspired by Alexis Shotwell's careful definition of the word (careful in its awareness of the noninnocence of all conceptions of future well-being) to describe "the contingent, without-guarantees, partially shared world that

recognizes both ethical entanglement and irreducible difference" (2016, 155). "*How* we pursue flourishing," in Shotwell's formulation, "will always involve an in-process, syncretic, speculative fabulation, an improvisational engagement with emergence" (2016, 9).

13 Both "art-for-art's sake" conservatives and radical leftists steer well clear of "pragmatism," which, as Levine notes, is "charged with confining us ever further within the brutal and corrupt systems of the present. Anything short of pulling this whole rotten society up by the roots is the same as quietism and complacency, wishy-washy liberalism, or worse, sinister neoliberalism" (2021, 236).

CHAPTER FOUR

1 They explain: "We have made BlackLife one word because we believe that living Black makes BlackLife inextricable from the mark of its flesh, both historically and in our current time. The mark of Black flesh is the foundation from which Black Life in all of its multiplicities, varieties, potentialities and possibilities proceeds from and is therefore intimately entangled" (Walcott and Abdillahi 2020, 9). With significant implications for urban resilience strategies, they also argue that "every policy proposal should be exposed to the Black Test. By that we mean it should meet the test of ameliorating Black dispossession and making BlackLife possible. If the policy does not meet the Black Test, then it is a failed policy, always already, from the first instance of its proposal" (95).

2 It's worth noting not only *that* race comes up in certain resilience studies but also *how* it comes up. Yoosun Park, Rory Crath, and Donna Jeffrey note that resilience research in social work tends to treat race as "just one more demographic detail of communities/individuals at risk, rather than a key factor for analysis and intervention" (2020, 10). That is, few studies cite racism as a structural factor affecting the life circumstances of the studied population, let alone an underlying determinant of the studies' own normative assumptions about what constitutes adaptive or maladaptive behaviours. An example of a resilience intervention that brackets racism while stressing parental responsibility is a Halton [Ontario] Catholic District School Board's (HCDSB) planned 2021 workshop for Black parents on "Raising Resilient Black Children." The workshop was postponed after drawing significant community criticism. At worst, the workshop might be seen to presume a lack of parenting skills on the part of Black parents. At best, as the grandparent of an HCDSB student noted, "It seems like they're saying, racism is here to stay, buckle up, we're giving you some tools, you can go ahead and use those tools" (Francis 2021).

3 In pointed contrast with images of white feminine fragility, the stereotype of the "strong Black woman" ostensibly celebrates "*those* Black mothers" while rationalizing an absence of care or social support and concealing Black

women's heightened risk of health problems, including heart disease, diabetes, and depression (Wallace [1978] 2015; Parks 2013; Harris 2014; Harris-Perry 2013).

4 Some of the earliest studies of childhood resilience focused on the children of mothers with mental illness (Garmezy 1974), and a "strong mother-child bond" and "family stability" were widely cited as protective factors for youth in the face of other risk factors, including poverty.

5 Michael Bucknor provides an incisive reading of *Brother*'s engagement with issues surrounding Black male intimacy. Portraying the risks of Black male-male intimacy in a racist, heteronormative culture, the novel also describes "a homosocial world [that] is both an escape from and a fortress against" that culture (2019, 3).

6 At issue, notes Science and Technology Studies researcher Lundy Braun, is not the veracity of the data that shows variations that correlate with race; the problem, rather, is the attribution of observed differences to a congenital fact of Black life without regard for "disproportionate exposures to toxic environments, differential access to high-quality care and the daily insults of racism in every sphere of life that manifest biologically" (2015, 4).

7 "I feared for my life" is the common defence in such incidents, including the 2014 fatal shooting of Michael Brown, an unarmed Black teenager, by white police officer Darren Wilson in Ferguson, MO. In his trial, Wilson described Brown as a "demon" bent on killing him, recalling, "I just felt the immense power that he had" (Sorkin 2014, 4). In the transcript of the trial, Amy Sorkin observes, "there is not really a cross-examination, or any interrogation of the portrait of a young man who would run, enraged and magically indifferent, toward a volley of bullets, as if this were somehow a familiar, easily recognizable character" (4).

8 In their study of school-based resilience programs, Kathryn Ecclestone, Lydia Lewis, and Peter Lund note the prevalence of CBT-inspired techniques of monitoring thoughts and feelings "and then developing 'appropriate' emotional reactions" (2015, 203). They note that this mode of "therapeutic governance" works to forestall political engagement with the larger systems that can inhibit resilience (198, 203; see also Dahlsted et al. 2011).

9 To think about how the pressure to self-monitor works in concert with the violent force of the law, it is worth recalling Foucault's observation regarding the history of power – that the regimes that dominated different periods (punishment, discipline, biopolitics) should be seen not as a series of substitutions but rather as successive "adjustments" of state power that "can be articulated with each other" to manage populations at different scales through diverse technologies (2003, 250).

10 Sharpe's observation, insistently linking the planetary dynamics of climate with the experiential dynamics of weather, inspires Kristen Simmon's concept of "settler atmospherics," which are "the normative and necessary violences found in settlement-accruing, adapting, and constricting indigenous

and black life in the U.S. settler state" (2017). Sharpe's attention to the climate of antiblackness also resonates with the concept of "weathering," coined by health researcher Arline Geronimus in 1992 to describe demonstrated links between Black mothers' heightened risks of death and their exposure to the life-depleting force of racism (Geronimus 1992).

11 Following the publication of *Brother*, Chariandy gave a talk at the newly renovated Cedarbrae branch of the Toronto Public Library that he loved as a child. Libraries, he noted, "were places of discovery and solace for me growing up ... Very often, a library was one of the places where I could escape that gaze [from police and others in authority directed at Black and other visible minority youth] and, in looking into a book, I could imagine different possibilities for myself and be exposed to different worlds" (Patch 2017).

12 Recalling Gilmore's definition of racism as "the state-sanctioned ... exploitation of group-differentiated vulnerabilities to premature death *in distinct yet densely interconnected political geographies*" (2002, 261, italics added), Jodi Melamed observes that the rarely quoted last part of Gilmore's statement is crucial to recognizing the geographical dynamic of racism by which differentially valued groups of humans were forcibly separated and brought together – "interconnected" – in the interests of capital accumulation (2015, 78).

13 One way that Black bodies are disciplined is through the pathologization and criminalization of Black fellowship. Staff members in an Ontario youth penal institution reportedly became so concerned when Black youth would socialize together that multiple staff meetings had to be called to address widespread fears that the Black youth were organizing a riot (Maynard 2017, 212).

14 In his reflections on the novel, Chariandy (2019) notes Michael's inchoate recognition, in this description, of the ancestral Indigenous presence in the valley.

15 According to Paul Miller, aka DJ Spooky, "The best DJs are griots" and sampling a process of narrative creation (2004, 21). Jelly's name also recalls jazz musician Jelly Roll Morton (1890–1941) – a connection I'm grateful to Michael Basseler for pointing out to me.

16 As Alexander Weheliye explains in *Phonographies: Grooves in Sonic Afro-Modernity*, music "renders futurity audible in its circumvention of strictly mimetic technes. In sonic Afro-modernity, sound, for a variety of social, ontological, historical, and aesthetic reasons ... holds out more flexible and future-directed provenances of black subjects' relation to and participation in the creation of Western modernity" (2005, 11).

17 The community is energized by youth, but it is notably Michael's mother, not Michael, who responds to Aisha's efforts to bring them together. Their leadership reflects the dynamic Keenanga-Yamahtta Taylor observes in Black Lives Matter in which, partly due to the absence of young Black men, "'missing' – snatched from society by imprisonment or premature death" (2016, 166), young Black women have been "a central organizing force" (163). She also notes that "despite the constant clamor of 'generational divide' today,

there is much fluidity between the youth and older African Americans, who are often the parents of the young people being killed by the police" (163).

18 Ben Saunders, a Black psychology professor in New York, recalls his recognition that, for Black men, the risk of being subject to police violence has no correlation to "right" or "wrong" choices: "Philando Castile was killed for cooperating," he notes. "I realized you can be killed for cooperating. That was liberating because I don't need to focus on cooperating as much" (Hackman 2016, 5).

19 In his genealogical analysis of resilience, Philippe Bourbeau cites Francis Bacon's seventeenth-century use of the word to describe the way sound can "bounce back," for example, in the form of an echo (2018, 25).

20 In a conversation with Lawrence Hill, Chariandy acknowledges the prevalence of the trope of the "strong Black mother" (particularly in the work of male writers) while also speaking to his interest (in both *Brother* and his 2007 novel, *Soucoyant*) in portraying Black mothers who embody vulnerability along with "resilience and an enduring kind of beauty" (Chariandy 2017b).

CHAPTER FIVE

1 Throughout the story, italics denote the narrator's dialogue with her friend, distinct from the exchanges with therapy lady.

2 I am grateful to Cheryl Lousley for drawing my attention to Carpenter's introduction to Merasty's memoir as a complicated instance of settler colonial resilience thinking.

3 Stout is also the author of the 2012 essay-memoir, "A Survivor Reflects on Resilience," in *Speaking my Truth: Reflections on Reconciliation and Residential Schools*, published by the Aboriginal Healing Foundation.

4 Elijah Harper was an Ojibwe-Cree residential school survivor who went on to become Chief of the Red Sucker Lake Nation and a member of the Manitoba MLA. In 1990, he famously halted the Meech Lake Accord that sought to bring Quebec into the Constitution on the basis of the exclusion of Indigenous people from the process.

5 The narrow approach to the abusive nature of residential school also ignores long-term physical injuries, which – even leaving aside more overt forms of abuse – included severe malnutrition, an assault to growing bodies whose effects have been shown to persist not only into adulthood but also to successive generation (Mosby and Galloway 2017).

6 Natalie Clark addresses the inadequacy of Western concepts of trauma in addressing the health needs of Indigenous girls. In a study based on work with girls who have experienced violence, she calls for an Indigenous intersectional framework that assists girls in understanding and locating their coping as responses to larger structural and systemic forces including racism, poverty,

sexism, colonialism, and a culture of violence enacted through state policy and practices (2014, 8).

7 Chapter 4 discusses this dynamic in relation to the different discussions of risk concerning white children, who are understood to require more freedom to take risks, and Black children, who are framed as risky/at risk and need of intervention.

8 This biopolitical dynamic in which the death of Indigenous people "comes as no surprise" resonates with anti-Black racism in which, as Ruth Wilson Gilmore notes, "premature death is an unfortunate given rather than an intolerable failure" (2002, 17). The expectation of premature Black and Indigenous death is discussed in chapters 3 and 6.

9 The termination of funding to the AHF in 2010 – Indian Affairs Minister Chuck Strahl maintained that the program "was never meant to last forever" and that redirecting funds to Health Canada would result in "better access" for victims (Voices-voix coalition 2012) – resulted in the termination of approximately one hundred and twenty-five projects.

10 Liboiron clearly outlines the mechanics of settler misunderstanding (part ignorant, part strategic) of the significance of land to Indigenous people (2021, 42–6), drawing a distinction between land, with a lower-case "l," to signify "the colonial worldview whereby landscapes are common, universal and everywhere, even with great variation" (6–7 n. 19) and Land, which is "fundamentally relational and specific to these relations" (45).

11 Anishinaabe writer Grace Dillon, cited in the introduction, reminds us that the SF use of the aeronautical term "Native slipstream," which refers to the flowing together of space and time, was not coined by cyberpunk writer Bruce Sterling, as SF studies usually claimed; it originated, rather, in the work of Gerald Vizenor and Cherokee writer Diane Glancy to describe and self-publish work deemed too "strange and unusual" by mainstream presses (Dillon and Marques 2021).

12 Adams focuses her research on the 164-manuscript page version of the Haudenosaunee Creation story told by Skanyatarí:yo John Arthur Gibson to ethnologist J.N.B. Hewitt, which is notable for its incorporation of detailed ethnobotanical data (Adams 2020b).

13 Adams reads the Creation story as "a sequence of instructions for addressing the loss of biome on an incomprehensibly big scale, starting with the acknowledgment of human-scale grief that has to happen before we can get down to the work of recovery" (2020a). In moving between the human and the biome, we should recall Max Liboiron's reminder that scale, properly understood, "is not about relative size. Scale is what relationships matter within a particular context" (2021, 84).

14 Offering an ironic rejoinder to Health Canada's efforts to foster a settler-colonial model of resilience in Indigenous youth, a participant in the Kahnawake resilience study observes: "The government has made us resilient

…Yeah, they tried hard but all it did was make us stronger …Well they tried to assimilate us and they tried, like with residential schools and then, it just backfired on them because it only made us more resilient and more, it made our skin tougher" (Philips, Dandeneau, and Kirmayer 2012, 22).

15 In relation to islands as sites of love, the meaning of the story's title, "it takes an ocean not to break," is ambiguous. The words come from the song "Terrible Love" by The National, which begins, "It's a terrible love that I'm walking with spiders" and concludes with the repeated line "it takes an ocean not to break" (Dessner and Berringer 2010). The meaning of the line "it takes an ocean not to break" might be glossed by references to a "ship of hopes" that later in the song becomes a "ship of woes," or even, ominously, by the line, "And I can't fall asleep/Without a little help." In Simpson's story, the ocean is literal (signaled in the drive to the coast) but also maybe figurative, its meaning complicated by ambiguous grammar: Who is the subject in the title? Is it the narrator who needs the sight, smell, sound, and feeling of ocean to help her to stay alive (in the same way as the existence of Turtle Island and all who live on her depend on the surrounding water)? Or do you have to *be* an ocean – fluid, life-giving, all-encompassing – not to break?

16 "biindigen" means "come in," "namadin" means "sit down" (Simpson 2013b, 135).

CHAPTER SIX

1 The connection between opportunism and opportunities is discussed in chapter 4.

2 The official catalyst for the Intervention was the 2007 publication of a report, *Little Children Are Sacred*, which summarized conditions of abuse and neglect that had been widely known about since the early 1990s. The federal government notably ignored nearly all the report's recommendations concerning the remediation of long-standing conditions of poor housing, inadequate infrastructure, and insufficient resources for health care and education, taking up only the recommendation for enhanced police presence, imposed along with a raft of other punitive measures. These measures included the suspension of the 1975 *Racial Discrimination Act*, the disbanding of local Aboriginal Councils, the abolition of the consideration of Indigenous customary law in sentencing, the quarantining of welfare, financial penalties for parents whose children were absent from school, and the abolition of federally funded employment programs.

3 Based on work with diverse Aboriginal groups, primarily in the north, anthropologist Deborah Bird Rose offers a general definition:

> Country in Aboriginal English is not only a common noun but also a proper noun. People talk about country in the same way that they would talk about a person: they speak to country, sing to country, visit country, worry about country, feel sorry for country, and long for

country. People say that country knows, hears, smells, takes notice, takes care, is sorry or happy. Country is not a generalised or undifferentiated type of place, such as one might indicate with terms like "spending a day in the country" or "going up the country." Rather, country is a living entity with a yesterday, today and tomorrow, with a consciousness, and will toward life. Because of this richness, country is home, and peace; nourishment for body, mind, and spirit; heart's ease. (1996, 7)

4 The policy states that "investment decisions should aim to: improve participation in education/training and the market economy on a sustainable basis; reduce dependence on welfare wherever possible; and promote personal responsibility, engagement and behaviours consistent with positive social norms" (COAG 2011, A-23).

5 See chapters 4 and 5 for discussions of the normalization of the premature death of Black and Indigenous people in North America.

6 The *Closing the Gap 2018* report features initiatives such as an investment of $135 million in Indigenous sport, which aims to "use sport and recreation to improve [Indigenous people's] wellbeing and resilience, improve educational attendance and attainment, engage youth, develop or upgrade infrastructure facilities and help to provide employment and training opportunities" (Turnbull 2018, 110).

7 Claims for the extraordinary nature of the Intervention gloss over its continuity with historical measures of colonial control. Barry Morris and Andrew Lattas explain, "Whether it be the 'murderous activities of the frontier' or Indigenous people's incarceration onto reserves that functioned almost as total institutions, Indigenous Australians have regularly been governed through extraordinary interventions that promise to be temporary until people have been normalised and transformed into self-governing disciplined subjects. As the ex-army officer and government minister who initiated the NT Intervention, Mal Brough, put it: 'Stabilise, normalise, exit'" (2010, 2).

8 Several commentators have looked at the Intervention through the Agambenian lens of bare life, including Grieves (2017), Kramer (2012), and Tedmanson and Wadiwal (2010). Others have pointed to the constituent role of the state of exception in colonial law (Hussain 2003) and the control of labour. "Emergency rule," Mark Neocleous suggests, "has been crucial to the consolidation of capitalist modernity" (2006, 204).

9 The promise of protection contradicts the stated aim of the National Strategy for Disaster Resilience to wean the population off "unrealistic expectations and unsustainable dependencies" (Commonwealth of Australia 2015, 1).

10 While acknowledging a national preoccupation with severe weather events, Leigh Dale cautions against reading Rudd's statement as reflective of general opinion about the threat of climate change, pointing out that "weather" in

Australia, "is allowed to be a crisis so climate cannot be" (email message to author, 10 October 2019).

11 In a way that echoes the situation in Canada, discussed in chapter 5, Rundle sees the rise of therapeutic discourse in the 1990s, concurrent with "the lapsing ... of a focus on genuine self-determination," as productive of an imaginative vacuum, lending support to a "mono-historical idea of the transition to modernity" (2007, 41). The gist of that idea was this:

> There was only one path for historical social development, and it was essentially to restage the enclosures, dissolving all common or collective land into individual titles. The considerable and overwhelming opposition to this process from Aboriginal people is easily handled by the classical liberal and Hayekian Right, since they believe that possessive individualism is simply a feature of essential human nature waiting to be brought to the surface, the white picket fence already whispering away in every Aboriginal heart. What would thus be an act of arbitrary social engineering – carving up land into a legal individual form and hoping that a psychology and culture to match it would develop from that fact – could be disguised as merely clearing away layers of inauthentic oppression ... so that the universal could re-emerge. (41)

12 In the end, even the Brolga must be sacrificed for the good of the world. When, amidst the flooding, Warren Finch is assassinated, his clans people come to claim his body. "The police were obliged under the regulations of emergency laws to intervene in the lives of all Aboriginal people, to throw the bush people out of the cathedral" (Wright 2016, 288) while welcoming in their place "important overseas people who used up vast amounts of their country's wealth by emptying barrels of jet fuel to fly over vast distances and oceans to get to the cathedral" (289).

13 The 2018 Resilient Australia National School Award, sponsored by the Australian Institute for Disaster Resilience (2018), went to the Firestick Project in which Wurundjeri Elder Uncle Dave Wandin taught students at Dixons Creek Primary School in Victoria (the site of devastating 2009 bush fires) about Aboriginal fire management. In the short video describing the project, Wandin explains over a didgeridoo and drum music soundtrack, "Teaching those children today will actually spread the message about what Indigenous burning is about. And through that, they will be the driving force in the future generations to lead the groundswell of caring for our country in a traditional and culturally sensitive manner that is governed by the country, not governed by people" (Australian Institute for Disaster Resilience 2018). In overall effect – and in pointed contrast to the damning assessment of Aboriginal family life in the NTNER – the video conveys a sense of the inherent wisdom of Aboriginal concepts of intergenerational responsibility for navigating an uncertain future.

14 Taleb himself, in Malcolm Gladwell's words, "turned the inevitability of disaster into an investment strategy" following the collapse of Long Term Capital Management in the late nineties (2002). Taleb argues, not surprisingly, that capitalism, which "revitaliz[es]" the world, by facilitating opportunities to leverage luck, is the best system through which to realize these goals" (2007, 222).

15 Drawing on Gayatri Spivak's argument in "Can the Subaltern Speak?," Honni van Rijswijk offers a convincing rationale for Wright's decision to make Oblivia silent, pointing out that "given the legal and political history of the figure of the 'abused Aboriginal child', it is impossible for Oblivia to tell the story of her rape without it being read as a narrative of community or familial dysfunction" (2017, 132).

16 Various commentators have commented on the novel's "challenging of form and style" (Gleeson-White 2017), noting that it is "a difficult narrative to follow" (Daley 2016) and "challenging to many of its readers" (Potter 2012) and characterized at times by a "persistently ambiguous and alienating poetic mode" (Skeat 2016, 1) and "determined descriptive weirdness" (Williamson 2013).

17 In his 2016 book *The Great Derangement: Climate Change and the Unthinkable*, Amitav Ghosh, like Beck, links the novel to the social changes that emerged in the wake of industrialism but arrives at the opposite conclusion. Ghosh cites the novel's emergence alongside the burgeoning of science and the birth of statistics "ruled by ideas of probability and improbability" (19) in support of his thesis that "serious fiction" cannot represent disasters of the multiscalar complexity and improbability of climate change. The emerging critical consensus (and the burgeoning field of cli-fi) suggests that Ghosh underestimated the capacities of literary fiction. As Sangeeta Ray notes (citing Ghosh's own fiction as examples), "the chronotope of the novel has always dealt with complex disaster" (2018; see also Trexler 2015; Singh 2017). And even as Ghosh describes the exclusion of "improbable" events from the realist terrain of the novel (floods, landslides, and tsunamis, for example), he acknowledges that the distinction between the probable and the improbable is actually not that clear: "*Improbable* is not the opposite of *probable*, but rather an inflexion of it, a gradient in a continuum of probability" (2016, 16). By focusing on the novel's achievement of a vision of "moderate and orderly" life (22), Ghosh plays down the process by which normality and the everyday asserts itself against the current of events that would otherwise overwhelm it; this is the terrain of the novel, which is also the terrain of resilience.

18 Angelo Gianfrancesco draws a more limited connection between the novel and resilience, focusing on the emergence in the nineteenth century of what he terms "une littérature de résilience" (2001). In authors ranging from Charles Dickens to Victor Hugo, he traces the recurrence of narratives focused on "the wounded child" who experiences transformation through adversity.

19 I have proposed elsewhere a concept of "compromised" resilience (O'Brien 2017), which resonates with Basseler's "dirty resilience" (2019a, 25) in its emphasis on impurity, entanglement, and complicated subjectivity.

20 Alison Ravenscroft cogently critiques the frequent application of the label of postcolonial magic realism to Wright's previous novel, *Carpentaria*, noting that such readings by non-Aboriginal critics have the effect of reducing Indigenous ontologies to tricky subversions of Western logic. In other words, "others' reality is produced as if it were a version of the colonisers' own, only a lesser one: less rational, less logical" (2012, 62).

21 While Povinelli cautions against inflecting ontological principles such as the Spinozan concept of *conatus* – "that which exists, *whether living or nonliving*, strives to persevere in being" (2016, 18, italics added) – with the biological condition of life. Rose uses the term "life" to encompass a wide variety of organic and inorganic entities and processes, arguing "life does want to live, it does want to be in connection, it does want flourishing relationships, it does want pattern and community" (2004, 49).

22 Explaining her preference for the term "recuperation" over words like "recovery" or "restoration," Rose highlights that "in contemporary usage it seems to communicate the humility of the project. Central to my argument is the proposition that there is no former time/space of wholeness to which we might return or which we might resurrect for ourselves … Nor is there a posited future wholeness which may yet save us. Rather, the work of recuperation seeks glimpses of illumination, and aims towards engagement and disclosure" (2004, 24).

23 In a tribute to the Aboriginal poet Oodgeroo Noonuccal, Wright says that she thinks it is "possible and necessary for a writer of any culture to reach across regional and international boundaries" (2008, 6). She has spoken and written about the inspiration she draws from writers including Mario Vargas Llosa, Jorge Luis Borges, Italo Calvino, James Joyce, Seamus Heaney, and Carlos Fuentes (Wright 2002, 2008; Azam 2014), in a quest to "develop [her] books as a mixture of traditional storytelling and storytelling across the world" (Azam 2014).

24 Wright describes her aim in writing *The Swan Book* in a similar way: "I wanted to demonstrate how we maintain an idea of sovereignty of the mind, even if we haven't got sovereignty of the country or the land" (Wright and Zable 2013, 2).

CONCLUSION

1 The use of metaphor as an instrument of colonial violence runs deep, as Tapji Garba and Sara-Maria Sorentino note in their critical reading of Tuck and Yang's essay. Citing the work of Saidya Hartman, Hortense Spillers, Frank Wilderson, and others, they point out that the effort to rescue the materiality

of land and Indigenous sovereignty from settler abstraction fails properly to account for the mechanism of slavery whereby Black lives become fungible – become, essentially, metaphorical (2020, 775).

2 The reverse might also be true – that we can no more dispense with resilience than we can dispense with narrative. Unless maybe it's time to forego both together, as Dionne Brand suggested in her 2021 piece in *The Toronto Star*, "On Narrative, Reckoning and the Calculus of Living and Dying." Decrying the tendency during COVID for people to wish for things to return to "normal," she suggested that "everything is up in the air, all narratives for the moment have been blown open – the statues are falling – all the metrics are off, if only briefly. To paraphrase Trouillot, we want 'a life that no narrative could provide, even the best fiction.' The reckoning might be now" (2020).

References

Adams, Amber Meadow. 2020a. "Behind the Essay: Amber Meadow Adams." [Interview on essay, "To my Grandmother, c/o the Mush Hole."] *Off Assignment*, 23 September 2020. www.offassignment.com/articles/amber-meadow-adams-2.

– 2020b. "Yotsi'tsishon and the Language of the Seed in the Haudenosaunee Story of Earth's Creation." *English Language Notes* 58 (1): 111–31.

– 2023. "The Vocabulary of Survival in Rotinonhsyón:ni Narrative." Paper presented at the Narratives of Sustenance in Broken Times Conference, McMaster University, Hamilton, Ontario, 30 June 2023.

Ahmed, Sara. 2010. *The Promise of Happiness*. Durham, NC: Duke University Press.

– 2012. *On Being Included: Racism and Diversity in Institutional Life*. Durham, NC: Duke University Press.

Albrechtsen, Janet. 2017. "Faux Leaders Worse than No Leaders at All." *The Australian*, 7 June 2017. www.theaustralian.com.

Amin, Massoud. 2019. "The Gift of Injustice: When Truth is Suppressed and Justice Denied." Linkedin article, 15 April 2019. linkedin.com/pulse/gift-injustice-when-truth-suppressed-justice-denied-massoud-amin/.

Andersson, Neil. 2008. "Editorial: Affirmative Challenges in Indigenous Resilience Research." *Pimatisiwin: A Journal of Aboriginal and Indigenous Community Health* 6 (2): 3–6.

Ansfield, Bench. 2015. "Still Submerged: The Uninhabitability of Urban Redevelopment." In *Sylvia Wynter: On Being Human as Praxis*, edited by Katherine McKittrick, 124–41. Durham, NC: Duke University Press.

Ansloos, Jeffrey, and Shanna Peltier. 2022. "A Question of Justice: Critically Researching Suicide with Indigenous Studies of Affect, Biosociality, and Land-Based Relations." *Health* 26 (1): 100–19.

Anzilotti, Eillie. 2019. "Why Did the Rockefeller Foundation Just Unceremoniously End its Successful Resilience Program?" *Fast Company*, 2 April 2019. www.fastcompany.com/90328267/the-rockefeller-foundation-is-unceremoniously-ending-its-successful-resilience-program.

Arora-Jonsson, Seema. 2016. "Does Resilience Have a Culture? Ecocultures and the Politics of Knowledge Production." *Ecological Economics* 121:98–107.

Åsberg, Cynthia. 2013. "Resilience is Cyborg: Feminist Clues to a Post-Disciplinary Environmental Humanities of Critique and Creativity." *Resilience: A Journal of the Environmental Humanities* 1 (1): 12–4.

Assari, Shervin. 2016. "Black Americans May Be More Resilient to Stress Than White Americans." *The Conversation*, 16 September 2016. theconversation.com/black-americans-may-be-more-resilient-to-stress-than-white-americans-62338.

Assari, Shervin, and Maryam Moghani Lankarani. 2016. "Association between Stressful Life Events and Depression: Intersections of Race and Gender." *Journal of Racial and Ethnic Health Disparities* 3:349–56.

Australian Government, Department of Home Affairs. "Organizational Resilience." Cyber and Infrastructure Security Centre. Last updated 29 March 2022. https://www.cisc.gov.au/what-is-the-cyber-and-infrastructure-security-centre/organisational-resilience.

Australian Institute for Disaster Resilience. 2018. "2018 Resilient Australia National School Award: Firestick Project." YouTube video, 7 November 2018. www.youtube.com/watch?v=GAby63zE_aE.

Azam, Mariam. 2014. "Alexis Wright: 'It Was Like Writing a Story to the Ancestors.'" *The Guardian*, 25 May 2014. www.theguardian.com/books/australia-culture-blog/2014/may/25/alexis-wright-it-was-like-writing-a-story-to-the-ancestors.

Baggini, Julian. 2016. "State School Pupils Lack Confidence – You Won't Fix That in the Classroom." *The Guardian*, 15 January 2016. theguardian.com/commentisfree/2016/jan/15/state-school-pupils-confidence-lessons-personality-private-education.

Baishya, Amit R., and Priya Kumar. 2022. "Ends of Worlds or the Continuation of the Planet? Postcolonial Theory, the Anthropocene, and the Nonhuman." *Postcolonial Studies*, 25 (3): 305–20.

Bannerji, Himani. 2000. *The Dark Side of the Nation: Essays on Multiculturalism, Nationalism and Gender*. Toronto: Women's Press.

Barras, Arnaud. 2016. "The Law of Storytelling: The Hermeneutics of Relationality in Alexis Wright's *The Swan Book*." *JASAL: Journal of the Association of Studies in Australian Literature* 15 (3): 1–12.

Basseler, Michael. 2019a. "Stories of Dangerous Life in a Post-Trauma Age: Toward a Critical Narratology of Resilience." In *Narrative in Culture*, edited by Astrid Erll and Roy Sommer, 15–36. Boston: De Gruyter.

– 2019b. "Fictions of Resilience: Narrating Environmental Catastrophe and Crisis in Cormac McCarthy's *The Road* (2006) and Jesmyn Ward's *Salvage the Bones* (2011)." In *The American Novel in the 21st Century: Cultural Contexts – Literary Developments – Critical Analyses*, edited by Michael Basseler and Ansgar Nünning, 169–86. Trier, GER: Wissenschaftlicher Verlag Trier.

BBC. 2020. "COVID: Melbourne Towers Lockdown 'Breached Human Rights.'" *BBC News*, 17 December 2020. www.bbc.com/news/world-australia-55342990.

Beck, Ulrich. 1992. *Risk Society: Towards a New Modernity*. Translated by Mark Ritter. Thousand Oaks, CA: SAGE Publications.

– 2007. *World at Risk*. Translated by Ciaran Cronin. Cambridge, UK: Polity Press.

Beilin, Ruth, and Cathy Wilkinson. 2015. "Introduction: Governing for Urban Resilience." *Urban Studies* 52 (7): 1205–17.

Belcourt, Billy Ray. 2020. *A History of My Brief Body*. Toronto: Penguin Canada.

Berkes, Fikret, Johan Colding, and Carl Folke. 2003. *Navigating Social-Ecological Systems: Building Resilience for Complexity and Change*. Cambridge, UK: Cambridge University Press.

Berkowitz, Michael. 2017. "Why Urban Resilience?" *Medium*, 20 July 2017. medium.com/cities-taking-action/why-urban-resilience-771c0ff2b864.

– 2018. "5 Years: A Growing and Evolving Resilience Movement." *Medium*, 18 May 2018. medium.com/@100ResilientCities/5-years-a-growing-and-evolving-resilience-movement-da6da606268.journals.openedition.org/factsreports/488.

Berlant, Lauren. 2011. *Cruel Optimism*. Durham, NC: Duke University Press.

Big-Canoe, Katie, and Chantelle A.M. Richmond. 2014. "Anishinaabe Youth Perceptions About Community Health: Toward Environmental Repossession." *Health and Place* 26:127–35.

Birch, Tony. 2016. "'The Lifting of the Sky': Life Outside the Anthropocene." In *Humanities for the Environment: Integrating Knowledge, Forging New Constellations of Practice*, edited by Joni Adamson and Michael Davis, 195–209. Oxfordshire, UK: Routledge.

Blaeser, Kimberley. 1996. *Gerald Vizenor: Writing in the Oral Tradition*. Norman: University of Oklahoma Press.

Bliss, Laura. 2019. "The Rise, Fall and Possible Rebirth of Resilient Cities." *Bloomberg CityLab*, 19 July 2019. www.bloomberg.com/news/articles/2019–06–12/the-demise-of-rockefeller-s-100-resilient-cities.

Bohland, Jim, Simin Davoudi, and Jennifer Lawrence. 2018. *The Resilience Machine*. Oxfordshire, UK: Routledge.

Bonanno, George A., and Erica D. Diminich. 2013. "Annual Research Review: Positive Adjustment to Adversity-Trajectories of Minimal-Impact Resilience and Emergent Resilience." *Journal of Child Psychology and Psychiatry* 54 (4): 378–401.

Boseley, Matilda. 2020. "Melbourne Public Housing COVID Lockdown Violated Human Rights, Victoria's Ombudsman Finds." *The Guardian*, 16 December 2020.

Bourbeau, Philippe. 2018. "A Genealogy of Resilience." *International Political Sociology* 12: 19–35.

Bracke, Sarah. 2016. "Bouncing Back: Vulnerability and Resistance in Times of Resilience." In *Vulnerability in Resistance*, edited by Judith Butler, Zeynep Gambetti, and Letitia Sabsey, 52–75. Durham, NC: Duke University Press.

Brand, Dionne. 1997. *Land to Light On*. Toronto: McClelland & Stewart.

– 2001. *A Map to the Door of No Return*. Toronto: Doubleday Canada.
– 2002. *thirsty*. Toronto: Penguin Canada.
– 2020. "On Narrative, Reckoning and the Calculus of Living and Dying." *Toronto Star*, 4 July 2020. www.thestar.com/entertainment/books/2020/07/04/dionne-brand-on-narrative-reckoning-and-the-calculus-of-living-and-dying.html.
Brand, Fridolin Simon, and Kurt Jax. 2007. "Focusing the Meaning(s) of Resilience: Resilience as a Descriptive Concept and a Boundary Object." *Ecology and Society* 12 (1). www.jstor.org/stable/26267855.
Brant, Beth. 1999. "The Good Red Road: Journeys of Homecoming in Native Women's Writing." In *Contemporary Native American Cultural Issues*, edited by Duane Champagne, 91–102. Lanham, MD: AltaMira.
Braun, Lundy. 2014. *Breathing Race into the Machine: The Surprising Career of the Spirometer*. Minneapolis: University of Minnesota Press.
– 2015. "Race, Ethnicity and Lung Function: A Brief History." *Canadian Journal of Respiratory Therapy* 51 (4): 99–201.
Braveheart-Jordan, Maria, and Lemyra DeBruyn. 1995. "So She May Walk in Balance: Integrating the Impact of Historical Trauma in Native American Indian Women." In *Racism in the Lives of Women: Testimony, Theory, and Guides to Antiracist Practice (Haworth Innovations in Feminist Studies)*, edited by Jean Adleman and Gloria Enguídanos, 345–68. Stoud, UK: Harrington Park/Haworth Press.
Brew, Nigel. 2017. "A Quick Guide to the History of Proposals for an Australian Department of Homeland Security." *Research Paper Series 2017–18*, 14 July 2017. Canberra, AU: Parliamentary Library. www.aph.gov.au/About_Parliament/Parliamentary_Departments/Parliamentary_Library/pubs/rp/rp1718/Quick_Guides/HomelandSecurity.
Brown, E. Richard. 1976. "Public Health in Imperialism: Early Rockefeller Programs at Home and Abroad." *American Journal of Public Health* 66 (9): 897–903.
Brown, Wendy. 1999. "Resisting Left Melancholy." *boundary 2* 26 (3): 20–7.
Bucknor, Michael. 2019. "'that body always just a skin away.' *sx salon* 30 (February). smallaxe.net/sxsalon/issues/sx-salon-30/articles.
Burstow, Bonnie. 2003. "Toward a Radical Understanding of Trauma and Trauma Work." *Violence Against Women* 9 (11): 1293–317.
Butler, Judith. 2004. *Precarious Life: The Powers of Mourning and Violence*. Brooklyn, NY: Verso Books.
Butler, Octavia E. 1998. "'Devil Girl from Mars': Why I Write Science Fiction." [Transcript of public address delivered at Massachusetts Institute of Technology, 19 February 1998.] *The Media in Transition*, 4 October 1998. web.mit.edu/m-i-t/articles/butler_talk_index.html.

Campbell, Mark. 2015. "Sonic Intimacies." *Decolonization, Indigeneity, Education & Society*, 25 March 2015. decolonization.wordpress.com/2015/03/25/sonic-intimacies-on-djing-better-future.
– 2019. "Harden." *sx salon* 30 (February). smallaxe.net/sxsalon/issues/sx-salon-30/articles.
Cappell, Elliott. 2017. "Making Toronto a Resilient City." Interview by Steve Paikin. *The Agenda*, TVO Today, 12 September 2017. www.tvo.org/transcript/2462441/making-toronto-a-resilient-city.
– 2019. "Ascent and Demise of 100 Resilient Cities: What Can We Learn?" LinkedIn article, 1 August 2019. www.linkedin.com/pulse/ascent-demise-100-resilient-cities-what-can-we-learn-elliott-cappell.
Carey, Christopher. 2020. "100 Resilient Cities Relaunches as an Independent Network." *Cities Today*, 7 February 2020. www.cities-today.com/100-resilient-cities-relaunches-as-an-independent-network/.
Carpenter, David. 2015. "Introduction." In *The Education of Augie Merasty*, authored by Joseph Auguste (Augie) Merasty, ix–xxvii. University of Regina Press.
Carpenter, Steve, Brian Walker, J. Marty Anderies, and Nick Abel. 2001. "From Metaphor to Measurement: Resilience of What to What?" *Ecosystems*, 4 (8): 765–81.
Carson, Rachel. 1962. *Silent Spring*. Boston, MA: Houghton Mifflin.
Casey, George W. Jr. 2011. "Comprehensive Soldier Fitness: A Vision for Psychological Resilience in the US Army." *American Psychologist* 66 (1): 1–3.
Castel, Robert. 1991. "From Dangerousness to Risk." In *The Foucault Effect: Studies in Governmentality*, edited by Graham Gordon, Colin Gordon, and Peter Miller, 281–98. Chicago: University of Chicago Press.
Cazdyn, Eric. 2012. *The Already Dead: The New Time of Politics, Culture, and Illness*, Durham, NC: Duke University Press.
Chariandy, David. 2017a. *Brother*. Toronto: McClelland & Stewart.
– 2017b. "David Chariandy in Conversation." Interview by Lawrence Hill. YouTube video, 24 November 2017. www.youtube.com/watch?v=lYGgXPy29jI.
– 2017c. "Why David Chariandry Wrote about 'the Resilience, the Imagination, and the Sheer Intelligence' of Scarborough." Interview by Shelagh Rogers. *The Next Chapter*, CBC, 25 September 2017. cbc.ca/radio/thenextchapter/david-chariandy-kathleen-winter-susan-perly-1.4300619/why-david-chariandy-wrote-about-the-resilience-the-imagination-the-sheer-intelligence-of-scarborough-1.4300655.
– 2019. "The Acknowledgments." *sx salon* 30 (February). smallaxe.net/sxsalon/issues/sx-salon-30/articles.
Chariandy, David, and Catherine Hernandez. 2017 "Scarborough Stories." Interview by Steve Paiken. *The Agenda*, TVO. 1 November 2017.

City of Copenhagen. 2018. "Copenhagen: Resilience and Liveability." *Field Actions Science Reports (FACTS)* 18: 30–3. journals.openedition.org/factsreports/4750.

City of Melbourne. 2016. *Resilient Melbourne*. The City of Melbourne, Global Resilient Cities Network, May 2016. www.melbourne.vic.gov.au/SiteCollectionDocuments/resilient-melbourne-strategy.doc.

City of Toronto. 2018. *Resilience Is*. The City of Toronto, Resilient Toronto, Toronto Foundation, 100 Resilient Cities, Produced by Lossless Creative. YouTube video, 1 August 2018. www.youtube.com/watch?v=REvAQz71x-gk&list=PLp11YxteHNp1JZC71Q.

– 2019. *Toronto's First Resilience Strategy*. The City of Toronto, Global Resilient Cities Network, June 2019. web.archive.org/web/20190614001921/https://www.toronto.ca/ext/digital_comm/pdfs/resilience-office/toronto-resilience-strategy.pdf.

Clark, Natalie. 2014. "Shock and Awe: Trauma as the New Colonial Frontier." *Humanities* 5 (14): 1–16.

Clarke, Tayah. 2023. "The Project of Reworlding: Building Towards a Non-Resilient Future." Unpublished essay. Microsoft Word document.

Coaffee, Jon, and Peter Lee. 2016. *Urban Resilience: Planning for Risk, Crisis and Uncertainty*. London, UK: Palgrave Macmillan.

COAG (Council of Australian Governments). 2011. *National Indigenous Reform Agreement (Closing the Gap)*. 4 March 2011. web.archive.org/web/20160623215=103/http://www.federalfinancialrelations.gov.au/content/npa/health_indigenous/indigenous-reform/national-agreement_sept_12.pdf.

Colombino, Annalisa, and Alberto Vanolo. 2017. "Turin and Lingotto: Resilience, Forgetting and the Reinvention of Place." *European Planning Studies* 25 (1): 10–28.

Colour the Trails. n.d. "About Colour the Trails." Last modified 31 April 2023. colourthetrails.com/about-colour-the-trails/.

Common Good. n.d. "Donate Now—Common Good." commongood.org. Last modified 1 February 2016. https://secure.givelively.org/donate/the-common-good-institute-inc.

Commonwealth of Australia. 2007. "Social Security and Other Legislation Amendment (Welfare Payment Reform) Bill 2007 and Four Related Bills Concerning the Northern Territory National Emergency Response." *Senate Standing Committee on Legal and Constitutional Affairs: Official Committee Hansard*. Canberra: Commonwealth of Australia, 10 August 2007. https://www.aph.gov.au/~/media/wopapub/senate/committee/legcon_ctte/completed_inquiries/2004_07/nt_emergency/report/report_pdf.ashx.

Commonwealth of Australia and Department of Home Affairs. 2011. *National Strategy for Disaster Resilience: Building the resilience of our nation to disasters*. National Emergency Management Committee, February 2011. Canberra: Commonwealth of Australia. https://www.homeaffairs.gov.au/emergency/files/national-strategy-disaster-resilience.pdf.

– 2015. *Critical Infrastructure Resilience Strategy: Policy Statement*. Commercial and Administrative Law Branch. Canberra: Commonwealth of Australia. www.cisc.gov.au/help-and-support-subsite/Files/critical_infrastructure_resilience_strategy_policy_statement.pdf.

Conrad, Joseph. (1899) 2007. *Heart of Darkness*. Edited by Robert Hampson and Owen Knowles. London: Penguin Classics.

Cooper, Melinda. 2010. "Turbulent Worlds: Financial Markets and Environmental Crisis." *Theory, Culture & Society* 27 (2–3): 167–90.

Cote, Muriel, and Andrea J. Nightingale. 2012. "Resilience Thinking Meets Social Theory: Situating Social Change in Socio-ecological Systems (SES) Research." *Progress in Human Geography* 36 (4): 475–89.

Coulthard, Glen Sean. 2007. "Subjects of Empire: Indigenous Peoples and the 'Politics of Recognition' in Canada." *Contemporary Political Theory* 6 (4): 437–60.

– 2014. *Red Skin White Masks*. Minneapolis: University of Minnesota Press.

Cronon, William. 1992. "A Place for Stories: Nature, History and Narrative." *The Journal of American History* 78 (4): 1347–76.

Cutter, Susan. 2016. "Resilience to What, Resilience for Whom?" *Geographical Journal* 182 (2): 110–13.

Cyrulnik, Boris. 2005. *The Whispering of Ghosts: Trauma and Resilience*. Translated by Susan Fairfield. New York: Other Press.

Dahlstedt, Magnus, Andreas Fejes, and Elin Shönning. 2011. "The Will to De(liberate): Shaping Governable Citizens Through Cognitive Behavioural Programmes in Schools." *Journal of Education Policy* 26 (3): 399–414.

Daley, Linda. 2016. "Fabulation: Toward Untimely and Inhuman Life in Alexis Wright's *The Swan Book*." *Australian Feminist Studies* 31 (89): 305–18.

Darwin, Charles. (1859) 2017. *On the Origin of the Species*. MacMillan Collector's Library. London: MacMillan Collector's Library.

Davidson, Debra J. "The Applicability of the Concept of Resilience to Social Systems: Some Sources of Optimism and Nagging Doubts." *Society and Natural Resources*, 23: 1135–49.

Deleuze, Gilles, and Félix Guattari. 1983. "What is a Minor Literature?" *Mississippi Review* 11, no. 3 (Winter/Spring): 13–33.

Dessner, Aaron Brooking, and Matthew Donald Berninger. 2010. "Terrible Love." Perf. by The National. Track 1, *High Violet*, 4AD, 2010, vinyl LP.

Diamond, Jared. 1999. *Guns, Germs and Steel: The Fates of Human Societies*. New York: W.W. Norton.

Diaz, Gloria, Gabrielle Cabrera, Carla Moore, and Laura Yakas. 2019. "Woke to Weary." *Public Culture* 31 (2): 373–91.

Díaz, Junot. 2012. "The Search for Decolonial Love: An Interview with Junot Díaz." Interview by Paula M. L. Moya. *Boston Review*, 26 June 2012. www.bostonreview.net/articles/paula-ml-moya-decolonial-love-interview-junot-diaz/.

Dicken, Emily, and Lily Yumagulova. 2016. "A Dialogue from First Nations on Emergency Management Across Canada." HAZNET: *The Magazine of the Canadian Risks and Hazards Network* 8 (2): 78–9.

Dillon, Grace. 2016. "Introduction: Indigenous Futurisms, Bimaashi Biidaas Mose, Flying and Walking towards You." *Extrapolation* 57 (1–2). go.gale.com/ps/i.do.

Dillon, Grace, and Pedro Neves Marques. 2021. "Taking the Fiction Out of Science Fiction: A Conversation about Indigenous Futurisms." *e-flux Journal* (120). www.e-flux.com/journal/120/417043/taking-the-fiction-out-of-science-fiction-a-conversation-about-indigenous-futurisms/.

Dorries, Heather, David Hugill, and Julie Tomiak. 2022. "Racial Capitalism and the Production of Settler Colonial Cities." *Geoforum* 132:263–70.

Douglas, Mary. 1966. *Purity and Danger: An Analysis of Concepts of Purity and Taboo.* Oxfordshire, UK: Routledge and Kegan Paul.

Doxtater, Michael. 2004. "Indigenous Knowledge in the Decolonial Era." *The American Indian Quarterly* 28 (3–4): 618–33.

Duffield, Mark. 2007. *Development, Security and Unending War: Governing the World of Peoples.* Cambridge, UK: Polity Press.

– 2011. "Environmental Terror: Uncertainty, Resilience and the Bunker." Working Paper 06-11. School of Sociology, Politics and International Studies, University of Bristol. https://www.bristol.ac.uk/media-library/sites/spais/migrated/documents/duffield-0611.pdf.

Dunne, Sean. 2014. "Stronger Than Ever: Why Resilience Is a Valuable Skill to Teach in Schools." *Independent School Parent,* 8 April 2014. independentschoolparent.com/pastoral/stronger-than-ever-why-resilience-is-a-valuable-skill-to-teach-in-schools.

Duran, Eduardo, and Bonnie Duran. 1995. *Native American Postcolonial Psychology.* Harrison, NY: SUNY Press.

Duran, Eduardo, Bonnie Duran, Maria Yellow Horse Brave Heart, and Susan Yellow-Horse Davis. 1998. "Healing the American Indian Soul Wound." In *International Handbook of Multigenerational Legacies of Trauma*, edited by Yael Danieli, 341–54. New York: Springer.

Ecclestone, Kathryn, Lydia Lewis, and Peter Lund. 2015. "Can a Rules Based Model Illuminate Pedagogical Practices?" *Pedagogy in Practice,* 1 (2): 36–65.

Edwards, Peter. 2010. "Shrugs Greet Historic $145M Toronto Land Claim Settlement." *The Toronto Star,* 8 June 2010. https://www.thestar.com/news/gta/shrugs-greet-historic-145m-toronto-land-claim-settlement/article_20387fa8-6849-57be-9391-71eac09958b7.html.

Eisenstadt, Michael. 2014. "Defeating ISIS: A Strategy for a Resilient Adversary and an Intractable Conflict." *Policy Notes*, The Washington Institute for Near East Policy, 20 November 2014.

EIU (The Economist Intelligence Unit). 2019. *Global Liveability Index 2019: A Free Overview,* The Economist Intelligence Unit, 22 October 2019. www.cbeinternational.ca/pdf/Liveability-Free-report-2019.pdf.

– 2021. *Global Liveability Index 2021: How the Covid-19 Pandemic Affected Liveability Worldwide*. The Economist Intelligence Unit, 22 2021.

Elliott, Jane. 2013. "Suffering Agency: Imagined Neoliberal Personhood in North America and Britain." *Social Text*, 31 (2): 83–101.

Eng, David L., and David Kazanjian. 2003. "Introduction: Mourning Remains." In *Loss*, edited by David L. Eng and David Kazanjian, 29–58. Berkeley: University of California Press.

Erikson, Kai. 1995. "Notes on Trauma and Community." In *Trauma: Explorations in Memory*, edited by Cathy Carruth, 183–199. Baltimore, MD: Johns Hopkins University Press.

Evans, Brad, and Julian Reid. 2014. *Resilient Life: The Art of Living Dangerously*. Cambridge, UK: Polity Press.

Evans-Campbell, Tessa. 2008. "Historical Trauma in American Indian/Native Alaska Communities: A Multi-Level Framework for Exploring Impacts on Individuals, Families and Communities." *Journal of Interpersonal Violence* 23:316–38.

Fast, Elizabeth, and Delphine Collin-Vézina. 2010. "Historical Trauma, Race-Based Trauma and Resilience of Indigenous Peoples: A Literature Review." *First Peoples Child and Family Review* 5 (1): 126–36.

Faulkner, Joanne. 2015. "'Our Own Hurricane Katrina': Aboriginal Disadvantage and Australian National Identity." *National Identities* 17 (2): 117–35.

Findlay, Stephanie, and Nicholas Kohler. 2010. "Too Asian." *Macleans*, 10 November 2010.

Fisher, Mark. 2009. *Capitalist Realism: Is There No Alternative?* Winchester, UK: Zero Books.

Fitzgibbon, Joanne, and Carrie L. Mitchell. 2019. "Just Urban Futures? Exploring Equity in '100 Resilient Cities.'" *World Development* 122:648–59.

Fitzpatrick, Scott J. 2016. "Ethical and Political Implications of the Turn to Stories in Suicide Prevention." *Philosophy, Psychiatry & Psychology* 23 (3–4): 265–76.

Folke, Carl. 2006. "Resilience: The Emergence of a Perspective for Social-Ecological Systems Analysis." *Global Environmental Change* 16:253–67.

Folke, Carl, Johan Colding, and Fikret Berkes. 2003. "Synthesis: Building Resilience and Adaptive Capacity in Social-Ecological Systems." In *Navigating Social-Ecological Systems: Building Resilience for Complexity and Change*, 352–87. Cambridge, UK: Cambridge University Press.

Folke, Carl, Thomas Hahn, Per Olsson, and John Norberg. 2005. "Adaptive Governance of Social-Ecological Systems." *Annual Review of Environment and Resources* 30:441–73.

Forbes, Stephen. 1925. "The Lake as a Microcosm." *Illinois Natural History Survey Bulletin* 15 (1–9): 537–50. https://doi.org/10.21900/j.inhs.v15.303.

Forster, E.M. (1924) 2005. *A Passage to India*. Edited by Pankaj Mishra. London: Penguin Classics.

Foucault, Michel. 2003. *Society Must Be Defended: Lectures at the Collège de France 1975–76*. Translated by David Macey. New York: Picador.

– 2009. *Security, Territory, Population: Lectures at the Collège de France 1977–1978*. Translated by Graham Burchell. NY: Picador.

Fraile-Marcos, Ana María. 2019. "Introduction: Glocal Narratives of Resilience and Healing." In *Glocal Narratives of Resilience*, 1–20. Oxfordshire, UK: Routledge.

Francis, Angelyn. 2021. "Halton Catholic District School Board's Workshop for Black Parents Postponed After Many Say It Misses the Mark." *Toronto Star*, 1 November 2021. www.thestar.com/news/gta/2021/11/01/halton-catholic-district-school-boards-workshop-for-black-parents-postponed-after-many-say-it-misses-the-mark.html.

Fraser, Nancy. 2017. "Progressive Neoliberalism vs Reactionary Populism: A Choice that Feminists Should Refuse." NORA – *Nordic Journal of Feminist and Gender Research* 24 (4): 281–4.

Freedman, Lynn, Shanon McNab, Sang Hee Won, Anna Abelson, and Amy Manning. 2020. "Disrespect and Abuse of Women of Color during Pregnancy and Childbirth: Findings from Qualitative Exploratory Research in New York City." *Averting Maternal Death and Disability* (Working Paper). Columbia Mailman School of Public Health, New York, NY, September 2020. https://www.publichealth.columbia.edu/file/7307/download?token=YUVlbgfA.

Friedersdorf, Conor. 2015. "The New Intolerance of Student Activism." *The Atlantic*, 9 November 2015. www.theatlantic.com/politics/archive/2015/11/the-new-intolerance-of-student-activism-at-yale/414810/.

Gagné, Marie-Anik. 1998. "The Role of Dependency and Colonialism in Generating Trauma in First Nations Citizens." In *International Handbook of Multigenerational Legacies of Trauma*, edited by Yael Danieli, 355–72. New York: Springer.

Garba, Tapji, and Sara-Maria Sorentino. 2020. "Slavery is a Metaphor." *Antipode Journal* 52 (3): 764–82.

Garmezy, Norman. 1974. "The Study of Competence in Children at Risk for Severe Psychopathology." In *The Child in his Family: Children at Psychiatric Risk*, 3rd ed, edited by James Anthony and Cyrille Koupernik, 77–97. Hoboken, NJ: Wiley.

Garmezy, Norman, Ann Masten, and Auke Tellegen. 1984. "The Study of Stress and Competence in Children: A Building Block for Developmental Psychopathology." *Child Development* 55:97–111.

Geronimus, Arline. 1992. "The Weathering Hypothesis and the Health of African-American Women and Infants: Evidence and Speculations." *Ethnicity and Disease* 2 (3): 207–21.

Ghosh, Amitav. 2016. *The Great Derangement: Climate Change and the Unthinkable*. University of Chicago Press.

Gianfrancesco, Angelo. 2001. "Une Littérature de Résilience?" In *La Résilience: Résister et se Construire*, edited by Michel Manciaux, 21–32. Mêdecine & Hygiène, RMS.

Gilbert, Jeremy. 2012. "Moving on from the Market Society: Culture (and Cultural Studies) in a Post-Democratic Age." OurKingdom Long Revolution Series, *openDemocracy*, 13 July 2012. www.opendemocracy.net/en/opendemocracyuk/moving-on-from-market-society-culture-and-cultural-studies-in-post-democra/.

Gilmore, Ruth Wilson. 2002. "Fatal Couplings of Power and Difference: Notes on Racism and Geography." *The Professional Geographer* 54 (1): 15–24.

Gladwell, Malcolm. 2002. "Blowing Up." *The New Yorker*, 29 April 2002. Archived at gladwell.com. web.archive.org/web/20040807112343/http://www.gladwell.com/2002/2002_04_29_a_blowingup.htm.

Glass, Deborah. 2020. *Investigation into the Detention and Treatment of Public Housing Residents Arising from a COVID-19 'Hard Lockdown' in July 2020* (Report). Victoria Ombudsman, 17 December 2020. www.ombudsman.vic.gov.au/our-impact/investigation-reports/investigation-into-the-detention-and-treatment-of-public-housing-residents-arising-from-a-covid-19-hard-lockdown-in-july-2020/.

Gleeson-White, Jane. 2017. "Country and Climate in Alexis Wright's *The Swan Book*." *AJE: Australasian Journal of Ecocriticism and Cultural Ecology* 6 (2016–2017): 29–38.

Glynn, Kevin, and Julia Cupples. 2022. "Stories of Decolonial Resilience." *Cultural Studies* 36 (6). doi/full/10.1080/09502386.2022.2144398.

Goff, Phillip Atiba, Matthew Christian Jackson, Carmen Marie Culotta, Brooke Allison, Lewis Di Leone, and Natalie Anne DiTomasso. 2014. "The Essence of Innocence: Consequences of Dehumanizing Black Children." *Journal of Personality and Social Psychology* 106 (4): 526–45.

Goh, Kian. 2021. *Form and Flow: The Spatial Politics of Urban Resilience and Climate Justice*. Cambridge: Massachusets Institute of Technology.

Goldman, Brian. 2016. "Has Old-Fashioned Fun been Trumped by Fears of Injury and Legal Action?" *Cross Country Canada*, CBC, 10 January 2016.

Gray, Peter. 2010. "The Decline of Play and Risk in Children's Mental Disorders." *Psychology Today*, 26 January 2010. www.psychologytoday.com/ca/blog/freedom-learn/201001/the-decline-play-and-rise-in-childrens-mental-disorders.greet_historic_145m_toronto_land_claim_settlement.html.

– 2015. "Declining Student Resilience: A Serious Problem for Colleges." *Psychology Today*, 22 September 2015. www.psychologytoday.com/ca/blog/freedom-learn/201509/declining-student-resilience-serious-problem-colleges.

Grieves, Victoria. 2017. "The Seven Pillars of Aboriginal Exception to the Australian State: Camps, Refugees, Biopolitics and the Northern Territory Emergency Response (NTER)." In *"And there'll be NO dancing": Perspectives on Policies Impacting Indigenous Australia since 2007*, edited by Elizabeth Baehr and

Barbara Schmidt-Haberkamp, 87–109. Cambridge, UK: Cambridge Scholars Publishing.

Griffiths, Tom, and Libby Robin, eds. 1997. *Ecology and Empire: Environmental History of Settler Societies*. Keele, UK: Keele University Press.

Gross, Lawrence William. 2014. *Anishinaabe Ways of Knowing and Being*. Farnham, UK: Ashgate Publishing.

Grossman, Michelle. 2013. "Prognosis Critical: Resilience and Multiculturalism in Contemporary Australia." *M/C Journal* 16 (5).

Grove, Richard H. 1995. *Green Imperialism*. Cambridge, UK: Cambridge University Press.

Gumbs, Alexis Pauline. 2019. "Being Ocean as Praxis: Depth Humanisms and Dark Sciences." *Qui Parle* 28 (2): 335–52.

Gurstein, Penny. 2018. "Liveability for Whom? Vancouver's Conundrum." *Livable Cities from a Global Perspective*, edited by Roger W. Caves and Fritz Wagner, 138–48. Oxfordshire, UK: Routledge.

Hackman, Rose. 2016. "It's Like We're Seen as Animals: Black Men on Their Vulnerability and Resilience." *The Guardian*, 12 July 2016. www.theguardian.com/world/2016/jul/12/black-men-america-violence-vulnerable-detroit.

Hage, Ghassan. 2000. *White Nation: Fantasies of White Supremacy in a Multicultural Society*. Oxfordshire, UK: Routledge.

– 2018. "Psychoanalysis and Cultural Studies." *Cultural Studies* 32 (6): 889–96.

Halls, Andrew. n.d. "Headmaster's Welcome." Kings College School. www.kcs.org.uk/ senior-school/head-masters-welcome.

– 2014a. "Strength and Self-Belief Can Help British Young People Be Happy Again." *The Sunday Times*, The Schools Blog, 23 March 2014.

– 2014b. "True Grit: Standing Up to the 21st-Century." *The Sunday Times*, The Schools Blog, 9 March 2014.

Hansen, John E., and Rose Antsanen. 2016. "Elders Teachings About Resilience and Its Implications for Education in Dene and Cree Communities." *The International Indigenous Policy Journal* 7 (1).

Haraway, Donna. 1985. "Teddy Bear Patriarchy: Taxidermy in the Garden of Eden, New York City, 1908–1936." *Social Text* 11 (1984–1985): 20–64.

– 2016. *Staying with the Trouble: Making Kin in the Cthulucene*. Durham, NC: Duke University Press.

Harding, Sandra. 2008. *Sciences from Below: Feminisms, Postcolonialities and Modernities*. Durham, NC: Duke University Press.

Hargreaves, Allison. 2009. "Compelling Disclosures: Colonial Violence and the Narrative Imperative in Feminist Anti-violence Discourse and Indigenous Women's Writing." *Canadian Women's Studies* 27 (2–3): 107–13.

Harris, Cheryl I. 1993. "Whiteness as Property." *Harvard Law Review* 106 (8): 1701–91.

Harris, Tamara Winfrey. 2014. "Precious Mettle: The Truth Behind the 'Strong Black Woman' Stereotype." *Bitch Magazine*, 13 May 2014. bitchmedia.org/article/precious-mettle-myth-strong-black-woman.

Harris-Perry, Melissa V. 2013. *Sister Citizen: Shame, Stereotypes, and Black Women in America*. New Haven, CT: Yale University Press.

Hartman, Saidiya. 2007. *Lose Your Mother: A Journey along the Atlantic Slave Route*. New York: Farrar, Straus and Giroux.

– 2008. "Venus in Two Acts." *small axe* 26:1–14.

Hassan, Genevieve. 2015. "*The Martian*: A 'Love Letter to Science.'" *BBC News*, 29 September 2015. www.bbc.com/news/entertainment-arts-34338556.

Hayles, N. Katherine. 2000. "Making the Cut: The Interplay of Narrative and System, or What System Theory Can't See." In *Observing Complexity: Systems Theory and Postmodernity*, edited by William Rasch and Cary Wolfe, 137–62. Chicago: University of Chicago Press. scholars.duke.edu/display/pub-1102152https://scholars.duke.edu/display/pub1102152.

Health Canada, First Nations and Inuit Health Branch. 2003a. "Acting on What We Know: Preventing Youth Suicide in First Nations." *The Report of the Advisory Group on Suicide Prevention*. Last modified 3 March 2013. Ottawa, ON: Health Canada.

HeavyRunner, Iris, and Joann Morris. 1997. "Traditional Native Culture and Resilience." *Research / Practice* 5 (1).

Heer, Jeet. 2010. "Too Brazen." *The Walrus Blog*, 24 November 2010.

Heidenreich, Adrian C. 2016. "The 1880 Crow Indian Delegation to Washington, D.C.: Cultural Identity, Colonial Policies, and Intercultural Images." *Montana State University Billings Library Lecture Series*, 18 October 2016.

Heinzen, Barbara, and Arthur Muliro. 2004. "The World is not Makeable." *Development* 47 (4): 9–14.

Henderson, Jennifer. 2023. "Neoliberal Gothic, Settler Social Imaginaries, and the Case for Decolonization on Two Fronts." In *Land/Relations*, edited by Larissa Lai and Smaro Kamboureli, 125–44. Waterloo: Wilfrid Laurier University Press.

Henderson, Jennifer, and Keith Denny. 2015. "The Resilient Child, Human Development and the 'Postdemocracy.'" *Biosocieties* 10 (July): 1–27.

Hernandez, Catherine. 2017. *Scarborough*. Toronto: Arsenal Pulp Press.

Hinkson, Melinda. 2007. "Introduction: In the Name of the Child." In *Coercive Reconciliation: Stabilise, Normalise, Exit Aboriginal Australia*, edited by Jon Altman and Melinda Hinkson, 1–14. Melbourne, AU: Arena Publications Association.

Hoad, Philip. 2015. "The Martian Shows Hollywood's Chinese Connection Has Lift Off." *The Guardian*, 20 November 2015. www.theguardian.com/film/filmblog/2015/nov/30/global-box-office-the-martian-the-good-dinosaur-creed.

Hoffman, Diane M. 2010. "Risky Investments: Parenting and the Production of the 'Resilient Child." *Health, Risk & Society* 12 (4): 385–94.

Hoffman, Kelly M., Sophie Trawalter, Jordan R. Axt, and M. Norman Oliver. 2015. "Racial Bias in Pain Assessment and Treatment Recommendations, and False Beliefs about Biological Differences between Blacks and Whites." *Proceedings of the National Academy of Sciences of the United States of America* 113 (16): 4296–301.

Hofman, Shar Zavareh. 2021. "100 Resilient Cities Program and the Role of the Sendai Framework and Disaster Risk Reduction for Resilient Cities." *Progress in Disaster Science* 11:1–11.

Holling, C.S. 1973. "Resilience and Stability of Ecological Systems." *Annual Review of Ecology and Systematics* 4:1–24.

– 2007. "Introduction: Reflections Part 1." *Resilience Science*, 21 February 2007. rs.resalliance.org/2007/02/21/introduction-reflections-part-1/.

Hornborg, Alf. 2013. "Revelations of Resilience: From the Ideological Disarmament of Disaster to the Revolutionary Implications of (P)anarchy." *Resilience: International Policies, Practices and Discourses* 1 (2): 116–29.

Howard, John. 2007. "To Stabilise and Protect: Little Children are Sacred." *The Sydney Papers* 19 (3): 68–76. search.informit.org/doi/epdf/10.3316/informit.018440362568649.

Howell, Alison, and Jijian Voronka. 2012. "Introduction: The Politics of Resilience and Recovery in Mental Health Care." *Studies in Social Justice* 6 (1): 1–7.

Hugill, David. 2017. "What Is a Settler-Colonial City?" *Geography Compass* 11 (5): e12315. doi.org/10.1111/gec3.12315.

Hussain, Nasser. 2003. *The Jurisprudence of Emergency: Colonialism and the Rule of Law.* Ann Arbor: University of Michigan Press.

Independent School Parent. 2014. "True Grit: Developing Emotional Resilience in Schools." *Independent School Parent*, 24 March 2014. www.independentschoolparent.com/education-news/true-grit-developing-emotional-resilience-in-schools/.

Jacobs, Jane M. 1996. *Edge of Empire: Postcolonialism and the City.* Oxfordshire, UK: Routledge.

– 2012. "Commentary: Property and Propriety: (Re)making the Space of Indigeneity in Australian Cities." *Postcolonial Studies* 15 (2):143–7.

Joseph, Jonathan. 2013. "Resilience as Embedded Neoliberalism: A Governmentality Approach." *Resilience: International Policies, Practices and Discourses* 1 (1): 38–52.

Juniper, Tony. 2011. "Will 2012 Be the Year of the R Word?" *The Guardian*, 14 December 2011. www.theguardian.com/sustainable-business/resiliance-sustainable-development.

Kanji, Azeezah, and A.J. Withers. 2021. "Encampment Evictions: Another Face of Colonial Violence in Canada." *Al Jazeera*, 22 July 2021. www.aljazeera.com/opinions/2021/7/20/encampment-evictions-another-face-of-colonial-violence-in-canada.

Karabel, Jerome. 2006. *The Chosen: The Hidden History of Admission and Exclusion at Harvard, Yale and Princeton*. Boston, MA: Mariner Books.

Kashef, Mohamad. 2016. "Urban Livability Across Disciplinary and Professional Boundaries." *Frontiers of Architectural Research* 5:239–53.

Kelbaugh, Douglas. 2019. *The Urban Fix: Resilience Cities in the War Against Climate Change, Heat Islands and Overpopulation*. Oxfordshire, UK: Routledge.

Khan, Shamus Rahman. 2011. *Privilege: The Making of an Adolescent Elite at St. Paul's School*. Princeton, NJ: Princeton University Press.

King, Tiffany Lethabo. 2019. *The Black Shoals: Offshore Formations of Black and Native Studies*. Durham, NC: Duke University Press.

King, Thomas. 1990. "Introduction." *All My Relations: An Anthology of Contemporary Canadian Native Fiction*, ix–xvi. Toronto: McClelland & Stewart.

Kirmayer, Laurence A., Stéphane Dandeneau, Elizabeth Marshall, Morgan Kahentonni Philips, and Karla Jessen Williamson. 2011. "Rethinking Resilience from Indigenous Perspectives." *Canadian Journal of Psychiatry* 56 (2): 84–91.

Knox, Todd H., Christi Deaton, Anne P. D'Adamo, and Leon Goe. 2000. "Ethnicity and Analgesic Practice." *Annals of Emergency Medicine* 35 (1): 11–16.

Kramer, Jillian. 2012. "Protecting White Australia: John Howard's Announcement of the Northern Territory Emergency Response and the Ongoing Colonial Project." *NEO* 5:1–16.

Kumar, Mohan B., and Michael Tjepkema. 2019. "Suicide among First Nations People, Métis and Inuit (2011–2016). Findings from the 2011 Canadian Census Health and Environment Cohort (CanCHEC)." *National Household Survey: Aboriginal Peoples*, Statistics Canada, 28 June 2019. www150.statcan.gc.ca/n1/pub/99–011-x/99–011-x2019001-eng.htm.

Laforme, Douglas. 2017. "What Could Canada Have Been if the Treaty Process Was Fair?" *Torontoist*, 7 June 2017. torontoist.com/2017/06/canada-treaty-process-fair/.

Latour, Bruno. 2004. "Why Has Critique Run out of Steam? From Matters of Fact to Matters of Concern." *Critical Inquiry* 30:225–48.

Lear, Jonathan. 2008. *Radical Hope: Ethics in the Face of Cultural Devastation*. Cambridge, MA: Harvard University Press.

Levine, Caroline. 2021. "The Long Lure of Anti-instrumentality: Politics, Aesthetics, and Sustainability." *Modern Fiction Studies* 67 (2): 225–46.

Levine, Madeline. 2006. *The Price of Privilege: How Parental Pressure and Material Advantage Are Creating a Generation of Disconnected and Unhappy Kids*. New York: HarperCollins.

Liboiron, Max. 2021. *Pollution is Colonialism*. Durham, NC: Duke University Press.

Linderman, Frank B. 1962. *Plenty-Coups: Chief of the Crows*, 2nd ed. Lincoln: University of Nebraska Press.

Lindroth, Marjo, and Heidi Sinevaara-Niskanen. 2019. "Colonialism Invigorated? The Manufacture of Resilient Indigeneity." *Resilience* 7 (3): 240–54.

Lindzon, Jared. 2019. "Top Takeaways from Toronto's Collision Tech Conference." *The Globe and Mail*, 28 May 2019. www.theglobeandmail.com/business/article-top-takeaways-from-torontos-collision-tech-conference/.

Liu, Sze Yan, Christina Florentini, Deborah Kaplan, Zinzi Bailey, Mary Huynh, and Katherine McVeigh. 2019. "Structural Racism and Severe Maternal Morbidity in New York State." *Clinical Medicine Insights: Women's Health* 12:1–8.

Lomborg, Bjørn. 2012. "Environmental Alarmism, Then and Now: The Club of Rome's Problem – and Ours." *Foreign Affairs* 91 (4): 24–40.

Longstaff, P.H., and Sung-Un Yang. 2008. "Communication Management and Trust: Their Role in Building Resilience to 'Surprises' Such As Natural Disasters, Pandemic Flu and Terrorism." *Ecology and Society* 13 (1).

Lousley, Cheryl. 2014. "'Third World' as Gothic Future: Specters of Bare Life at the World Commission on Environment and Development." Paper presented at the American Comparative Literature Association conference, New York University, New York, 20 March 2014.

– 2015. "Dionne Brand's Environmental Poetics." TOPIA 34:39–61.

Louv, Richard. 2005. *Last Child in the Woods: Saving Our Children from Nature-Deficit Disorder.* Chapel Hill, NC: Algonquin Books.

Love, Keosha. n.d. *Keosha Love: Artist, Activist and Educator.* Accessed 14 September 2022. www.keoshalove.com/about.html.

Luthar, Suniya S., Dante Cicchetti, and Bronwyn Becker. 2000. "The Construct of Resilience: A Critical Evaluation and Guidelines for Future Work." *Child Development* 71 (3): 543–62.

Mackey, Eve. 2002. *The House of Difference: Cultural Politics and National Identity in Canada*. Toronto: University of Toronto Press.

MacKinnon, Danny, and Kate Driscoll Derickson. 2012. "From Resilience to Resourcefulness: A Critique of Resilience Policy and Activism." *Progress in Human Geography* 37 (2): 1–18.

Mangham, C., P. McGrath, G. Reid, and M. Stewart. 1995. "Resiliency: Relevance to Health Promotion: Discussion Paper." Ottawa: Office of Alcohol, Drugs and Dependency Issues, Health Canada.

Manyena, Bernard, Geoff O'Brien, Phil O'Keefe, and Joanne Rose. 2011. "Disaster Resilience: A Bounce Back or Bounce Forward Ability?" *Local Environment: The International Journal of Justice and Sustainability* 16 (5): 417–24.

Marano, Hara Estroff. 2004. "A Nation of Wimps." *Psychology Today*, 1 November 2004. www.psychologytoday.com/ca/articles/200411/nation-wimps.

Markusen, Ann. 1999. "Fuzzy Concepts, Scanty Evidence, Policy Distance: The Case for Rigour and Policy Relevance in Critical Regional Studies." *Regional Studies* 37:701–17.

Martineau, Jarrett, and Eric Ritskes. 2014. "Fugitive Indigeneity: Reclaiming the Terrain of Decolonial Struggle through Indigenous Art." *Decolonization: Indigeneity, Education & Society* 3 (1): I–XII.

Masten, Ann. S. 2001. "Ordinary Magic: Resilience Processes in Development." *American Psychologist* 56 (3): 227–38.
Maynard, Robyn. 2017. *Policing Black Lives: State Violence in Canada from Slavery to the Present*. Halifax, NS: Fernwood Publishing.
Maynard, Robyn, and Leanne Betasamosake Simpson. 2022. *Rehearsals for Living*. Chicago: Haymarket Books.
McArthur, Jenny, and Enora Robin. 2019. "Victims of Their Own (Definition of) Success: Urban Discourse and Expert Knowledge Production in the Liveable City." *Urban Studies* 56 (9): 1711–28.
McAvoy, Jean. 2014. "Psy Disciplines." In *Encyclopedia of Critical Psychology*, edited by T. Teo, 1527–9. New York: Springer.
McClintock, Pamela. 2015. "How NASA Kept Things Real with *The Martian*." *Hollywood Reporter*, 30 September 2015. www.hollywoodreporter.com.
McCormick, Rod. M. 2009. "All My Relations." In *Mentally Healthy Communities: Aboriginal Perspectives*, edited by Canadian Institute for Health Information. Ottawa, ON: Canadian Institute for Health Information. publications.gc.ca/collection_2009/icis-cihi/H118-58-2009E.pdf.
McDonald, Glenn. 2015. "*The Martian*: Technology, Wonder, and a Love Letter to NASA." *Yahoo*.com, 2 October 2015. www.yahoo.com/tech/the-martian-technology-wonder-and-a-love-letter-202317268.html.
McFate, Jessica Lewis. 2015. "The ISIS Defense in Iraq and Syria: Countering an Adaptive Enemy." *Middle East Security Report* 27, Institute for the Study of War, May 2015. New York: McGraw Hill. www.understandingwar.org/report/isis-defense-iraq-and-syria-countering-adaptive-enemy.
McKittrick, Katherine. 2006. *Demonic Grounds: Black Women and the Cartographies of Struggle*. Minneapolis: University of Minnesota Press.
– 2016. "Rebellion, Invention, Groove." *small axe* 49:79–91.
McKittrick, Katherine, and Clyde Woods. 2007. "'No One Knows the Mysteries at the Bottom of the Ocean.'" In *Black Geographies and the Politics of Place*, 1–13. Toronto: Between the Lines Books; Boston: South End Press.
McRobbie, Angela. 1994. *Postmodernism and Popular Culture*. Oxfordshire, UK: Routledge.
McWade, Brigit. 2016. "Recovery-as-Policy as a Form of Neoliberal State Making." *Intersectionalities: A Global Journal of Social Work Analysis, Research, Polity and Practice* 5 (3): 62–81.
Meadows, Donella H., Dennis L. Meadows, Jorgen Randers, and William W. Behrens III. 1972. *The Limits to Growth: A Report for the Club of Rome's Project on the Predicament of Mankind*. New York: New American Library.
Melamed, Jodi. 2015. "Racial Capitalism." *Critical Ethnic Studies* 1 (1): 76–85.
Menzies, Peter. 2010. "Intergenerational Trauma from a Mental Health Perspective." *Native Social Work Journal* 7:63–85.
Merchant, Carolyn. 2003. "Shades of Darkness: Race and Environmental History." *Environmental History* 8 (3).

Methmann, Chris, and Angela Oels. 2015. "From 'Fearing' to 'Empowering' Refugees: Governing Climate-Induced Migration in the Name of Resilience." *Security Dialogue* 46 (1): 51–68.

Mignolo, W.D., and M.V. Tlostanova, 2006. "Theorizing from the Borders: Shifting to Geo- and Body-Politics of Knowledge." *European Journal of Social Theory* 9 (2): 205–21.

Miller, Paul. 2004. *Rhythm Science*. Cambridge: Massachusetts Institute of Technology Press.

Million, Dian. 2008. "Felt Theory." *American Quarterly* 60 (2): 267–72.

– 2013. *Therapeutic Nations: Healing in an Age of Indigenous Human Rights*. Tucson: Arizona University Press.

Milner, Natalie. 2014. "Great Expectations." *Independent School Parent*, 29 June 2014. independentschoolparent.com/pastoral/great-expectations.

Mohamud, Jamilla. 2020a. "Anti-Black Racism in the Liveable City and Canada" (Blog). Ontario Professional Planners Institute, 1 July 2020. ontarioplanners.ca/blog/planning-exchange/july-2020/anti-black-racism-in-the-liveable-city-and-canada.

– 2020b. "The Paradox of Black Life: Discourses of Urban (Un)liveability." MA thesis, Environmental Studies, York University. yorkspace.library.yorku.ca/xmlui/bitstream/handle/10315/38252/JM%20MES%20MP%20final.pdf?sequence=1&isAllowed=y.

Moreton-Robinson, Aileen. 2015. *The White Possessive: Property, Power, and Indigenous Sovereignty*. Minneapolis: University of Minnesota Press.

Morris, Barry, and Andrew Lattas. 2010. "Embedded Anthropology and the Intervention." *Arena* 107, August 2010. arena.org.au/embedded-anthropology-and-the-intervention/.

Mosby, Ian, and Tracey Galloway. 2017. "'Hunger Was Never Absent.' How Residential School Diets Shaped Current Patterns of Diabetes among Indigenous People." *Canadian Medical Association Journal* 189 (32): 1043–5.

Mueller, Tim B. 2013. "The Rockefeller Foundation, the Social Sciences, and the Humanities in the Cold War." *Journal of Cold War Studies* 15 (3): 108–35.

Myers, Steven Lee. 2021. "The Moon, Mars and Beyond: China's Ambitious Plans in Space." *The New York Times*, 15 October 2021. nytimes.com/article/china-mars-space.html.

Nadasy, Paul. 1999. "The Politics of TEK: Power and the 'Integration' of Knowledge." *Arctic Anthropology* 36 (1–2): 1–18.

Neale, Timothy, and Eve Vincent. 2016. "Instabilities and Inequalities: Relations between Indigenous People and Environmentalism in Australia Today." In *Unstable Relations: Indigenous People and Environmentalism in Contemporary Australia*, edited by Timothy Neale and Eve Vincent, 1–24. Perth, AU: University of Western Australia Publishing.

Nelson, Alan. 2002. "Unequal Treatment: Confronting Racial and Ethnic Disparities in Health Care." *Journal of the National Medical Association* 94 (8): 666–8.

Nelson, Glenn. 2015. "Why Are Our Parks So White?" *New York Times*, 12 July 2015. www.nytimes.com/2015/07/12/opinion/sunday/diversify-our-national-parks.html.

Neocleous, Mark. 2006. "The Problem with Normality: Taking Exception to 'Permanent Emergency.'" *Alternatives* 31:191–213.

Nixon, Rob. 2011. *Slow Violence and the Environmentalism of the Poor*. Cambridge, MA: Harvard University Press.

Noe, Bernie. 2013. "Building Resilience in Students. Lakeside School, Seattle." Lakeside School, 14 June 2013. Accessed 20 July 2018, link no longer available.

O'Brien, Susie. 2014. "'Graceful Failure': The Privatization of Resilience." *Review of Education, Pedagogy and Cultural Studies* 36 (4): 260–73.

– 2017. "Resilience Stories: Narratives of Adaptation, Refusal and Compromise." *Resilience: Journal of the Environmental Humanities* 4 (1): 43–65.

– 2019. "'The Story You Don't Want to Tell': Decolonial Resilience in Thomas King's *The Back of the Turtle*." In *Glocal Narratives of Resilience*, edited by Ana María Fraile-Marcos, 39–55. Oxfordshire, UK: Routledge.

– 2023. "EN/CULTRST/GLOB 773 'Revolt and Remember': Resilience in the Postcolonial Environmental Humanities." Syllabus. Hamilton, ON: McMaster University.

Olsson, Lennart, Anne Jerneck, Henrik Thoren, Johannes Persson, and David O'Byrne. 2005. "Why Resilience is Unappealing to Social Science: Theoretical and Empirical Investigations of the Scientific Use of Resilience." *Science Advances* 1 (4).

Olsson, Per, Lance H. Gunderson, Steve R. Carpenter, Paul Ryan, Louis Lebel, Carl Folke, and C. S. Holling. 2006. "Shooting the Rapids: Navigating Transitions to Adaptive Governance of Social-Ecological Systems." *Ecology and Society* 11 (1).

O'Malley, Pat. 2010. "Resilient Subjects: Uncertainty, Warfare and Liberalism." *Economy and Society* 39 (4): 488–509.

Oxford English Dictionary. 2023. s.v. "Volume." https://www.oed.com/search/advanced/Meanings?textTermTexto=volume&textTermOpto=WordPhrase.

Park, Neville. 2016. "Famous Quotes Reimagined in the Voice of John Tory." *Torontoist*, 18 April 2016. torontoist.com/2016/04/famous-quotes-reimagined-in-the-voice-of-john-tory/.

Park, Yoosun, Rory Crath, and Donna Jeffrey. (2020). "Disciplining the Risky Subject: A Discourse Analysis of Resilience in the Discourse of Social Work." *Journal of Social Work* 20 (2): 1–21.

Parker, John N., and Edward J. Hackett. 2012. "Hot Spots and Hot Moments in Scientific Collaborations and Social Movements." *American Sociological Review* 77 (1): 21–44.

Parks, Sheri. 2013. *Fierce Angels: Living with a Legacy from the Sacred Dark Feminine to the Strong Black Woman*. Chicago: Chicago Review Press.

Patch, Nick. 2017. "David Chariandy Rewrites Scarborough in His New Book *Brother*." *Toronto Star*, 26 September 2017. www.thestar.com/entertainment/books/2017/09/22/david-chariandy-rewrites-scarborough-in-his-new-book-brother.html.

Paterson, Chris, Claire Tyler, and Jen Lexmond with CentreForum, All-Party Parliamentary Group on Social Mobility, Character Counts. 2014. *Character and Resilience Manifesto* (Report). CentreForum, 1 February 2014. www.bl.uk/collection-items/character-and-resilience-manifesto.

Peet, Richard. 1985. "The Social Origins of Environmental Determinism." *Annals of the Association of American Geographers* 75 (3): 309–33.

Perrow, Charles. 1999. *Normal Accidents: Living with High Risk Technologies*. Princeton, NJ: Princeton University Press.

Peterson, Christopher, and Martin E.P. Seligman. 2004. *Character Strengths and Virtues: A Handbook and Classification*. Worcester, MA: American Psychological Association.

Phillips, Jason. 2013. "Drop the Worry Ball: How to Parent in the Age of Entitlement." *The PATH Newsletter*. Dundas, ON: Dundas Valley Montessori School. http://dvms.ca/category/the-path-montessori-news-research-people-and-voices/.

Phillips, Morgan Kahentonni, Stéphane Dandeneau, and Laurence J. Kirmayer. 2012. "Roots of Resilience: Stories of Resilience, Healing and Transformation in Kahnawake." *Community Report*. Network for Aboriginal Mental Health Research.

Porter, Libby, and Simin Davoudi. 2012. "The Politics of Resilience for Planning: A Cautionary Note." *Planning Theory & Practice* 13 (2): 329–33.

Porter, Libby, and Oren Yiftachel. 2019. "Urbanizing Settler-Colonial Studies: Introduction to the Special Issue." *Settler Colonial Studies* 9 (2):177–86.

Potter, Emily. 2012. "Introduction: Making Indigenous Place in the Australian City." *Postcolonial Studies* 15 (2): 131–42.

Povinelli, Elizabeth. 2011. *Economies of Abandonment: Social Belonging and Endurance in Late Liberalism*. Durham, NC: Duke University Press.

– 2016. *Geontologies: A Requiem for Late Liberalism*. Durham, NC: Duke University Press.

– 2017. "The Ends of Humans: Anthropocene, Autonomism, Antagonism, and the Illusions of Our Epoch." *South Atlantic Quarterly* 116 (2): 293–310.

Prevatt, Frances F. 2003. "The Contributions of Parenting Practices in a Risk and Resiliency Model of Children's Adjustment." *British Journal of Developmental Psychology* 21:469–80.

Ranganthan, Malini, and Eve Bratman. 2021. "From Urban Resilience to Abolitionist Climate Justice in Washington, DC." *Antipode: A Radical Journal of Geography* 53 (1): 115–37.

Ravenscroft, Alison. 2010. "Dreaming of Others: Carpentaria and its Critics." *Cultural Studies Review* 16 (2): 194–225.
– 2012. *The Postcolonial Eye*. Farnham, UK: Ashgate.
Ray, Sangeeta. 2018. "Reading Form in the Age of the Anthropocene." Keynote address given at Planetary Cultural and Literary Studies: New Epistemologies and Relational Futures in the Age of the Anthropocene/ Études culturelles et littéraires planétaires: Nouvelles épistémologies et avenirs relationnels à l'ère de l'anthropocène, University of Montreal, Montreal, QC, 9–12 April 2018.
Regis, Mike, dir. 2019. *Resilient People: Joe, Husam & Keosha*. The City of Toronto, YouTube video, 4 March 2019. www.youtube.com/watch?v=jz3ToRGf3EI. resources/UR/Resilient-Cities-Resilient-Lives-Learning-from-the-100RC-Network.pdf.
Rifkin, Mark. 2013. "Settler Common Sense." *Settler Colonial Studies* 3 (3–4): 322–40.
Robin, Libby. 2014. "Resilience in the Anthropocene: A Biography." In *Rethinking Invasion Ecologies from the Environmental Humanities*, edited by Jodi Frawley and Iain McCalman, 45–63. Oxfordshire, UK: Routledge.
Robinson, Cedric J. 1983. *Black Marxism: The Making of the Black Radical Tradition*. London, UK: Zed Books.
Rockefeller Foundation. n.d. "A Legacy of Making Opportunity Universal." The Rockefeller Foundation. Last modified 5 April 2023. www.rockefeller foundation.org./video/the-rockefeller-foundation-a-legacy-of-making-opportunity-universal/.
– 2020. "Our History." The Rockefeller Foundation. Last modified 18 September 2020. www.rockefellerfoundation.org/about-us/our-history/.
Rodin, Judith. 2013. "33 Resilient Cities Announced by Rockefeller Foundation." The Rockefeller Foundation, 13 December 2013. www.rockefellerfoundation.org/blog/33-resilient-cities-announced-by-the-rockefeller-foundation/. Accessed July 5, 2021.
– 2014. *The Resilience Dividend: Managing Disruption, Avoiding Disaster, and Growing Stronger in an Unpredictable World*. London, UK: Profile Books.
Rose, Deborah Bird. 1996. *Nourishing Terrains: Australian Aboriginal Views of Landscape and Wilderness*. Canberra, AU: Australian Heritage Commission.
– 2004. *Reports from a Wild Country: Ethics for Decolonization*. Kensington, AU: University of New South Wales Press.
Rose, Nikolas. 1996. "Authority and the Genealogy of Subjectivity." In *Detraditionalization: Critical Reflections on Authority and Identity*, edited by Paul Heelas, Scott Lash, and Paul Morris, 294–327. Cambridge, MA: Blackwell Publishers.
– 2011. "Identity, Genealogy, History." *Questions of Cultural Identity*, edited by Stuart Hall and Paul du Gay, 128–150. London: SAGE Publications. https://doi.org/10.4135/9781446221907.

Ross, Andrew. 1994. *The Chicago Gangster Theory of Life: Nature's Debt to Society.* Brooklyn, NY: Verso Books.

Rotarangi, Stephanie, and Darryn Russell. 2009. "Social-Ecological Resilience Thinking: Can Indigenous Culture Guide Environmental Management?" *Journal of the Royal Society of New Zealand* 39 (4): 209–13.

Rudd, Kevin. 2008. "The First National Security Statement to the Parliament Address by the Prime Minister of Australia, The Hon. Kevin Rudd MP" (Speech). *Parliamentary Debates: House of Representatives: Official Hansard* 18. Canberra: Commonwealth of Australia, 4 December 2008. https://parlinfo.aph.gov.au/parlInfo/search/display/display.w3p;query=Id:%22chamber/hansardr/2008-12-04/0045%22.

Rundle, Guy. 2007. "Military Humanitarianism in Australia's North." In *Coercive Reconciliation: Stabilise, Normalise, Exit Aboriginal Australia,* edited by Jon Altman and Melinda Hinkson, 37–46. Melbourne, AU: Arena Publications.

Russell, Alex, and Tim Falconer. 2014. *Drop the Worry Ball: How to Parent in the Age of Entitlement.* New York: HarperCollins.

Ruth, Matthias, and Rachel S. Franklin. 2014. "Livability for All? Conceptual Limits and Practical Implications." *Applied Geography* 49:18–23.

Said, Edward. 1993. *Culture and Imperialism.* New York: Knopf.

Schambra, William A. 2013. "Philanthropy's Original Sin." *The New Atlantis* (39). www.thenewatlantis.com/publications/philanthropys-original-sin.

Schwartz, Peter. 2004. *Inevitable Surprises: Thinking Ahead in a Time of Turbulence,* Sheridan, WY: Gotham Books.

Scott, Ridley, dir. 2015. *The Martian.* Los Angeles, CA: 20th Century Studios. 144 minutes.

Scranton, Roy. 2015a. *Learning to Die in the Anthropocene: Reflections on the End of a Civilization.* San Francisco, CA: City Lights Publishers.

– 2015b. "We're Doomed. Now What?" Opinionator, *New York Times,* 21 December 2015. archive.nytimes.com/opinionator.blogs.nytimes.com/2015/12/21/were-doomed-now-what/.

Scrymgour, Marion. 2014. "Lessons Learned: Looking Back and Looking Forward after the 'Intervention.'" *Indigenous Law Bulletin* 8 no. 16 (January). www5.austlii.edu.au/au/journals/IndigLawB/2015/3.pdf.

Seligman, Martin. 2011. "Building Resilience." *Harvard Business Review,* April 2011, 100–6.

Semple, Ellen Churchill. 1903. *American History and Its Geographic Conditions.* Boston, MA: Houghton Mifflin.

Sharifi, Ayoob, and Yoshiki Yamagata. 2016. "Urban Resilience Assessment: Multiple Dimensions, Criteria, and Indicators." In *Urban Resilience,* edited by Yoshiki Yamagata and Hiroshi Maruyama, 259–276. New York: Springer.

Sharpe, Christina. 2016. *In the Wake: On Blackness and Being.* Durham, NC: Duke University Press.

Shiva, Vandana. 2016. *The Violence of the Green Revolution: Third World Agriculture, Ecology, and Politics*. Lexington: University Press of Kentucky.

Shotwell, Alexis. 2016. *Against Purity Politics*. Minneapolis: University of Minnesota Press.

Simmonds, Michael, and Kate White. 2018. "Weathering Life's Storms." *The Torch*, Havergal College, Spring 2018, 12–13.

Simpson, Audra. 2011. *Mohawk Interruptus: Political Life across the Borders of Settler States*. Durham, NC: Duke University Press.

Simpson, Leanne Betasamosake. 2008. "Oshkimaadiziig, the New People." *Lighting the Eighth Fire: The Liberation Resurgence and Protection of Indigenous Nations*. Winnipeg, MB: ARP Books.

– 2013a. "Embodying the Transformation of Idle No More: In Conversation with Leanne Simpson." Interview by Naomi Klein. *rabble.ca*, 6 March 2013.

– 2013b. *Islands of Decolonial Love*. Winnipeg, MB: ARP Books.

– 2017. *As We Have Always Done: Indigenous Freedom Through Radical Resistance*. Minneapolis: University of Minnesota Press.

Sinclair, Murray. 2015. "Statement from the Chair, Justice Murray Sinclair." In *Canada's Residential Schools: The History, Part 1 Origins to 1939*, edited by Truth and Reconciliation Commission, vii-x. Montreal, QC: McGill-Queen's University Press. publications.gc.ca/collections/.

Singh, Vandana. 2017. "The Unthinkability of Climate Change: Thoughts on Amitav Ghosh's *The Great Derangement*." *Strange Horizons*. strangehorizons.com/non-fiction/reviews/the-unthinkability-of-climate-change-thoughts-on-amitav-ghoshs-the-great-derangement/.

Skeat, Jean. 2016. "Political Poetics and the Power of Things: Nonhuman Agency and Climate Change in Alexis Wright's *The Swan Book*." *Transformations: Journal of Media and Culture* 27.

Skenazy, Lenore. 2009. *Free-Range Kids: Giving Our Children the Freedom We Had without Going Nuts with Worry*. Hoboken, NJ: Jossey-Bass.

– 2015. "Mob of Yale Students Scream Profanities about Hallowe'en Costume Insensitivity." Free-Range Kids, 7 November 2015. www.freerangekids.com/mob-of-yale-students-scream-profanities-about-halloween-costume-insensitivity/.

Solnit, Rebecca. 2009. *Paradise Built in Hell: The Extraordinary Communities That Arise in Disaster*. New York: Viking.

– 2012. "The Rain on Our Parade: A Letter to My Dismal Allies." *TomDispatch*, 27 September 2012. tomdispatch.com/rebecca-solnit-we-could-be-heroes/.

– 2016. *Hope in the Dark: Untold Histories, Wild Possibilities*. Chicago: Haymarket Books.

Sorkin, Amy. 2014. "Darren Wilson's Demon." *The New Yorker*, 26 November 2014. www.newyorker.com/news/amy-davidson/demon-ferguson-darren-wilson-fear-black-man.

Spear, Wayne K. 2014. *Full Circle: The Aboriginal Healing Foundation & the Unfinished Work of Hope, Healing and Reconciliation*. Ottawa, ON: Aboriginal Healing Foundation.

Spencer, Jasmine. 2019. "The Buffalo, the Chickadee, and the Eagle: A Multispecies Textual History of Plenty Coups's Multivocal Autobiography." *American Indian Quarterly* 43 (2): 168–203.

Stevenson, Lisa. 2014. *Life Beside Itself: Imagining Care in the Canadian Arctic*. Berkeley: University of California Press.

Stout, Madeline Dion. 2012. "A Survivor Reflects on Resilience." In *Speaking My Truth: Reflections on Reconciliation and Residential Schools*, edited by Mike DeGagné, Jonathan Dewar, and Glen Lowry, 47–52. Ottawa, ON: Aboriginal Healing Foundation.

Stout, Madeline Dion, and Gregory Kipling. 2003. *Aboriginal People, Resilience and the Residential School Legacy*. Ottawa, ON: The Aboriginal Healing Foundation. www.ahf.ca/downloads/resilience.pdf.

Strathern, Marilyn. 1992. *Reproducing the Future: Anthropology, Kinship and the New Reproductive Technologies*. Oxfordshire, UK: Routledge.

Strycharczyk, Doug, and Charles Elvin. 2014. *Developing Resilient Organizations: How to Create an Adaptive, High-Performance and Engaged Organization*. London, UK: Kogan Page.

Swing, William. 2009. "Foreword." In *Migration, Environment and Climate Change: Assessing the Evidence*, edited by Frank Laczko and Christine Aghazarm. Geneva, CH: International Organization for Migration. publications.iom.int/system/files/pdf/migration_and_environment.pdf.

Taleb, Nicholas Nassim. 2007. *The Black Swan: The Impact of the Highly Improbable*. New York: Random House.

Taylor, Keeanga Yamahtta. 2016. *From #BlackLivesMatter to Black Liberation*. Chicago: Haymarket Books.

Tedmanson, Deirdre, and Dinesh Wadiwel Neoptolemas. 2010. "The Governmentality of New Race/Pleasure? Wars." *Culture and Organization* 16 (1): 7–22.

Thobani, Sunera. 2007. *Exalted Subjects: Studies in the Making of Race and Nation in Canada*. Toronto: University of Toronto Press.

Thomas, Destiny. 2020a. "Opinion: Urbanism is Complicit in Infra-Structural Racism – And Reparations Have a Place in the Built Environment." *Streetsblog, USA*, 27 July 2020. usa.streetsblog.org/2020/07/27/opinion-urbanism-is-complicit-in-infra-structural-racism-and-reparations-have-a-place-in-the-built-environment/.

– 2020b. "'Safe Streets' Are Not Safe for Black Lives." *Bloomberg*, 8 June 2020. www.bloomberg.com/news/articles/2020–06–08/-safe-streets-are-not-safe-for-black-lives.

Tobias, Joshua K., and Chantelle A.M. Richmond. 2014. "'That Land Means Everything to Us as Anishinaabe ...' Environmental Dispossession and Resilience on the North Shore of Lake Superior" *Health and Place* 29:26–33.

Tomiak, Julie. 2017. "Contesting the Settler City: Indigenous Self-Determination, New Urban Reserves, and the Neoliberalization of Colonialism." *Antipode* 49 (4): 928–45.

Tootonsab, Zahra. 2023. "Resilience and Sheltering." Unpublished manuscript. Microsoft Word document.

Tory, John, Eileen De Villa, and Matthew Pegg. 2021. *COVID-19 Briefing July 21*. The City of Toronto. YouTube video, 21 July 2021. youtube.com/watch?v=axdlhAGN3SI.

Tough, Paul. 2011 "What If the Secret to Success Is Failure?" *New York Times Magazine*, 14 September 2011. www.nytimes.com/2011/09/18/magazine/what-if-the-secret-to-success-is-failure.html.

– 2012. *How Children Succeed: Grit, Curiosity and the Hidden Power of Character*. New York: Mariner Books.

Tousignant, Michel, and Nibisha Sioui. 2009. "Resilience and Aboriginal Communities in Crisis: Theory and Interventions." *Journal of Aboriginal Health* 5 (1): 42–61.

Travers, Peter. 2015. "*The Martian*." *Rolling Stone*, 30 September 2015. www.rollingstone.com/tv-movies/tv-movie-reviews/the-martian-122671/.

Trexler, Adam. 2015. *Anthropocene Fictions: The Novel in a Time of Climate Change*. Charlottesville: University of Virginia Press.

Truffaut-Wong, Olivia. 2015. "How Matt Damon Trained for *The Martian* and Put Humor, Not Science, First." *Bustle*, 12 October 2015. www.bustle.com/articles/116417-how-matt-damon-trained-for-the-martian-put-humor-not-science-first.

Truth and Reconciliation Commission of Canada. 2015. "Honouring the Truth, Reconciling for the Future." In *Summary of the Final Report of the Truth and Reconciliation Commission of Canada*. Truth and Reconciliation Commission of Canada. publications.gc.ca/collections/collection_2015/trc/IR4-7-2015-eng.pdf.

Tuck, Eve. 2009. "Suspending Damage: A Letter to Communities." *Harvard Educational Review* 79 (3): 409–27.

Tuck, Eve, and K. Wayne Yang. 2012. "Decolonization is Not a Metaphor." *Decolonization: Indigeneity, Education & Society* 1 (1).

Turnbull, Malcolm. 2018. *Closing the Gap: Prime Minister's Report 2018*. Canberra: Commonwealth of Australia.

Turner, Pat, and Nicole Watson. 2007. "The Trojan Horse." In *Coercive Reconciliation: Stabilise, Normalise, Exit Aboriginal Australia*, edited by Jon Altman and Melinda Hinkson, 205–12. Arena Publications.

Ungar, Michael. 2009. *Too Safe for Their Own Good: How Risk and Responsibility Help Teens Thrive*. Toronto: McClelland and Steward.

United Nations Office for Disaster and Risk Reduction. 2018. "Building Urban Resilience with Nature: A Practitioner's Guide to Action." *PreventionWeb*,

November 2018. www.preventionweb.net/publication/building-urban-resilience-nature-practitioners-guide-action.

Vale, Lawrence J., and Thomas J. Campanella, eds. 2005. *The Resilient City: How Modern Cities Recover from Disaster.* New York: Oxford University Press.

Van Rijswijk, Honni. 2017. "Archiving the Northern Territory Intervention in Law and in the Literary Counter-Imaginary" In *Evidence and the Archive: Ethics, Aesthetics and Emotion,* edited by Katherine Biber and Trish Luker, 119–35. Oxfordshire, UK: Routledge.

Vizenor, Gerald. 1996. *Manifest Manners: Postindian Warriors of Survivance.* Lincoln: University of Nebraska Press.

– 2008. "Aesthetics of Survivance: Literary Theory and Practice." In *Survivance: Narratives of Native Presence,* 1–23. Lincoln: University of Nebraska Press.

– 2019. *Native Provenance: The Betrayal of Cultural Creativity.* Lincoln: University of Nebraska Press.

voices-voix Coalition. 2012. "Aboriginal Healing Foundation." *voices-voix: Defending Advocacy and Dissent in Canada,* 28 November 2012. web.archive.org/web/20130929120646/http://voices-voix.ca/en/facts/profile/aboriginal-healing-foundation.

Wack, Pierre. 1985a. "Scenarios: Shooting the Rapids." *Harvard Business Review,* September 1985, 139–50.

– 1985b. "Scenarios: Uncharted Waters Ahead." *Harvard Business Review,* September 1985, 73–89.

Walcott, Rinaldo. 2019. "The End of Diversity." *Public Culture* 31 (2): 393–408.

Walcott, Rinaldo, and Idil Abdillahi. 2020. *Black Life: Post-BLM and the Struggle for Freedom.* Winnipeg, MB: ARP Books.

Walker, Brian, and David Salt. 2006. *Resilience Thinking: Sustaining Ecosystems and People in a Changing World,* Washington, DC: Island Press.

Walker, Jeremy, and Melinda Cooper. 2011. "Genealogies of Resilience: From Systems Ecology to the Political Economy of Crisis Adaptation." *Security Dialogues* 42 (2): 143–61.

Wallace, Michelle. (1978) 2015. *Black Macho and the Myth of the Superwoman.* London, UK: Verso Books.

Walsh, Paul. 2017. "Charges: U Prof Conceals Felony Allegation While Purchasing 14 Pistols." *GOPUSA,* 7 September 2017. web.archive.org/web/20170907012543/https://www.gopusa.com/why-did-professor-massoud-amin-buy-14-guns-in-3-weeks/.

Wang, Janet F. 1999. "Foreword." *Holistic Nursing Practice* 13 (3): vi–ix.

Ward, Jesmyn. 2011. *Salvage the Bones.* New York: Bloomsbury.

Watson, Irene. 2005. "Settled and Unsettled Spaces: Are We Free to Roam?" *Australian Critical Race and Whiteness Studies Association Journal* 1:40–52.

– 2009. "In the Northern Territory Intervention, What is Saved or Rescued and at What Cost?" *Cultural Studies Review* 15:45–60.

Watts, Vanessa. 2013. "Indigenous place-thought & agency amongst humans and non-humans (First Woman and Sky Woman go on a European world tour!)." *Decolonization: Indigeneity, Education & Society* 2 (1): 20–34.

Weale, Sally. 2016. "Extrovert Character Traits Shaped by Background, Study Finds." *The Guardian*, 14 January 2016. https://www.theguardian.com/society/2016/jan/14/extrovert-character-traits-shaped-by-background-study-finds.

Webber, Sophie, Helga Leitner, and Eric Sheppard. 2021. "Wheeling Out Urban Resilience: Philanthrocapitalism, Marketization and Local Practise." *Annals of the American Association of Geographers* 111 (2): 343–63.

Weheliye, Alexander G. 2005. *Phonographies: Grooves in Sonic Afro-Modernity*. Durham, NC: Duke University Press.

Weinberger, Sarah. 2017. "Shared Path: Bridging Indigenous and Settler Notions of Urban Planning: An Annotated Interview with Carolyn King" *Journal of Law and Social Policy* 27 (9).

Weir, Andy. 2011. *The Martian: A Novel*. New York: Random House.

Wenzel, Jennifer. 2014. "CO2 and the Coeval." Paper presented at the American Comparative Literature Association conference, New York University, New York, 20 March 2014.

Werner, Emmy E., and Ruth S. Smith, 1982. *Vulnerable but Invincible: A Longitudinal Study of Resilient Children and Youth*. New York: McGraw Hill.

Wesley-Esquimaux, Cynthia C. 2009. "Trauma to Resilience: Notes on Decolonization." In *Restoring the Balance: First Nations Women, Community, and Culture*, edited by Gail Guthrie Valaskakis, Madeleine Dion Stout, and Eric Guimond, 213–34. Winnipeg, MB: University of Manitoba Press.

Wesley-Esquimaux, Cynthia C., and Magdalene Smolewski. 2004. *Historic Trauma and Aboriginal Healing*, Ottawa, ON: Aboriginal Healing Foundation.

Whyte, Kyle Powys. 2018. "Settler Colonialism, Ecology and Environmental Injustice." *Environment and Society: Advances in Research* 9:125–44.

Wikipedia. 2023. "Conor Friedersdorf." Last modified 8 July 2023. en.wikipedia.org/wiki/Conor_Friedersdorf.

Williams, Monnica T., Anjalika Khanna Roy, Marie-Paule MacIntyre, and Sonya Faber. 2022. "The Traumatizing Impact of Racism in Canadians of Colour." *Current Trauma Reports* 8 (2): 17–34.

Williamson, Geordie. 2013. "Alexis Wright Stages a Counter Intervention with *The Swan Book*." *The Australian*, 10 August 2013.

Wolcott, Victoria. 2012. *Race, Riots, and Roller Coasters: The Struggle over Segregated Recreation in America*. Philadelphia: University of Pennsylvania Press.

Wolfe, Patrick. 2006. "Settler Colonialism and the Elimination of the Native." *Journal of Genocide Research* 8 (4): 387–409.

Wolfenstein, Martha. 1958. "The Emergence of Fun Morality." In *Mass Leisure*, edited by Eric Larrabee and Rolf Meyersohn, 86–95. Florence, MA: The Free Press. Previously published in the *Journal of Social Issues* 7, no. 4 (1951): 15–25.

Woods, Angela, Akiko Hart, and Helen Spandler. 2019. "The Recovery Narrative: Politics and Possibilities of a Genre." *Culture, Medicine and Psychiatry* 46 (March): 221–47.

Wright, Alexis. 2002. "The Politics of Writing." *Southerly* 62 (2): 10–20.

– 2008. "A Weapon of Poetry: Alexis Wright Remembers Oodgeroo Noonucal." *Overland* 193:19–24.

– 2016. *The Swan Book*. London, UK: Constable and Robinson.

– 2022. "The Inward Migration in Apocalyptic Times." *Emergence Magazine*, 26 October 2022. emergencemagazine.org/essay/the-inward-migration-in-apocalyptic-times/.

Wright, Alexis, and Arnold Zable. 2013. "The Future of Swans." *Overland* 213. https://overland.org.au/previous-issues/issue-213/feature-alexis-wright-and-arnold-zable/.

Wynter, Sylvia. 1994. "'No Humans Involved': An Open Letter to My Colleagues." *Forum N.H.I.: Knowledge for the 21st Century* 1 (1): 1–15. https://people.ucsc.edu/~nmitchel/sylvia.wynter_-_no.humans.allowed.pdf.

– 2003. "Unsettling the Coloniality of Being/Power/Truth/Freedom: Towards the Human, After Man, Its Overrepresentation – An Argument." *The New Centennial Review* 3 (3): 257–337.

Wynter, Sylvia, and Katherine McKittrick. 2015. "Unparalleled Catastrophe for Our Species? Or, to Give Humanness a Different Future: Conversations." In *Sylvia Wynter: On Being Human as Praxis*, edited by Katherine McKittrick, 10–89. Durham, NC: Duke University Press.

Yaeger, Patricia. 2013. "Beasts of the Southern Wild and Dirty Ecology." *Southern Spaces*. https://southernspaces.org/2013/beasts-southern-wild-and-dirty-ecology/.

Zebrowski, Christopher. 2009. "Governing the Network Society: A Biopolitical Critique of Resilience." *Political Perspectives* 3 (1).

– 2015. *The Value of Resilience: Securing Life in the Twenty-first Century*. Oxfordshire, UK: Routledge.

Zhang, X., and H. Li. 2017. "Urban Resilience and Urban Sustainability: What We Know and What Do Not Know." *Cities* 72:141–8.

Zolli, Andrew, and Ann Marie Healy. 2012. *Resilience: Why Things Bounce Back*. New York: Simon & Schuster.

Index